Mathematics, Cryptocurrencies and Blockchain Technology

Mathematics, Cryptocurrencies and Blockchain Technology

Editors

José Luis Miralles-Quirós

María Mar Miralles-Quirós

MDPI • Basel • Beijing • Wuhan • Barcelona • Belgrade • Manchester • Tokyo • Cluj • Tianjin

Editors

José Luis Miralles-Quirós
Faculty of Economic and Business Sciences,
University of Extremadura,
06006 Badajoz, Spain

María Mar Miralles-Quirós
Faculty of Economic and Business Sciences,
University of Extremadura,
06006 Badajoz, Spain

Editorial Office

MDPI
St. Alban-Anlage 66
4052 Basel, Switzerland

This is a reprint of articles from the Special Issue published online in the open access journal *Mathematics* (ISSN 2227-7390) (available at: https://www.mdpi.com/journal/mathematics/special_issues/Mathematics_Cryptocurrencies_Blockchain_Technology).

For citation purposes, cite each article independently as indicated on the article page online and as indicated below:

LastName, A.A.; LastName, B.B.; LastName, C.C. Article Title. *Journal Name* **Year**, *Volume Number*, Page Range.

ISBN 978-3-0365-4571-4 (Hbk)
ISBN 978-3-0365-4572-1 (PDF)

Contents

About the Editors

José Luis Miralles-Quirós

José Luis Miralles-Quirós is an Associate Professor of Financial Economics and Accounting at the University of Extremadura in Spain. His research has primarily focused on providing shareholders' investment strategies that would beat the market in adverse situations using sophisticated mathematical approaches. Meanwhile, his research also includes the analysis of companies' environmental, social, and corporate governance activities and their connection to shareholders' value creation. These works have been published in prestigious journals such as Business Strategy and the Environment, Corporate Social Responsibility and Environmental Management, Energy Economics, International Review of Economics and Finance, Journal of Business Ethics, Journal of International Financial Markets, Institutions & Money, Mathematics, and North American Journal of Economics and Finance, among others.

María Mar Miralles-Quirós

María Mar Miralles-Quirós is an Associate Professor of Financial Economics and Accounting and the Director of the Research Group on Markets and Financial Assets at the University of Extremadura in Spain. Her research has focused on providing shareholders' investment strategies that would beat the market using sophisticated mathematical approaches, as well as the analysis of companies' sustainable activities and their connection to shareholders' value creation. Her research works have been published in prestigious journals such as Business Strategy and the Environment, Corporate Social Responsibility and Environmental Management, Energy Economics, International Review of Economics and Finance, Journal of Business Ethics, Journal of International Financial Markets, Institutions & Money, Mathematics, and North American Journal of Economics and Finance, among others.

mathematics

MDPI

Editorial

Mathematics, Cryptocurrencies and Blockchain Technology

José Luis Miralles-Quirós * and María Mar Miralles-Quirós

Faculty of Economic and Business Sciences, University of Extremadura, 06006 Badajoz, Spain; marmiralles@unex.es
* Correspondence: miralles@unex.es

This book contains the successful invited submissions [1–9] to a Special Issue of *Mathematics* on the subject area of "Mathematics, Cryptocurrencies and Blockchain Technology".

Blockchain is the innovative database technology that is at the heart of nearly all cryptocurrencies and has already significantly changed the future of money, finance, supply chain management and more. In this Special Issue, we focus on the pricing mathematics underlying mathematical and computational methods that can be useful tools for prediction or for estimating the reasonable value of something.

This Special Issue includes the most important studies of the Cryptocurrencies and Blockchain Technologies, such as the analysis of the Bitcoin price dynamics, the macroeconomic consequences of introducing Central Bank Digital Currencies (CBDC), and concerns about sustainable development or the Blockchain token economy.

Chen and Huang [1] focus on the issue of the fact that cryptocurrencies involve significant jump risks and conduct an in-depth investigation of hedging strategies. They find that the inclusion of jumps in returns and volatilities is significant in the historical time series of Bitcoin prices. In a similar order, considering Blockchain technology's potential to revolutionize stock trading, Cohen [2] proposes a trading system based on second order stochastic dominance to different cryptocurrencies. He finds that the system is able to predict long trends but also to outperform the Buy and Hold strategy in most cases.

The COVID-19 pandemic and its consequences were also discussed in this Special Issue. Boguslavsky et al. [3] state, after performing gallop polls, that one of the main reasons for the significant rise in cryptocurrencies is that they are an "epidemiologically safe" means of transaction.

Pinto-Gutiérrez et al. [4] and Guo et al. [5] focus their studies on Tokens and Non-Fungible Tokens (NFTs), which offer to their holders a medium to purchase various goods, services or privileges. The former show that Bitcoin returns can predict the following week's NFT growth after using different vector autoregressive models, while the latter propose a "dual incentive value-based" paradigm to improve profitability in Blockchain token economy. For that reason, they develop a business study case for improving merchants' environmental states and show that merchants obtain greater profits following the proposed paradigm.

As mentioned above, this Special Issue also pays attention to one of humanity's greatest problems, the development of a sustainable world. Syed et al. [6] focus on the relationship between green bonds and Bitcoin and find that positive shocks of Bitcoins exert a positive influence on green bonds. There is also a space for machine-learning models and their use to discriminate between malicious and non-malicious tokens in different scenarios, such as the paper of Mazorra et al. [7], but also for predicting Bitcoin's prices, as Ye et al. [8] propose.

Finally, we should point out the study of Syarifudding and Bakhtiar [9] who develop a medium-sized dynamic stochastic general equilibrium model to assess the macroeconomic consequences of introducing interest-bearing CBDC, finding that they offer a significant number of macroeconomic benefits.

The response to our call had the following statistics:

Citation: Miralles-Quirós, J.L.; Miralles-Quirós, M.M. Mathematics, Cryptocurrencies and Blockchain Technology. *Mathematics* **2022**, *10*, 2038. https://doi.org/10.3390/math10122038

Received: 8 June 2022
Accepted: 10 June 2022
Published: 12 June 2022

Submissions (12);
Publications (9);
Rejections (3);
Article types: Research Articles (9);
Authors' geographical distribution (published papers):
China (3);
Spain (2);
Chile (1);
Colombia (1);
India (1);
Indonesia (1);
Israel (1);
Pakistan (1);
Russia (1);
Taiwan (1).

We found the edition and selections of papers for this book very inspiring and rewarding. We thank the editorial staff and reviewers for their efforts and help during the process.

Author Contributions: This work is an outcome of the joint efforts of the two authors. Both authors conceived the research idea, reviewed the related literature and contributed to the interpretation of the results. They also wrote the manuscript and thoroughly read and approved the final version. All authors have read and agreed to the published version of the manuscript.

Funding: The authors gratefully acknowledge support from the Junta de Extremadura (Counselling of Economy, Science and Digital Agenda) and the European Regional Development Fund ("A way of doing Europe") under the VI Action Plan for Research and Development 2017/20 through grant GR21019.

Data Availability Statement: Not applicable.

Conflicts of Interest: The authors declare no conflict of interest.

References

1. Chen, K.; Huang, Y. Detecting Jump Risk and Jump-Diffusion Model for Bitcoin Options Pricing and Hedging. *Mathematics* **2021**, *9*, 2567. [CrossRef]
2. Cohen, G. Trading Cryptocurrencies Using Second Order Stochastic Dominance. *Mathematics* **2021**, *9*, 2861. [CrossRef]
3. Boguslavsky, D.; Sharova, N.; Sharov, K. Cryptocurrency as Epidemiologically Safe Means of Transactions: Diminishing Risk of SARS-CoV-2 Spread. *Mathematics* **2021**, *9*, 3263. [CrossRef]
4. Pinto-Gutiérrez, C.; Gaitán, S.; Jaramillo, D.; Velasquez, S. The NFT Hype: What Draws Attention to Non-Fungible Tokens? *Mathematics* **2022**, *10*, 335. [CrossRef]
5. Guo, C.; Zhang, P.; Lin, B.; Song, J. A Dual Incentive Value-Based Paradigm for Improving the Business Market Profitability in Blockchain Token Economy. *Mathematics* **2022**, *10*, 439. [CrossRef]
6. Syed, A.; Ahmed, F.; Kamal, M.; Ullah, A.; Ramos-Requena, J. Is There an Asymmetric Relationship between Economic Policy Uncertainty, Cryptocurrencies, and Global Green Bonds? Evidence from the United States of America. *Mathematics* **2022**, *10*, 720. [CrossRef]
7. Mazorra, B.; Adan, V.; Daza, V. Do Not Rug on Me: Leveraging Machine Learning Techniques for Automated Scam Detection. *Mathematics* **2022**, *10*, 949. [CrossRef]
8. Ye, Z.; Wu, Y.; Chen, H.; Pan, Y.; Jiang, Q. A Stacking Ensemble Deep Learning Model for Bitcoin Price Prediction Using Twitter Comments on Bitcoin. *Mathematics* **2022**, *10*, 1307. [CrossRef]
9. Syarifuddin, F.; Bakhtiar, T. The Macroeconomic Effects of an Interest-Bearing CBDC: A DSGE Model. *Mathematics* **2022**, *10*, 1671. [CrossRef]

mathematics

Article

Detecting Jump Risk and Jump-Diffusion Model for Bitcoin Options Pricing and Hedging

Kuo-Shing Chen [1,*] and Yu-Chuan Huang [2]

1 Department of Accounting, Ming Chuan University, 250 Zhong Shan N. Rd., Sec. 5, Taipei 111, Taiwan
2 Department of Accounting Information, College of Business, Southern Taiwan University of Science and Technology, Tainan 710, Taiwan; jenhuang@stust.edu.tw
* Correspondence: moses@mail.mcu.edu.tw; Tel.: +886-9-21225936

Abstract: In this paper, we conduct a fast calibration in the jump-diffusion model to capture the Bitcoin price dynamics, as well as the behavior of some components affecting the price itself, such as the risk of pitfalls and its ambiguous effect on the evolution of Bitcoin's price. In addition, in our study of the Bitcoin option pricing, we find that the inclusion of jumps in returns and volatilities are significant in the historical time series of Bitcoin prices. The benefits of incorporating these jumps flow over into option pricing, as well as adequately capture the volatility smile in option prices. To the best of our knowledge, this is the first work to analyze the phenomenon of price jump risk and to interpret Bitcoin option valuation as "exceptionally ambiguous". Crucially, using hedging options for the Bitcoin market, we also prove some important properties: Bitcoin options follow a convex, but not strictly convex function. This property provides adequate risk assessment for convex risk measure.

Keywords: blockchain; convex risk measure; jump-diffusion model; fintech; option pricing

Citation: Chen, K.-S.; Huang, Y.-C. Detecting Jump Risk and Jump-Diffusion Model for Bitcoin Options Pricing and Hedging. *Mathematics* **2021**, *9*, 2567. https://doi.org/10.3390/math9202567

Academic Editors: José Luis Miralles-Quirós and María Mar Miralles-Quirós

Received: 5 September 2021
Accepted: 5 October 2021
Published: 13 October 2021

1. Introduction

In the Fintech era, Bitcoin has shown remarkable performance in the decade since Nakamoto (2008) invented the cryptocurrency, due the blockchain-based and decentralized system. It has also risen rapidly in market capitalization since the COVID-19 pandemic outbreak. In the past decade, Bitcoin prices have been extremely volatile, and its abnormal return expands the potential in phases of extreme price; unpredictable and massive crashes broke out after the 2017/18 crash. Consequently, the price of Bitcoin appears to jump. As shown in Figure 1, the price of Bitcoin rose by more than 1900 percent in 2017, starting the year at around USD 1000 and grazing almost USD 20,000 in mid-December. However, there is still no clear explanation as to why there is a price jump, that is, a sudden spike in interest. Bitcoin is notoriously volatile and has seen multiple booms and crashes. As previously stated, these peaks are in line with price bubbles, and the current Bitcoin market is comparable to the internet bubble of the late 1990s. A popular ambiguity model in finance is the ambiguous volatility approach. Models with ambiguous volatility and jumps in returns and volatility are quite different to contingent claims usages which have no analytic solutions. A more effective approach was proposed by the implied diffusion approach of Poisson jumps by Dupire [1] and Andersen and Andreasen [2]. They show significant evidence that this technique exhibits some dominant in terms of capturing the form of a smile or a skew of implied volatilities. In addition, there are several studies addressing the valuation of options under jump-diffusion processes. In response, Ma et al. [3] apply in univariate and self-exciting (i.e., Hawkes) jump-diffusion models to the valuation of European-type contingent claims. Moreover, two different hedging strategies, which are used for the option under a jump-diffusion model, were explored by He et al. [4]. Briefly, there are two crucial problems when the underlying asset follows Merton [5] and Bates' [6] jump-diffusion process. First, the calibration is an ill-posed inverse problem, even for simple jump-diffusion models, and may lead to calibration bias of model parameters that have serious effects on hedging performance and valuation of derivatives, see Cont and Tankov [7]. Second, a contingent claim cannot be hedged perfectly with standard marketed instruments available when the underlying asset returns follows a jump-diffusion with possible jump size taking values on a continuum, see, e.g., Gómez-Valle and Martínez-Rodríguez [8].

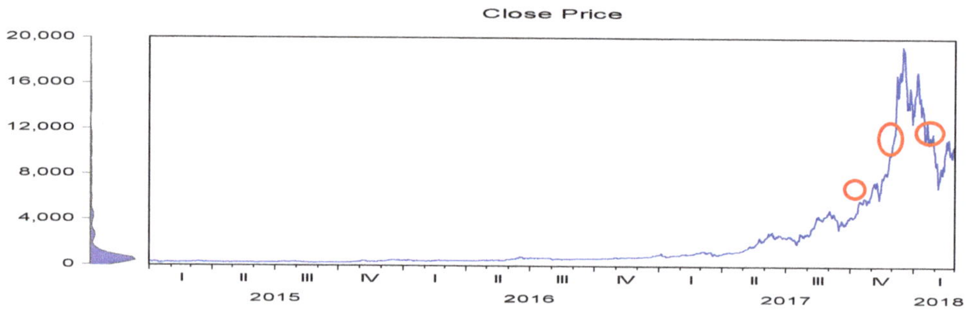

Figure 1. Market Price of Bitcoin in the Bitcoin/USD exchange rate from 1 January 2015 to 28 February 2018. Notes. Jump effect of Bitcoin price revaluation on Bitcoin/USD exchange rate, huge jump starting from Q3/2017.

The purpose of this paper is to address the important issue that cryptocurrencies involve significant jump risks, in which they behave in a highly volatile manner, are vulnerable to hacking, and most transactions are aimed at speculative investments in Bitcoin. The volatility and speculative nature of cryptocurrencies indicates the necessity for diversification and hedging across market platforms (see Luther and White [9]). The conclusion reached so far is that Bitcoin are considered a store of value asset class or speculative investment, rather than a currency. As for the empirics of Bitcoin's price, volatility observed in this market is a major concern, for example, Yermack [10] argued that Bitcoin prices are considerably more volatile than gold prices. In addition, Dowd and Hutchinson [11] draw a very drastic conclusion: "Bitcoin will bite the dust". Furthermore, the preliminary findings of current works (e.g., Ardia et al. [12], Fang et al. [13], Bouri et al. [14], Bouri and Gupta [15], and Cao and Celik [16]), argue that the heightened volatility of Bitcoin prices is likely to be driven by the uncertainty macroeconomics, e.g., the US–China trade war and the COVID-19 pandemic outbreak. Recently, a few studies have been devoted to combining the Bitcoin literature with that on option pricing to construct Bitcoin option pricing models with dynamic jumps. There are several notable papers on this topic, such as Scaillet, Treccani, and Trevisan [17], Siu and Elliott [18], Jalan, Matkovskyy, and Saqib [19], which have documented the earlier analysis. However, these literatures do not provide a specific measure by detecting jumps for implied volatility in jump-diffusion models, and the option is hedged with the underlying Bitcoin.

In this paper, we focus on theoretical properties for the suggested model; the choice for the most suitable model parameters among the ones proposed in the literature is made in view of market data considering historical volatility and jumps (e.g., Hilliard et al [20]). It is worth noting that a market for these contingent claims has recently appeared in the existing literature, such as Kapetanios, Neumann, and Skiadopoulos [21] and Qiao et al. [22].

Our study makes the following contributions: From a theoretical viewpoint, it contributes to a recently emerged literature in two ways. First, the model is proven to elaborate on how Bitcoins can be captured using a fast calibration in the Bates jump-diffusion process. Second, we conduct an in-depth investigation of hedging strategies with perfect replication of a contingent claim. The paper empirically analyses the behavior of Bitcoin prices; we contribute to the literature by fitting the calibrated model combining the ambiguous parameters and detecting spurious jump component from Table 1.

Table 1. Descriptive statistics on significant jumps using LM statistics.

	Q1		Q2		Q3		Q4	
	No. of Jumps	*P(Jump freq.)*	**No. of Jumps**	*P(Jump freq.)*	**No. of Jumps**	*P(Jump freq.)*	**No. of Jumps**	*P(Jump freq.)*
2015	45	0.125	52	0.1429	61	0.1685	44	0.1196
# Observations	360		364		368		368	
2016	45	0.1236	42	0.1154	47	0.1291	37	0.1016
# Observations	364		364		368		368	
2017	38	0.1056	36	0.0989	50	0.1359	41	0.1114
# Observations	360		364		368		368	
2018	35	0.1483						
# Observations	236							
# jumps	573							
(Mean)	**(0.124)**							
(Std. dev.)	(0.02)							
(Total Obs.	4,620							

Regarding number of jumps and jump intensity, we further provide the total number jumps (# jumps), their proportion (%) over sample observations, i.e., expressed as (P(jump) = 100(#jumps/#obs.)), and their mean and standard deviation of full sample observations (values in parentheses). Quarterly estimates for BTC and no. of jumps represents number of detected jumps, and P (jump freq.) implies the proportion of observations with a significant jump arrivals at $\alpha = 0.05$. LM statistics represent the Lee and Mykland [23] jump test statistic.

The rest of the paper is s organized as follows. In Section 2, we briefly describe the jump detection technique to capture the Bitcoin price dynamics and calculus the intensity of the jumps. In Section 3 we introduce a quasi-closed formula for European-style options for Bitcoin derivations pricing and computation of Greeks. Section 4 is devoted to a numerical application and some preliminary results. Finally, Section 5 offers some concluding remarks. Most technical proofs are provided in the Appendix.

2. Methodology

2.1. Jump Detection Methodology

The evolution of Bitcoin prices under jump-diffusion processes can be expressed the following stochastic differential equation as:

$$d\log P_t = \mu_t dt + \sigma(t)dW_t + Y_t dJ_t \tag{1}$$

where μ_t, σ(t) and W_t are the drift and volatility stochastic processes and the Brownian motion, respectively, such that $d\log P_t$ denotes an Itô process with continuous sample paths; J_t is a counting process that controls the jumps arrival; and Y_t represents the jump size.

Due to competing approaches, the study uses Lee and Mykland's [23] jump detection technique to identify whether there are any arrival jumps in Bitcoin prices for a review of frequency jump detection. Moreover, the jump detection test proposed by Lee and Mykland [23] can identify jumps that occur at any time during the trading day in financial assets, whereas the other jump tests in the existing literature can merely examine the daily discontinuous sample-path, see Dumitru and Urga [24]. The discrete time returns of Equation (1) are expressed as follows:

$$R_t = \log(P_t) - \log(P_{t-1}) \tag{2}$$

where R_t is the log return. Additionally, to formally define our empirical volatility measures on the trading day t, we sum the squared j-th intraday returns by:

$$RV_t = \sum_{j=1}^{M} R_{t,j}^2 \tag{3}$$

where M refers to the number of observations within the measurement time frame. Multiply the above estimator by $\pi/2$, a consistent estimator for quadratic variance in the arrival jumps, to obtain the realized bipower variation (BV) as follows:

$$BV_t \equiv \frac{\pi}{2}\frac{M}{M-1}\sum_{j=2}^{M}|R_{t,j}||R_{t,j-1}| \tag{4}$$

where the $\frac{M}{M-1}$ term indicates a finite sample correction. Therefore, an empirically more robust measure was developed by Huang and Tauchen [25] as the following relative jump statistic, defined as:

$$RJ_t = \frac{RV_t - BV_t}{RV_t} \tag{5}$$

or the corresponding (approximate) logarithmic form can be expressed as:

$$RJ_t \equiv \log RV_t - \log BV_t \tag{6}$$

In addition, both BV_t and RJ_t, in order to capture the distinct components, are calculated for the total daily price variation. Therefore, the jump detection statistic is defined as:

$$\mathcal{L}(i) = \frac{R_{t,i}}{\hat{\sigma_{t,i}}} \tag{7}$$

where $\hat{\sigma_{t,i}}^2 = \frac{1}{K-2}\sum_{j=i-K+2}^{i-1}|R_{t,j}||R_{t,j-1}|$, and K is the window size. Additionally, Lee and Mykland [23] construct a rejection region to test the null hypothesis of no jump at $(t_{i-1}, t_i]$ at a given significance level α meeting the following condition:

$$\frac{|\mathcal{L}(i)| - C_n}{S_n} > -\log(-\log(1-\alpha)) \tag{8}$$

where $C_n = \frac{\sqrt{2\log n}}{0.7979} - \frac{\log \pi + \log(\log n)}{1.5958\sqrt{2\log n}}$, $S_n = \frac{1}{1.5958\sqrt{2\log n}}$. The null hypothesis of no jumps is rejected whenever $\frac{\mathcal{L}(i) - C_n}{S_n} > \beta^*$ exceeds the critical value β^* under a significance level of $\alpha = 0.05$. For a given confidence level α is obtained with β^* such that $exp(-e^{-\beta^*}) = 1 - \alpha = 0.95$, namely, $\beta^* = -\log(-\log(0.95)) = 2.9702$. This procedure can be expected to detect only a spurious jump in a given sample of n observations. Finally, by the above procedure, we can obtain the jump intensity, and these results can later be applied as a setting parameter to calibrate in the Bates model.

2.2. The Bitcoin and Its Options Market Model

To model uncertainty, we consider a complete, filtered, probability space $(\Omega, \mathcal{F}, \mathbb{P})$ with a right-continuous filtration $(\mathcal{F}_t)_{t>0}$ that satisfies the usual conditions of completeness on which is defined the price process $S = (S_t)_t$ of a Bitcoin asset. This asset serves us later as underlying European derivatives. Using Ito's Lemma, the corresponding model for the Bitcoin price under the physical probability measure $\mathbb{P}$, the Bitcoin price whose return dynamics are given by the following:

$$\frac{dS_t}{S_t} = \left(\mu - \lambda\bar{k}\right)dt + \sigma W_t + kdN_t \tag{9}$$

where μ,σ are the instantaneous expected return and the instantaneous volatility, respectively, scaled to correspond to the unit time interval; W_t denotes a standard Wiener process under the market measure $\mathbb{P}$. The N_t follows a Poisson counting process, with the mean number of jumps per unit time λ under the measure $\mathbb{P}$ so that arrival jump intensity is also given by:

$$dN_t = \begin{cases} 0 \text{ with probability } & 1-\lambda dt, \\ 1 \text{ with probability } & \lambda dt. \end{cases} \tag{10}$$

where k is magnitude of the sudden jumps, the expected proportional jump size takes the form:

$$\bar{k} \equiv \mathbb{E}_{\mathbb{P}}\left(e^J - 1\right).$$

We next extend the jump-diffusion model and obtain a diffusion approximation as the following right-continuous process, also called the Levy–Itô decomposition:

$$S_t = S_0 + \left[b - \lambda\bar{k}\right] t + \sigma W^{\mathbb{Q}}(t) + k \sum_{i=1}^{N(t)} J_i \tag{11}$$

where S_0 is the initial price level of Bitcoin and b is cost-of-carry for Bitcoin options. Their price dynamics follow the stochastic differential equation described by:

$$\frac{dS_t}{S_t} = \left(b - \lambda\bar{k}\right)t + \sigma W^{\mathbb{Q}}(t) + (J_i - 1)dNt \tag{12}$$

Suppose $\mathbb{Z}_t$ is a jump-diffusion process with evolution given by:

$$\mathbb{Z}_t = \mathbb{Z}_0 + \int_0^t a_s\, d_s + \int_0^t \sigma dW + \sum_{i=1}^{N_t} \Delta\mathbb{Z}_i \tag{13}$$

where a_s is the drift term, σ is the volatility term, and $\Delta\mathbb{Z}_i$ corresponds to jump i in the Bitcoin price. Then, using Ito's formula for jump-diffusions, the stochastic equation can be further obtained as follows:

$$lnS_t = lnS_0 + \left[b - \lambda\bar{k} - \frac{\sigma^2}{2}\right](t) + \sigma W_t + \sum_{i=1}^{Nt} lnJ_i \tag{14}$$

We next obtain the following after taking the exponential of the previous equation

$$S_t = S_0 \exp\left\{\left(b - \frac{\sigma^2}{2}\right)t + \sigma W_t\right\} \exp\left(\sum_{i=1}^{Nt} lnj_i\right) \tag{15}$$

It is worth recalling the assumption that the price fluctuation of Bitcoin follows a log-normal diffusion process with jumps. Specifically, using the previous definition of the price log-return jump size, that is $lnj_i \equiv J_i$. Then, for a given under jump-diffusion, the corresponding Bitcoin price fluctuations process S_t satisfies the stochastic equation

$$S_t = S_0 exp\left[\left(b - \frac{\sigma^2}{2}\right)t + \sigma W_t\right]\left(\prod_{i=1}^{N_t} J_i\right) \tag{16}$$

2.3. Fourier Transform and Moments of Bitcoin's Returns Dynamic

From the above model, several interesting implicit parameters, such as implied total annual volatility, can also be found. When the underlying process under $\mathbb{P}$ is defined by Equation (9), then the log return process is given by:

$$\begin{aligned} Ln\tfrac{S_t}{S_0} &= \left[\left(\alpha - \tfrac{1}{2}\sigma^2 - \lambda\bar{k}\right)t + \sigma W_t + \sum_{i=1}^{N_t} ln(j_i)\right] \\ &= \left[\left(\alpha - \tfrac{1}{2}\sigma^2 - \lambda\bar{k}\right)t + \sigma W_t + \textstyle\sum_{i=1}^{N_t} ln(j_i)\right] \end{aligned} \tag{17}$$

The characteristic function of the Bitcoin's log-return process can be expressed as the following expectation by using the Fourier transform of the log-return density function.

$$\begin{aligned}
&\mathcal{F}_\omega(ln\tfrac{S_t}{S_0}) = E\left[exp\left(i\omega\, ln\tfrac{S_t}{S_0}\right)\right] \\
&= E\left[exp\left(i\omega\left(\alpha-\tfrac{1}{2}\sigma^2-\lambda\bar{k}\right)t\right)\right]E[exp(i\omega\,\sigma W_t)]E[exp(\textstyle\sum_{i=1}^{N_t} i\omega J_i\,)] \\
&= exp\left[i\omega\left(\alpha-\tfrac{1}{2}\sigma^2-\lambda\bar{k}\right)t\right]exp\left[\tfrac{1}{2}(i\omega\,\sigma)^2t\right]E[exp(\textstyle\sum_{i=1}^{N_t} i\omega ln(j_i)\,)] \\
&= exp\left[i\omega\left(\alpha-\tfrac{1}{2}\sigma^2-\lambda\bar{k}\right)t-\tfrac{1}{2}(\omega\,\sigma)^2t\right]\,[exp(\lambda tE(j^{i\omega}-1)\,)] \\
&= exp\left[i\omega\alpha t-\tfrac{1}{2}i\omega\sigma^2t-i\omega\lambda\bar{k}t-\tfrac{1}{2}\omega^2\sigma^2t+\lambda tE(j^{i\omega}-1)\right] \\
&\mathcal{F}_\omega\left(ln\tfrac{S_t}{S_0}\right) = exp\left\{i\omega\alpha t-\tfrac{1}{2}i\omega(1-i\omega\,)\sigma^2t+\lambda[E(j^{i\omega}-1)-i\omega\bar{k}]t\right\}
\end{aligned} \tag{18}$$

Accordingly, the density function is based on the PDF of Poisson counter data, using the property of the law of iterated expectation and progresses to the Taylor expansion of exponential function. Note that all j_i are identically distributed as j. Expectation of $E(j^{i\omega}-1)$ is also expressed with the law of iterated expectations. Therefore, moments of the returns dynamic can be calculated by the inverse Fourier transforms of the characteristic function. The mean and the volatility of Bitcoin's log-returns process are obtained by the derivatives of the aforementioned characteristic function as follows:

$$\begin{aligned}
E\left(ln\tfrac{S_t}{S_0}\right) &= (-i)\tfrac{\partial\mathcal{F}}{\partial\omega}|_{\omega=0} = \left[\alpha-\tfrac{1}{2}\sigma^2+\lambda E(lnj)-\lambda\bar{k}\right]t \\
Var\left(ln\tfrac{S_t}{S_0}\right) &= (-i)^2\tfrac{\partial^2\mathcal{F}}{\partial\omega^2}|_{\omega=0} = \{\sigma^2+\lambda[E(lnj)]^2+\lambda Var(lnj)\}t
\end{aligned}$$

When the jump size is log-normal, $ln(j_t)$~$N\left(\alpha_j-\frac{1}{2}\sigma_j^2,\ \sigma_j^2\right)$ or $j\sim logN[e^{\alpha_j},\ e^{2\alpha_j}(e^{\sigma_j}-1)]$

$$E\left(ln\frac{S_t}{S_0}\right) = \left[\alpha-\frac{1}{2}\sigma^2+\lambda\left(\alpha_j-\frac{1}{2}\sigma_j^2\right)-\lambda\bar{k}\right]t \tag{19}$$

Hence, the total variance of the natural logarithm of the Bitcoin price under a jump-diffusion process is given by:

$$Var\left(ln\frac{S_t}{S_0}\right) = \left\{\sigma^2+\lambda\left[\left(\alpha_j-\frac{1}{2}\sigma_j^2\right)^2+\sigma_j^2\right]\right\}t \tag{20}$$

In the risk-neutral probability process $J^{\mathbb{Q}} = lnj^{\mathbb{Q}}$~$N\left(\alpha_j-\gamma\sigma_j^2-\frac{1}{2}\sigma_j^2,\ \sigma_j^2\right)$. Consequently:

$$\mathcal{F}_\omega^{\mathbb{Q}}\left(ln\frac{S_t}{S_0}\right) = exp\left[i\omega rt-\frac{1}{2}i\omega(1-i\omega\,)\sigma^2t+\lambda^{\mathbb{Q}}t\left[E^{\mathbb{Q}}\left(j^{i\omega}-1\right)-i\omega\bar{k}^{\mathbb{Q}}\right]\right] \tag{21a}$$

$$E^{\mathbb{Q}}\left(ln\frac{S_t}{S_0}\right) = \left[r-\frac{1}{2}\sigma^2+\lambda^{\mathbb{Q}}\left(\alpha_j-\gamma\sigma_j^2-\frac{1}{2}\sigma_j^2\right)-\lambda^{\mathbb{Q}}\bar{k}^{\mathbb{Q}}\right]t \tag{21b}$$

$$Var^{\mathbb{Q}}\left(ln\frac{S_t}{S_0}\right) = \left\{\sigma^2+\lambda^{\mathbb{Q}}\left[\left(\alpha_j-\gamma\sigma_j^2-\frac{1}{2}\sigma_j^2\right)^2+\sigma_j^2\right]\right\}t \tag{21c}$$

Equations (21a)–(21c) synthesize and depict completely the mapping from the risk-neutral measures $\mathbb{P}$ to $\mathbb{Q}$ for transform analysis of affine jump-diffusion options pricing, given the assumption that the representative investor has a CRRA utility. The next theorem provides the European call option price.

2.4. Pricing Contingent Claims of Bitcoin under Jump-Diffusion

In the market model outlined above, pricing contingent claims of Bitcoin can be expressed, and its value is given by:

$$C_a(S,X,\tau) = \sum_{i=0}^{\infty} \frac{e^{-\lambda^{\mathbb{Q}}\tau}\left(\lambda^{\mathbb{Q}}\tau\right)^i}{i!} C_{BS}(S,X,b,\tau,r,\sigma_s) \tag{22}$$

Or equivalently as follows:

$$C_{ai}(S,X,\tau) = \mathcal{P}_{Oi}(\lambda\tau)\left[S_t e^{-b\tau} N(d_{1i}) - X e^{-r\tau} N(d_{2i})\right] \tag{23a}$$

A European put option has an analogous jump-diffusion formula

$$P_{ui}(S,X,\tau) = \mathcal{P}_{Oi}(\lambda\tau)\left[X e^{-r\tau} N(-d_{2i}) - S_t e^{-b\tau} N(-d_{1i})\right] \tag{23b}$$

where

$$\mathcal{P}_{oi}(\lambda\tau) = \sum_{i=0}^{\infty} \frac{e^{-\lambda^{\mathbb{Q}}\tau}\left(\lambda^{\mathbb{Q}}\tau\right)^i}{i!}$$

and:

- X: the strike price of Bitcoin; S_t: the underlying price of Bitcoin at time t.
- σ_s: Volatility of the price variation based on no jump.
- r : risk-free rate, λ and b are as before.

In Proposition 1, we offer a pricing method that can calculate C_a. To price Bitcoin, a risk–neutrality measure $\mathbb{Q}$ is required which is equivalent to real-world measure $\mathbb{P}$, such that the discounted asset price process is a martingale. Alternative interpretation of Bitcoin pricing with jump-diffusion $\mathbb{Q}$ is a risk-neutral measure. Therefore, the Merton options pricing formula can be interpreted as the weighted sum of individual Black–Scholes values, that the probability of i jumps will occur during the life of the option.

Proposition 1. *Suppose the Bitcoin price follows the dynamics of (16), and the corresponding model for the European call option price C_a is given by*

$$C_a(S,X,\tau) = \sum\nolimits_{i=0}^{\infty} \frac{e^{-\lambda^*\tau}(\lambda^*\tau)^i}{i!}\left[S_t N(d_{1i}) - X e^{-\bar{r}_i\tau} N(d_{2i})\right] \tag{24}$$

where

$$d_{2i} = \frac{ln\frac{S_t}{X} + (\bar{r}_i - \lambda^* k^* + \frac{\sigma_i^2}{2})\tau}{\sigma_s^2\tau + i\sigma_J^2}$$

and

$$d_{2i} = d_{1i} - \sigma_i\sqrt{\tau}$$

with

$$\begin{aligned}
&\bar{\alpha} \equiv \alpha + \gamma\sigma_J^2 \\
&\lambda^* = \lambda^*(1+k^*) \\
&k^* = exp\left(\bar{\alpha} + \sigma_J^2/2\right) - 1 \\
&\bar{r}_i = (b - \lambda k)\tau + \left(\bar{\alpha} - \sigma_J^2/2\right)i \\
&\sigma_i^2 = \sigma_s^2\tau + i\sigma_J^2 \text{ or } \sigma_i = \sqrt{\sigma_s^2\tau + i\sigma_J^2} \\
&\tau \equiv T - t \text{ time to expiration}
\end{aligned}$$

Proof of Proposition 1. A Bitcoin option with a payoff of the form $\phi(S_\tau) = (S_\tau - X)^+$ on the underlying asset S_τ can be written as $\phi(S_\tau)e^{-rt}$, which is a martingale under $\mathbb{Q}$. The expectation operator $\mathbb{E}_{\mathbb{Q}}[.]$ under the risk-neutral measure, which is a conditional expectation of the discounted final payoff with a solution for option prices, can be denoted as:

$$\phi(S_\tau) = e^{rt}\mathbb{E}_{\mathbb{Q}}\left[\frac{\phi(S_\tau)}{e^{rt}}\middle|\mathcal{F}_t\right] \tag{25}$$

Note that the option price discounted by the money market account e^{-rt} is a martingale in the martingale measure $\mathbb{Q}$. Substituting $b = r\text{-}g$ into (14) with the non-dividend yield on Bitcoin option, that is $g = 0$, we can proceed to the next step. Let $\mathbb{A} = \{S_\tau > X\}$ be the event that the option is in-the-money at maturity. Event $\mathbb{A}$ is equivalent to the event that:

$$\sigma_i W_\tau + \sum_{i=1}^{N_\tau} J_i > ln\frac{S_t}{X} - \left(r - \lambda^* k^* - \frac{\sigma_i^2}{2}\right)\tau \tag{26}$$

Hence, in (25), the call option price is

$$\begin{aligned}\phi(S_\tau) &= e^{-rt}\mathbb{E}_{\mathbb{Q}}[(S_t - X)\mathbb{I}_A] \\ &= S_t e^{-r\tau}\mathbb{E}_{\mathbb{Q}}\left[e^{-\frac{\sigma_i^2}{2}\tau + \sigma_i W_\tau + \sum_{i=1}^{N_\tau} J_i - \lambda^* k^* \tau})\mathbb{I}_A\right] - Xe^{-r\tau}\mathbb{E}_{\mathbb{Q}}\mathbb{I}_A \\ &= S_t\widetilde{\mathbb{Q}}(A) - Xe^{-r\tau}\mathbb{Q}(A)\end{aligned} \tag{27}$$

wherein (27), the Radon–Nikodym derivative is

$$\left.\frac{d\widetilde{\mathbb{Q}}}{d\mathbb{Q}}\right|_\tau = e^{-\frac{\sigma_i^2}{2}\tau + \sigma_i W_\tau + \sum_{i=1}^{N_\tau} J_i - \lambda^* k^* \tau}$$

from which we note that

$$\mathbb{Q}(A) = \sum_{i=0}^{\infty} \frac{e^{-\lambda^*\tau}(\lambda^*\tau)^i}{i!} N(d_{2i}) \tag{28}$$

where

$$d_{2i} = \frac{ln\frac{S_t}{X} + (\overline{r}_i - \lambda^* k^* + \frac{\sigma_i^2}{2})\tau}{\sigma_s^2\tau + i\sigma_J^2}$$

For a selected γ and ν in the Radon–Nikodym derivative, we can obtain from the application of the derivative Cheang et al. [26] that the jump-sizes will follow normally distributed with mean $\overline{\alpha} = \alpha + \gamma\sigma_j^2$ with the same variance σ_j^2 under the equivalent martingale measure $\mathbb{Q}$. Moreover, under the measure $\widetilde{\mathbb{Q}}$ and the Wiener component $\sigma_i\widetilde{W}_\tau$ is normally distributed and J is normally distributed and the Poisson process N_t has the new intensity of the jump-arrivals $\lambda^* = \lambda^*(1 + k^*)$.

Hence:

$$\widetilde{\mathbb{Q}}(A) = \sum_{i=0}^{\infty} \frac{e^{-\lambda^*\tau}(\lambda^*\tau)^i}{i!} N(d_{1i}) \tag{29}$$

where

$$d_{1i} = d_{2i} + \sigma_i\sqrt{\tau}$$

By plugging Equations (28) and (29) into Equation (27), we can obtain Equation (24). Consequently, the proof of Proposition 1 is completed. □

Throughout this paper, we shall consider the Bates model as an extension of a Merton jump-diffusion model. The diffusion based on stochastic volatility models cannot capture the asymmetry of short-term price returns to describe implied volatility skews of the options for short maturities. The combined stochastic volatility and jump-diffusion (SVJD) processes introduced by Bates can deal with this puzzle by incorporating jump components to the Heston stochastic volatility model. The benefit of the Bates model also reflects the 'jump fear' of the participants had experienced from the markets crash. The SVJD processes also provide the explanation to the distinction between skew and smile with respect to the asymmetry of jumps expected by the index options market, e.g., the fear of a great downward jump causes a downward skew (Cont and Tankov [7]). Therefore, Proposition 1 describes the closed-form expression for the Bates model.

Proposition 2. *In the market model outlined above, consider a European call option, C_a with maturity t or T , and strike X written on a futures contract with maturity T, where $t \leq T$. Whereas Bitcoin prices follow a jump-diffusion process, the closed form solutions of contingent claims Call/Put can be obtained from:*

$$C_a(S, X, \tau) = \mathcal{P}_{Oi}(\lambda\tau)\left[S_t e^{-b_i\tau} N(d_{1i}) - Xe^{-r\tau} N(d_{2i})\right] \tag{30}$$

$$P_u(S, X, \tau) = \mathcal{P}_{Oi}(\lambda\tau)\left[Xe^{-r\tau} N(-d_{2i}) - S_t e^{-b_i\tau} N(-d_{1i})\right] \tag{31}$$

where

$$\mathcal{P}_{oi}(\lambda\tau) = \sum_{i=0}^{\infty} \frac{e^{\lambda^*\tau}(\lambda^*\tau)^i}{i!}$$

$$d_{1i} = \frac{ln\frac{S_t}{X} + b_i + \frac{\sigma_i^2}{2}}{\sigma_i},\ d_{2i} = \frac{ln\frac{S_t}{X} + b_i - \frac{\sigma_i^2}{2}}{\sigma_i}$$

and

$$b_i = (b - \lambda k)\tau + \left(\sigma_s - \frac{\sigma_J^2}{2}\right)i$$

$$k^* \equiv exp\left(\sigma_s - \frac{\sigma_J}{2}\right) - 1,$$

$$d_{2i} \equiv d_{1i} - \sigma_i$$

$$\sigma_i^2 = \sigma_s^2\tau + i\sigma_J^2, \text{ or } \sigma_i = \sqrt{\sigma_s^2\tau + i\sigma_J^2}$$

Proof. See Appendix A. Appendix A provides the proof of Proposition 2 and the X_t values are the terminal Bitcoin drawn from the distribution of the equation. On the other hand, notice that if the $\sum_{i=0}^{\infty} \frac{e^{\lambda^*\tau}(\lambda^*\tau)^i}{i!}$ term of Equation (30) can be simplified into 1, then Equation (30) can be written as the B-S formula, one:

$$C_{ai}(S, X, \tau) = S_t e^{-b_i\tau} N(d_{1i}) - Xe^{-r\tau} N(d_{2i}) \tag{32}$$

□

Remark 1. *In the proof of Proposition 2, the decomposition of the option price in Equation (32) is similar to that obtained by Geman et al. [27] for the pure-diffusion case. As the jump size becomes smaller and smaller, that is, the jump rate is equal to zero, $\lambda = 0$, then the pricing formulae again degenerate to the Black–Scholes option formula. Substituting the Black–Scholes call/put price into Equations (30) and (31), yield the value of a call/put option, respectively.*

3. Option Hedging for Bitcoin Market

For each option pricing model, certain risk metrics can be computed and be managed their risk by analyzing Greeks. The sensitivities of the option price can represent the different dimensions of the risk in a Bitcoin option.

3.1. Option Hedging for Bitcoin Derivatives and Computation of Greeks

Before proceeding, it should be mentioned that option Greeks are widely adopted to measure risk exposure and hedging. More precisely, Appendix B provides the proof for the derivation results of Delta, Gamma, Theta, Vega, and the option *Rho*, and are summarized as follows:

1. Delta (Δ)

$$\Delta_{C_a} = \mathcal{P}_{oi}(\lambda\tau).e^{-b_i\tau}N(d_{1i}) \tag{33}$$

$$\Delta_{P_u} = \mathcal{P}_{oi}(\lambda\tau).e^{-b_i\tau}[N(d_{1i}) - 1] \tag{34}$$

The algorithm describes the first-order sensitivity of call options price with respect to the underlying rate is known to option traders as 'Delta', i.e., Δ_{C_a}.

2. Gamma (**Γ**)

Gamma represents the second derivative of the option's price concerning the underlying price. Hedges of gamma risk are generally accompanied by a delta hedge, with an option's delta being the first partial derivative of the option price with respect to changes in the underlying asset's price.

$$\boldsymbol{\Gamma}_{C_a} = \mathcal{P}_{oi}(\lambda\tau)\,\frac{e^{-b_i\tau}}{\sigma_i\sqrt{\tau}S_t}N'(d_{1i}) \tag{35}$$

$$\boldsymbol{\Gamma}_{P_u} = \mathcal{P}_{oi}(\lambda\tau)\,\frac{e^{-b_i\tau}}{\sigma_i\sqrt{\tau}S_t}N'(d_{1i}) \tag{36}$$

where $N'(d_i) = \frac{1}{\sqrt{2\pi}}e^{-\frac{d_i^2}{2}}$.

3. Theta (**Θ**)

$$\begin{aligned}\boldsymbol{\Theta}_{C_a} = {} & [b_i\mathcal{P}_{oi}(\lambda\tau) + \lambda\mathcal{P}_{oi-1}(\tau) - \lambda\mathcal{P}_{oi}(\tau)][S_te^{-b_i\tau}N(d_{1i})] - \\ & [r\mathcal{P}_{oi}(\lambda\tau) + \lambda\mathcal{P}_{oi-1}(\tau) - \lambda\mathcal{P}_{oi}(\tau)][Xe^{-r\tau}N(d_{2i})]\end{aligned} \tag{37}$$

$$\begin{aligned}\boldsymbol{\Theta}_{P_u} = {} & [r\mathcal{P}_{oi}(\lambda\tau) + \lambda\mathcal{P}_{oi-1}(\tau) - \lambda\mathcal{P}_{oi}(\tau)][Xe^{-r\tau}N(-d_{2i})] - [b_i\mathcal{P}_{oi}(\lambda\tau) + \\ & \lambda\mathcal{P}_{oi-1}(\tau) - \lambda\mathcal{P}_{oi}(\tau)][S_te^{-b_i\tau}N(-d_{1i})]\end{aligned} \tag{38}$$

4. Vega (**ν**)

Vega indicates the amount that an options option's price changes in reaction to changes by one percentage point in the implied volatility of the underlying asset. One approach to managing risk is to establish a hedge against the implied volatility exposure of the underlying asset.

$$\boldsymbol{\nu}_{C_a} = \mathcal{P}_{oi}(\lambda\tau)S_te^{-b_i\tau}\sqrt{\tau}N'(d_{1i}) > 0 \tag{39}$$

$$\boldsymbol{\nu}_{P_u} = \mathcal{P}_{oi}(\lambda\tau)S_te^{-b_i\tau}\sqrt{\tau}N'(d_{1i}) > 0 \tag{40}$$

5. ***Rho***

$$\boldsymbol{Rho}_{C_a} = \mathcal{P}_{oi}(\lambda\tau)X\tau e^{-r\tau}N(d_{2i}) > 0 \tag{41}$$

$$\boldsymbol{Rho}_{P_u} = -\mathcal{P}_{oi}(\lambda\tau)\tau Xe^{-r\tau}N(-d_{2i}) < 0 \tag{42}$$

3.2. Derivation of Sensitivity for Bitcoin Options Respective with Exercise Price

Proposition 3 incorporates our results in as far as the jump components for the European-style options contracts.

Proposition 3. *In the Poisson jump-component type model with lognormally distributed jump sizes at the Bitcoin price, the value of a European call option under the locally risky minimizing hedging strategy is given by $C_a(S, X, \tau)$. The Bitcoin option is convex in (S, X). However, the function is not strictly convex. In addition, the specific property of a put option $P_u(S, X, \tau)$ is similar to a call option.*

Proof. Before proving the proposition we first outline the following definitions:

Definition 1. *A matrix A is positive semidefinite if and only if all its principal n minors (not just leading) are nonnegative.*

Definition 2. *Let $f : U \to \mathbb{R}$ be a twice differentiable function $f''(x)$, where $U \in\to \mathbb{R}^n$ is a convex open subset. It follows that: f is positive semidefinite on $\mathbb{R}^n$ if and only if all its principal minors are positive or zero. Its second derivative Hessian matrix $f''(x)$ is positive semidefinite for $x \in U$ if and only if a function f is convex. If $f''(x)$ is positive definite for every $x \in U$, then f is strictly convex.*

Then, in sensitivity analysis, the optimal hedge is approximated at first-order by the ratio. For a European call option on a Bitcoin option, the sensitivity can be shown as:

$$\frac{\partial C_a}{\partial X} = -\mathcal{P}_{oi}(\lambda\tau)e^{-r\tau}N(d_{2i}) \tag{43}$$

The derivation for Equation (41) with respect to X,S are written as

$$\begin{aligned}
\frac{\partial^2 C_a}{\partial X^2} &= \frac{-\partial \mathcal{P}_{Oi}(\lambda\tau)e^{-r\tau}N(d_{2i})}{\partial X} = \frac{\mathcal{P}_{Oi}(\lambda\tau)e^{-r\tau}N'(d_{2i})}{X\sigma\sqrt{\tau}} > 0\\
\frac{\partial^2 C_a}{\partial X \partial S} &= \frac{-\partial \mathcal{P}_{Oi}(\lambda\tau)e^{-r\tau}N(d_{2i})}{\partial S} = \frac{-\mathcal{P}_{Oi}(\lambda\tau)e^{-r\tau}N'(d_{2i})}{S\sigma\sqrt{\tau}} < 0\\
\frac{\partial^2 C_a}{\partial S \partial X} &= \frac{\partial \mathcal{P}_{Oi}(\lambda\tau).e^{-b_i\tau}N(d_{1i})}{\partial X} = \frac{-\mathcal{P}_{Oi}(\lambda\tau)e^{-b_i\tau}N'(d_{1i})}{X\sigma\sqrt{\tau}} < 0
\end{aligned}$$

For simplicity, the term of $\frac{\partial^2 C_a}{\partial S^2}$ yields $\frac{\mathcal{P}_{oi}(\lambda\tau)e^{-b_i\tau}}{\sigma_i\sqrt{\tau}S_t}N'(d_{1i})$.

The above equations can be rearranged in the following matrix form and the Hessian matrix of a Bitcoin option can now be written as:

$$\begin{bmatrix} \frac{\partial^2 C_a}{\partial S^2} & \frac{\partial^2 C_a}{\partial S \partial X} \\ \frac{\partial^2 C_a}{\partial X \partial S} & \frac{\partial^2 C_a}{\partial X^2} \end{bmatrix} = \begin{bmatrix} \frac{\mathcal{P}_{oi}(\lambda\tau)e^{-b_i\tau}}{\sigma_i\sqrt{\tau}S_t}N'(d_{1i}) & \frac{-\mathcal{P}_{Oi}(\lambda\tau)e^{-b_i\tau}N'(d_{1i})}{X\sigma\sqrt{\tau}} \\ \frac{-\mathcal{P}_{Oi}(\lambda\tau)e^{-r\tau}N'(d_{2i})}{S\sigma\sqrt{\tau}} & \frac{\mathcal{P}_{Oi}(\lambda\tau)e^{-r\tau}N'(d_{2i})}{X\sigma\sqrt{\tau}} \end{bmatrix} \tag{44}$$

The leading principal minors of the Hessian matrix is $\frac{\mathcal{P}_{oi}(\lambda\tau)e^{-b_i\tau}}{\sigma_i\sqrt{\tau}S_t}N'(d_{1i}) > 0$ and $\det|H| = 0$. Therefore, according to Definition 1, the Hessian matrix is a positive semidefinite matrix, which indicates that $C_a(S, X, \tau)$ is convex in (S, X). In addition, according to Definition 2, $C_a(S, X, \tau)$ is not a strictly convex function. Consequently, the corresponding delta of a long position in a Bitcoin call option is a strictly positive (negative) number; or equivalently, the call option price is a strictly increasing function of the Bitcoin price. For a European put option on a Bitcoin option, the sensitivity can be shown as:

$$\frac{\partial P_u}{\partial X} = \mathcal{P}_{oi}(\lambda\tau)e^{-r\tau}N(-d_{2i}) \tag{45}$$

The process of derivation Equation (45) is shown as:

$$
\begin{aligned}
\frac{\partial P_u}{\partial X} &= \mathcal{P}_{oi}(\lambda\tau)\left[e^{-r\tau}N(-d_{2i}) + Xe^{-r\tau}\frac{\partial N(-d_{2i})}{\partial X} - S_t e^{-b_i\tau}\frac{\partial N(-d_{1i})}{\partial X}\right] \\
&= \mathcal{P}_{oi}(\lambda\tau)\left\{e^{-r\tau}[-N(d_{2i})] + Xe^{-r\tau}\frac{\partial[-N(d_{2i})]}{\partial d_{2i}}\frac{\partial d_{2i}}{\partial X} - S_t e^{-b_i\tau}\frac{\partial[-N(d_{1i})]}{\partial d_{1i}}\frac{\partial d_{1i}}{\partial X}\right\} \\
&= \mathcal{P}_{oi}(\lambda\tau)\left\{e^{-r\tau}[-N(d_{2i})] - Xe^{-r\tau}\left(\frac{1}{\sqrt{2\pi}}e^{-\frac{d_{1i}^2}{2}}.\frac{S_t}{X}.e^{\bar{r}_i\tau}\right)\left(\frac{1}{\sigma_i\sqrt{\tau}}\right).\frac{-1}{X} + S_t e^{-b_i\tau}\frac{1}{\sqrt{2\pi}}e^{-\frac{d_{1i}^2}{2}}.\left(\frac{1}{\sigma_i\sqrt{\tau}}\right).\frac{-1}{X}\right\} \\
&= \mathcal{P}_{oi}(\lambda\tau)\left\{e^{-r\tau}[-N(d_{2i})] + \frac{1}{\sigma_i\sqrt{2\pi\tau}}e^{-\frac{d_{1i}^2}{2}}.\frac{S_t}{X}.e^{-b_i\tau} - \frac{1}{\sigma_i\sqrt{2\pi\tau}}e^{-\frac{d_{1i}^2}{2}}\left(\frac{S_t}{X}.e^{-b_i\tau}\right)\right\} \\
&= \mathcal{P}_{Oi}(\lambda\tau)e^{-r\tau}N(-d_{2i})
\end{aligned}
$$

Next, the derivation for Equation (45) with respect to X,S are written as:

$$
\begin{aligned}
\frac{\partial^2 P_u}{\partial S\partial X} &= \frac{\partial \mathcal{P}_{Oi}(\lambda\tau).e^{-b_i\tau}[N(d_{1i})-1]}{\partial X} = \frac{-\mathcal{P}_{Oi}(\lambda\tau)e^{-b_i\tau}N'(d_{1i})}{X\sigma\sqrt{\tau}} < 0 \\
\frac{\partial^2 P_u}{\partial X\partial S} &= \frac{\partial \mathcal{P}_{Oi}(\lambda\tau).e^{-r\tau}N(-d_{2i})}{\partial S} = \frac{-\mathcal{P}_{Oi}(\lambda\tau)e^{-r\tau}N'(d_{2i})}{S\sigma\sqrt{\tau}} < 0 \\
\frac{\partial^2 P_u}{\partial X^2} &= \frac{\partial \mathcal{P}_{Oi}(\lambda\tau)e^{-r\tau}N(-d_{2i})}{\partial X} = \frac{-\mathcal{P}_{Oi}(\lambda\tau)e^{-r\tau}N'(d_{2i})}{-X\sigma\sqrt{\tau}} > 0
\end{aligned}
$$

After slightly rearranging the above equations, these equations correspond to the Hessian matrix of a Bitcoin put option is shown as:

$$
\begin{bmatrix} \frac{\partial^2 P_u}{\partial S^2} & \frac{\partial^2 P_u}{\partial S\partial X} \\ \frac{\partial^2 P_u}{\partial X\partial S} & \frac{\partial^2 P_u}{\partial X^2} \end{bmatrix} = \begin{bmatrix} \frac{\mathcal{P}_{oi}(\lambda\tau)e^{-b_i\tau}}{\sigma_i\sqrt{\tau S_t}}N'(d_{1i}) & \frac{-\mathcal{P}_{Oi}(\lambda\tau)e^{-b_i\tau}N'(d_{1i})}{X\sigma\sqrt{\tau}} \\ \frac{-\mathcal{P}_{Oi}(\lambda\tau)e^{-r\tau}N'(d_{2i})}{S\sigma\sqrt{\tau}} & \frac{\mathcal{P}_{Oi}(\lambda\tau)e^{-r\tau}N'(d_{2i})}{X\sigma\sqrt{\tau}} \end{bmatrix} = 0 \tag{46}
$$

Similarly, the leading principal minors of the Hessian matrix are also $\frac{\mathcal{P}_{oi}(\lambda\tau)e^{-b_i\tau}}{\sigma_i\sqrt{\tau S_t}}N'(d_{1i}) > 0$ and $\det|H| = 0$. Therefore, according to Definition 1, the Hessian is a positive semidefinite matrix. Similarly, $P_u(S,X,\tau)$ is convex in (S,X). According to Definition 2, $P_u(S,X,\tau)$ is not a strictly convex function. Thus, the proof of Proposition 3 is completed. □

In general, the price of a Bitcoin put option serves in the same direction as a short position in the specific portfolio. In particular, to short the specified number of underlying Bitcoin shares is necessary to hedge a written put option for investors.

More generally, we can adopt the preceding convex property for the contingent claim function based on convex risk measures of probability measures, making it useful for other applications beyond estimation. Next, we proceed to capture parameter uncertainty by using convex risk measures for all derivatives without exposure to model (parameter) risk. Due to the uncertainty that emerges from the estimator's volatility and possible bias, adequately specified parameters of a financial model are applied to the case of historical estimation. Hedging contingent claims with computation of Greeks is assumed in different model approaches based on convex risk measures in order to incorporate parameter risk and to transform it into Bitcoin derivatives prices, extending the results in Cont and Tankov [7] and Bannör and Scherer [28].

4. Numerical Application

The estimation procedures for fast calibration in the jump-diffusion model will be exhibited as follows:

First, estimates for the jump intensity parameter λ from Table 1 will be needed. The Bitcoin market data employed for the jump detection on the empirical research will be described. As closed-form solutions are available for the Bates implied volatility from the asymptotic formulas, this approach improves the calibration efficiency.

Second, with the setting parameters received from the calibration procedures, Bitcoin option prices, with Bates' semi-closed form solution (Equation (30)), were computed. The calibration results are shown as volatility surface and smiles.

For the empirical investigation in the study, we select the historical Bitcoin data from 1 January 2015 to 28 February 2018, which consists of 4620 daily collected data. The dataset is adopted from the Bitcoin Price Index (BPI) traded daily on CoinDesk (https://www.coindesk.com/price/bitcoin/ (accessed on 01 October 2018)). In practice, the Bitcoin Price Index of CoinDesk indicates an average Bitcoin price across leading Bitcoin exchanges and their rate between the US dollar (USD) and the Bitcoin. The Bitcoin return profile of log-returns representing $\mathbb{R}_t = \log(S_t/S_{t-1})$ is shown in Figure 2. The magnitude of log-returns depicts from 0.25 to -0.25 and exhibits asymmetry phenomenon. Additionally, Figures 2 and 3 display both the persistence and asymmetry features in Bitcoin return volatility. As expected, the RV_t, BV_t, and RJ_t are all robust in detecting irregular jump arrivals and market structure noise. To further analyze the jump dynamics, we provide quarterly statistics of the significant jump components for a critical value of $\alpha = 0.05$ in Table 1. The observations have a jump range of 0.099 to 0.169 for the sample period, with an average of 0.124. As a comparison shown in Table 1, the intensity of the exact jump is the highest during the Q3 in any given year of the sample period. For example, in 2015, there are 45, 52, 61, and 44 jumps in Q1, Q2, Q3, and Q4, respectively. Similar patterns exist in other years. The jump intensity also varies across years. Hence, jumps appear to be time-varying.

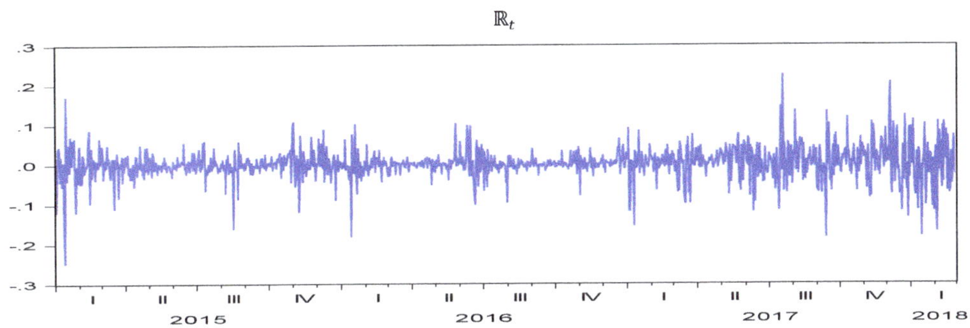

Figure 2. Return, Logarithmic Returns of Bitcoin. The top panel of the graph illustrates the daily returns of Bitcoin over the period time and the bottom panel of the graph illustrates the daily logarithmic returns of Bitcoin.

The following empirical results illustrate some of the rich implications of pricing contingent claims on Bitcoin following jump-diffusions. The real-world probabilities calculated from historical price data is referred to as physical or market probabilities measure $\mathbb{P}$. Accordingly, the estimated model parameters can be used in the option pricing under the risk-neutral pricing measure $\mathbb{Q}$ for price all options. Consider constructing a portfolio that includes a contingent claim (e.g., a call option) having price S, an underlying asset whose price follows the process given in Equation (16). For the simulations, we used the following model parameters: cost-of-carry (b) = 5%, the riskless interest rate $r = 0.02$, option's time to maturity (τ) = 1, 3, or 6 months(M), and nonzero value of the mean jump size or expected jump size $\bar{k} = -0.05$. The Bitcoin price at time t = 0 is set to $S_0 = 11{,}000$, which is the average price from 26–31 January, 2018, and ${\sigma_B}^2 = 0.25$ refers to the annualized 5- or 30-day historical volatility of the Bitcoin Price Index (BPI). Early examples of the use of this for jump components can be found in Haug [29], Beckers [30], and Ball and Torous [31]. More importantly, in Tables 2 and 3, the base parameters of the jump intensity λ are set to 9.89%, 13.5%, and 16.85%, the magnitudes are filtered from the empirical outcomes in Table 1, include jump means $u_{j,t}$= 0.124, and jump volatilities $\delta = 0.02$.

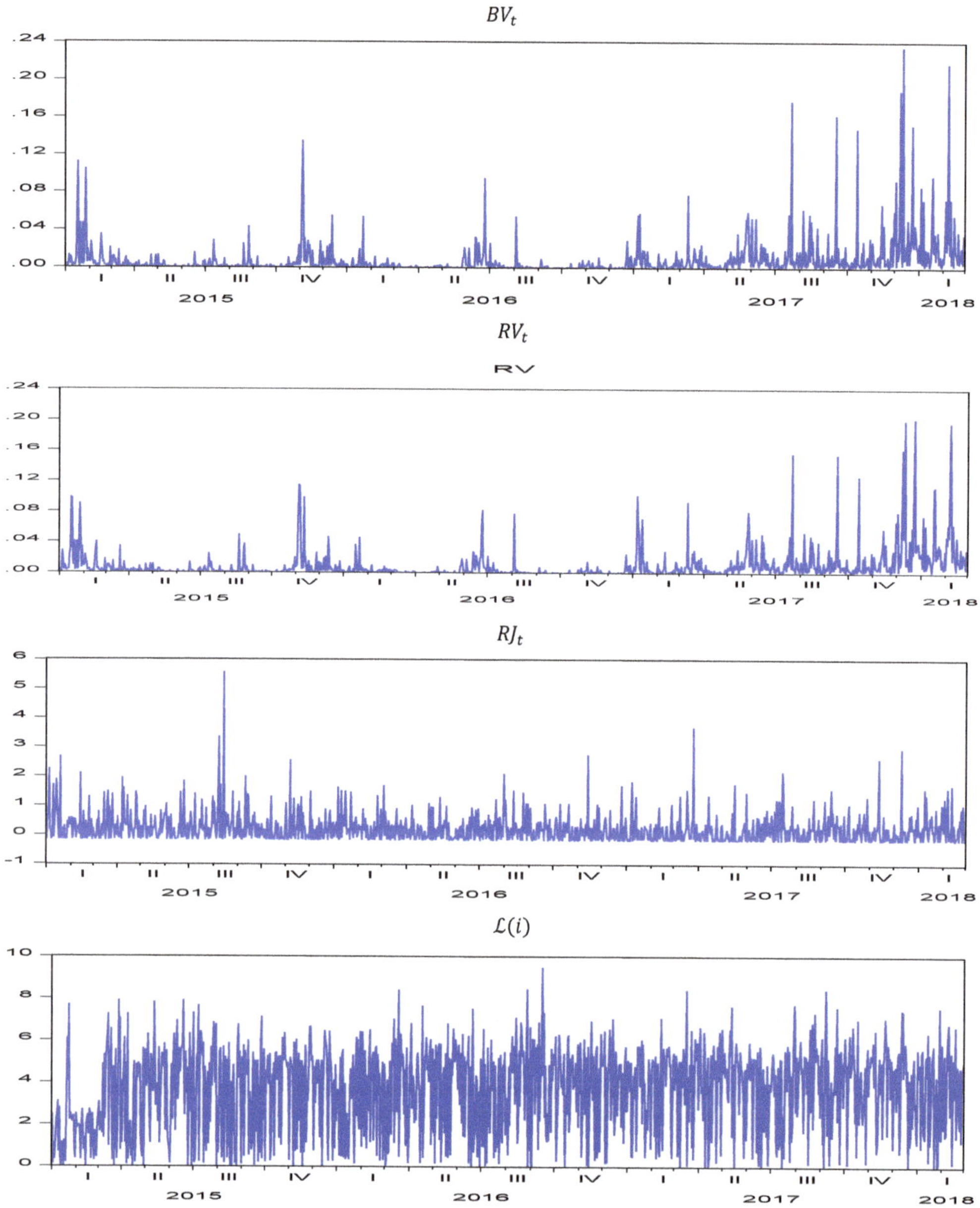

Figure 3. Time series of the Bipower variation, realized volatility, and the relative jump and jump statistic component for Bitcoin prices. The top panel of the figure depicts the *BVt* (Equation (4)), the second panel plots for respective graphs the daily realized volatility *RVt* (Equation (3)); the third panel plots the relative jump component *RTt* (Equation (6)); and the bottom panel depicts the jump statistic $\mathcal{L}(i)$ (Equation (7)) at significance $\alpha = 0.05$.

Table 2. Calculating Bitcoin Call Option Valuation with Merton Jump-Diffusion.

		$S = 11{,}000$, $\delta = 0.02$, $r = 0.02$,			$\bar{k} = -0.05$, $b = 5$ (%)					
${\sigma_B}^2$	**Strike**	$\lambda = 9.89\%$ Time to Maturity			$\lambda = 13.5\%$ Time to Maturity			$\lambda = 16.85\%$ Time to Maturity		
		1M	**3M**	**6M**	**1M**	**3M**	**6M**	**1M**	**3M**	**6M**
0.1	9000	2014.78	2044.27	2088.59	2014.79	2044.28	2088.58	2014.80	2044.29	2088.57
	10,000	1016.44	1053.38	1119.73	1016.43	1053.37	1119.72	1016.45	1053.39	1119.74
	11,000	134.84	245.47	363.59	134.83	245.45	363.58	134.85	245.49	363.57
	12,000	0.13	11.66	55.22	0.14	11.67	55.23	0.12	11.68	55.24
	13,000	0.01	0.08	3.65	0.01	0.07	3.66	0.01	0.06	3.64
0.25	9,000	2015.28	2069.29	2185.76	2015.27	2069.28	2185.76	2015.28	2069.30	2185.76
	10,000	1046.95	1203.09	1407.02	1046.94	1203.08	1407.02	1046.95	1203.07	1407.02
	11,000	323.31	570.56	820.85	323.30	570.57	820.85	323.31	570.57	820.85
	12,000	46.99	216.75	434.98	46.99	216.74	434.97	46.99	216.76	434.98
	13,000	3.06	66.48	211.10	3.05	66.49	211.11	3.06	66.58	211.10
0.5	9000	2065.65	2324.81	2670.25	2065.64	2324.80	2670.26	2065.65	2324.831	2670.27
	10,000	1239.45	1642.23	2069.64	1239.46	1642.24	2069.63	1239.45	1642.25	2069.65
	11,000	637.06	1111.34	1580.02	637.07	1111.33	1580.03	637.06	1111.37	1580.04
	12,000	279.18	723.76	1191.25	279.17	723.77	1191.26	279.18	723.78	1191.27
	13,000	105.35	455.94	889.10	105.36	455.92	889.11	105.35	455.95	889.15

European options prices were computed using equation (22). Numerical results are based on historical parameter estimates and then calibration of the Merton volatility jump-diffusion model is simultaneously applied to call options. Calibrated parameters as follows: initial volatility = 10%, 25%, and 50%, and mean jump size is −0.05. In addition, jump intensity λ = 0.0989, 0.135, and 0.1685, jump means = 0.124, and jump standard deviation = 0.02, among the jump distribution are calculated from Table 1.

Table 3. Calculating Bitcoin Call Option Valuation with Bates Jump-Diffusion.

		$S = 11{,}000$, $\delta = 0.02$, $r = 0.02$,			$\bar{k} = -0.05$, $b = 5$ (%)					
${\sigma_B}^2$		$\lambda = 9.89\%$ Time to Maturity			$\lambda = 13.5\%$ Time to Maturity			$\lambda = 16.8\%$ Time to Maturity		
		1M	**3M**	**6M**	**1M**	**3M**	**6M**	**1M**	**3M**	**6M**
0.1	9000	2050.00	2187.91	2410.51	2057.83	2227.12	2488.79	2065.43	2259.81	2550.17
	10,000	1114.09	1350.15	1646.38	1146.09	1426.31	1764.11	1171.19	1482.95	1850.13
	11,000	381.98	704.14	1040.01	447.37	806.26	1183.55	489.41	878.62	1285.27
	12,000	49.05	295.50	603.86	89.59	392.93	750.66	121.84	463.55	855.31
	13,000	0.32	94.32	320.94	3.76	161.27	450.09	11.37	215.11	545.86
0.25	9000	2060.35	2249.91	2539.11	2071.18	2292.66	2615.41	2080.69	2326.57	2674.05
	10,000	1161.11	1472.97	1840.52	1193.35	1541.26	1941.94	1218.07	1592.42	2017.41
	11,000	486.37	874.77	1280.33	534.45	957.44	1396.49	569.87	1018.31	1481.99
	12,000	113.63	468.59	856.52	169.57	548.11	974.78	197.93	607.68	1062.35
	13,000	21.77	226.28	552.67	35.06	289.33	662.17	47.64	338.81	744.89
0.5	9000	2128.68	2495.99	2961.99	2143.91	2535.12	3022.75	2156.08	2565.66	3069.84
	10,000	1332.08	1834.29	2375.33	1358.67	1883.84	2446.11	1379.26	1922.06	2500.62
	11,000	737.67	1306.54	1886.12	769.45	1361.35	1962.91	793.95	1403.54	2021.95
	12,000	359.96	905.03	1485.66	387.99	959.66	1564.53	409.98	1001.94	1625.31
	13,000	164.43	611.86	1,162.73	174.89	662.07	1,240.36	190.58	701.33	1,300.48

European options prices were computed using Equation (30). Calibration of the Bates volatility jump-diffusion model is simultaneously applied to call options. Calibrated parameters are the same as Table 2.

In Tables 2 and 3, the empirical outcomes are provided for pricing call options under the Merton and Bates models, respectively. Tables 2 and 3 summarize the options pricing under the jump-diffusion process for the setting parameters against several strikes (in columns). As expected, the values of in-the-money (ITM) options decrease with respect to strike prices while out of the money (OTM) values show similar results obtained by the calibration procedure. The pricing values, which are tabulated with different choices of strike price X, frequency of Poisson events λ, and volatility σ, are key differences for ATM prices values of Bitcoin options, while ITM and OTM options in Bitcoin are very small. This may be justified by the fact that Bitcoin investors consider ambiguity neutrality with respect to probabilistically sophisticated preferences to ambiguity averse market makers, even the OTM and ITM ones, as the underlying value is expected to blow up. However, Bitcoin investors prefer ATM options that are more likely to be exercised under ambiguous Bitcoin market making, especially on jump-diffusion. Our findings should be interpreted with caution. What we document here are the price of a call/put option is a strictly decreasing (increasing) function of Bitcoin price depicted as Figure 4A,B, and which is violated from the traditional theoretical call/put values (Theoretically, a long call option can only increase the value of the option. Hence, the delta of a long call option is always positive. Another way to look at this would be in terms of replicating a Bitcoin with options. The delta of a long call option goes up when their underlying Bitcoin goes up. Therefore, more shares of underlying assets, which are represented by the replicated options, should be held to hedge a written call option). Such deviations may be the result of the jump risk of option prices in the Bitcoin market (The value of a call option increases when the price of Bitcoin increases, so the delta of a call option is positive. Conversely the value of a put option decreases when the price of Bitcoin increases, so the delta of the put option is negative). If an option holder can always realize the option's theoretical value by selling (or delta hedging) in the market, only a European call option is better than a Bitcoin call, as it can be exercised just before stock becomes an ex-dividend.

Figure 4A–F depict the calibration results of the Greeks for Bitcoin options. As shown in Figure 4A,B, the surfaces of the delta of call and put options display non-convex. These Figures illustrate the difficulty of using the method based on convex risk measures to quantify parameter risk. However, the Vega of call and put options, as depicted in Figure 4D, appear to adequately specify the risk parameters with convex risk measures. Moreover, Figure 4C shows that the volatility surfaces obtained using jump diffusion model exhibit both smiles and skews for short maturities, which is also shown in Figure 4E. The findings interpret that the benefits of incorporating these jumps flow over into option pricing, as well as accurately capture the volatility smile in option prices (see Duan et al. [32]). Compared to the study of Cretarola et al. [33], they have not considered Bitcoin prices with jump innovations and not found volatility skews or smiles in Bitcoin options.

To summarize, jump-diffusion models shed light on an explanation of the implied volatility smile phenomenon as the implied volatility is different from the historical volatility as well as varies as a function of strikes (see Tankov et al. [34]). Our observations meet our expectations concerning Figure 5, which shows possible implied volatility patterns (as a function of strikes) in the Merton–Bates jump-diffusion model.

Stability across Strikes

Calibrated parameters for the Greek of above equations are set to time to maturity (τ) = 3 month(M), risk-free rate (r) = 2%, cost of carry (b) = 5%, volatility ${\sigma_B}^2 = 0.5$, jump size (kbar) = −5%, jump intensity $\lambda = 0.124$, and jump standard deviation $\delta = 0.02$. The setting values of the asset price (S), strike price (X) for the European call option considered are 11,000 for above Figure 4A–F.

Based on the same maturities, it is clear from the graphs in Figure 5 that the parametrization of the implied volatility smile in the Bates model converges to a flat smile and is more stable across different strikes than in the Merton model. For example, in the Bates model, this convergence is possible as the smile captures the presence of jumps whereas the term structure of implied volatility is taken into account using the cost-of-carry component. Moreover, the result is in line with Mijatović and Tankov [35] regarding the function of both the jump activity index of the jump component and the diffusion process component. We should emphasize that it only serves as an illustration, to indicate that the model can yield a close fit even to a very sharp volatility phenomenon. Similar examples are discussed in Kuo [36].

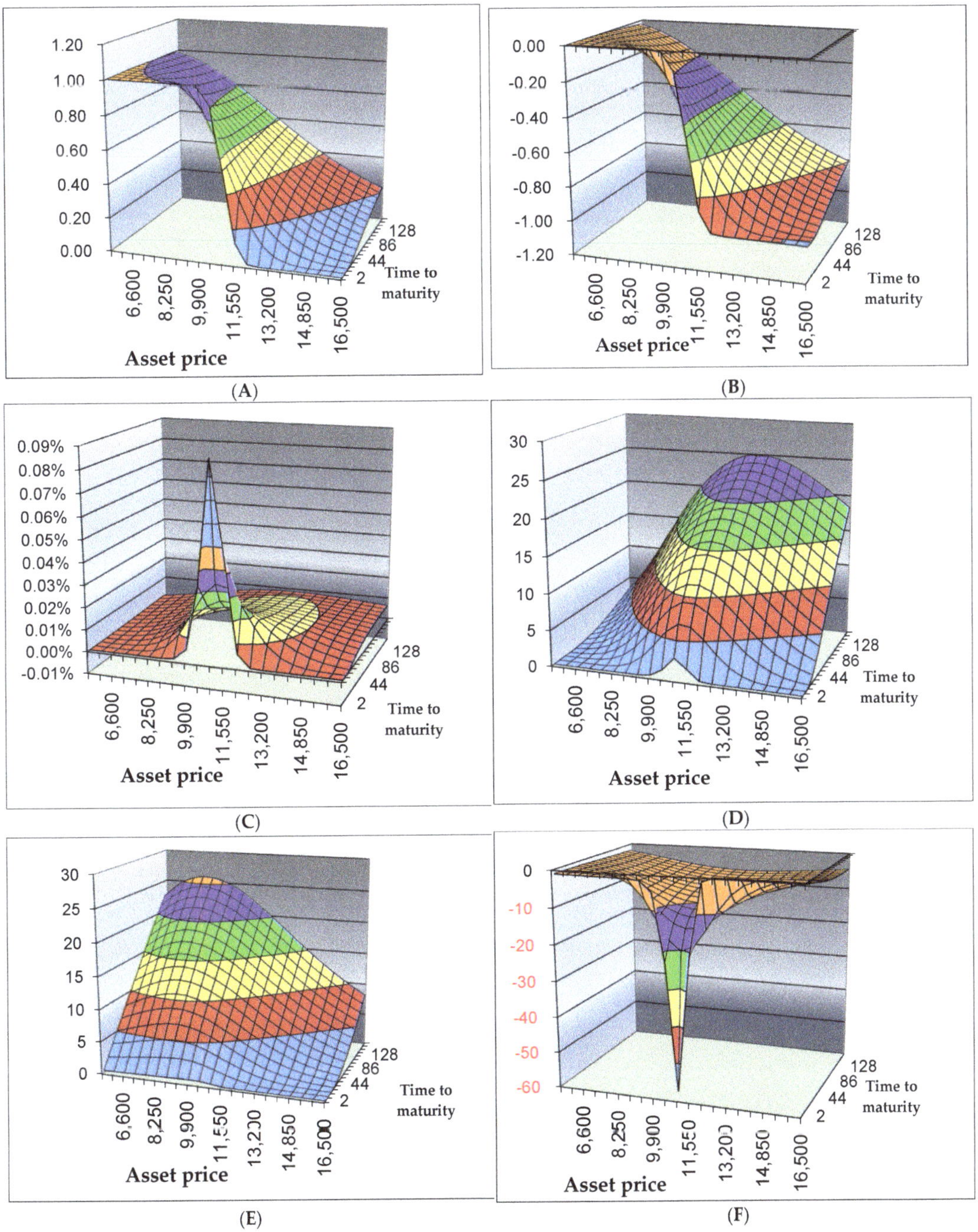

Figure 4. (**A**) The surface of Call options' Delta; (**B**) The surface of put options' Delta; (**C**) The surface of call and put options' Gamma; (**D**) Implied volatilities for call and put options' Vega; (**E**) Volatility surface of call options' Rho on Bitcoin price; (**F**) Theta of European call options.

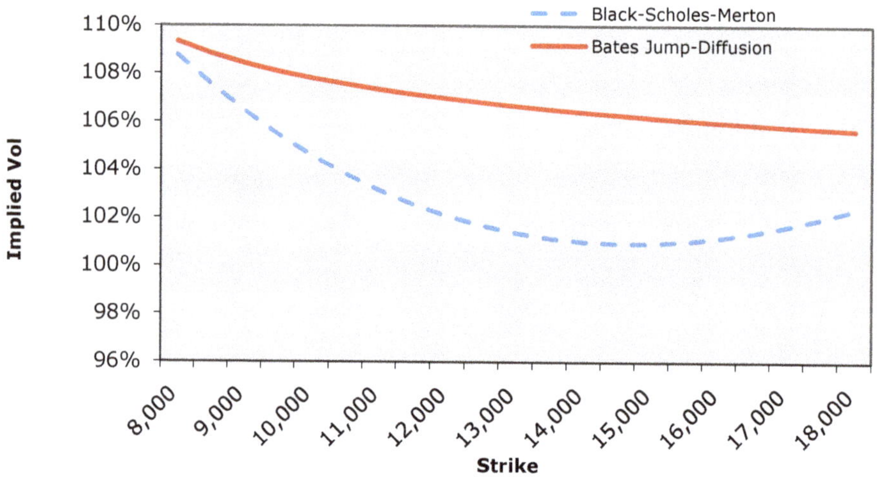

Figure 5. Volatility Smile Fitting. Figure depicts the volatility smile that the parametrization of the implied volatility smile in terms of the strike. This figure plots implied volatilities of call options on the Bitcoin price index as a function of their strikes and maturities for the Bates' model (red solid line) and the BSM model (blue dotted line). More importantly, the Bates' volatility jump-diffusion model is consistent with an asymmetric volatility smile. This model assumes jump risk is systematic and appears to be a much closer match to reality than Merton due to the simultaneous asset price jumps and amplitudes, possibly by varying amounts.

5. Concluding Remarks

Overall, Bitcoin prices exhibit highly volitile behavior due to the interventions, speculative investment interest, and the numerous news-driven shocks in the market (see Scaillet et al. [17]). In this paper, we adopt the idea that Bitcoin prices are influenced by jump-diffusion and confidence about the underlying technology; as a consequence, such a jump-diffusion may spread to Bitcoin prices causing an ambiguous effect.

To describe the jump risk distribution more accurately, this paper applies the jump detection approach to identify realized jumps on the Bitcoin market and to estimate the jump parameters of intensity, mean, and variance. Crucially, similar to Tauchen et al. [37], we find that the jump intensity varies among the 2015–2018Q1 from 9.89% to 16.85%. Applying this to the Bitcoin market, this finding reports some important implications in jump frequencies and volatilities across the sample period over time.

Moreover, based on risk-neutral measures, we derive a quasi-closed formula for European-style Bitcoin derivatives under the Merton–Bates jump-diffusion risk and their Greeks, and a numerical application is provided.

To shed some light on Bitcoin hedging, this paper introduces the computation of Greeks relationships for Bitcoin options as asset replication in frictionless markets. Market makers or confidence about cryptocurrencies are not directly observed, but some major factors may be considered as target variables, such as the number and volume of Bitcoin option transactions. More unconventional problems in the current analysis are left for future research. As suggested in Figure 2A,B, we must ensure that the introduced model is capable of capturing jumps in the Bitcoin market by simply calibrating the model parameters.

As future work, we could better fit the model by incorporating the GARCH-Jump process (e.g., Chan and Maheu [38], Duan et al. [39], and Gronwald [40]) for the volatility of Bitcoin options or considering a new variable such as the stochastic volatility. Therefore, its resolution will be considerably more complex, and could be very interesting research.

Author Contributions: Writing—original draft preparation, K.-S.C. and Y.-C.H.; writing—review and editing, K.-S.C., Y.-C.H.; Methodology, K.-S.C.; Resources, Y.-C.H. All authors have read and agreed to the published version of the manuscript.

Funding: This research received no external funding.

Institutional Review Board Statement: Not Applicable.

Informed Consent Statement: Not Applicable.

Data Availability Statement: Not Applicable.

Acknowledgments: The authors are especially grateful to the anonymous referees for their constructive suggestions and helpful comments to improve our paper.

Conflicts of Interest: The authors declare no conflict of interest.

Appendix A

The proof of Proposition 2 follows along the line of Chen [41]. To find the stochastic jump-diffusion (SJD) formula of Bates and evaluate the options under a risk-neutral measure $\mathbb{Q}$. First, the risk-neutral price C_a at time $\tau \in$ [0,t) of European-style call options at strike price X and underlying options on the Bitcoin price S expiring in τ under the martingale measure $\mathbb{Q}$, can be written by:

$$C_a\left(S, X, \tau, r, \sigma_s^2\right) = e^{-r\tau} \sum_{i=0}^{\infty} \{P_i(i\ jumps)\} E_Q[\max(S_t - X, 0) | i\ jumps] \tag{A1}$$

$$= e^{-r\tau} \sum_{i=0}^{\infty} \frac{e^{\lambda\tau}(\lambda\tau)^i}{i!} E_Q\left[\max\left(S_t\, ke^{-\lambda\tau} - X, 0\right)\right] \tag{A2}$$

$$= \sum_{i=0}^{\infty} \frac{e^{\lambda\tau}(\lambda\tau)^i}{i!} E_Q\left[e^{-r\tau}\max\left(S_t\, ke^{-\lambda\tau} - X, 0\right)\right] \tag{A3}$$

$$= \sum_{i=0}^{\infty} \frac{e^{\lambda\tau}(\lambda\tau)^i}{i!} E_Q\left[C_{BS}\left(S_t\, ke^{-\lambda\tau}, X, \tau, r, \sigma_s^2\right)\right] \tag{A4}$$

where $S_t = S_0 \exp\left[\left(\mu - \frac{\sigma_s^2}{2}\right)t + \sigma_s dW_t\right]$ denotes the underlying prices of Bitcoin under risk measure in Black and Scholes' model (C_{BS}). Thus we proceed to prove the relationship:

$$\begin{aligned} &\tfrac{e^{\lambda\tau}(\lambda\tau)^i}{i!} E_Q\left[C_{BS}\left(S_t\, ke^{-\lambda\tau}, X, \tau, r, \sigma_S^2\right)\right] \\ &= \tfrac{e^{\lambda^*\tau}(\lambda^*\tau)^i}{i!}\left[S_t N(d_{1i}) - Xe^{-r\tau}N(d_{2i})\right] \end{aligned} \tag{A5}$$

Under the risk-neutral measure $\mathbb{Q}$, the undelying Bitcoin prices dynamic $\widetilde{\mathbb{S}}_t$ can be written as:

$$\widetilde{\mathbb{S}}_t = \widetilde{\mathbb{S}}_0 exp\left[\left(u - \lambda k - \frac{\sigma_i^2}{2}\right)\tau + \sigma_i W_t + \sum_{n=1}^{N(t)} J_n\right]$$

Therefore,

$$\begin{aligned} E_Q\left[C_{BS}\left(S_t\, e^J e^{-\lambda\tau}, X, \tau, r, \sigma_s^2\right)\right] = E_Q\left[\frac{\left(\widetilde{\mathbb{S}}_t\, e^J e^{-\lambda_t} N\left(\frac{S_t}{X} + J - \lambda\tau + \left(r + \frac{\sigma_i^2}{2}\right)\tau\right)\right)}{\sigma_s\sqrt{\tau}}\right] \\ -E_Q\left[\left(X\, e^{-\lambda\tau} N\left(\frac{S_t}{X} + J - \lambda\tau + \left(r - \frac{\sigma_i^2}{2}\right)\tau\right)\right)/\sigma_s\sqrt{\tau}\right] \end{aligned} \tag{A6}$$

$$= E_Q\left[\frac{\left(\widetilde{\mathbb{S}}_t\, e^J e^{-\lambda\tau} N\left(\frac{S_t}{X}+(r-\lambda k)\tau+\left(\sigma_s-\sigma_J^2\right)\tau\right)\right)}{\sigma_s\sqrt{\tau}}\right]$$
$$-E_Q\left[\left(X\, e^{-\lambda\tau} N\left(\frac{S_t}{X}+(r-\lambda k)\tau+\left(\sigma_s+\frac{\sigma_J^2}{2}\right)\tau\right)\right)/\sigma_i\sqrt{\tau}\right] \quad (A7)$$

$$= \widetilde{\mathbb{S}}_t e^{-\lambda\tau} e^{\frac{\sigma_J^2}{2}} N\left(\frac{1}{\sigma_i\sqrt{\tau}}\left[ln\frac{S_t}{X}+(r-\lambda k)\tau+\left(\sigma_s+\sigma_J^2\right)\tau\right]\right)$$
$$-Xe^{-\lambda\tau} N\left(\frac{1}{\sigma_i\sqrt{\tau}}\left[ln\frac{S_t}{X}+(r-\lambda k)\tau+\left(\frac{\sigma_i^2}{2}\right)\tau\right]\right) \quad (A8)$$

$$= \widetilde{\mathbb{S}}_t e^{-\lambda\tau} e^{\frac{\sigma_J^2}{2}} N\left(\frac{1}{\sigma_i\sqrt{\tau}}\left[ln\frac{S_t}{X}+\left(r-\lambda k+\frac{\sigma_J^2}{2}\right)\tau+\left(\sigma_s+\frac{\sigma_J^2}{2}\right)\tau\right]\right)$$
$$-Xe^{-\lambda\tau} N\left(\frac{1}{\sigma_i\sqrt{\tau}}\left[ln\frac{S_t}{X}+\left(r-\lambda k+\frac{\sigma_J^2}{2}\right)\tau+\left(\frac{\sigma_S^2}{2}+\frac{\sigma_J^2}{2}\right)\tau\right]\right) \quad (A9)$$

$$= \widetilde{\mathbb{S}}_t e^{-\lambda\tau} e^{\frac{\sigma_J^2}{2}} N\left(\frac{1}{\sigma_i\sqrt{\tau}}\left[ln\frac{S_t}{X}+b_i\tau+\left(\sigma_s+\frac{\sigma_J^2}{2}\right)\tau\right]\right)$$
$$-Xe^{-\lambda\tau} N\left(\frac{1}{\sigma_i\sqrt{\tau}}\left[ln\frac{S_t}{X}+b_i\tau-\left(\frac{\sigma_S^2}{2}+\frac{\sigma_J^2}{2}\right)\tau\right]\right) \quad (A10)$$

By Girsanov's theorem and taking the logarithm on the equation, we then arrange the results as follows:

$$\sum_{i=0}^{\infty}\frac{e^{\lambda^*\tau}(\lambda^*\tau)^i}{i!}\left\{S_t N\left(\frac{1}{\sigma_i\sqrt{\tau}}\left[ln\frac{S_t}{X}+(r-\lambda k)\tau+\left(\sigma_s+\frac{\sigma_J^2}{2}\right)\tau\right]\right)\right.$$
$$\left.-Xe^{-\lambda\tau} N\left(\frac{1}{\sigma_i\sqrt{\tau}}\left[ln\frac{S_t}{X}+b_i\tau-\left(\frac{\sigma_S^2}{2}+\frac{\sigma_J^2}{2}\right)\tau\right]\right)\right\} \quad (A11)$$

$$=\sum_{i=0}^{\infty}\frac{e^{\lambda^*\tau}(\lambda^*\tau)^i}{i!}S_t e^{-b_i\tau}N\left(\frac{ln\frac{S_t}{X}+b_i+\frac{\sigma_i^2}{2}}{\sigma_i}\right)-Xe^{-r\tau}\sum_{i=0}^{\infty}\frac{e^{\lambda^*\tau}(\lambda^*\tau)^i}{i!}N\left(\frac{ln\frac{S_t}{X}+b_i-\frac{\sigma_i^2}{2}}{\sigma_i}\right) \quad (A12)$$

$$=\sum_{i=0}^{\infty}\frac{e^{\lambda^*\tau}(\lambda^*\tau)^i}{i!}\left[S_t e^{-b_i\tau}N(d_{1i})\right]-Xe^{-\lambda\tau}\sum_{i=0}^{\infty}\frac{e^{\lambda^*\tau}(\lambda^*\tau)^i}{i!}.N(d_2) \quad (A13)$$

where $d_{1i} = \frac{ln\frac{S_t}{X}+b_i+\frac{\sigma_i^2}{2}}{\sigma_i}$, $d_{2i} = \frac{ln\frac{S_t}{X}+b_i-\frac{\sigma_i^2}{2}}{\sigma_i}$ and $b_i = (r-\lambda k)\tau+\left(\sigma_S^2-\frac{\sigma_J^2}{2}\right)i$, $\sigma_i=\sqrt{\sigma_S^2\tau+i\sigma_J^2}$

Finally, the desired result is obtained as follows:

$$C_a(S,X,\tau)=\sum_{i=0}^{\infty}\frac{e^{\lambda^*\tau}(\lambda^*\tau)^i}{i!}\left[S_t e^{-b_i\tau}N(d_{1i})-Xe^{-r\tau}N(d_{2i})\right]$$

The derivation of put options is analogous to the above procedures.

This completes the proof of Proposition 2.

Appendix B. Risk Metrics of the Model of Bates (1991)

In this appendix, we make various technical remarks on the different kinds of Bitcoin options which are necessary for our proofs to hold. Instead of hedging the position with the underlying asset, we consider here a strategy in which we invest in another European option (call or put). Other important risk metrics are delta Δ, Vega Λ, and gamma $\mathbf{\Gamma}$ under Bates' model is derived as follows:

Appendix B.1. Derivation of Delta for Different Kinds of Bitcoin Derivatives

Recall that the prices of a European call/put option based on Black–Scholes formulas with the dividend yield paid by the contingent claims are written as follows:

$$C_a(S,X,\tau) = \mathcal{P}_{Oi}(\lambda\tau)\left[S_t e^{-b\tau}N(d_{1i}) - Xe^{-r\tau}N(d_{2i})\right]$$

and

$$P_u(S,X,\tau) = \mathcal{P}_{Oi}(\lambda\tau)\left[Xe^{-r\tau}N(-d_{2i}) - S_t e^{-b\tau}N(-d_{1i})\right]$$

The similar proof of the derivatives of the Greeks letters on the standard Black–Scholes one can be found in, e.g., Haug [29] and Chen et.al. [42]. First of all, we want to derive the formula of Delta. To make the following derivations more easily, we calculate Equation (A14) and Equation (A15) in advance.

$$N'(d_{1i}) = \frac{\partial N(d_{1i})}{\partial d_{1i}} = \frac{1}{\sqrt{2\pi}}e^{-\frac{d_{1i}{}^2}{2}} \tag{A14}$$

$$N'(d_{2i}) = \frac{\partial N(d_{2i})}{\partial d_{2i}} \tag{A15}$$

$$= \frac{1}{\sqrt{2\pi}}e^{-\frac{d_{2i}{}^2}{2}} = \frac{1}{\sqrt{2\pi}}e^{-\frac{(d_{1i}-\sigma_i\sqrt{\tau})^2}{2}} = \frac{1}{\sqrt{2\pi}}e^{-\frac{d_{1i}^2}{2}}.e^{d_{1i}\sigma_s\sqrt{\tau}}.\, e^{-\frac{\sigma_s^2\tau}{2}}$$
$$\frac{1}{\sqrt{2\pi}}e^{-\frac{d_{1i}^2}{2}}.e^{ln\frac{S_t}{X}+(\bar{r}_i+\frac{\sigma_i^2}{2})\tau}.\, e^{-\frac{\sigma_s^2\tau}{2}} = \mathcal{P}_{Oi}(\lambda\tau)\frac{1}{\sqrt{2\pi}}e^{-\frac{d_{1i}^2}{2}}.\,\frac{S_t}{X}.e^{\bar{r}_i\tau}$$

For a European call option on a dividend-paying contingent claim, the Equation (30) applies; delta can be written as:

$$\Delta = \mathcal{P}_{Oi}(\lambda\tau).e^{-b_i\tau}N(d_{1i}) \tag{A16}$$

The derivation process of (A16) is:

$$\begin{aligned}
\Delta &= \tfrac{\partial C_a}{\partial S_t} = \mathcal{P}_{Oi}(\lambda\tau)\left[e^{-b_i\tau}N(d_{1i}) + S_t e^{-b_i\tau}\tfrac{\partial N(d_{1i})}{\partial S_t} - Xe^{-r\tau}\tfrac{\partial N(d_{2i})}{\partial S_t}\right] \\
&= \mathcal{P}_{Oi}(\lambda\tau)\left[e^{-b_i\tau}N(d_{1i}) + S_t e^{-b_i\tau}\tfrac{\partial N(d_{1i})}{\partial d_{1i}}\tfrac{\partial d_{1i}}{\partial S_t} - Xe^{-r\tau}\tfrac{\partial N(d_{2i})}{\partial d_{2i}}\tfrac{\partial d_{2i}}{\partial S_t}\right] \\
&= \mathcal{P}_{Oi}(\lambda\tau)e^{-b_i\tau}N(d_{1i}) + S_t e^{-b_i\tau}\frac{1}{S_t\sigma_s\sqrt{2\pi\tau}}e^{-\frac{d_{1i}^2}{2}} - S_t e^{-b_i\tau}\frac{1}{S_t\sigma_s\sqrt{2\pi\tau}}e^{-\frac{d_{1i}^2}{2}} \\
&\xrightarrow{yields} \mathcal{P}_{Oi}(\lambda\tau).e^{-b_i\tau}N(d_{1i})
\end{aligned}$$

For brevity, a European call option on continuously compounded dividend yield, delta can be written as:

$$\Delta = \mathcal{P}_{Oi}(\lambda\tau).e^{-b_i\tau}[N(d_{1i}) - 1] \tag{A17}$$

The derivation process of (A17) is:

$$\begin{aligned}
\Delta &= \tfrac{\partial P_u}{\partial S_t} = Xe^{-r\tau}\tfrac{\partial N(-d_{2i})}{\partial S_t} - e^{-b_i\tau}N(-d_{1i}) - S_t e^{-b_i\tau}\tfrac{\partial N(-d_{1i})}{\partial S_t} \\
&= Xe^{-r\tau}\tfrac{\partial[1-N(d_{2i})]}{\partial d_{2i}}\tfrac{\partial d_{2i}}{\partial S_t} - e^{-b_i\tau}[1-N(d_{1i})] - S_t e^{-b_i\tau}\tfrac{\partial[1-N(d_{1i})]}{\partial d_{1i}}\tfrac{\partial d_{1i}}{\partial S_t} \\
&= Xe^{-r\tau}\frac{1}{\sqrt{2\pi}}e^{-\frac{d_{1i}^2}{2}}.\frac{S_t}{X}e^{b_i\tau}\frac{1}{S_t\sigma_s\sqrt{\tau}} - e^{-b_i\tau}[1-N(d_{1i})] + S_t e^{-b_i\tau}\frac{1}{\sqrt{2\pi}}e^{-\frac{d_{1i}^2}{2}}\frac{1}{S_t\sigma_s\sqrt{\tau}} \\
&= -S_t e^{-b_i\tau}\frac{1}{S_t\sigma_s\sqrt{2\pi\tau}}e^{-\frac{d_{1i}^2}{2}} + e^{-b_i\tau}[N(d_{1i})-1] + S_t e^{-b_i\tau}\frac{1}{S_t\sigma_s\sqrt{2\pi\tau}}e^{-\frac{d_{1i}^2}{2}} \\
&\xrightarrow{yields} \mathcal{P}_{oi}(\lambda\tau).e^{-b_i\tau}[N(d_{1i})-1]
\end{aligned}$$

Q.E.D

Appendix B.2. Derivation of Gamma for Different Kinds of Bitcoin Options

In the model approach outlined above, the derivation process of Equations (35) and (36) as follows

$$\Gamma = \frac{\partial^2 C_a}{\partial S_t^2} = \frac{\partial\left(\frac{\partial C_a}{\partial S_t}\right)}{\partial S_t} = \frac{\partial\left[e^{-b_i\tau}N(d_{1i})\right]}{\partial S_t} = \mathcal{P}_{Oi}(\lambda\tau)e^{-b_i\tau}\frac{\partial[N(d_{1i})]}{\partial d_{1i}}\frac{\partial d_{1i}}{\partial S_t} = \mathcal{P}_{Oi}(\lambda\tau)e^{-b_i\tau}N'(d_{1i})\frac{\frac{1}{S_t}}{\sigma_i\sqrt{\tau}} \\ = \mathcal{P}_{Oi}(\lambda\tau)\frac{e^{-b_i\tau}}{\sigma_i\sqrt{\tau}S_t}N'(d_{1i}) \tag{A18}$$

Alternative, for a European put option, gamma can be given as

$$\Gamma = \frac{\partial^2 P_u}{\partial S_t^2} = \frac{\partial\left(\frac{\partial P_u}{\partial S_t}\right)}{\partial S_t} = \frac{\partial\left[e^{-b_i\tau}N(d_{1i})-1\right]}{\partial S_t} = \mathcal{P}_{Oi}(\lambda\tau)e^{-b_i\tau}\frac{\partial[N(d_{1i})-1]}{\partial S_t}\frac{\partial d_{1i}}{\partial S_t} = \\ \mathcal{P}_{Oi}(\lambda\tau)e^{-b_i\tau}N'(d_{1i})\frac{\frac{1}{S_t}}{\sigma_i\sqrt{\tau}} = \mathcal{P}_{Oi}(\lambda\tau)\frac{e^{-b_i\tau}}{\sigma_i\sqrt{\tau}S_t}N'(d_{1i}). \tag{A19}$$

Q.E.D

Appendix B.3. Derivation Process of Vega for Different Kinds of Bitcoin Options

The derivation process of Equation (39) can be shown as

$$\begin{aligned}
\mathrm{v} &= \frac{\partial C_a}{\partial \sigma_i} = \mathcal{P}_{Oi}(\lambda\tau)[S_t e^{-b_i\tau}\frac{\partial N(d_{1i})}{\partial \sigma_i} - Xe^{-r\tau}\frac{\partial N(d_{2i})}{\partial \sigma_i}] \\
&= \mathcal{P}_{Oi}(\lambda\tau)[S_t e^{-b_i\tau}\frac{\partial N(d_{1i})}{\partial d_{1i}}\frac{\partial d_{1i}}{\partial \sigma_i} - Xe^{-r\tau}\frac{\partial N(d_{2i})}{\partial d_{2i}}\frac{\partial d_{2i}}{\partial \sigma_i}] \\
&= \mathcal{P}_{Oi}(\lambda\tau)\left\{S_t e^{-b_i\tau}\left(\frac{1}{\sqrt{2\pi}}e^{-\frac{d_{1i}^2}{2}}\right)\left(\frac{\sigma_i^2\tau^{3/2} - \left[ln\frac{S_t}{X} + (\overline{r}_i + \frac{\sigma_i^2}{2})\tau\right]\sqrt{\tau}}{\sigma_i^2\tau}\right) - \right. \\
&\left. Xe^{-r\tau}\left(\frac{1}{\sqrt{2\pi}}e^{-\frac{d_{1i}^2}{2}}.\frac{S_t}{X}.e^{\overline{r}_i\tau}\right)\left(\frac{-\left[ln\frac{S_t}{X} + (\overline{r}_i + \frac{\sigma_i^2}{2})\tau\right]\sqrt{\tau}}{\sigma_i^2\tau}\right)\right\} \\
&= \mathcal{P}_{Oi}(\lambda\tau)\left\{S_t e^{-b_i\tau}\left(\frac{1}{\sqrt{2\pi}}e^{-\frac{d_{1i}^2}{2}}\right)\left(\frac{\sigma_i^2\tau^{\frac{3}{2}} - \left[ln\frac{S_t}{X} + (\overline{r}_i + \frac{\sigma_i^2}{2})\tau\right].\sqrt{\tau}}{\sigma_i^2\tau}\right) - \right. \\
&\left. \left(S_t e^{-b_i\tau}\frac{1}{\sqrt{2\pi}}e^{-\frac{d_{1i}^2}{2}}\right)\left(\frac{-\left[ln\frac{S_t}{X} + (\overline{r}_i + \frac{\sigma_i^2}{2})\tau\right].\sqrt{\tau}}{\sigma_i^2\tau}\right)\right\} \\
&= \mathcal{P}_{Oi}(\lambda\tau)\left[S_t\frac{1}{\sqrt{2\pi}}e^{-\frac{d_{1i}^2}{2}}\left(\frac{\sigma_i^2\tau^{\frac{3}{2}}}{\sigma_i^2\tau}\right)\right] = \mathcal{P}_{Oi}(\lambda\tau)\left[S_t e^{-b_i\tau}\sqrt{\tau}N'(d_{1i})\right]
\end{aligned} \tag{A20}$$

Similarly, the derivation process of Equation (40) as follows

$$\begin{aligned}
\mathrm{v} &= \frac{\partial P_u}{\partial \sigma_i} = \mathcal{P}_{Oi}(\lambda\tau)\left[Xe^{-r\tau}\frac{\partial N(-d_{2i})}{\partial \sigma_i} - S_t e^{-b_i\tau}\frac{\partial N(-d_{1i})}{\partial \sigma_i}\right] \\
&= \mathcal{P}_{Oi}(\lambda\tau)\left[Xe^{-r\tau}\frac{\partial[1-N(d_{2i})]}{\partial d_{2i}}\frac{\partial d_{2i}}{\partial \sigma_i} - S_t e^{-b_i\tau}\frac{\partial[1-N(d_{1i})]}{\partial d_{1i}}\frac{\partial d_{1i}}{\partial \sigma_i}\right] \\
&= \mathcal{P}_{Oi}(\lambda\tau)\left\{Xe^{-r\tau}\left(\frac{1}{\sqrt{2\pi}}e^{-\frac{d_{1i}^2}{2}}.\frac{S_t}{X}.e^{\overline{r}_i\tau}\right)\left(\frac{-\left[ln\frac{S_t}{X} + (\overline{r}_i + \frac{\sigma_i^2}{2})\tau\right].\sqrt{\tau}}{\sigma_i^2\tau}\right) + \right. \\
&\left. S_t e^{-b_i\tau}\left(\frac{1}{\sqrt{2\pi}}e^{-\frac{d_{1i}^2}{2}}\right)\left(\frac{\sigma_i^2\tau^{3/2} - \left[ln\frac{S_t}{X} + (\overline{r}_i + \frac{\sigma_i^2}{2})\tau\right].\sqrt{\tau}}{\sigma_i^2\tau}\right)\right\} \\
&= \mathcal{P}_{Oi}(\lambda\tau)\left\{-\left(S_t e^{-b_i\tau}\frac{1}{\sqrt{2\pi}}e^{-\frac{d_{1i}^2}{2}}\right)\left(\frac{-\left[ln\frac{S_t}{X} + (\overline{r}_i + \frac{\sigma_i^2}{2})\tau\right].\sqrt{\tau}}{\sigma_i^2\tau}\right) + \right. \\
&\left. S_t e^{-b_i\tau}\left(\frac{1}{\sqrt{2\pi}}e^{-\frac{d_{1i}^2}{2}}\right)\left(\frac{\sigma_i^2\tau^{\frac{3}{2}} - \left[ln\frac{S_t}{X} + (\overline{r}_i + \frac{\sigma_i^2}{2})\tau\right].\sqrt{\tau}}{\sigma_i^2\tau}\right)\right\} \\
&= \mathcal{P}_{Oi}(\lambda\tau)S_t e^{-b_i\tau}\frac{1}{\sqrt{2\pi}}e^{-\frac{d_{1i}^2}{2}}\left(\frac{\sigma_i^2\tau^{\frac{3}{2}}}{\sigma_i^2\tau}\right) = \mathcal{P}_{Oi}(\lambda\tau)S_t e^{-b_i\tau}\sqrt{\tau}N'(d_{1i}) \quad \text{Q.E.D}
\end{aligned} \tag{A21}$$

Appendix B.4. Derivation Process of Rho for Different Kinds of Bitcoin Options

The derivation process of Equation (41) as follows

$$\begin{aligned}
Rho &= \tfrac{\partial C_a}{\partial r} = \mathcal{P}_{Oi}(\lambda\tau)\left[S_t e^{-b_i\tau}\tfrac{\partial N(d_{1i})}{\partial r} + \tau X e^{-r\tau}N(d_{2i}) - Xe^{-r\tau}\tfrac{\partial N(d_{2i})}{\partial r}\right] \\
&= \mathcal{P}_{Oi}(\lambda\tau)\left[S_t e^{-b_i\tau}\tfrac{\partial N(d_{1i})}{\partial d_{1i}}\tfrac{\partial d_{1i}}{\partial r} + \tau X e^{-r\tau}N(d_{2i}) - Xe^{-r\tau}\tfrac{\partial N(d_{2i})}{\partial d_{2i}}\tfrac{\partial d_{2i}}{\partial r}\right] \\
&= \mathcal{P}_{Oi}(\lambda\tau)\left[S_t e^{-b_i\tau}\tfrac{1}{\sqrt{2\pi}}e^{-\frac{d_{1i}^2}{2}}.\left(\tfrac{\sqrt{\tau}}{\sigma_i}\right) + \tau X e^{-r\tau}N(d_{2i}) - Xe^{-r\tau}\left(\tfrac{1}{\sqrt{2\pi}}e^{-\frac{d_{1i}^2}{2}}.\tfrac{S_t}{X}.e^{\bar{r}_i\tau}\right)\left(\tfrac{\sqrt{\tau}}{\sigma_i}\right)\right] \\
&= \mathcal{P}_{Oi}(\lambda\tau)\left[S_t e^{-b_i\tau}\tfrac{1}{\sqrt{2\pi}}e^{-\frac{d_{1i}^2}{2}}.\left(\tfrac{\sqrt{\tau}}{\sigma_i}\right) + \tau X e^{-r\tau}N(d_{2i}) - S_t e^{-b_i\tau}\tfrac{1}{\sqrt{2\pi}}e^{-\frac{d_{1i}^2}{2}}.\left(\tfrac{\sqrt{\tau}}{\sigma_i}\right)\right] \\
&= \mathcal{P}_{Oi}(\lambda\tau)X\tau e^{-r\tau}N(d_{2i})
\end{aligned} \tag{A22}$$

Similarly, the derivation process of Equation (42) can be shown as

$$\begin{aligned}
Rho &= \tfrac{\partial P_u}{\partial r} = -\tau X e^{-r\tau}N(-d_{2i}) + Xe^{-r\tau}\tfrac{\partial N(-d_{2i})}{\partial r} - S_t e^{-b_i\tau}\tfrac{\partial N(-d_{1i})}{\partial r} \\
&= Xe^{-r\tau}\tfrac{\partial[1-N(d_{2i})]}{\partial d_{2i}}\tfrac{\partial d_{2i}}{\partial r} - \tau X e^{-r\tau}[1-N(d_{2i})] - S_t e^{-b_i\tau}\tfrac{\partial[1-N(d_{1i})]}{\partial d_{1i}}\tfrac{\partial d_{1i}}{\partial r} \\
&= -Xe^{-r\tau}\left(\tfrac{1}{\sqrt{2\pi}}e^{-\frac{d_{1i}^2}{2}}.\tfrac{S_t}{X}.e^{\bar{r}_i\tau}\right)\left(\tfrac{\sqrt{\tau}}{\sigma_i}\right) + \tau X e^{-r\tau}[1-N(d_{2i})] + S_t e^{-b_i\tau}\tfrac{1}{\sqrt{2\pi}}e^{-\frac{d_{1i}^2}{2}}.\left(\tfrac{\sqrt{\tau}}{\sigma_i}\right) \\
&= -S_t e^{-b_i\tau}\tfrac{1}{\sqrt{2\pi}}e^{-\frac{d_{1i}^2}{2}}.\left(\tfrac{\sqrt{\tau}}{\sigma_i}\right) + \tau X e^{-r\tau}[1-N(d_{2i})] + S_t e^{-b_i\tau}\tfrac{1}{\sqrt{2\pi}}e^{-\frac{d_{1i}^2}{2}}.\left(\tfrac{\sqrt{\tau}}{\sigma_i}\right) \\
&= -\mathcal{P}_{Oi}(\lambda\tau)\tau X e^{-r\tau}N(-d_{2i})
\end{aligned} \tag{A23}$$

Q.E.D

B.5. Derivation of Theta for Different Kinds of Bitcoin Options

Proof. Available from the author upon request. □

References

1. Dupire, B. Pricing with a smile. *Risk* **1994**, *7*, 18–20.
2. Andersen, L.; Andreasen, J. Jump-diffusion processes: Volatility smile fitting and numerical methods for option pricing. *Rev. Deriv. Res.* **2000**, *4*, 231–262. [CrossRef]
3. Ma, Y.; Shrestha, K.; Xu, W. Pricing vulnerable options with jump clustering. *J. Futur. Mark.* **2017**, *37*, 1155–1178. [CrossRef]
4. He, C.; Kennedy, J.S.; Coleman, T.F.; Forsyth, P.A.; Li, Y.; Vetzal, K.R. Calibration and hedging under jump diffusion. *Rev. Deriv. Res.* **2006**, *9*, 1–35. [CrossRef]
5. Merton, R. Option pricing when underlying stock returns are discontinuous. *J. Financ. Econ.* **1976**, *3*, 124–144. [CrossRef]
6. Bates, D.S. The crash of '87: Was it expected? The evidence from options markets. *J. Financ.* **1991**, *46*, 1009–1044. [CrossRef]
7. Cont, R.; Tankov, P. Non-Parametric calibration of jump-diffusion option pricing models. *J. Comput. Financ.* **2004**, *7*, 1–49. [CrossRef]
8. Gómez-Valle, L.; Martínez-Rodríguez, J. Including jumps in the stochastic valuation of freight derivatives. *Mathematics* **2021**, *9*, 154. [CrossRef]
9. Luther, W.J.; White, L.H. Can Bitcoin become a major currency? *Cayman Financ. Rev.* **2014**, *36*, 78–79. [CrossRef]
10. Yermack, M. *Is Bitcoin a Real Currency? An Economic Appraisal*; NBER Working Paper 19747; National Bureau of Economic Research: Cambridge, MA, USA, 2013.
11. Dowd, K.; Hutchinson, M. Bitcoin will bite the dust. *Cato J.* **2015**, *35*, 357–382.
12. Ardia, D.; Bluteau, K.; Rüede, M. Regime changes in bitcoin GARCH volatility dynamics. *Financ. Res. Lett.* **2019**, *29*, 266–271. [CrossRef]
13. Fang, L.; Bouri, E.; Gupta, R.; Roubaud, D. Does global economic uncertainty matter for the volatility and hedging effectiveness of Bitcoin? *Int. Rev. Financ. Anal.* **2019**, *61*, 29–36. [CrossRef]
14. Bouri, E.; Roubaud, D.; Shahzad, S.J.H. Do Bitcoin and other cryptocurrencies jump together? *Q. Rev. Econ. Financ.* **2020**, *76*, 396–409. [CrossRef]
15. Bouri, E.; Gkillas, K.; Gupta, R.; Pierdzioch, C. Forecasting Realized Volatility of Bitcoin: The Role of the Trade War. *Comput. Econ.* **2021**, *57*, 29–53. [CrossRef]

16. Cao, M.; Celik, B. Valuation of bitcoin options. *J. Futur. Mark.* **2021**, *41*, 1007–1026. [CrossRef]
17. Scaillet, O.; Treccani, A.; Trevisan, C. High-frequency jump analysis of the Bitcoin market. *J. Financ. Econ.* **2020**, *18*, 209–232.
18. Siu, T.K.; Elliott, R.J. Bitcoin option pricing with a SETAR-GARCH model. *Eur. J. Financ.* **2021**, *27*, 564–595. [CrossRef]
19. Jalan, A.; Matkovskyy, R.; Saqib, A. The Bitcoin options market: A first look at pricing and risk. *Appl. Econ.* **2021**, *53*, 2026–2041. [CrossRef]
20. Hilliard, J.E.; Reis, J.A. Jump processes in commodity futures prices and options pricing. *Am. J. Agric. Econ.* **1999**, *81*, 273–286. [CrossRef]
21. Kapetanios, G.; Konstantinidi, E.; Neumann, M.; Skiadopoulos, G. Jumps in option prices and their determinants: Real-time evidence from the E-mini S&P 500 option market. *J. Financ. Mark.* **2019**, *46*, 100506.
22. Qiao, G.; Yang, J.; Li, W. VIX forecasting based on GARCH-type model with observable dynamic jumps: A new perspective. *N. Am. J. Econ. Financ.* **2020**, *53*, 101186. [CrossRef]
23. Lee, S.S.; Mykland, P.A. Jumps in financial markets: A new nonparametric test and jump dynamics. *Rev. Financ. Stud.* **2008**, *21*, 2535–2563. [CrossRef]
24. Dumitru, A.-M.; Urga, G. Identifying Jumps in Financial Assets: A Comparison Between Nonparametric Jump Tests. *J. Bus. Econ. Stat.* **2012**, *30*, 242–255. [CrossRef]
25. Huang, X.; Tauchen, G. The relative contribution of jumps to total price variance. *J. Financ. Econ.* **2005**, *3*, 456–499. [CrossRef]
26. Cheang, G.H.L.; Chiarella, C. *A Modern View on Mertons Jump-Diffusion Model*; Research paper No. 287; University of Technology Sydney, Quantitative Finance Research Centre: Sidney, Australia, 2011.
27. Geman, H.; El Karoui, N.; Rochet, J.C. Changes of numeraire, changes of probability measure and option pricing. *J. Appl. Probab.* **1995**, *32*, 443–458. [CrossRef]
28. Bannör, F.K.; Scherer, M. Capturing parameter uncertainty with convex risk measures. *Eur. Actuar. J.* **2013**, *3*, 97–132. [CrossRef]
29. Haug, E.G. *The Complete Guide to Option Pricing Formulas*, 2nd ed.; McGraw–Hill: New York, NY, USA, 2007.
30. Beckers, S. A note on estimating the parameters of the diffusion–jump model of stock returns. *J. Financ. Quant. Anal.* **1981**, *16*, 127–140. [CrossRef]
31. Ball, C.A.; Torous, W.N. A simplified jump process for common stock returns. *J. Financ. Quant. Anal.* **1983**, *18*, 53–65. [CrossRef]
32. Duan, J.C.; Ritchken, P.H.; Sun, Z. *Jump Starting GARCH Pricing and Hedging Option with Jumps in Returns and Volatilities*; Working Paper; National University of Singapore: Singapore, 2007.
33. Cretarola, A.; Figà-Talamanca, G.; Patacca, M. Market attention and Bitcoin price modeling: Theory, estimation and option pricing. *Decis. Econ. Financ.* **2020**, *43*, 187–228. [CrossRef]
34. Tankov, P.; Voltchkova, E. Pricing, Hedging, and Calibration in Jump-Diffusion Models. In *Frontiers in Quantitative Finance*; Cont, R., Ed.; Wiley: Hoboken, NJ, USA, 2008. [CrossRef]
35. Mijatović, A.; Tankov, P. A new look at short-term implied volatility in asset price models with jumps. *Math. Financ.* **2016**, *26*, 149–183. [CrossRef]
36. Kou, S.G. A jump-diffusion model for option pricing. *Manag. Sci.* **2002**, *48*, 1086–1101. [CrossRef]
37. Tauchen, G.; Zhou, H. Realized jumps on financial markets and predicting credit spreads. *J. Econ.* **2011**, *160*, 102–118. [CrossRef]
38. Chan, W.H.; Maheu, J.M. Conditional Jump Dynamics in Stock Market Returns. *J. Bus. Econ. Stat.* **2002**, *20*, 377–389. [CrossRef]
39. Duan, J.-C.; Ritchken, P.; Sun, Z. Approximating GARCH-jump models, jump-diffusion processes, and option pricing. *Math. Financ.* **2006**, *16*, 21–52. [CrossRef]
40. Gronwald, M. Is Bitcoin a Commodity? On price jumps, demand shocks, and certainty of supply. *J. Int. Money Financ.* **2019**, *97*, 86–92. [CrossRef]
41. Chen, K.-S. Research on Equity Release Mortgage Risk Diversification with financial innovation: Reinsurance Usage. *J. Risk Model Valid.* **2016**, *10*, 35–55. [CrossRef]
42. Chen, H.Y.; Lee, C.F.; Shih, W.K. Derivation and application of Greek letters: Review and integration. In *Handbook of Quantitative Finance and Risk Management, Part III*; Springer: Berlin/Heidelberg, Germany, 2010; pp. 491–503.

mathematics MDPI

Article

Trading Cryptocurrencies Using Second Order Stochastic Dominance

Gil Cohen

Department of Management, Western Galilee Academic College, Acre 2412101, Israel; gilc@wgalil.ac.il

Abstract: This research is the first attempt to customize a trading system that is based on second order stochastic dominance (SSD) to five known cryptocurrencies' daily data: Bitcoin, Ethereum, XRP, Binance Coin, and Cardano. Results show that our system can predict price trends of cryptocurrencies, trade them profitably, and in most cases outperform the buy and hold (B&H) simple strategy. Our system's best performance was achieved trading XRP, Binance Coin, Ethereum, and Bitcoin. Although our system has also generated a positive net profit (NP) for Cardano, it failed to outperform the B&H strategy. For all currencies, the system better predicted long trends than short trends.

Keywords: cryptocurrencies; Bitcoin; Ethereum; algorithmic trading; artificial intelligence

Citation: Cohen, G. Trading Cryptocurrencies Using Second Order Stochastic Dominance. *Mathematics* **2021**, *9*, 2861. https://doi.org/10.3390/math9222861

Academic Editors: José Luis Miralles-Quirós and María Mar Miralles-Quirós

Received: 24 October 2021
Accepted: 10 November 2021
Published: 11 November 2021

Publisher's Note: MDPI stays neutral with regard to jurisdictional claims in published maps and institutional affiliations.

1. Introduction

The use of algorithmic trading systems is widespread among investment houses and professional traders who uses algorithmic trading as their major investment tool. In recent years, investors have realized that those systems are necessary for processing efficiently a huge amount of financial data and replace many hours of human analysis. Researchers and practitioners have tried to identify cryptocurrencies' price behaviors and by doing so improve their ability to forecasts future prices. Different processes were used to identify and forecasts cryptocurrencies' price behaviors, including linear and nonlinear and other technical tools. This research makes the first attempt to predict price trends of major cryptocurrencies using second order stochastic dominance (SSD) conditions. The concept of stochastic dominance arises in decision analysis in situations where one probability distribution over possible outcomes can be ranked as superior to another. Our aim is to detect stochastic dominance superiority changes and exploit them for profitable trading.

We tested our system for five major cryptocurrencies: Bitcoin, Ethereum, XRP (Ripple), Binance Coin, and Cardano. Cryptocurrency such as Bitcoin is traded on special exchanges including Etoro and CoinBase. The biggest exchange in the world by far is called Binance. That exchange has developed its own cryptocurrency called Binance Coin to make it easier to pay for the exchange services, and this currency held in 2021 the third largest market value of all cryptocurrencies. Cardano was launched in 2017 as a third generation blockchain that aimed to directly compete with other decentralized platforms as a more scalable, secure, and efficient alternative. By August 2021, Cardano had the third highest market value after Bitcoin and Ethereum. We found that the system can predict price trends of cryptocurrencies, trade them profitably, and in most cases outperform the buy and hold (B&H) simple strategy.

2. Literature Review

Researchers have documented that the cryptocurrency market is largely affected by herding behavior (Vidal Tomas et al. [1]; Gama Silva et al. [2]); therefore, techniques such as machine learning and technical analysis improve price forecasting when they integrate additional variables related to sentiment (see for example Ortu et al. [3]). Because of this market behavior, some trading algorithms combines market data with social media data (Liu [4], Sohangir et al. [5]). The social media information is extracted mainly from Google and Twitter along with popular investor idea exchange platforms such as Seeking Alpha (https://seekingalpha.com/Seekingalpha.com, accessed on 1 November 2021) and Investopedia (https://www.investopedia.com/, accessed on 1 November 2021). Kim et al. [6] tried to predict fluctuations in the prices of cryptocurrencies by analyzing comments in online communities. They found that positive comments significantly affected the price fluctuations of Bitcoin, whereas the prices of two other cryptocurrencies, Ripple (XRP) and Ethereum, were strongly influenced by negative comments. Garcia and Schweizer [7] also demonstrated the existence of a relationship between returns and Twitter valence and polarization. Matta et al. [8] reported significant cross correlation values between the volume of online searches and Bitcoin's trading volume.

In contrast to stock markets, cryptocurrencies are less regulated and therefore carry extra risks (Baek and Elbeck [9]). In such a dynamic trading environment, algorithmic trading systems can provide fast and useful information (Chow et al. [10]; Liu et al. [11]; Cohen [12]; Cohen [13]). Balcilar et al. [14] found that when extreme events are excluded, volume is an important predictor of Bitcoin's price. Brandvold et al. [15] investigated the role of various of cryptocurrency exchanges in the price discovery process and concluded that information sharing is dynamic and evolves significantly over time. Feng et al. [16] found evidence of informed trading in the Bitcoin market prior to major events. Moreover, they noticed that informed traders prefer to build their positions two days before large positive events and one day before large negative events. This result serves as proof of market inefficiency that differentiates uninformed traders from informed traders.

3. Data and Methodologies

Our data consisted of daily price and returns of the five most popular cryptocurrencies that are valued together at more than \$1.5 trillion (at the end of August 2021). The time scope for this research varied from the beginning of January 2015 for Bitcoin and the beginning of May 2018 for Cardano until the end of September 2021. We programed a trading system that uses second order stochastic dominance (SSD) to predict short term price trends of the examined crypto currencies. SSD implies that if two separate distributions A and B exist, A has a second order stochastic dominance over B if A holds less risk in terms of particle variations and has at least as high mean value. Concerning the cumulative distribution functions F_A and F_B, a is second order stochastic dominant over B if the area under F_A from minus infinity to x is less than or equal to the area under F_B for all x (Equation (1)).

$$\int_{-\infty}^{x} [F_B(t) - F_A(t)]dt \geq 0 \quad (1)$$

where t = particle at time t, of the stochastic distribution.

The necessary conditions for second order stochastic dominance are given in Equation (2):

$$E_A(x) \geq E_B(x)$$
$$Min_A(x) \geq Min_B(x) \quad (2)$$

The SSD requirements fit trading, since investors rely heavily on the financial asset distribution function when they make investment decisions, and in that process, they usually put more weight on the downside of the investment opportunity since they are guided by fear of loss and risk aversion. In a recent study, McCarthy and Hillenbrand [17] found that extrapolative beliefs and risk aversion are important drivers of stock prices, together explaining 86% of movements in the S&P500 index.

To allow a stronger impact of a new price information over an old one, we used Exponential Moving Average (EMA_x) instead of $E_A(x)$, as noted in Equation (3).

$$EMA_x = R(x) * k + EMA_{x-1} * (1 - k) \quad (3)$$

where EMA_x = current exponential moving average, $R(x)$ = today's return, EMA_{x-1} = yesterday's exponential moving average return, N = number of days of the EMA, and $k = \frac{2}{N+1}$.

We then integrated Equations (2) and (3) to produce long and short trading signals. A long signal is generated if the following conditions are met (Equation (4)):

$$EMA_x > EMA_{x-1} \text{ and } Min_x \geq Min_{x-1} \quad (4)$$

A short signal is generated if the following conditions are met (Equation (5)):

$$EMA_x < EMA_{x-1} \text{ and } Min_x \leq Min_{x-1} \quad (5)$$

Figure 1 shows a bar chart of Bitcoin against the U.S. dollar, demonstrating that in an uptrend, the average daily return is growing along with a higher minimum daily return. On the other hand, a downtrend is characterized with lower average and lower minimum daily returns.

Figure 1. Uptrends and a downtrend of Bitcoin's daily price.

Each bar in Figure 1 contains information of the open, close, high, and low of the daily prices. A long red bar symbolizes a large daily price drop, and a long red bar symbolizes a major price rise. The system is designed to buy or sell one cryptocurrency at a time for easy comparison to the buy and hold (B&H) strategy. A specific number of days is entered into the system for it to calculate two consecutive EMAs and distributions and to establish whether the SSD condition of the current distribution over the latter exists. If such dominance is recognized, the system generates long or short trade. Once a position is realized, the system will stay in that position until an opposite dominance occurs. This trading system is highly sensitive to the range of days for which the SSD and EMAs are calculated. When it relies on a large number of days for those calculations, the number of executed trades drop dramatically, since it becomes difficult to recognize a continuous trend for every financial asset and especially for cryptocurrencies that are characterized with frequent trend shifts. Therefore, we altered the number of days systematically starting with one day until the number of recorded trades dropped to zero. We then reported the results of the best setups that produced the highest net profit (NP) generated by the trading system and the Profit Factor (PF), which is the gross profits divided by gross losses. For example, if the profit factor is 1.3, the system generated 30% more profits than losses. In order to document the downside risk, for each strategy, we calculated Maximum Draw Down (MDD), which is the maximum observed loss of a single trade without taking into consideration the frequency of large losses. Since the cryptocurrencies market varies dramatically over time because of its complexity and relatively infancy (see, for example, Fry and Cheah [18]; Fry [19]), we followed the changes of the average NP and MDD per trade over time for each cryptocurrency. Moreover, we also separated all trades to long and short trades to find out whether our system has different forecasting power for uptrends and downtrends.

4. Results

We start our results section by examining Figure 2, which represents Bitcoin price movement for a two-month random sample. Figure 2 show that the Bitcoin price oscillated at a reasonable scope before hitting a sharp movement because of a major outside shock, and then its volatility quadrupled in the next coming days.

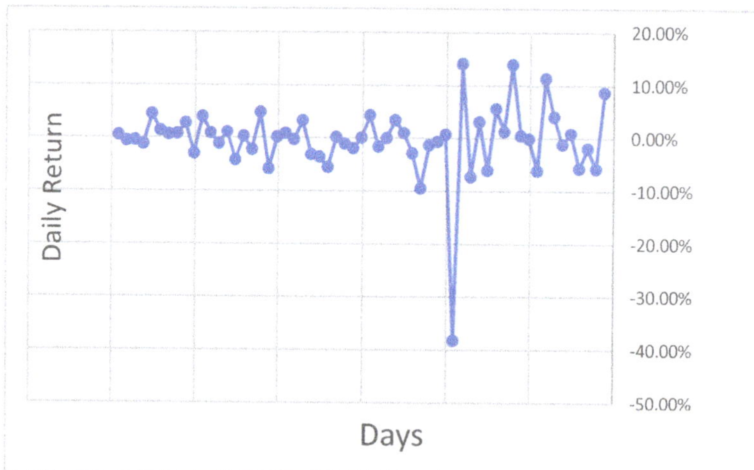

Figure 2. Two months of Bitcoin daily price oscillation.

The results of the SSD-based trading system of the five cryptocurrencies are summarized in Tables 1–5. The results reported in the tables are the best results our system achieved by altering the number of days until reaching the highest NP and PF. Each table also shows the dollar and percentage gap of the system's NP versus the B&H strategy for the entire examined period. Moreover, the tables also contain information about long and short trades for each cryptocurrency.

Table 1. Results for Bitcoin trades.

Days		10	11	12	13	14	15
B&H$		60,361	60,361	60,361	60,361	60,361	60,361
All Trades	NP	52,121	56,436	71,825	73,051	62,445	50,040
	PF	1.56	1.65	1.93	1.98	1.78	1.64
	MDD	11,424	7515	5952	5716	6751	10,425
$ Gap		−8240	−3925	11,464	12,690	2084	−10,321
% Gap		−13.6%	−6.5%	19%	21%	3.45%	−17%
Long Trades	NP	56,272	58,457	66,158	67,070	61,767	48,747
	PF	2.68	2.90	3.25	3.40	3.10	2.62
Short Trades	NP	−4151	−2021	5667	5981	678	1293
	PF	0.93	0.96	1.12	1.13	1.01	1.03

Table 2. Results for Ethereum trades.

Days		22	23	24	25	26	27
B&H$		3741	3741	3741	3741	3741	3741
All Trades	NP	4385	4653	4741	4018	4357	4215
	PF	2.36	2.49	2.54	2.24	2.48	2.39
	MDD	262	181	199	257	311	411
$ Gap		644	912	1000	277	616	474
% Gap		17.2%	24.4%	26.7%	7.4%	16.5%	12.7%
Long Trades	NP	3719	3869	3916	3556	3724	3655
	PF	4.11	4.23	4.20	3.69	4.01	3.80
Short Trades	NP	666	784	825	462	633	560
	PF	1.32	1.40	1.45	1.24	1.37	1.32

Table 3. Results for XRP trades.

Days		12	13	14	15	16	17
B&H$		0.39	0.39	0.39	0.39	0.39	0.39
All Trades	NP	1.22	2.39	1.39	1.46	1.23	1.15
	PF	1.40	2.05	1.51	1.57	1.47	1.44
	MDD	0.17	0.21	0.25	0.33	0.26	0.28
$ Gap		0.83	2.00	1.00	1.07	0.84	0.76
% Gap		207%	502%	250%	274%	215%	195%
Long Trades	NP	0.81	1.39	0.91	0.94	0.83	0.77
	PF	1.70	2.45	1.65	1.70	1.59	1.56
Short Trades	NP	0.41	1.00	0.48	0.52	0.41	0.38
	PF	1.21	1.76	1.36	1.43	1.33	1.29

Table 4. Results for Binance Coin trades.

Days		23	24	25	26	27	28
B&H$		472.6	472.6	472.6	472.6	472.6	472.6
All Trades	NP	732	755	805	826	780	783
	PF	3.36	3.72	4.21	4.48	4.29	4.35
	MDD	15.8	26.7	22.4	20.8	30.4	19.6
$ Gap		259.4	282.4	332.4	353.4	307.4	310.4
% Gap		54.9%	59.7%	70.3%	74.7%	65%	65.7%
Long Trades	NP	600	612	637	648	624	626
	PF	6.75	8.30	8.79	10.55	10.15	10.40
Short Trades	NP	132	143	168	178	156	157
	PF	1.64	1.74	1.99	2.06	1.92	1.93

Table 5. Results for Cardano trades.

Days		50	51	52	53	54	55
B&H$		1.85	1.85	1.85	1.85	1.85	1.85
All Trades	NP	1.66	1.69	1.68	1.76	1.75	1.75
	PF	2.06	2.09	2.08	2.18	2.17	2.19
	MDD	0.26	0.25	0.36	0.31	0.41	0.36
$ Gap		−0.19	−0.16	−0.17	−0.09	−0.10	−0.10
% Gap		−10.3%	−8.6%	−9.2%	−4.8%	−5.4%	−5.4%
Long Trades	NP	1.86	1.88	1.87	1.92	1.92	1.93
	PF	3.34	3.42	3.41	3.640	3.63	3.72
Short Trades	NP	−0.20	−0.19	−0.20	−0.16	−0.17	−0.18
	PF	0.73	0.75	0.74	0.79	0.78	0.76

Table 1 demonstrates that the best setup for Bitcoin trading through our system is 13 days, producing 73,051 NP, which is 21% over the B&H strategy. The PF of this setup is 1.98, which means there are 98% more winning trades than loosing trades. The MDD calculations indicate that the trading strategy is least risky when it is based on 13 days. Table 1 also show that our SSD-based system better predicts Bitcoin's uptrends than downtrends. We also find high dependency of the system performance on its daily selected setup. Figure 3 show that the average NP and MDD per trade varies over time using the best setup for Bitcoin.

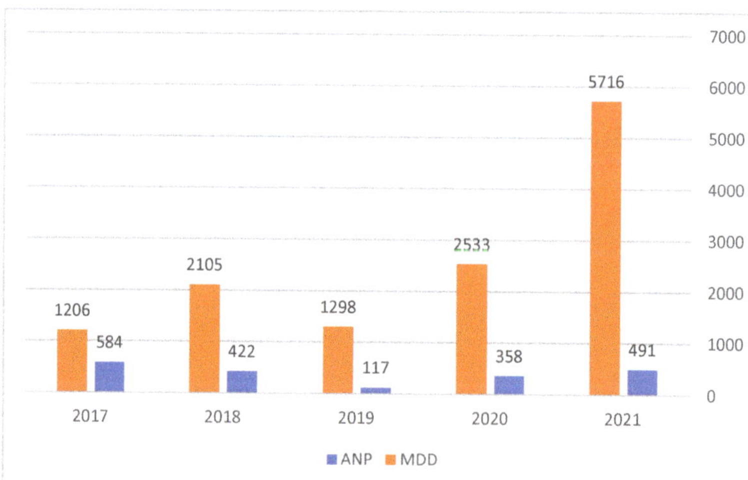

Figure 3. Bitcoin average NP and MDD per trade for 2017–2021. Note: ANP = average trade net profit, MDD = maximum loss per trade. The data for 2021 is until the end of September 2021.

Figure 3 shows that our system's best performance was achieved in 2017, resulting in an ANP of $584, and the MDD was $1206. The year 2021 had the highest MDD for the system with $491 average NP per trade. Table 2 summarizes the results of our system for Ethereum trades.

Table 2 demonstrates that Ethereum price trends changed slower than did Bitcoin's. The best trend prediction was achieved using a 24 day setup for Ethereum compared to 13 days for Bitcoin. Using a 24 day setup, our system produced 4741 NP, which is 26.7% more than the B&H strategy and $199 MDD. The PF at this setup is 2.54, which represents

154% more winning trades than loosing trades. Moreover, our system results are more robust for Ethereum trades than for Bitcoin trades. Again, as for Bitcoin, the system predicts better Ethereum long trends than short trends. Figure 4 demonstrates the average NP and MDD per trade varies over time using the best setup for Ethereum.

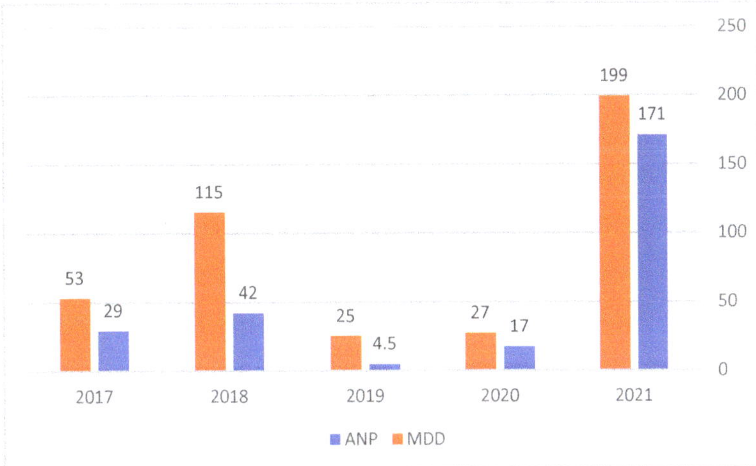

Figure 4. Ethereum average NP and MDD per trade for 2017–2021. Note: ANP = average trade net profit, MDD = maximum loss per trade. The data for 2021 is until the end of September 2021.

Figure 4 shows that the highest ANP and MDD per trade were achieved in 2021. These results reflect the large appreciation in the Ethereum price during 2021 and the ability of our system to detect uptrends. Table 3 summarizes the results of our system for XRP trades.

Table 3 shows that our system outperformed the B&H strategy by 502% ($2) with $0.21 MDD, for the 13 days setup, making the system a better fit for XRP trends prediction than for Bitcoin or Ethereum. The system is robust for 12 to 17 day setups, resulting in 1.57 average PF. As for the Bitcoin and Ethereum, the XRP system better predicts long trends than short trends. Figure 5 shows the average NP and MDD per trade varies over time using the best setup for XRP.

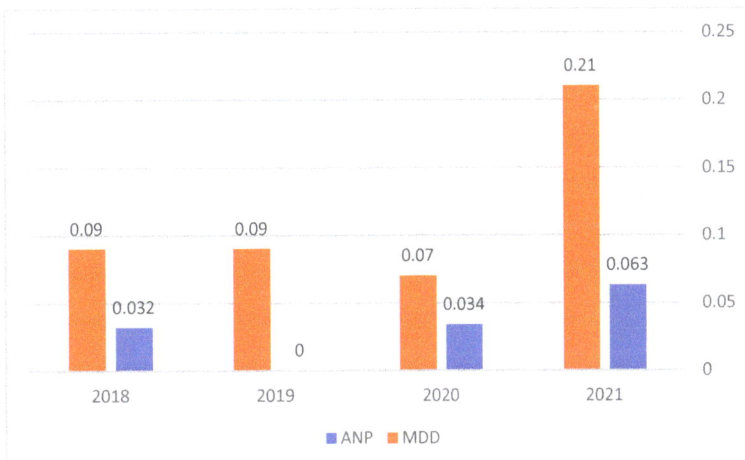

Figure 5. XRP average NP and MDD per trade for 2018–2021. Note: ANP = average trade net profit, MDD = maximum loss per trade. The data for 2021 is until the end of September 2021.

Figure 5 shows that as the price of the XRP appreciated in the market, our system better generated profits and was subjected to higher risks (ANP of 0.063 and MDD of 0.21). Table 4 summarizes the results of our system for Binance Coin trades.

Table 4 shows that the SSD system fits to trade Binance Coin. The best setup was 26 days, resulting in $826 NP, which represents a 74.7% return over the B&H strategy and $20.8 MDD. Setups from 23 to 28 days produced better results than the B&H strategy by more than 50%. The system performances are excellent for long trades (PF = 10.55 for the 26 day setup) and good for short trades (PF = 2.06 for the 26 day setup). Figure 6 show that the average NP and MDD per trade varies over time using the best setup for XRP.

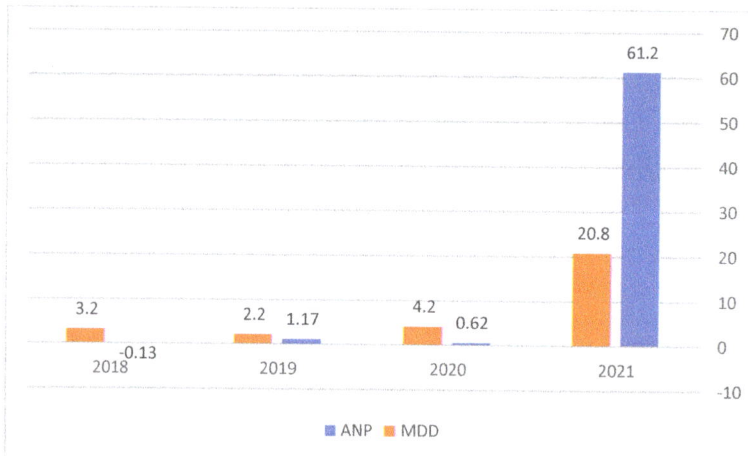

Figure 6. Binance Coin average NP and MDD per trade for 2018–2021. Note: ANP = average trade net profit, MDD = maximum loss per trade. The data for 2021 is until the end of September 2021.

Figure 6 show that the main profits were accumulated by our system in 2021. From January 2021 till the end of September 2021, the Binance Coin rose from $42 to $387.5 (822%). The MDD also rose dramatically in 2021, indicating the higher risk involved in trading the Binance Coin using our system. Table 5 summarizes the results of our system for Cardano trades.

Table 5 shows that the system's best performance was achieved using a much longer period than the other examined cryptocurrencies and with worse results. The best result was achieved using a 53 day setup, which was $1.76 NP and which was beaten by the B&H strategy by 4.8% and $0.31 MDD. Although the system generated positive NP for long trades, it generated net losses for all short trades. Figure 7 demonstrates that the average NP and MDD per trade varies over time using the best setup for Cardano.

Figure 7 show that in 2021, our system's performance and risk rose dramatically in comparison to 2019 and 2020. The ANP was $0.1 compared to $0.03 and $0.02 in 2019 and 2020, respectively. The MDD also rose to $0.31, signaling that the risk involved in trading rose dramatically.

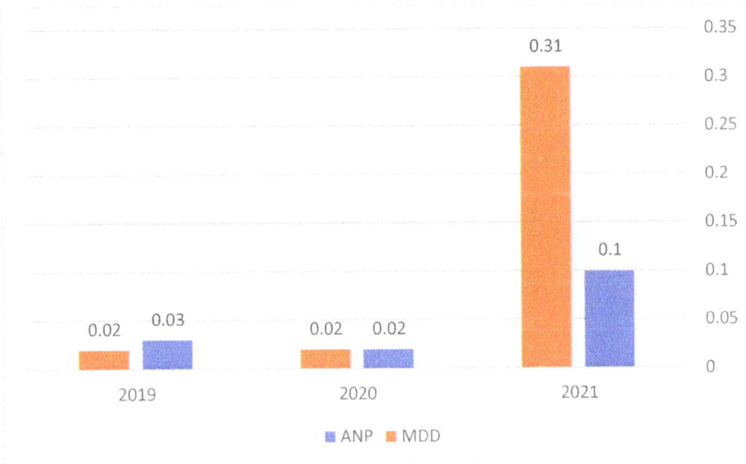

Figure 7. Cardano average NP and MDD per trade for 2019–2021. Note: ANP = average trade net profit, MDD = maximum loss per trade. The data for 2021 is until the end of September 2021.

5. Conclusions and Future Research

This research is the first attempt to design and test cryptocurrency trading systems based on second order stochastic dominance. The time scope used in this research varies from the beginning of January 2015 for Bitcoin and the beginning of May 2018 for Cardano until the end of September 2021. Results show that our system can predict price trends of cryptocurrencies and in most cases outperform the B&H simple strategy. Our system's best performance was achieved trading XRP, Binance Coin, Ethereum, and Bitcoin. Although our system also generated a positive NP for Cardano, it failed to outperform the simple B&H strategy. For all currencies the system better predicts long trends than short trends. The best short trends predicted were achieved trading XRP and the worst trading Cardano. Future research can try to predict cryptocurrency prices using stochastic behaviors and try to predict intraday price movements using those behaviors.

Funding: This research was funded by West Galilee College.

Data Availability Statement: Upon request.

Conflicts of Interest: The author declares no conflict of interest.

References

1. Vidal-Tomás, D.; Ibáñez, A.M.; Farinós, J.E. Herding in the cryptocurrency market: CSSD and CSAD approaches. *Financ. Res. Lett.* **2019**, *30*, 181–186. [CrossRef]
2. Gama Silva, P.V.J.; Klotzle, M.C.; Pinto, A.C.F.; Gomes, L.L. Herding behavior and contagion in the cryptocurrency markets. *J. Behav. Exp. Financ.* **2019**, *22*, 41–50. [CrossRef]
3. Ortu, M.; Uras, N.; Conversano, C.; Destefanis, G.; Bartolucci, S. On Technical trading and social media indicators in cryptocurrencies' price classification through deep learning. *arXiv* **2021**, arXiv:2102.08189.
4. Liu, X. Target and position article—Analyzing the impact of user-generated content on B2B Firms' stock performance: Big data analysis with machine learning methods. *Ind. Mark. Manag.* **2020**, *86*, 30–39. [CrossRef]
5. Sohangir, S.; Wang, D.; Pomeranets, A.; Khoshgoftaar, T.M. Big data: Deep learning for financial sentiment analysis. *J. Big Data* **2018**, *5*, 3. [CrossRef]
6. Kim, Y.B.; Kim, J.G.; Kim, W.; Im, J.H.; Kim, T.H.; Kang, S.J.; Kim, C.H. Predicting fluctuations in cryptocurrency transactions based on user comments and replies. *PLoS ONE* **2016**, *11*, 8. [CrossRef] [PubMed]
7. Garcia, D.; Schweizer, F. Social signals and algorithmic trading of bitcoin. *Rev. Sociol. Open Sci.* **2015**, *2*, 9. [CrossRef] [PubMed]
8. Matta, M.; Lunesu, L.; Marchesi, M. The Predictor Impact of Web Search Media on Bitcoin Trading Volumes. In Proceedings of the 7th International Joint Conference on Knowledge Discovery, Knowledge Engineering and Knowledge Management, Lisbon, Portugal, 12–14 November 2015.
9. Baek, C.; Elbeck, M. Bitcoin as an investment or speculative vehicle? A first look. *Appl. Econ. Lett.* **2014**, *22*, 30–34. [CrossRef]

10. Chow, Y.S.; Robbins, H.; Siegmund, D. *Great Expectations: The Theory of Optimal Stopping*; Houghton Mifflin: Boston, MA, USA, 1971.
11. Liu, Y.; Yang, A.; Zhang, J.; Jingjing, Y. An optimal stopping problem of detecting entry points for trading modeled by geometric Brownian motion. *Comput. Econ.* **2020**, *55*, 827–843. [CrossRef]
12. Cohen, G. Forecasting bitcoin trends using algorithmic learning systems. *Entropy* **2020**, *8*, 838. [CrossRef] [PubMed]
13. Cohen, G. Optimizing candlesticks patterns for bitcoin's trading systems. *Rev. Quant. Financ. Account.* **2021**, *57*, 1155–1167. [CrossRef]
14. Balcilar, M.; Bouri, E.; Gupta, R.; Roubaud, D. Can volume predict Bitcoin returns and volatility? A quantiles-based approach. *Econ. Model.* **2017**, *64*, 74–81. [CrossRef]
15. Brandvold, M.; Molner, P.; Vagstad, K.; Valstad, O.C.A. Price discovery on Bitcoin exchanges. *J. Int. Financ. Mark. Inst. Money* **2015**, *36*, 18–35. [CrossRef]
16. Feng, W.; Wang, Y.; Zang, Z. Informed trading in the Bitcoin market. *Financ. Res. Lett.* **2018**, *26*, 63–70. [CrossRef]
17. McCarthy, O.; Hillenbrand, S. Heterogeneous Investors and Stock Market Fluctuations. SSRN. Available online: https://papers.ssrn.com/sol3/papers.cfm?abstract_id=3944887 (accessed on 1 November 2021).
18. Fry, J.; Cheah, E.T. Negative bubbles and shocks in cryptocurrency markets. *Int. Rev. Financ. Anal.* **2016**, *47*, 343–352. [CrossRef]
19. Fry, J. Booms, busts and heavy tails: The story of Bitcoin and cryptocurrency markets? *Econ. Lett.* **2018**, *171*, 225–229. [CrossRef]

mathematics

Article

Cryptocurrency as Epidemiologically Safe Means of Transactions: Diminishing Risk of SARS-CoV-2 Spread

Dmitry V. Boguslavsky, Natalia P. Sharova * and Konstantin S. Sharov

Koltzov Institute of Developmental Biology of Russian Academy of Sciences, 26 Vavilov Street, 119334 Moscow, Russia; boguslavsky@rambler.ru (D.V.B.); const.sharov@mail.ru (K.S.S.)
* Correspondence: npsharova@bk.ru; Tel.: +7-499-135-7674; Fax: +7-499-135-8012

Abstract: In comparison with other respiratory viruses, the current COVID-19 pandemic's rapid seizing the world can be attributed to indirect (contact) way of transmission of SARS-CoV-2 virus in addition to the regular airborne way. A significant part of indirect transmission is made through cash bank notes. SARS-CoV-2 remains on cash paper money for period around four times larger than influenza A virus and is absorbed by cash notes two and a half times more effectively than influenza A (our model). During the pandemic, cryptocurrencies have gained attractiveness as an "epidemiologically safe" means of transactions. On the basis of the authors' gallop polls performed online with social networks users in 44 countries in 2020–2021 (the total number of clear responses after the set repair 32,115), around 14.7% of surveyed participants engaged in cryptocurrency-based transactions during the pandemic. This may be one of the reasons of significant rise of cryptocurrencies rates since mid-March 2020 till the end of 2021. The paper discusses the reasons for cryptocurrency attractiveness during the COVID-19 pandemic. Among them, there are fear of SARS-CoV-2 spread via cash contacts and the ability of the general population to mine cryptocurrencies. The article also provides a breakdown of the polled audience profile to determine the nationalities that have maximal level of trust to saving and transacting money as cryptocurrencies.

Keywords: COVID-19; Bitcoin; Ether; Ethereum; contact way of disease transmission; respiratory virus; cash money

Citation: Boguslavsky, D.V.; Sharova, N.P.; Sharov, K.S. Cryptocurrency as Epidemiologically Safe Means of Transactions: Diminishing Risk of SARS-CoV-2 Spread. *Mathematics* **2021**, *9*, 3263. https://doi.org/10.3390/math9243263

Academic Editors: José Luis Miralles-Quirós and María Mar Miralles-Quirós

Received: 18 November 2021
Accepted: 14 December 2021
Published: 15 December 2021

1. Introduction

In spring 2020, on the verge of the "coronacrisis", the event that combined healthcare, economic, financial, administrative, political, employment, and social crises, many markets experienced a dramatic fall. The situation was exacerbated by massive layoffs. Most importantly, central banks in the period of COVID-19 pandemic mainly eased their monetary policy to help different sectors of their economies to overcome the crisis, e.g., the USD interest rate was diminished from 2.25% in January 2020 to 0.25% in April 2020 and it has remained at this level thus far [1]. This was an unprecedented Federal Open Market Committee's decision, as in the post-war period of US history the USD interest rate was never this low. Even after the "great financial crisis" of the 21st century broke out in 2008, the interest rate was 0.50. As a result, fixed-income investments became not as popular as they were before the pandemic. Treasury notes, bonds, and interest rate swaps plunged after the FOMC decision. Federal funds rate dropped to 0.00–0.25% and Eurodollar futures, consequently, jumped [2]. Simultaneously, the financial crisis distracted many investors from the traditional assets such as stocks. At this uneasy time, electronic money, including cryptocurrencies, came to the foreground. Luo et al. [3] and Shovkhalov with Idrisov [4] showed that price-based monetary policy has strong anti-interference, as an increase in e-money supply leads to weakening of the effect of monetary policy.

The correlation of almost all stock, futures and spot markets worldwide was unprecedented at the beginning of the pandemic [5–8]. Almost all world financial assets behaved in a very similar, nearly identical manner in February–March 2020 [9]. Previously such a behavior was observed only in 2008 [10,11]. After the global fall in February–March 2020, world markets began to revive by degrees. Most of the stock markets, both in economically developed countries and emerging economies, are higher at the end of 2021 than they were at the beginning of 2020 [12].

Figure 1 shows the behavior of different financial assets since February 2019 till September 2020 (the end of the first wave of the COVID-19 pandemic). We can observe a mixed behavior of traditional assets and a sharp rise in cryptocurrencies price (Bitcoin and Ether).

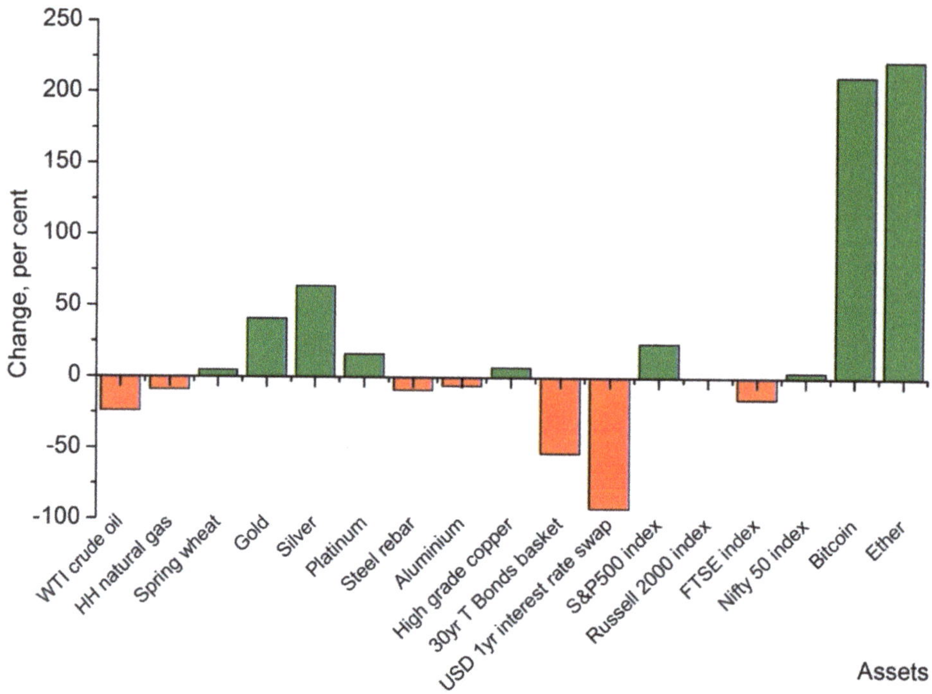

Figure 1. Relative change in price of different assets: energy resources; grains; precious, ferrous and non-ferrous metals; bonds; interest rate swaps; several world stock indices; and cryptocurrencies, since February 2019 till September 2020 (the end of the first wave of the COVID-19 pandemic). The data are taken from the following sources: New York Mercantile Exchange; Chicago Board of Trade; London Bullion Market; Singapore Exchange; London Metal Exchange; BrokerTec; London Clearing House LCH ClearNet; Chicago Mercantile Exchange; Intercontinental Exchange; National Stock Exchange of India; and several cryptocurrency exchanges.

In February–March 2020, i.e., the very beginning of the pandemic, there was a clear fall of price of most popular financial assets such as world stock indexes or energy resources. An especially uncommon, almost absurd situation, was observed with crude oil, whose prices fell below zero (in this scenario a crude oil producer must pay money for storage instead of receiving it for crude oil sale). Bitcoin and Ether prices also underwent this temporary slippage, but to a much lesser degree. By the end of the first wave of the pandemic cryptocurrencies outperformed every other asset in the world significantly.

The COVID-19 pandemic did not undermine the growing tendency of cryptocurrencies. On the contrary, the whole period of the pandemic caused a substantial rise in Bitcoin prices thus far (15 November 2021), bringing it to its historical maximums (+810%). We take Bitcoin as a reference for all cryptocurrencies, but for some other cryprocurrencies the rise of their price was even more expressed since January 2020 up to now (15 November 2021) (e.g., +3738% for Ether).

This behavior is quite uncommon for the pandemic time. No other financial asset experienced such a rise in price in the COVID-19 times [13,14]. Instead, economic stagnation, diminishing investment activities, and widening the bond–swap spread are common phenomena now [15–20]. However, cryptocurrencies outperformed any "traditional" market. This growth was not broken even by the events which were deemed to impact cryptocurrencies negatively, e.g., the prohibition of mining farms in PRC on the grounds of environmental impact or the notorious Elon Musk's refusal to sustain cryptocurrencies. It may be partly explained by the "safe haven" effect [21–23]. The Chinese government's prohibition of mining as well as restrictions in some other parts of the world were caused by the huge environmental impact of mining farms. In Asia, Latin America, and Africa, the impact of cryptocurrency mining is especially large [24–26]. However, environmental-based restrictions did not break the growing trend of cryptocurrencies during the pandemic.

To be sure, during the last five to six years there was a growing trend in prices and trading volumes of cryptocurrencies. From 2015 thus far, the Bitcoin price rose from 200 USD to 60,000 USD and the volume from dozens and hundreds of Bitcoins a day to some 50,000 Bitcoins a day, i.e., around 3 billion USD a day (in total on different cryptocurrency exchanges) [27–29]. This growing trend was accounted for by the involvement of both the general population and several large investors (large net-worth individuals and a few banks) that supported cryptocurrencies from the very beginning. Some of the large players were attracted by the unclear legislation associated with use of cryptocurrency payments, savings, trading, and other transactions, e.g., the absence of tax deductions applicable to cryptocurrency-based operations [30–32]. The other investors were distracted from cryptocurrencies for the very same reason of lack of legal regulation. To sum up, up until the pandemic, cryptocurrencies experienced many periods of ebbs and flows. However, only now can we observe such a rocketing. In the paper, we suppose that this growth can be partially caused by the pandemic along with the other reasons, as the pandemic may have raised the attractiveness of cryptocurrency on the whole.

A few authors suggested that cryptocurrencies became to be regarded as safe havens in the global COVID-related instability [33–38]. Kim and Lee [39] and Lahmiri and Bekiros [40] argue that the COVID-19 pandemic influenced cryptocurrencies prices negatively, making them extremely volatile and unpredictable. However, in the works of Woebbeking [41], Drożdż et al. [42], Friti et al. [43], and Zhu et al. [44] an opposite viewpoint is proposed: the pandemic was the main reason for stabilizing and supporting the growing trend of cryprocurrencies.

In the paper, we suggest a reason for an exceptional growth of cryptocurrencies during the COVID-19 pandemic. We believe that it was cryptocurrency that began to be regarded as an epidemiologically safe means of transactions and a possible substitution for cash money.

Of course, cash money was always regarded as a probable means of transmitting different respiratory pathogens, even before the current pandemic. However, it is interesting to compare the transmissibility of SARS-CoV-2 virus through cash notes with respiratory viruses close in structure and properties such as influenza A virus. Besides, since this pandemic caused enormous media coverage, people began to pay larger attention to epidemiological safety in their payments than they did before. This may be supported by the fact that there are many media news regarding coronavirus and cash money unsafety, and we could find few such news during any previous epidemics of the last two decades, e.g., SARS 2002–2004, "bird flu" H5N1, H1N1 epidemics, etc.

We suggest a hypothesis that the significant rise of cryptocurrencies in 2020–2021 may be mainly explained by the large inflow of small investors (general population) to cryptocurrency trading that were searching for an epidemiologically safe means of transactions during the time of pandemic.

The article has the following structure. We shall analyze the validity of such allegations about cash money as a means of spreading the virus. Then we shall investigate the connection between disbelief towards cash money and approving/supporting cryptocurrencies instead of credit/debit card operations. We shall study the situation in different countries and finally evaluate the possible future scenarios of cryptocurrency behavior in the time of pandemic.

2. Methods

2.1. Cohorts

We investigated social networks users' opinion regarding cryptocurrencies, cash money, and the COVID-19 spread in 44 countries. The initial number of responses was 86,841. After the set repair, the final number of responses suitable for analysis was 32,115.

2.2. Time of Study

The main results have been obtained in the interval 15 March 2020 to 15 November 2021.

2.3. Software

Origin 8.1 (OriginLab Corp., Northampton, MA, USA) was used for modelling, statistical calculations and visualization.

2.4. Type of Study

The study is a biosocial analysis of different strata's attitudes performed along with computational modelling.

2.5. Description of the Interviewing Procedure

The interviewing was performed as follows.

1. A C++-based program was written to screen through the following networks: Facebook, Instagram, VK, Google+, and Twitter, for accounts that contained at least 20 posts with the following keywords: cryptocurrency (with and without a space), cryptocurrencies (with and without a space), crypto, cryptotrading (with and without a space), cryptomining (with and without a space), cryptocurrency exchange (with and without a space), cryptocurrencies exchange (with and without a space), cryptocurrency wallet (with and without a space), cryptocurrencies wallet (with and without a space), mining, mining farm, Bitcoin, Ether, Ethereum, blockchain (with and without a space), blockchain technology (with and without a space in the first word), BTC, ETH, Bitfinex, Bitstamp, Bitbay, Btcmarkets, Cex.io, Coinbase, Exmo, Gemini, Kraken, for the period since 15 March 2020. Versions in different languages of the keywords were used (excepting the names of the cryptocurrency exchanges listed here);
2. If the screening procedure returned an account, the other C++- and Silverlight-based program submitted a private message to the account with an invitation to join the current research;
3. If the account's holder responded, the response was stored in the special database on our server to be analyzed further;
4. The languages used in the screening and invitation were Arabic, Central Thai, Chinese (simplified), Chinese (traditional), English, Farsi, French, German, Greek, Italian, Japanese, Korean, Malay, Portuguese, Russian, Spanish, Turkish, and Vietnamese. These sets of languages were deemed a priori suitable to encompass the majority of social networks users;
5. In the poll, the social networks users had to respond to the three questions with answers YES (1), NO (2) or -/–/— (different forms of dash that stood for IT'S DIFFICULT TO SAY) (3):
   (1) Do you engage in any transactions with cryptocurrency (mining, speculation, savings, payment, etc.)? (Q1)

(2) If cryptocurrencies were widely recognized as means of transactions, regulated and guaranteed against fraud/hacking/loss, would you prefer them to ordinary cashless bank transactions, e.g., payments with bank-issued debit/credit cards? (Q2)

(3) Do you regard cash money as an epidemiologically risky means of transactions during the COVID-19 pandemic? (Q3)

The fourth input factor was the level of ordinary (bank) cashless operations in a country in 2015–2019. The data for this factor were collected from the following sources: (1) the number of non-cash transactions per inhabitant, 2014–2019 [45]; (2) overview of preferred methods of payment around the world [46], and proportion of non-cash payments in selected countries worldwide in 2015 [47]. The data published by other researchers/statistical agencies were only used in point 4.

The respondents were asked to answer with only pre-defined replies {YES, NO, ... (versions in other languages), -, –, —, or 1, 2, 3}.

2.6. Country Choice

The countries with the number of responses suitable for further analysis larger than the pre-defined conditional threshold (i.e., responses left in the set after repair) were included in the study. In our case, this minimal number was arbitrarily chosen as 500. We received 44 countries that fitted our criterion. Introducing the threshold is a measure of increasing the significance of the sample set for the research.

2.7. Data Cleaning and Set Repairing

We eliminated spoilt and strange responses as well as responses with low credibility in an algorithmic way.

1. First, a program screened through the database and carried out the simplest linguistic analysis. It removed all responses in which at least one field was blank or at least one field did not contain at least one intelligible word in the language list used.
2. Second, a program screened through the database and eliminated all responses with at least one field different from {YES, NO, ... (versions in other languages), -, –, —, 1, 2, 3}. Different letter cases (upper case, lower case, or a combination thereof) and different languages from the list could be used.

As a result, we have chosen 47,823 clean responses that may have been analyzed further of 86,841 responses initially stored in the database. So, the clean set of responses was 55.07% of the initial one. Of this intermediate set we excluded the responses of minors, outliers with an age of more than 64 y.o., and all responses where the respondent's age could not be determined. This gave us 32,115 responses (67.15% of the intermediate set and 36.98% of the initial unrepaired set).

2.8. Final Set Characteristics

The main characteristics of the final sample set after repair are summarized in Table 1.

2.9. Methodology to Assess Risk of SARS-CoV-2 Surface Contact Transmission through Bank Notes

To estimate the rate of transmitting SARS-CoV-2 by cash bank notes, we may apply a modified SIR (Susceptible–Infected–Recovered) model with the virus shedding assumption [48–50]. In this model, in addition to the direct airborne route of infection transmission, an infected person sheds SARS-CoV-2 virions on surfaces that become objects of indirect infection. It has been repeatedly demonstrated that SARS-CoV-2 has longer average times of decay on surfaces in comparison with many other respiratory viruses, e.g., influenza, parainfluenza, adenoviruses, or other coronaviruses [51–54]. Though there were supposedly no works concerning SARS-CoV-2 virions adhesion on cash bank notes thus far, Xue et al. [55], Azuma et al. [56] and Marquès et al. [57] showed that SARS-CoV-2 virion particles behave differently on different surfaces. Paper, especially paper with a layer of dust, fat, and other contaminants (this may be a good approach to describe cash notes in circulation), can absorb SARS-CoV-2 large virions (around 100–200 nm in diameter) effectively [58,59].

Table 1. Main demographics of the respondents and their cryptocurrency-related profile. Detected algorithmically on the basis of the data provided in social networks accounts (if any) or from the questionnaire. Student distribution of the sample set was assumed, CI = 95%, $p = 0.05$.

Age	Range: 18–64 years *; mean 32.4 ± 10.2 y.o.
Gender	13,654 females (42.52% **)
IT-related occupation	8366 (26.05%)
Active lifestyle (based on analysis of photo captions posted in the last three years)	10,077 (31.38%)
Self-employed (if stated overtly in the social account profile)	5228 (16.28%)
Academic training (if stated overtly in the social account profile):	
• Student (undergraduate or post-graduate)	7420 (23.10%)
• Bachelor degree	5238 (16.31%)
• Master degree	4904 (15.27%)
• PhD degree or higher	82 (0.26%)
Engaged in any operations with any of cryptocurrencies	4728 (14.72%)
Time of using any of cryptocurrencies in group of those persons who use them	Mean 1.1 ± 0.7 years
Interest in cryptocurrencies emerged after the beginning of the COVID-19 pandemic, independently of using cryptocurrencies in practice or not (based on the posts content analysis)	18,106 (56.38%)
Engaged in crypto mining	2264 (7.05%)
Engaged in crypto trading	3588 (11.17%)
Engaged in crypto savings	1012 (3.15%)
Engaged in crypto exchange with other wallets/cryptocurrencies	709 (2.21%)
Regular online payments with cryptocurrencies	134 (0.42%)

* Responses received from minors were not included in the sample set; ** Hereinafter the percentage of the total final set.

Combining an advanced technique by Fred Brauer in his book "Mathematical Models in Population Biology and Epidemiology" [60] and a number of papers in periodicals [61–65] with our SIR modified model [48], we receive an additional group of the population that sheds the virus through the bank notes V_{shed}. In his works, some of which are published in co-authorship, Fred Brauer proposed a methodology of calculating/receiving/assessing age of infection [60,61], final size equation [60,61], contact networks [62], indirect transmission [63], epidemic progression with time [64], and behavior change during an epidemic [65]. We then receive the first order Markov differential equation

$$\frac{dV_{shed}}{dt} = \sigma I - \tau V, \tag{1}$$

where I is the number of infected individuals, σ is the rate of shedding the virus on cash notes and τ is the decay rate of SARS-CoV-2 on surface. We use the word "decay" conditionally, as it may include different processes whose result would be the loss of infectivity of the virus: virus mechanical removal from the note, agglomeration of viruses, biochemical destruction, photo destruction by sun UV radiation, etc. [66,67]. Hirose et al. stressed that during any epidemic, cash money circulation is an important factor of transmitting the disease [67].

The total number of people in the group is N:

$$N = S + I + R, \tag{2}$$

where S is the subgroup of susceptible persons and R recovered. The SIR model assumes that

$$\begin{cases} \frac{dS}{dt} = -\beta_{air}SI - \beta_{surf}SV, \\ \frac{dI}{dt} = \beta_{air}SI + \beta_{surf}SV - \alpha I, \\ \frac{dR}{dt} = \alpha I \end{cases} \tag{3}$$

where β_{air} is the rate of airborne infection, β_{surf} is the rate of transmission via surfaces, and α is the rate of recovery. For simplicity of the model, let us suppose that all surface transmission of SARS-CoV-2 is done through cash bank notes. For model (3), basic reproduction number r_0:

$$r_0 = \frac{\beta_{air}N}{\alpha} + \frac{\beta_{surf}\sigma N}{\alpha\tau}. \tag{4}$$

Equation (4) is a construction based on the simplest model described in the works [60,61,63]. It was received taking into account the Brauer's viewpoint on basic reproduction number and final size relation. It contains two terms. The former describes the airborne (common) way of pandemic transmission, the latter the transmission through bank notes. $r_{0,air}$ for SARS-CoV-2 is estimated as 1.6–2.6 for different environments [68–70]. In our works [28,33,50] we found that combined r_0 may be assessed as 2.0–5.6 for different environments. Therefore, we can attribute the difference to the second term in Equation (4), i.e., $r_{0,surf}$. However, in real life the basic reproduction number depends on more parameters than Equation (4) assumes.

The approach described above is the simplest approach in which we assumed the immediate infection/decay of the virus on the cash notes. In reality, the situation is more complex. In its circulation in the population, a bank note may be infected by different people with different amounts of SARS-CoV-2 virions several times. Naturally, it can infect several people. This leads to necessity in presenting infection potential of a bank note and virus shedding as functions of time: $SR = SR(t,\ t_{inf})$—shedding rate of a person during the time of being infectious t_{inf}; $AV = AV(t,\ t_{shed})$—"active virus," i.e., the part of virions absorbed on bank notes that are still infectious for people, t_{shed} earlier. Then, we may calculate the amount of active virions that can still be dangerous to people operating with the bank note at moment t, by substituting a new variable $T = t - t_{inf}$ for integration:

$$Local\ AV = \int_0^t SR\left(t_{inf}\right)AV\left(t - t_{inf}\right)dt_{inf} = \int_0^t SR(t-T)AV(T)dT. \tag{5}$$

For the full course of COVID-19 pandemic, we have

$$Total\ AV = \int_0^\infty \int_0^t SR(t-T)AV(T)dTdt. \tag{6}$$

Integrating by variable substitution and the order interchange, we receive

$$\begin{aligned} Total\ AV &= \int_0^\infty \left(\int_T^\infty SR(t-T)dt\right)AV(T)dT = \int_0^\infty \left(\int_0^\infty SR(\mathfrak{T})d\mathfrak{T}\right)AV(T)dT \\ &= \int_0^\infty SR(\mathfrak{T})d\mathfrak{T} \int_0^\infty AV(T)dT. \end{aligned} \tag{7}$$

From Equations (4) and (7), it is easy to write the expression for basic reproduction number $r_{0,surf}$:

$$r_{0,\ surf} = \frac{\beta_{surf}}{\alpha\tau}N\int_0^\infty SR(\mathfrak{T})d\mathfrak{T}\int_0^\infty AV(T)dT. \tag{8}$$

To estimate whether the pandemic will continue in an imagined population that applies all epidemiological measures to prevent the SARS-CoV-2 airborne spread ($r_{0,air} = 0$), only through cash circulation, let us consider the initial moment $t = 0$. At the very beginning of SARS-CoV-2 spread in this biosocial group, we would have the following system of equations:

$$\begin{cases} S = N, \\ t = 0, \\ V_{shed} = 0, \\ TotalAV = 0. \end{cases} \tag{9}$$

From Equation (3), for $\frac{dS}{dt}$ and Equation (9) it can be seen that at the beginning of the pandemic in a given theoretical society where only cash notes circulation contributes to SARS-CoV-2 spread,

$$\frac{dS}{dt} = -\beta_{surf} N \int_0^{\infty} \left(\int_0^{\infty} -\frac{dS}{dT}(t - T - \mathfrak{T}) AV(T) dT \right) SR(\mathfrak{T}) d\mathfrak{T}. \tag{10}$$

For Equation (10) to have a solution like

$$S(t) = S_{init} e^{kt}, \tag{11}$$

its characteristic equation should be

$$\beta_{surf} N \int_0^{\infty} e^{-k\mathfrak{T}} SR(\mathfrak{T}) d\mathfrak{T} \int_0^{\infty} e^{-kT} AV(T) dT = 1. \tag{12}$$

Finally, it is easy to observe from Equations (8) and (12) that at the beginning of the epidemic

$$r_{0,\ surf} = \frac{1}{\alpha\tau} \frac{\int_0^{\infty} SR(\mathfrak{T}) d\mathfrak{T} \int_0^{\infty} AV(T) dT}{\int_0^{\infty} e^{-k\mathfrak{T}} SR(\mathfrak{T}) d\mathfrak{T} \int_0^{\infty} e^{-kT} AV(T) dT}. \tag{13}$$

From Equation (13), we see that in our imagined society there will be no pandemic spread due to cash circulation, if parameter $k < 0$. Otherwise, the virus will spread in the population through operations with bank notes.

Substituting the experimentally obtained figures for $r_{0,surf}$ estimates that may be derived from [48,54,71] to Equation (13), we can compare SARS-CoV-2 virions behavior during adhesion on bank notes with the behavior of other respiratory viruses, e.g., influenza viruses [72–76]. The works of Otter et al. [72] and Cortes and Zuñiga [73] compare the transmission of coronaviruses SARS 2002–2004 and MERS with that of influenza viruses. Lauterbach et al. provides data on surface transmission of influenza A virus [74]. The study of Ikeda et al. describes adhesion of influenza A virus on different surfaces and provides parameters of adhesion [75]. Robinson et al. describes surface transmission and inactivation of different respiratory viruses in different ambience [76].

3. Results and Discussion

3.1. Comparison of SARS-CoV-2 and Influenza A Transmission Potential through Paper Cash Money

Figure 2 shows comparative decay of Influenza A (calculated with data provided in our works [48,54,71] and works of other researchers [72–76]) and SARS-CoV-2 on dirty paper surfaces that may be a good approximation for cash bank notes in circulation. Calculation is made with respect to basic reproduction numbers $r_{0,air}$ and $r_{0,surf}$ for influenza A and SARS-CoV-2 viruses (Equation (13)) for idealized environments where cash money are the only surfaces with shed viruses. Modelling is made so that Equation (1) has a solution as an exponential-type decay.

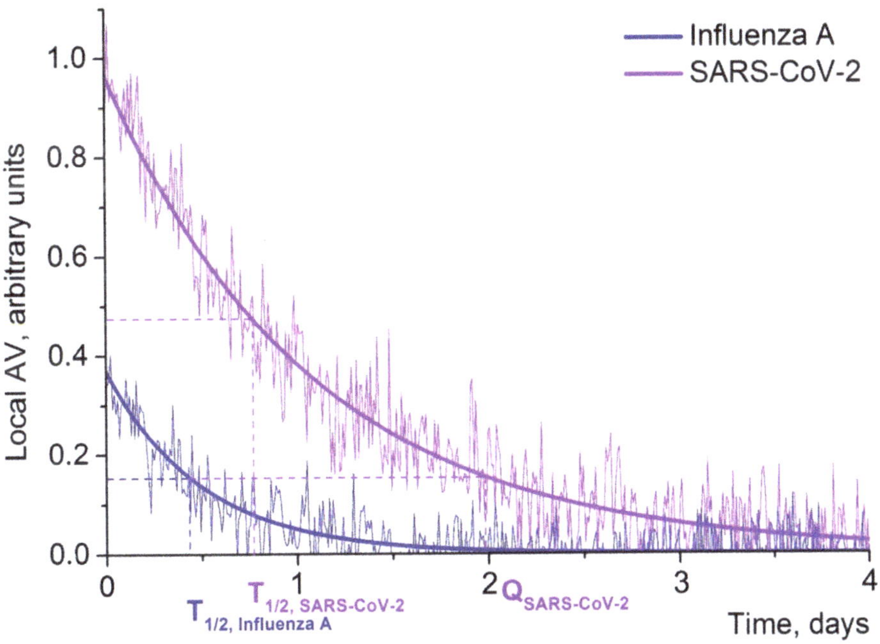

Figure 2. Modelling the decay of active viruses on dirty and fat paper surfaces (approximation for cash bank notes) in ideal conditions free of UV radiation and mechanical stir. The initial amounts of virions shed on the surfaces are equal for the two viruses. Poisson noise 5%. Modelling is made in OriginPro 8.1 (OriginLab Corp., Northampton, MA, USA) with the use of nonlinear curve simulation instrument based on multiparametric input.

From Figure 2 one can observe that the half-life time of SARS-CoV-2 active virions $T_{1/2,SARS\text{-}CoV\text{-}2}$ on dirty and fat paper is nearly two times larger than half-life time of influenza A active virions $T_{1/2,Influenza\ A}$. Besides, to reach the level of influenza A active virions on dirty paper at the time of half-life, it will take SARS-CoV-2 approximately two days, i.e., the period four times greater than the period for influenza A (point $Q_{SARS\text{-}CoV\text{-}2}$ on the time scale). This evidences SARS-CoV-2 greater stability on porous surfaces (unclear, whether this implies mechanical stability or biochemical stability). Then, $AV_{SARS\text{-}CoV\text{-}2}(0)$ is around 2.5 times more than $AV_{Influenza\ A}(0)$. It may be explained by greater adhesion capacity of SARS-CoV-2 with respect to dirty, viscous, and hydrophobic paper surfaces, as in the modelling the initial quantities of viruses shed were equal for SARS-CoV-2 and influenza A.

Assuming that all surface transmission of the viruses is made through cash bank notes (a theoretical scenario), we may conclude that cash money has larger epidemiological risk for transmitting SARS-CoV-2 than influenza A (and possibly many other respiratory viruses). In reality the transmission of an epidemic is more complex and it may include different surfaces and airborne ways. However, the main conclusion will be the same as for our idealized model: during the COVID-19 and similar pandemics, cash money becomes a risky substance for spreading the pathogen. Currencies with plastic cash money such as Hong Kong dollars or Macanese patacas may be less risky but they are rare in the world, as the overwhelming majority of currencies are still printed on paper. We did not conduct any special research on the matter, however. We supposed it on the basis of several studies that demonstrated lower transmissibility of respiratory viruses through plastic surfaces than through paper surfaces [72–76].

3.2. Growth of Population Interest in Cryptocurrencies as Possible Substitutes for Cash Money

Figure 3 shows the in-group percentage of respondents who answered YES to question 1, by country (green bars), and part of the population who preferred bank debit/credit/online payments in 2015–2019 (grey bars). It is to emphasize that green bars demonstrate the in-group percentage of those people who used cryptocurrencies in 2020–2021 and participated in our study, and they do not show the percentage of the total population of these countries who use cryptocurrencies. Obviously, the latter may be different from the data we collected and showed as green bars. Therefore, Figure 3 must be understood in a semi-quantitative sense and the data depicted as green bars used with caution. Nonetheless, Figure 3 allows one to make an estimation of cryptocurrency popularity among social network users. Besides, it demonstrates the trends that push new countries ahead in using cryptocurrencies in our days.

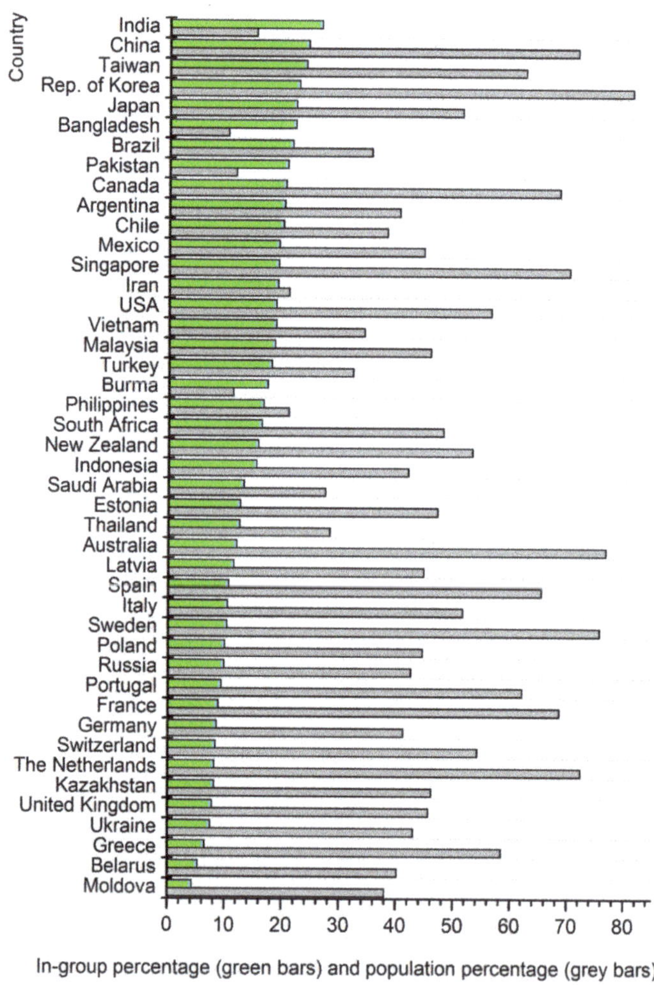

Figure 3. Part of respondents who engaged in any transactions with any cryptocurrencies in the groups of respondents studied our investigation (2020–2021), per cent (green bars), and mean part of population that was using non-cash bank payments (debit/credit cards or online payments) in these countries in 2015–2019 on a regular basis (third-party data, grey bars).

In our research, the leader of using cryptocurrencies was India. China followed, despite the recent prohibition of the Chinese government to mine cryptocurrencies because of the environmental impact. As we can see, Figure 3 demonstrates a picture a little different from the data provided by Statista.com website, according to which the top six crypto countries in 2020 were Nigeria, Vietnam, Philippines, Turkey, Peru, and Switzerland [77]. That may be partly explained by different methodologies applied by Statista.com for their evaluations and by us in the current research and different set composition.

In Table 2, we provide Pearson correlation coefficients C_{xy} between people who responded YES to the above three queries and the fourth factor of level of non-cash bank payments in a country in 2015–2019.

Table 2. Pearson correlation coefficients C_{xy} between YES reply proportion in different countries to the queries at the corresponding significance levels p_{xy}. Strong correlation is highlighted in bold.

	Q1	Q2	Q3	Bank Non-Cash
Q1		0.6402	**0.8404** *	−0.1932
Q2	$p \leq 2.87 \times 10^{-6}$		0.5904	0.1619
Q3	$\boldsymbol{p \leq 9.66 \times 10^{-13}}$ *	$p \leq 2.46 \times 10^{-5}$		−0.1730
Bank Non-Cash	$p \leq 0.2090$	$p \leq 0.2939$	$p \leq 0.2615$	

* Strong correlation is highlighted in bold.

A few important observations may be drawn from Figure 3 and Table 2:

1. There is almost no correlation (even very slight anti-correlation) between Q1 (Figure 3, green bars) and bank non-cash transactions level (Figure 3, grey bars). From this, it may be deduced that cryptocurrencies are mainly used by different groups of population than devoted supporters of only credit/debit cards/online payments who totally reject using cash. Of course, a person may use both these ways of non-cash transactions (bank-controlled and cryptocurrencies) but the preferences may be different on the scale of the whole population of a country, e.g., in India we may currently observe the highest level of cryptocurrency attractiveness, while the level of using non-cash bank operations was one of the lowest in the world in 2015–2019;
2. There is still no data in statistical agencies on using debit/credit card/online payments in the time of the COVID-19 pandemic. However, there are reasons to believe that the pandemic increased the level of non-cash bank payments somewhat proportionally with respect to the pre-COVID level, according to the data provided by Statista [78], European Central Bank [79], and a set of papers on non-cash payments chosen by Science Direct [80]. With all that said, the demand for cash money also significantly increased, as works [81–86] demonstrate, despite the decline in cash day-to-day operations of individuals. Guttmann et al. presented a report on cash demand during the pandemic made by the Reserve Bank of Australia [81]. Náñez Alonso et al. discussed changes in cash demand in rural areas of Spain, which were caused by COVID-19 [82]. In a Bank of Canada Staff Discussion Paper, Chen et al. compared the demand and use of cash [83]. In a National Bank of Poland working paper, Wisniewski et al. analyzed the level of transition from cash to cashless payments during the pandemic [84]. Alvarez and Argente [85] as well as Rogoff and Scazzero [86] described new trends of cash management after 2020. All these works prove that the cash volume increased during the COVID-19 pandemic. However, this may be a result of inflation, whose level was relatively high in different parts of the world during the pandemic (partly caused by low interest rates). We may hypothesize that persons who widely used card payments before the pandemic, increased the frequency of card use. However, the groups of population who became interested in cryptocurrencies at the time of the pandemic may differ from those who prefer online bank payments and bank card operations on regular basis;
3. The correlation between Q1 and Q2 is considerable. There were people who replied YES to Q2 but NO to Q1. Therefore, we may anticipate that in case of larger regulation

and protection of cryptocurrencies, the proportion of those who approve and use cryptocurrencies, may rise significantly;

4. The correlation between Q1 and Q3 is very strong (highlighted in bold in Table 1). It means we may assume that the COVID-19 pandemic was one of the main reasons for the raising fascination of cryptocurrencies;
5. The country composition is different for supporting cryptocurrency-based operations and non-cash bank operations. On the whole, with a few exceptions, we can see that economically developed countries tend to group at the lower part of Figure 3 (lower level of trust for cryptocurrency), whereas the level of non-cash bank transactions may be substantial in these countries. On the contrary, the population of many emerging countries (mainly Asian states) currently has the highest interest in cryptocurrencies independently of the level of non-cash card and online payments made by this population.

3.3. Temporal Change of Attitudes towards Cryptocurrencies in the Course of COVID-19 Pandemic

Figure 4 demonstrates the temporal change of the weighted average of YES proportion to queries Q1, Q2, and Q3 (all respondents from all countries) with regard to Bitcoin prices. Each measurement was made at the middle of the month since March 2020 to November 2021. The Pearson correlation coefficients in regard to time change are provided in Table 3.

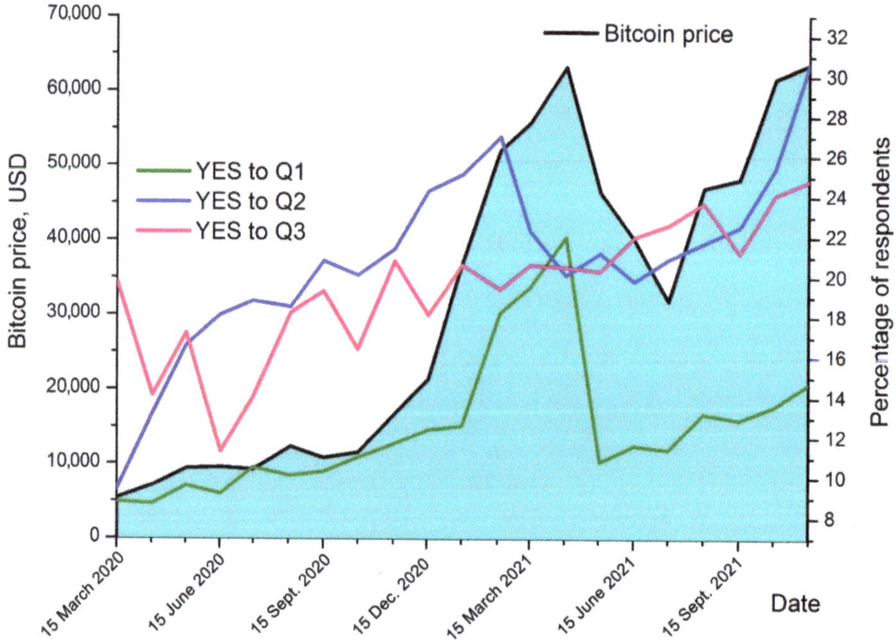

Figure 4. Bitcoin price (left axis) and weighted average proportion of respondents who answered YES to queries Q1, Q2, and Q3 (right axis), depending on time. Fixings were made at the middle of each month from 15 March 2020 to 15 November 2021.

Table 3. Pearson correlation coefficients B_{xy} between temporal changes of weighted average YES proportion in the whole set and Bitcoin prices, at the corresponding significance levels $p_{B,\,xy}$.

	Q1 (*t*)	Q2 (*t*)	Q3 (*t*)	Bitcoin Price (*t*)
Q1 (*t*)		0.5271	0.4187	**0.7878** *
Q2 (*t*)	$p_B \leq 0.0141$		0.5236	**0.6953** *
Q3 (*t*)	$p_B \leq 0.0589$	$p_B \leq 0.0149$		**0.7254** *
Bitcoin Price (*t*)	$\mathbf{p_B \leq 2.24 \times 10^{-5}}$ *	$\mathbf{p_B \leq 4.67 \times 10^{-4}}$ *	$\mathbf{p_B \leq 1.98 \times 10^{-4}}$ *	

* Strong correlations are highlighted in bold.

It is noteworthy that the Bitcoin price is highly correlated with the sentiments of people who are interested in cryptocurrencies. These are sentiments about Bitcoin future (Q1 and Q2) and the fear of using cash bank notes during the pandemic (Q3). This makes cryptocurrencies the assets whose price is currently largely determined by psychological factors influencing the behavior of the general population, in comparison with more "traditional" financial assets, where institutional interest plays considerable role.

4. Limitations

The major limitations of the study are the following:

- Our results reflect participation of only one social group in using cryptocurrencies, i.e., active users of social networks Facebook, Instagram, VK, and Google+. Therefore, our approach is not very representative. The results for the total population of the countries studied may be different;
- We may have overlooked a few countries with a considerable level of using cryptocurrencies due to introducing a minimum threshold on number of responses, e.g., Nigeria, Peru, or Colombia [77];
- We widely used the concept of correlation between different factors. However, correlation is not capable of showing the direction of causative relations, nor does it take into account the multitude of possible factors. Therefore, we may have missed several factors in the sociological survey. As well, we did;
- We assumed that the main reason for tremendous cryptocurrency growth was the COVID-19 pandemic. However, it may be only one of several important factors;
- We focused on Bitcoin, but we did not study a variety of cryptocurrencies and their behavior during the pandemic;
- We compared the level of using cryptocurrencies in 2020–2021 with the level of non-cryptocurrency bank cashless payments in 2015–2019. Strictly speaking, that may have blurred the results to a certain degree;
- We did not study the involvement of large institutional investors in cryptocurrencies trading during the pandemic. However, without studying this field the full picture of the cryptocurrency–pandemic relation is hardly attainable;
- We only compared SARS-CoV-2 with influenza A virus in terms of transmissibility through cash bank notes. It would be interesting to compare it with other respiratory viruses and epidemics;
- We did not investigate psychological attitudes of the general population towards cryptocurrencies as a substitute for banks monopoly on producing money and how this may have contributed to the rise of cryptocurrencies rates during the pandemic. Taking into account psychological attractiveness of cryptocurrencies as a competitor to the money produced by banks may be a serious factor of cryptocurrencies rocketing during the COVID-19 pandemic;
- We did not compare paper money and plastic money in terms of epidemiological risk;
- We did not assess epidemiological risk of using debit/credit cards kept in wallets along with cash money;
- We did not distinguish between different ways of using cryptocurrencies, i.e., the ever-changing levels of mining, trading, keeping in cryptocurrency wallets, payments, etc.

- We applied a very strict algorithmic set repair that led to a substantial contraction of the set [Final Set (after repair) = 37% × Initial Set (before repair)] algorithmically without any complex linguistic analysis of the responses.
- We did not perform any manual analysis of the responses. That may have excluded many relevant responses from the further analysis, e.g., those that were input in the questionnaire in a different form from the sample we proposed {YES, NO, ... (versions in other languages), -, –, —, or 1, 2, 3}.

Of all of the limitations stated above, we regard the following two the most important: (1) research of using cryptocurrency not in the whole population, but in a group that cannot give the full representativeness; and (2) absence of a multifaceted comparative study of cryptocurrencies/cash/bank cards and other online payments in the time of pandemic due to lack of third-party data. Addressing these limitations can provide a guidance how to devise and conduct a future research.

5. Conclusions

The COVID-19 pandemic caused fear of using cash bank notes as an epidemiologically risky means of transactions and simultaneous surge of almost all cryptocurrencies rates. We may hypothesize that this surge is explained by the growth of the general population's interest in cryptocurrencies as more suitable means for new types of social relations in the global world where epidemiological measures must be ensured and observed. Heldt [87] and Biały [88] write that caution for cash money may be one of the ways to enhance the culture of communication during the pandemic events. Using cryptocurrencies is a possible option to make such an enhancement. Santos et al. [89], Naughton et al. [90], VanMeter et al. [91], and Sassin [92] emphasize the appeal of new electronic techniques of financial transactions for many people in the situation of a crisis-related uncertainty and cryptocurrencies may have attractiveness as a psychological safe haven. Besides, based on works of Wilder-Smith et al. [93], Peeri et al. [94], Nomura et al. [95], Maria and José Luis Miralles-Quirós [96], and Dwita et al. [97] we may suppose that cryptocurrencies may be a part of the Sustainable Finance paradigm.

In our model described in this article, we proved that the fear of cash money as a SARS-CoV-2 spreader is explainable. A significant part of indirect transmission of SARS-CoV-2 virus is made through cash bank notes circulation. SARS-CoV-2 remains on cash paper money for a period around four times larger than the influenza A virus and it is absorbed by cash notes two and a half times more effectively than influenza. With all that said, it should be stressed that using cash money is not any more dangerous to people during the pandemic than wearing clothes, driving cars, or buying utilities. However, due to the persistence of cash money in our life and frequent incompliance with routine safety measures by people during the pandemic (e.g., neglect of elementary washing hands after dealing with cash notes) make cash notes an important factor in spreading the pathogen.

Our conclusions about the use of cash bank notes on the whole agrees with the recent research of Bank of England that says "The COVID pandemic has changed the way that people shop. In response to social distancing guidelines, more people are shopping online, meaning fewer cash payments". [98].

However, our estimations of coronavirus viability on paper cash surfaces do not coincide with the results obtained on behalf of the BoE [98]. The authors of the report on virus viability published by the BoE [98] ("Cash in the time of COVID" BoE paper, Box 2) argue that it is difficult to get the coronavirus from the cash notes or coins. However, the results obtained by Blutest Laboratories Ltd., Glasgow, UK, (the BoE's contractor) cannot be unambiguously interpreted in the context of our investigation for the following reasons. 1. The laboratory did not used SARS-CoV-2, the causative pathogen of COVID-19. Instead, they used a surrogate coronavirus, but they did not specify which one. As it is known, coronaviral infections represent the group of infectious diseases caused by RNA-containing viruses of the order *Nidovirales*, family *Coronaviridae*, which affect many species of birds and mammals [99]. These viruses are numerous and currently there are more than a hundred representatives known to scientists [100]. A number of coronaviruses are pathogenic to humans, e.g., HKU1, NL63, OC43, and E229 coronaviruses cause mild human diseases [101,102]. All coronaviruses deviate from each other in size, physical conformation, and physical properties [103] and to substitute the causative agent of COVID-19 by another member of the family was possibly not the best option, as the results obtained by Blutest Laboratories Ltd. can hardly be extrapolated to SARS-CoV-2. 2. In the report published by the BoE the researchers do not provide information on the sample set of surfaces. We have no idea on the number of experiments and statistics used. 3. The authors of this report do not provide data on the techniques used to bring samples of virions to the surfaces they studied. Was it an aerosol, spray, gas, liquid, or large-droplet injection? 4. They do not provide technical data on amplification and detection of the viral RNA to assess the amount of remaining virions. To measure a virus quantity on a surface is not a trivial task and, therefore, to use the data provided by Blutest Laboratories Ltd., a reader must be fully aware of the methodology. In any case, the BoE report says that the transmission level of the novel coronavirus SARS-CoV-2 is negligibly small by cash bank notes during the pandemic. We cannot agree due to the lack of information given by the authors from Blutest Laboratories Ltd.

As epidemiologically safe means of transactions, cryptocurrencies could be attractive as a perspective for possible substitutes for cash, were they more regulated, protected, and broadly accepted as a legal means of payment, and the transactions based on them guaranteed by different institutions. The preference of cryptocurrencies to bank non-cash operations by the growing number of people (especially persons of young age, having an active lifestyle, or engaged in IT-related professions) during the pandemic may also be explained by the psychological appeal of cryptocurrencies as money that is produced by individuals, not by banks who produce customary money (USD, EUR, etc.).

Our paper helps to see a broad perspective of cryptocurrencies development during a crisis time. We studied the "coronacrisis", but the conclusions may be applied to different crisis events and pivotal points in the development of societies.

In a global world without borders, we may anticipate unstable epidemiological situation in the decades to come. In this situation, if cryptocurrencies are recognized as legal means of savings and payments by different governments, as it is already done with Bitcoin in El Salvador, we may see them achieve tremendous success.

Author Contributions: Conceptualization, K.S.S.; methodology, D.V.B. and K.S.S.; software, D.V.B. and K.S.S.; validation, D.V.B., N.P.S. and K.S.S.; formal analysis, D.V.B. and K.S.S.; investigation, D.V.B., N.P.S. and K.S.S.; resources, N.P.S.; data curation, D.V.B. and K.S.S.; writing—original draft preparation, K.S.S.; writing—review and editing, D.V.B., N.P.S. and K.S.S.; visualization, D.V.B. and K.S.S.; supervision, N.P.S.; project administration, N.P.S.; funding acquisition, N.P.S. All authors have read and agreed to the published version of the manuscript.

Funding: This work has been funded by Government program of basic research in Koltzov Institute of Developmental Biology of Russian Academy of Sciences in 2021, No. 0088-2021-0008.

Institutional Review Board Statement: Not applicable.

Conflicts of Interest: The authors declare no conflict of interest.

Ethics: All results are anonymized and no identifying information about the social network users' accounts was collected or disclosed in the research. The participating users who disclosed their real names were included in the cohorts but this information was stored on our server and was not used at any stage of the work. Since no experiments were carried out on biological organisms, no special ethics permission from the affiliated institution was required.

References

1. Interest Rates, Discount Rate for United States. Available online: https://fred.stlouisfed.org/series/INTDSRUSM193N (accessed on 4 December 2021).
2. Trading Economics. Available online: https://tradingeconomics.com/united-states/interest-rate#:~{}:text=Interest%20Rate%20in%20the%20United,percent%20in%20December%20of%202008.&text=United%20States%20Fed%20Funds%20Rate%20%2D%20data%2C%20historical%20chart%2C%20forecasts,updated%20on%20December%20of%202021 (accessed on 4 December 2021).
3. Luo, S.; Zhou, G.; Zhou, J. The Impact of Electronic Money on Monetary Policy: Based on DSGE Model Simulations. *Mathematics* **2021**, *9*, 2614. [CrossRef]
4. Shovkhalov, S.; Idrisov, H. Economic and Legal Analysis of Cryptocurrency: Scientific Views from Russia and the Muslim World. *Laws* **2021**, *10*, 32. [CrossRef]
5. Jareño, F.; González, M.D.L.O.; López, R.; Ramos, A.R. Cryptocurrencies and oil price shocks: A NARDL analysis in the COVID-19 pandemic. *Resour. Policy* **2021**, *74*, 102281. [CrossRef] [PubMed]
6. Umar, Z.; Jareño, F.; de la González, M. The impact of COVID-19-related media coverage on the return and volatility connectedness of cryptocurrencies and fiat currencies. *Technol. Forecast. Soc. Chang.* **2021**, *172*, 121025. [CrossRef]
7. Umar, Z.; Gubareva, M. A time–frequency analysis of the impact of the COVID-19 induced panic on the volatility of currency and cryptocurrency markets. *J. Behav. Exp. Financ.* **2020**, *28*, 100404. [CrossRef]
8. Mnif, E.; Jarboui, A.; Mouakhar, K. How the cryptocurrency market has performed during COVID-19? A multifractal analysis. *Financ. Res. Lett.* **2020**, *36*, 101647. [CrossRef]
9. Corbet, S.; Hou, Y.; Hu, Y.; Larkin, C.; Oxley, L. Any port in a storm: Cryptocurrency safe-havens during the COVID-19 pandemic. *Econ. Lett.* **2020**, *194*, 109377. [CrossRef]
10. Wątorek, M.; Kwapień, J.; Drożdż, S. Financial Return Distributions: Past, Present, and COVID-19. *Entropy* **2021**, *23*, 884. [CrossRef]
11. Casti, J.L. From Social Mood to Collective Events: Measuring the Path by Sociometers. *Beacon J. Stud. Ideol. Ment. Dimens.* **2021**, *4*, 020110153. Available online: https://hdl.handle.net/20.500.12656/thebeacon.4.020110153 (accessed on 14 October 2021).
12. Verma, P.; Dumka, A.; Bhardwaj, A.; Ashok, A.; Kestwal, M.C.; Kumar, P. A Statistical Analysis of Impact of COVID19 on the Global Economy and Stock Index Returns. *SN Comput. Sci.* **2021**, *2*, 27. [CrossRef]
13. Sassin, W. Die Grenzen Der Ökonomie: Globalisierung—Vom Füllhorn Zum Giftbecher? *Eur. Crossrd.* **2020**, *1*, 010410216. Available online: https://hdl.handle.net/20.500.12656/eurcrossrd.1.010410216 (accessed on 3 November 2021).
14. Sassin, W. Der Konflikt Zwischen Ideologien und Einer Nüchternen Und Umfassenden Sichtweise: Nachhaltig Gegen Resilient? *Beacon J. Stud. Ideol. Ment. Dimens.* **2020**, *3*, 020440211. Available online: https://hdl.handle.net/20.500.12656/thebeacon.3.020440211 (accessed on 6 October 2021).
15. Donskikh, O.A. Moral and Ideological Consequences of Pandemic. *Beacon J. Stud. Ideol. Ment. Dimens.* **2020**, *3*, 020510125. Available online: https://hdl.handle.net/20.500.12656/thebeacon.3.020510125 (accessed on 14 November 2021).
16. Elleby, C.; Dominguez, I.P.; Adenauer, M.; Genovese, G. Impacts of the COVID-19 Pandemic on the Global Agricultural Markets. *Environ. Resour. Econ.* **2020**, *76*, 1067–1079. [CrossRef]
17. Mazur, M.; Dang, M.; Vega, M. COVID-19 and the march 2020 stock market crash. Evidence from S&P1500. *Financ. Res. Lett.* **2020**, *38*, 101690. [CrossRef]
18. Pinilla, J.; Barber, P.; Vallejo-Torres, L.; Rodríguez-Mireles, S.; López-Valcárcel, B.; Serra-Majem, L. The Economic Impact of the SARS-CoV-2 (COVID-19) Pandemic in Spain. *Int. J. Environ. Res. Public Health* **2021**, *18*, 4708. [CrossRef]
19. Mahata, A.; Rai, A.; Nurujjaman, M.; Prakash, O.; Bal, D.P. Characteristics of 2020 stock market crash: The COVID-19 induced extreme event. *Chaos Interdiscip. J. Nonlinear Sci.* **2021**, *31*, 053115. [CrossRef]
20. Sassin, W. Globalisierung und Digitalisierung—Die Exponentielle Ausbreitung Ansteckender Information und Deren Mögliche Eindämmung. *Beacon J. Stud. Ideol. Ment. Dimens.* **2020**, *3*, 010510201. Available online: https://hdl.handle.net/20.500.12656/thebeacon.3.010510201 (accessed on 11 September 2020).
21. O'Sullivan, A. Ungoverned or anti-governance? How Bitcoin threatens the future of Western institutions. *J. Int. Aff.* **2018**, *71*, 90–102.
22. Suoquin, F. Auf Der Suche Nach Dem Wesen Der Evolution. Deutschland Nach Dem Zweiten Weltkrieg, Die USA Und Die Europäische Union Als Beispiele Für Den Übergang Zur Nächsten Evolutionsstufe Des Homo Sapiens. *Eur. Crossrd.* **2020**, *1*, 020210220. Available online: https://hdl.handle.net/20.500.12656/eurcrossrd.1.020210220 (accessed on 1 December 2020).
23. Matkovskyy, R.; Jalan, A. Can Bitcoin Be an Inflation Hedge? Evidence from a Quantile-on-Quantile Model. *Rev. Econ.* **2021**, *7*, 1021–1041. [CrossRef]
24. Meynkhard, A. Energy Efficient Development Model for Regions of the Russian Federation: Evidence of Crypto Mining. *Int. J. Energy Econ. Policy* **2019**, *9*, 16–21. [CrossRef]
25. Alonso, S.N.; Jorge-Vázquez, J.; Fernández, M.E.; Forradellas, R.R. Cryptocurrency Mining from an Economic and Environmental Perspective. Analysis of the Most and Least Sustainable Countries. *Energies* **2021**, *14*, 4254. [CrossRef]
26. Goodkind, A.L.; Jones, B.A.; Berrens, R.P. Cryptodamages: Monetary value estimates of the air pollution and human health impacts of cryptocurrency mining. *Energy Res. Soc. Sci.* **2019**, *59*, 101281. [CrossRef]
27. BTC/USD. Available online: https://www.investing.com/crypto/bitcoin/btc-usd-advanced-chart (accessed on 3 December 2020).

28. Bitcoin Trading Volume. Available online: https://data.bitcoinity.org/markets/volume/30d?c=e&t=b (accessed on 3 December 2020).
29. Total Bitcoin Trading Volume on Major Cryptocurrency Exchanges. Available online: https://www.blockchain.com/charts/trade-volume (accessed on 3 December 2020).
30. Chu, D. Broker-dealers for virtual currency: Regulating cryptocurrency wallets and exchanges. *Colum. Law Rev.* **2018**, *118*, 2323–2360.
31. Ducas, E.; Wilner, A. The security and financial implications of blockchain technologies: Regulating emerging technologies in Canada. *Int. J. Can. J. Glob. Policy Anal.* **2017**, *72*, 538–562. [CrossRef]
32. Turpin, J.B. Bitcoin: The Economic Case for a Global, Virtual Currency Operating in an Unexplored Legal Framework. *Indiana J. Glob. Leg. Stud.* **2014**, *21*, 335. [CrossRef]
33. Zhang, Y.; Zhu, P.; Xu, Y. Has COVID-19 Changed the Hedge Effectiveness of Bitcoin? *Front. Public Health* **2021**, *9*, 704900. [CrossRef] [PubMed]
34. Conlon, T.; Corbet, S.; McGee, R.J. Are cryptocurrencies a safe haven for equity markets? An international perspective from the COVID-19 pandemic. *Res. Int. Bus. Financ.* **2020**, *54*, 101248. [CrossRef] [PubMed]
35. Hou, J.; Liu, J.; Jie, Y. Examining the Psychological State Analysis Relationship Between Bitcoin Prices and COVID-19. *Front. Psychol.* **2021**, *12*, 647691. [CrossRef] [PubMed]
36. Chen, T.; Lau, C.K.M.; Cheema, S.; Koo, C.K. Economic Policy Uncertainty in China and Bitcoin Returns: Evidence From the COVID-19 Period. *Front. Public Health* **2021**, *9*, 651051. [CrossRef]
37. James, N.; Menzies, M.; Chan, J. Changes to the extreme and erratic behaviour of cryptocurrencies during COVID-19. *Phys. A Stat. Mech. Its Appl.* **2020**, *565*, 125581. [CrossRef]
38. Mahdi, E.; Leiva, V.; Mara'Beh, S.; Martin-Barreiro, C. A New Approach to Predicting Cryptocurrency Returns Based on the Gold Prices with Support Vector Machines during the COVID-19 Pandemic Using Sensor-Related Data. *Sensors* **2021**, *21*, 6319. [CrossRef]
39. Kim, K.; Lee, M. The Impact of the COVID-19 Pandemic on the Unpredictable Dynamics of the Cryptocurrency Market. *Entropy* **2021**, *23*, 1234. [CrossRef]
40. Lahmiri, S.; Bekiros, S. The impact of COVID-19 pandemic upon stability and sequential irregularity of equity and cryptocurrency markets. *Chaos Solitons Fractals* **2020**, *138*, 109936. [CrossRef]
41. Woebbeking, F. Cryptocurrency volatility markets. *Digit. Financ.* **2021**, *3*. [CrossRef]
42. Drożdż, S.; Kwapień, J.; Oświęcimka, P.; Stanisz, T.; Wątorek, M. Complexity in Economic and Social Systems: Cryptocurrency Market at around This Is Correct COVID-19. *Entropy* **2020**, *22*, 1043. [CrossRef]
43. Ftiti, Z.; Louhichi, W.; Ben Ameur, H. Cryptocurrency volatility forecasting: What can we learn from the first wave of the COVID-19 outbreak? *Ann. Oper. Res.* **2021**, 1–26. [CrossRef]
44. Zhu, P.; Zhang, X.; Wu, Y.; Zheng, H.; Zhang, Y. Investor attention and cryptocurrency: Evidence from the Bitcoin market. *PLoS ONE* **2021**, *16*, e0246331. [CrossRef]
45. Non-Cash Payments Volume. Available online: https://worldpaymentsreport.com/non-cash-payments-volume-3/#transactions-per-inhabitant (accessed on 17 November 2021).
46. World Economic Forum. Available online: https://www.weforum.org/agenda/2021/01/this-chart-shows-cash-cashless-finance-payment-methods-global-preference (accessed on 17 November 2021).
47. Proportion of Non-Cash Payments in Selected Countries Worldwide in 2015. Available online: https://www.statista.com/statistics/585966/share-of-cashless-transactions-by-country (accessed on 17 November 2021).
48. Sharov, K.S. Creating and applying SIR modified compartmental model for calculation of COVID-19 lockdown efficiency. *Chaos Solitons Fractals* **2020**, *141*, 110295. [CrossRef]
49. Valba, O.V.; Avetisov, V.A.; Gorsky, A.S.; Nechaev, S.K. Evaluating Ideologies of Coronacrisis-Related Self-Isolation and Frontiers Closing by SIR Compartmental Epidemiological Model. *Beacon J. Stud. Ideol. Ment. Dimens.* **2020**, *3*, 020210318. Available online: https://hdl.handle.net/20.500.12656/thebeacon.3.020210318 (accessed on 11 September 2021).
50. Sharov, K.S. 8806 Russian patients demonstrate T cell count as better marker of COVID-19 clinical course severity than SARS-CoV-2 viral load. *Sci. Rep.* **2021**, *11*, 9440. [CrossRef]
51. Malik, Y.A. Properties of Coronavirus and SARS-CoV-2. *Malays. J. Pathol.* **2020**, *42*, 3–11.
52. Meyerowitz, E.A.; Richterman, A.; Gandhi, R.T.; Sax, P.E. Transmission of SARS-CoV-2: A Review of Viral, Host, and Environmental Factors. *Ann. Intern. Med.* **2021**, *174*, 69–79. [CrossRef]
53. Fathizadeh, H.; Maroufi, P.; Momen-Heravi, M.; Dao, S.; Köse, Ş.; Ganbarov, K.; Pagliano, P.; Esposito, S.; Kafil, H.S. Protection and disinfection policies against SARS-CoV-2 (COVID-19). *Infez. Med.* **2020**, *28*, 185–191.
54. Sharov, K.S. HIV/SARS-CoV-2 co-infection: T cell profile, cytokine dynamics and role of exhausted lymphocytes. *Int. J. Infect. Dis.* **2020**, *102*, 163–169. [CrossRef]
55. Xue, X.; Ball, J.K.; Alexander, C.; Alexander, M.R. All Surfaces Are Not Equal in Contact Transmission of SARS-CoV-2. *Matter* **2020**, *3*, 1433–1441. [CrossRef]
56. Azuma, K.; Yanagi, U.; Kagi, N.; Kim, H.; Ogata, M.; Hayashi, M. Environmental factors involved in SARS-CoV-2 transmission: Effect and role of indoor environmental quality in the strategy for COVID-19 infection control. *Environ. Health Prev. Med.* **2020**, *25*, 1–16. [CrossRef]

57. Marquès, M.; Domingo, J.L. Contamination of inert surfaces by SARS-CoV-2: Persistence, stability and infectivity. A review. *Environ. Res.* **2020**, *193*, 110559. [CrossRef]
58. Zhou, L.; Yao, M.; Zhang, X.; Hu., B.; Li., X.; Chen, H.; Zhang, L.; Liu, Y.; Du, M.; Sun, B.; et al. Breath-, air- and surface-borne SARS-CoV-2 in hospitals. *J. Aerosol. Sci.* **2021**, *152*, 105693. [CrossRef]
59. Ren, S.-Y.; Wang, W.-B.; Hao, Y.-G.; Zhang, H.-R.; Wang, Z.-C.; Chen, Y.-L.; Gao, R.-D. Stability and infectivity of coronaviruses in inanimate environments. *World J. Clin. Cases* **2020**, *8*, 1391–1399. [CrossRef] [PubMed]
60. Henson, S.M.; Brauer, F.; Castillo-Chavez, C. Mathematical Models in Population Biology and Epidemiology. *Am. Math. Mon.* **2003**, *110*, 254. [CrossRef]
61. Brauer, F. Age-of-infection and the final size relation. *Math. Biosci. Eng.* **2008**, *5*, 681–690. [CrossRef] [PubMed]
62. Brauer, F. Preface. *J. Biol. Dyn.* **2010**, *4*, 429–430. [CrossRef]
63. Brauer, F. A new epidemic model with indirect transmission. *J. Biol. Dyn.* **2016**, *11*, 285–293. [CrossRef]
64. Davoudi, B.; Moser, F.; Brauer, F.; Pourbohloul, B. Epidemic progression on networks based on disease generation time. *J. Biol. Dyn.* **2013**, *7*, 148–160. [CrossRef]
65. Brauer, F. A simple model for behaviour change in epidemics. *BMC Public Health* **2011**, *11*, S3. [CrossRef]
66. Tien, J.H.; Earn, D.J.D. Multiple Transmission Pathways and Disease Dynamics in a Waterborne Pathogen Model. *Bull. Math. Biol.* **2010**, *72*, 1506–1533. [CrossRef]
67. Hirose, R.; Ikegaya, H.; Naito, Y.; Watanabe, N.; Yoshida, T.; Bandou, R.; Daidoji, T.; Itoh, Y.; Nakaya, T. Survival of SARS-CoV-2 and influenza virus on the human skin: Importance of hand hygiene in COVID-19. *Clin. Infect. Dis.* **2020**, *73*, e4329–e4335. [CrossRef]
68. Jung, S.-M.; Akhmetzhanov, A.R.; Hayashi, K.; Linton, N.M.; Yang, Y.; Yuan, B.; Kobayashi, T.; Kinoshita, R.; Nishiura, H. Real-Time Estimation of the Risk of Death from Novel Coronavirus (COVID-19) Infection: Inference Using Exported Cases. *J. Clin. Med.* **2020**, *9*, 523. [CrossRef]
69. Kuniya, T. Prediction of the Epidemic Peak of Coronavirus Disease in Japan. *J. Clin. Med.* **2020**, *9*, 789. [CrossRef]
70. Delikhoon, M.; Guzman, M.I.; Nabizadeh, R.; Baghani, A.N. Modes of Transmission of Severe Acute Respiratory Syndrome-Coronavirus-2 (SARS-CoV-2) and Factors Influencing on the Airborne Transmission: A Review. *Int. J. Environ. Res. Public Health* **2021**, *18*, 395. [CrossRef]
71. Sharov, K.S. Trends in adaptation of fifteen European countries population to SARS-CoV-2 in March–May 2020: Can Taiwanese experience be adopted? *J. Formos. Med. Assoc.* **2020**, *120*, 679–687. [CrossRef]
72. Otter, J.A.; Donskey, C.; Yezli, S.; Douthwaite, S.; Goldenberg, S.D.; Weber, D.J. Transmission of SARS and MERS coronaviruses and influenza virus in healthcare settings: The possible role of dry surface contamination. *J. Hosp. Infect.* **2016**, *92*, 235–250. [CrossRef]
73. Cortes, A.A.; Zuñiga, J.M. The use of copper to help prevent transmission of SARS-coronavirus and influenza viruses. A general review. *Diagn. Microbiol. Infect. Dis.* **2020**, *98*, 115176. [CrossRef]
74. Lauterbach, S.E.; Wright, C.M.; Zentkovich, M.M.; Nelson, S.W.; Lorbach, J.N.; Bliss, N.T.; Nolting, J.M.; Pierson, R.M.; King, M.D.; Bowman, A.S. Detection of influenza A virus from agricultural fair environment: Air and surfaces. *Prev. Veter.-Med.* **2018**, *153*, 24–29. [CrossRef]
75. Ikeda, K.; Tsujimoto, K.; Suzuki, Y.; Koyama, A.H. Survival of influenza A virus on contaminated student clothing. *Exp. Ther. Med.* **2015**, *9*, 1205–1208. [CrossRef]
76. Robinson, M.; Drossinos, Y.; Stilianakis, N.I. Indirect transmission and the effect of seasonal pathogen inactivation on infectious disease periodicity. *Epidemics* **2013**, *5*, 111–121. [CrossRef]
77. Share of Respondents Who Indicated They Either Owned or Used Cryptocurrencies in 55 Countries Worldwide in 2020. Available online: https://www.statista.com/statistics/1202468/global-cryptocurrency-ownership (accessed on 3 December 2021).
78. Number of Non-Cash Transactions Worldwide from 2013 to 2018, with Forecasts from 2019 to 2023, by Region. Available online: https://www.statista.com/statistics/265767/number-of-cashless-transactions-worldwide-by-region (accessed on 18 November 2021).
79. Payments Statistics: 2020. European Central Bank. Available online: https://www.ecb.europa.eu/press/pr/stats/paysec/html/ecb.pis2020~{}5d0ea9dfa5.en.html (accessed on 18 November 2021).
80. Noncash Payments. Science Direct. Available online: https://www.sciencedirect.com/topics/economics-econometrics-and-finance/noncash-payments (accessed on 18 November 2021).
81. Guttmann, R.; Pavlik, C.; Ung, B.; Wang, G. Cash Demand during COVID-19. Available online: https://www.rba.gov.au/publications/bulletin/2021/mar/pdf/cash-demand-during-covid-19.pdf (accessed on 5 December 2021).
82. Alonso, S.N.; Jorge-Vazquez, J.; Forradellas, R.R. Detection of Financial Inclusion Vulnerable Rural Areas through an Access to Cash Index: Solutions Based on the Pharmacy Network and a CBDC. Evidence Based on Ávila (Spain). *Sustainability* **2020**, *12*, 7480. [CrossRef]
83. Chen, H.; Engert, W.; Huynh, K.; Nicholls, G.; Nicholson, M.; Zhu, J. Cash and COVID-19: The Impact of the Pandemic on the Demand for and Use of Cash (No. 2020-6). Bank of Canada Staff Discussion Paper. 2020. Available online: https://www.bankofcanada.ca/2020/07/staff-discussion-paper-2020-6 (accessed on 4 December 2021).
84. Wisniewski, T.P.; Polasik, M.; Kotkowski, R.; Moro, A. Switching from Cash to Cashless Payments during the COVID-19 Pandemic and Beyond. NBP Working Paper no. 337. Available online: https://www.nbp.pl/publikacje/materialy_i_studia/337_en.pdf (accessed on 4 December 2021).

85. Alvarez, F.; Argente, D. Cash-Management in Times of COVID-19. *BE J. Macroecon.* **2021**. [CrossRef]
86. Rogoff, K.; Scazzero, J. COVID Cash. CMFA Working Paper 002. Available online: https://scholar.harvard.edu/files/rogoff/files/cato_journal_covid_cash_november_2021.pdf (accessed on 4 December 2021).
87. Heldt, A. Let's Meet Halfway: Sharing New Responsibilities in a Digital Age. *J. Inf. Policy* **2019**, *9*, 336–369. Available online: https://papers.ssrn.com/sol3/papers.cfm?abstract_id=3459965 (accessed on 12 November 2020). [CrossRef]
88. Biały, B. Social Media—From Social Exchange to Battlefield. *Cyber Def. Rev.* **2017**, *2*, 69–90. Available online: https://cyberdefensereview.army.mil/CDR-Content/Articles/Article-View/Article/1589009/social-mediafrom-social-exchange-to-battlefield (accessed on 7 October 2020).
89. Santos, K.O.B.; Fernandes, R.D.C.P.; De Almeida, M.M.C.; Miranda, S.S.; Mise, Y.F.; De Lima, M.A.G. Trabalho, saúde e vulnerabilidade na pandemia de COVID-19. *Cad. De Saúde Pública* **2020**, *36*, e00178320. [CrossRef]
90. Naughton, S.X.; Raval, U.; Harary, J.M.; Pasinetti, G.M. The role of the exposome in promoting resilience or susceptibility after SARS-CoV-2 infection. *J. Expo. Sci. Environ. Epidemiol.* **2020**, *30*, 776–777. [CrossRef]
91. VanMeter, K.C.; Bhakdi, S.; Gerilovych, A.P. COVID-19 Outbreak Role in the Development of Societies: Questions and Inconsistencies. *Beacon J. Stud. Ideol. Ment. Dimens.* **2020**, *3*, 011140018. Available online: https://hdl.handle.net/20.500.12656/thebeacon.3.011140018 (accessed on 28 September 2021).
92. Sassin, W. Behindert Die Demokratie Die Nachhaltigkeit in Eurasien? *Eur. Crossrd.* **2020**, *1*, 020000201. Available online: https://hdl.handle.net/20.500.12656/eurcrossrd.1.020000201 (accessed on 4 November 2021).
93. Wilder-Smith, A.; Chiew, C.J.; Lee, V.J. Can we contain the COVID-19 outbreak with the same measures as for SARS? *Lancet Infect. Dis.* **2020**, *20*, e102–e107. [CrossRef]
94. Peeri, N.C.; Shrestha, N.; Rahman, M.S.; Zaki, R.; Tan, Z.; Bibi, S.; Baghbanzadeh, M.; Aghamohammadi, N.; Zhang, W.; Haque, U. The SARS, MERS and novel coronavirus (COVID-19) epidemics, the newest and biggest global health threats: What lessons have we learned? *Int. J. Epidemiol.* **2020**, *49*, 717–726. [CrossRef]
95. Nomura, S.; Yoneoka, D.; Tanoue, Y.; Kawashima, T.; Shi, S.; Eguchi, A.; Miyata, H. Time to Reconsider Diverse Ways of Working in Japan to Promote Social Distancing Measures against the COVID-19. *J. Hered.* **2020**, *97*, 457–460. [CrossRef]
96. Miralles-Quirós, M.M.; Miralles-Quirós, J.L. Sustainable Finance and the 2030 Agenda: Investing to Transform the World. *Sustainability* **2021**, *13*, 10505. [CrossRef]
97. Mariana, C.D.; Ekaputra, I.A.; Husodo, Z.A. Are Bitcoin and Ethereum safe-havens for stocks during the COVID-19 pandemic? *Financ. Res. Lett.* **2020**, *38*, 101798. [CrossRef] [PubMed]
98. Caswell, E.; Smith, M.H.; Learmonth, D.; Pearce, G. Cash in the Time of COVID. Quarterly Bulletin of Bank of England of 2020 Q4. Available online: https://www.bankofengland.co.uk/quarterly-bulletin/2020/2020-q4/cash-in-the-time-of-covid (accessed on 4 December 2021).
99. Gerilovych, A.P.; Stegniy, B.T.; Kornieikov, O.M.; Muzyka, D.V.; Gerilovych, I.O.; Bolotin, V.I.; Kovalenko, L.V.; Arefiev, V.L.; Zlenko, O.B.; Kolchyk, O.V. *Coronavirus Infections of Animals and Humans: Biological and Epidemiological Properties of Causative Agents*; Springer: Singapore, 2021; pp. 17–36. [CrossRef]
100. Payne, S. Family Coronaviridae. *Viruses* **2017**, 149–158. [CrossRef]
101. Roussel, Y.; Giraud-Gatineau, A.; Jimeno, M.-T.; Rolain, J.-M.; Zandotti, C.; Colson, P.; Raoult, D. SARS-CoV-2: Fear versus data. *Int. J. Antimicrob. Agents* **2020**, *55*, 105947. [CrossRef] [PubMed]
102. Sharov, K.S. Adaptation of a Russian population to SARS-CoV-2: Asymptomatic course, comorbidities, mortality, and other respiratory viruses—A reply to Fear versus Data. *Int. J. Antimicrob. Agents* **2020**, *56*, 106093. [CrossRef]
103. To, K.K.W.; Hung, I.F.N.; Chan, J.F.W.; Yuen, K.-Y. From SARS coronavirus to novel animal and human coronaviruses. *J. Thorac. Dis.* **2013**, *5*, S103–S108. [CrossRef]

mathematics

Article

The NFT Hype: What Draws Attention to Non-Fungible Tokens?

Christian Pinto-Gutiérrez [1,*], Sandra Gaitán [2], Diego Jaramillo [2] and Simón Velasquez [2]

1 Faculty of Business and Economics, Universidad de Talca, Talca 3460000, Chile
2 Center for Research in Economics and Finance (CIEF), School of Economics and Finance, Universidad EAFIT, Medellin 050022, Colombia; sgaitanr@eafit.edu.co (S.G.); djaramillp@eafit.edu.co (D.J.); svelasquep@eafit.edu.co (S.V.)
* Correspondence: cristian.pinto@utalca.cl; Tel.: +56-71-220-0200

Abstract: Non-fungible tokens (NFTs) can be used to represent ownership of digital art or any other unique digital item where ownership is recorded in smart contracts on a blockchain. NFTs have recently received enormous attention from both cryptocurrency investors and the media. We examine why NFTs have gotten so much attention. Using vector autoregressive models, we show that Bitcoin returns significantly predict next week's NFT growth in popularity, measured by Google search queries. Moreover, wavelet coherence analysis suggests that Bitcoin and Ether returns are significant drivers of next week's attention to NFTs. These results indicate that the remarkable increases in prices of major cryptocurrencies can explain the hype around NFTs.

Keywords: NFT; non-fungible tokens; investor attention; cryptocurrency

Citation: Pinto-Gutiérrez, C.; Gaitán, S.; Jaramillo, D.; Velasquez, S. The NFT Hype: What Draws Attention to Non-Fungible Tokens?. *Mathematics* **2022**, *10*, 335. https://doi.org/10.3390/math10030335

Academic Editors: José Luis Miralles-Quirós and María Mar Miralles-Quirós

Received: 22 December 2021
Accepted: 18 January 2022
Published: 22 January 2022

1. Introduction

The non-fungible token (NFT) market has shown a significant increase in popularity in 2021. In just one year, the NFT market went from total daily sales of about USD 183,121 in 2020 to an average of USD 38 million in 2021 (data from https://nonfungible.com/market/history, accessed on 22 December 2021). Some NFT examples include the sale made by the artist Beeple, who sold a piece of digital art for USD 69 million, or the sale of the first Tweet made by Twitter CEO Jack Dorsey for USD 2.9 million. Two others popular NFTs are the CryptoPunks and Decentraland. The entire CryptoPunks collection, created in 2017 by Larva Labs, surpassed USD 1 billion in sales in 2021. Meanwhile, MANA, the native token of Decentraland, a metaverse platform where users can buy and sell virtual properties, spiked 400% and hit an all-time high market capitalization of more than USD 6 billion after Facebook announced it was changing its name to Meta.

NFTs are tokens stored on a blockchain that can be used to represent ownership of digital assets like artworks, recordings, virtual real estate and pets. NFTs are sold on specialized marketplaces, such as OpenSea, Axie Marketplace, and Rarible. On these platforms, investors can also exchange the property right to the asset underlying the NFT. And because NFTs use smart contract technology, they can be set up so that the original artist can earn a percentage of all subsequent sales. The main difference between NFTs and cryptocurrencies, such as bitcoin, is that cryptocurrencies are fungible or interchangeable; they are all worth the same amount. However, NFTs are non-fungible, meaning that an NFT cannot be exchanged for another since each one is unique. Precisely, this uniqueness enables the use of NFTs to authenticate ownership of digital assets. Furthermore, each NFT is stored on a public and transparent blockchain (often Ethereum's). Thus, NFTs are decentralized applications with high levels of verifiability, tamper resistance, usability, atomicity, and traceability. For additional details about the technicalities of NFTs, please see Wang et al. (2021) [1].

In 2021, public attention towards NFTs exploded, and the NFT market has become quite popular among investors and collectors. For instance, the largest NFT marketplace, OpenSea, has more than one million users buying and selling digital art and collectibles via their platform (data from https://dune.xyz/rchen8/opensea, accessed on 22 December 2021). Thus, why have NFTs received such attention? In this paper, we examine the factors that explain investor attention to non-fungible tokens. This rise in awareness can be attributed to several factors, including the excitement around blockchain technology. We argue that rising cryptocurrency prices may have played a role in the surge of NFTs. We posit that NFT markets have benefited from the hype around major cryptocurrencies, particularly Bitcoin, as the digital currency with the largest market capitalization. Bitcoin has attracted significant attention recently, and it has undeniably assumed an important role in global financial markets. We also examine the effects of Ether, as NFTs are primarily registered on Ethereum smart contracts and often valued in Ether.

The literature on NFT markets is scarce. Prior papers have examined the factors that determine the prices of NFTs, finding a positive relationship between the prices of cryptocurrencies and the prices of NFTs [2,3]. The literature has also suggested that NFTs are difficult assets to value. For instance, Dowling (2021a) [4] shows that Decentraland is inefficiently priced and characterized by a steady rise in value. Chohan (2021) [5] claims that demand forces determining NFT prices are fundamentally dependent upon inherent scarcity and a buyer's readiness to purchase a one-of-a-kind item. Oppositely, other studies contradict this, stating that scarcity is not necessarily relevant in all NFTs. For example, Serada et al. (2020) [6] analyze CryptoKitties, an online game where players collect, breed, buy, and sell various kinds of virtual cats. They found that the least common game tokens experience rapid devaluation quickly if not enough players are in the game. Nadini et al. (2021) [7] created a superb overview of some central NFT features that span the six main NFT categories, including art, games, and collectibles. The findings show that past sale history is the best predictor of NFT prices, as one would expect. In addition, NFT-specific properties like a digital object's appearance also increase price predictability.

This paper provides novel evidence for the factors that draw investors' attention to the NFT market. To our knowledge, this is the first study to examine the levels of attention to non-fungible tokens. The NFT market started getting mainstream attention in early 2021, coinciding with a price run-up in all major cryptocurrencies. Accordingly, using a database featuring weekly data on Google search activity for the topic "non-fungible token" and two of the most popular NFTs, "Cryptopunk" and "Decentraland," between 2017 and 2021, we explore if NFT attention is related to cryptocurrency pricing. We test this hypothesis using various time-series econometric models, ranging from vector autoregressive (VAR) regressions to wavelet coherence analysis. We select the empirical models based on the experience of prior literature. Other studies examining investor attention to cryptocurrencies have primarily used VAR models (see, for example, [8–12]). Meanwhile, wavelet coherence models have recently been used in the financial literature to examine the dynamic relations among cryptocurrencies (see, for instance, [2,13–16]).

Using vector autoregressive (VAR) models, we find that the previous week's bitcoin returns significantly drive attention to NFTs. Moreover, when wavelet coherence analysis is used, we find that investors are more attracted to NFTs after increases in both Bitcoin and Ether returns. These results are consistent with the notion that as Bitcoin and other cryptocurrencies have boomed in price and popularity over the last few years, NFTs have also soared. In other words, the results suggest that the hype around cryptocurrencies could explain the NFT growth in popularity.

Our study has implications for financial practices, particularly for digital artists, collectors, and cryptocurrency investors. We believe our results will help NFT market participants better understand this disruptive innovation and the impacts that the accelerated growth of NFTs has on decentralized markets.

We organize the rest of the paper as follows. First, Section 2 provides the materials and methods used. Then, Section 3 presents our main results. Finally, Section 4 shows the conclusion and examines the implications of our findings.

2. Materials and Methods

2.1. Methodology

We first study the dynamics between cryptocurrency returns and NTF attention by estimating vector autoregressive (VAR) models with exogenous variables. VAR models are used to capture the complex dynamics of multiple time series. Prior studies analyzing investor attention to cryptocurrencies have mainly used VAR models (see, for example, [8–12]). In this paper, we estimate VAR models with exogenous variables. These exogenous variables include economic factors that could also determine investor attention to NFT markets. For example, we have variables such as CBOE Volatility Index (VIX), gold, and S&P 500 returns. We also control for the level of attention toward Bitcoin and Ethereum. The VAR model we evaluate in this study consists of the following two equations:

$$NFT\ attention_t = \alpha + \sum_{j=1}^{p} \beta' NFT\ attention_{t-j} + \sum_{j=1}^{p} \beta' Crypto\ return_{t-j} + \delta' Z_{t-1} + \mu_t, \quad (1)$$

$$Crypto\ return_t = \alpha + \sum_{j=1}^{p} \beta' NFT\ attention_{t-j} + \sum_{j=1}^{p} \gamma' Crypto\ return_{t-j} + \delta' Z_{t-1} + \mu_t. \quad (2)$$

Our primary dependent variable is NFT attention, which represents the weekly time series measuring the frequency of Google searches with the topic "non-fungible token" together with the term "NFT" at the worldwide level. We also use the weekly search volume for the topic "Cryptopunk" and "Decentraland", two of the most popular NFTs. Google search data are being increasingly utilized in financial and cryptocurrency literature to measure investor attention. For instance, Urquhart (2018) [8] and Lin (2021) [10] use Google data to gauge investors' interest in Bitcoin and several different cryptocurrencies. One of the main benefits of Google searches is that, under a single topic, its algorithms can cover various languages and group different searches with the same meaning [17].

In Equations (1) and (2), α is a vector of constants, β is a vector of coefficients on the first endogenous variable (the weekly NTFs Google attention), and γ is a vector of coefficients on the second endogenous variable (either weekly Bitcoin price returns or weekly Ethereum price returns). The vector Z_t represents the exogenous control variables, and δ is the vector of coefficients on these control variables. Finally, μ_t is a vector of independent white noise innovations. In Equations (1) and (2), the value p denotes the number of lags. We determine the optimal number lags using several information criteria, including the Akaike information criterion (AIC), Hannan–Quinn information criterion (HQIC), Schwarz-Bayesian information criteria (SBIC), and final prediction error (FPE).

Next, we use the wavelet coherence technique to investigate co-movement between cryptocurrency returns and NFT levels of attention. Wavelet coherence analysis enables investigation of any detectable co-movement between two-time series (bivariate wavelets) in the domains of time and frequency, whereas standard time series modeling does not. Nonstationary signals can also be analyzed with wavelet coherence. Recent studies by Dowling (2021b), Goodell and Goutte (2021), and Qiao et al. (2020) [2,13,14] employed wavelet coherence for cryptocurrency analyses.

We use cross-wavelets in keeping with Torrence and Compo (1998) [18]. The cross-wavelet transform explores the simultaneity of two signals in the frequency and the time domains, and the wavelet coherence analysis clarifies the correlation of this cross transform. The cross wavelet transform of two times-series is defined by the complex conjugate of their cross wavelet transform, $W_x(a,b)$ and $W_y(a,b)$, as:

$$W_{xy}(a,b) = W_x(a,b) * W_y(a,b), \quad (3)$$

where a is associated with the location and b to the scale. $W_x(a,b)$ and $W_y(a,b)$ are the wavelet transformations of the times series x (either Bitcoin or Ether returns) and y (NFT attention), respectively. The value of $W_{xy}(a,b)$ indicates the strength of the correlation between the two examined series.

Then, $R^2(a,b)$ returns the magnitude-squared wavelet coherence, which measures the correlation between signals x and y in the time-frequency plane. Torrence and Webster (1999) [19] define the wavelet squared coherence as follows:

$$R^2(a,b) = \frac{\left|S\left(b^{-1}W_{xy}(a,b)\right)\right|^2}{S\left(b^{-1}W_x(a,b)\right)^2 S\left(b^{-1}W_y(a,b)\right)^2}, \tag{4}$$

where S refers to a smoothing process over time and scale. $R^2(a,b)$ is a value between 0 and 1 that captures the co-movement between the time series x and y. The higher the value of $R^2(a,b)$, the higher the co-movement between the two variables. Wavelet squared coherence is restricted to positive values as opposed to the classical correlation of two time series. This means determining whether the co-movement between the variables is positive or negative is not possible. Thus, we use the phase difference of Torrence and Compo (1998) [18] to separate out the positive and negative co-movements. The phase difference is required to present lead-lag relationships as a function of frequency. It gives a graphical presentation of the wavelet squared coherence analysis considering the causal relationships between the two-time series. The phase difference can be provided by

$$\Phi_{xy} = \arctan\left(\frac{Im\left\{S\left(b^{-1}W_{xy}(a,b)\right)\right\}}{Re\left\{S\left(b^{-1}W_{xy}(a,b)\right)\right\}}\right), \tag{5}$$

where Im and Re are the imaginary and real operators, respectively. To indicate the direction of influence, we incorporate phase positions in the wavelet analysis.

2.2. Data

We collected Google search activity for the keywords "NFT + non-fungible token" (the plus sign means that results can include searches containing the words "NFT" or "non-fungible token"), "Cryptopunk", "Decentraland", "Bitcoin", and "Ethereum" from Google Trends (https://trends.google.com/, accessed on 9 August 2021) between 1 December 2017 and 30 July 2021. The Google search index ranges between 0 and 100. Average weekly NFT sales in USD are available from nonfungible.com (https://nonfungible.com, accessed on 9 August 2021). This data source has been previously used in NFT research (see, for example, [2,4]). We also collected weekly Bitcoin and Ethereum prices between the exact same dates from coinmarketcap.com (https://coinmarketcap.com, accessed on 9 August 2021). This data source has been widely used in cryptocurrency research (see, e.g., [20–22]). VIX index, S&P 500 index, and gold prices are from Yahoo Finance (https://finance.yahoo.com, accessed on 9 August 2021).

Table 1 provides descriptive statistics for the final sample. The results show that the weekly average Google search volume for the topic "non-fungible token + NFT" is 7.93. The weekly average search volume for "Cryptopunk" is 3.93, and the average search volume for "Decentraland" is 7.63. The average weekly return and standard deviation for Bitcoin were 0.76% and 11.91%, respectively. The average weekly return and standard deviation for Ether were 1.02% and 15.00%, respectively. We employ augmented Dickey-Fuller tests (ADF) to examine the stationarity of time-series variables. This analysis is essential as non-stationary data could lead to spurious regression results. The results reported in Table 1 show that, for some series, we cannot reject the null hypothesis of non-stationarity. In particular, we find that unit-roots are present in most Google search indexes. To normalize and detrend these series, we use the first differences of Google search queries in all empirical models in the subsequent sections. In the case of the Bitcoin and Ether returns series, the null hypothesis of a unit root is discarded. Likewise, the series we use as control variables are all stationary according to the ADF test.

Table 1. Descriptive statistics of key variables.

	Observations	Mean	Media	SD	Min	Max	Skewness	Kurtosis	ADF Test
NFT attention	193	7.93	1.00	19.81	0.00	100.00	3.18	12.66	−1.52
CryptoPunk attention	193	3.93	0.00	11.38	0.00	100.00	4.78	32.69	−0.43
Decentraland attention	193	7.63	3.00	13.66	0.00	100.00	3.63	19.53	−3.95 ***
Bitcoin return	193	0.76	0.75	11.91	−53.94	31.51	−0.53	5.17	−13.98 ***
Ether return	193	1.02	1.18	15.00	−65.97	49.89	−0.46	5.54	−12.62 ***
VIX return	193	0.16	−1.68	17.00	−46.09	85.37	0.96	6.41	−15.43 ***
Gold return	193	0.14	0.20	2.08	−9.90	10.10	−0.11	8.31	−17.17 ***
S&P 500 return	193	0.27	0.59	2.86	−16.23	11.42	−1.30	11.39	−15.19 ***
Bitcoin attention	193	16.27	10.00	14.04	6.00	83.00	2.16	7.85	−3.58 ***
Ethereum attention	193	14.03	6.00	17.92	2.00	100.00	2.38	9.37	−2.24
CryptoPunk return	191	4.87	1.32	63.88	−177.31	208.32	0.06	3.44	−21.98 ***
Decentraland return	179	2.76	−0.97	67.62	−227.13	207.45	0.06	4.65	−18.97 ***

Note: This table reports summary statistics for the dependent, independent, and control variables used in this study. The last column shows augmented Dickey-Fuller (ADF) tests to examine the stationarity of time-series data. All variables are defined in Appendix A. *** indicate that the Dickey-Fuller test statistic is significantly larger than the critical value at the 1%.

3. Results

Table 2 shows the estimated results for VAR models. Columns 1 and 2 report the results when we use Google searches for the topic "non-fungible token" together with the term "NFT". Columns 3 and 4 present the results for the key term "Cryptopunk". Columns 5 and 6 present the results for the term "Decentraland". In column 1, we find that past Bitcoin returns significantly influence search queries for NFT at lag 1 and 4, respectively, indicating that an increase in returns will lead to a rise in search queries in the following weeks. We also employ Granger causality tests to investigate the causal relationships between Bitcoin returns and attention to NFTs. We present Granger causality tests for each VAR model at the bottom of Table 2. The Granger causality test indicates that past Bitcoin returns provide significant information about future NFT search queries. In column 2, the estimation results reveal that past NFT search queries do not significantly influence Bitcoin returns as the coefficients are statistically insignificant. The Granger causality test also supports this finding, failing to reject the null hypothesis that NFT search queries does not cause Bitcoin returns. We find similar results when we analyze the dynamic relationship between Bitcoin returns and search queries for specific NFTs. Furthermore, these results remain even after controlling for other economic factors such as CBOE Volatility Index (VIX) returns, gold returns, and S&P 500 returns. Thus, these results support the hypotheses suggesting that an increase in Bitcoin returns will lead to greater attention to other crypto assets such as NFTs.

Table 3 shows the estimated results for VAR models when we use Ether returns. Although NFTs are normally registered on an Ethereum blockchain, we do not find any significant relationship between Ether returns and attention to NFTs when we use VAR models. Furthermore, Granger causality tests also show no meaningful causal relationships between Ether returns and NFT attention.

Table 2. Dynamic relationships among NFT attention and Bitcoin returns.

	ΔNFT + Non-Fungible Tokens	Bitcoin Return	ΔCryptoPunk	Bitcoin Return	ΔDecentraland	Bitcoin Return
	(1)	(2)	(3)	(4)	(5)	(6)
ΔNFT attention t-1	0.1341 *	0.1829	−0.2068 *	0.0677	−0.2799 ***	−0.0327
	(1.8302)	(0.8562)	(1.8806)	(0.3778)	(3.8149)	(0.2673)
ΔNFT attention t-2	0.3235 ***	−0.1923	−0.1756	0.0870	−0.1820 **	0.0425
	(4.5670)	(0.9313)	(1.5079)	(0.4587)	(2.3972)	(0.3361)
ΔNFT attention t-3	−0.1944 ***	−0.1244	0.2142 *	0.2004	−0.1005	0.2011
	(2.6200)	(0.5749)	(1.8522)	(1.0642)	(1.3672)	(1.6426)
ΔNFT attention t-4	−0.1223 *	0.3184	−0.0509	0.0440	−0.0467	−0.1380
	(1.7283)	(1.5428)	(0.4595)	(0.2442)	(0.6327)	(1.1215)
Bitcoin return t-1	0.0556 **	0.0069	0.0603	0.0128	0.1087 **	0.0432
	(2.1739)	(0.0930)	(1.3078)	(0.1709)	(2.3429)	(0.5586)
Bitcoin return t-2	−0.0286	−0.0070	0.1322 ***	−0.0295	0.1045 **	−0.0065
	(1.0645)	(0.0899)	(2.7199)	(0.3723)	(2.1046)	(0.0781)
Bitcoin return t-3	0.0070	0.0938	0.0131	0.0823	−0.0371	0.0807
	(0.2813)	(1.2892)	(0.2912)	(1.1219)	(0.7938)	(1.0368)
Bitcoin return t-4	0.0637 **	−0.0107	0.0026	−0.0097	0.0518	−0.0181
	(2.5245)	(0.1456)	(0.0577)	(0.1313)	(1.0692)	(0.2238)
Exogenous Controls:						
VIX return t-1	0.0011	−0.0027	0.0008	−0.0069	−0.0668	−0.0001
	(0.0417)	(0.0357)	(0.0172)	(0.0921)	(1.4132)	(0.0015)
Gold return t-1	−0.3016 **	−0.8107 *	−0.3271	−0.8532 *	0.0857	−0.6342
	(2.0328)	(1.8741)	(1.2189)	(1.9527)	(0.3402)	(1.5114)
S&P 500 return t-1	0.0429	0.1559	−0.1134	0.1776	−0.3700	0.1548
	(0.2677)	(0.3339)	(0.3939)	(0.3789)	(1.3214)	(0.3319)
ΔBitcoin attention t-1	−0.0325	−0.0646	0.0112	−0.0874	−0.0083	−0.2024
	(0.5749)	(0.3926)	(0.1166)	(0.5598)	(0.0869)	(1.2687)
NFT return t-1			0.0038	0.0082	−0.0073	0.0043
			(0.4614)	(0.6073)	(0.9768)	(0.3418)
Constant	0.1017	0.6930	0.5000	0.6854	0.0071	1.0141
	(0.3600)	(0.8416)	(0.9770)	(0.8224)	(0.0147)	(1.2506)
Observations	189	189	187	187	178	178
R2	0.212	0.0476	0.1244	0.0446	0.1495	0.0693
H0: Bitcoin return does not Granger-cause NFT attention	14.585 ***		9.1201 *		11.795 **	
Prob > chi2	0.006		0.058		0.019	
H0: NFT attention does not Granger-cause Bitcoin return	2.9402		1.2094		5.777	
Prob > chi2	0.568		0.877		0.216	

Note: This table presents the parameter estimates from vector autoregressive (VAR) models for Bitcoin returns and NFT attention. The key independent variable is the first differences (Δ) of NTF attention from Google search activity for the keywords "NFT + non-fungible token", "Cryptopunk", "Decentraland". t values are in parentheses. All variables are defined in Appendix A. ***, **, and * indicate that the coefficient is significantly different from zero at the 1%, 5%, and 10% levels, respectively.

Table 3. Dynamic relationships among NFT attention and Ether returns.

	ΔNFT + Non-Fungible Tokens	Ether Return	ΔCryptoPunk	Ether Return	ΔDecentraland	Ether Return
	(1)	(2)	(3)	(4)	(5)	(6)
ΔNFT attention t-1	0.1768 **	0.2538	−0.1129	−0.1201	−0.2507 ***	−0.0253
	(2.4669)	(0.9336)	(1.0393)	(0.4997)	(3.4229)	(0.1546)
ΔNFT attention t-2	0.3163 ***	−0.5096 *	−0.1087	0.2110	−0.1649 **	−0.0143
	(4.4703)	(1.8990)	(0.9621)	(0.8440)	(2.1956)	(0.0849)
ΔNFT attention t-3	−0.1626 **	−0.0936	0.3096 ***	0.0424	−0.0625	0.3265 **
	(2.3019)	(0.3495)	(2.7317)	(0.1692)	(0.8868)	(2.0698)
ΔNFT attention t-4	−0.1381 *	0.5839 **	0.0021	0.0637	−0.0343	−0.1064
	(1.9423)	(2.1656)	(0.0190)	(0.2650)	(0.4703)	(0.6514)
Ether return t-1	0.0341	0.1175	0.0086	0.1257	0.0536	0.1082
	(1.6196)	(1.4728)	(0.2341)	(1.5474)	(1.4360)	(1.2954)
Ether return t-2	−0.0317	0.0422	0.0484	0.0024	0.0485	−0.0165
	(1.5223)	(0.5339)	(1.2928)	(0.0285)	(1.2779)	(0.1936)
Ether return t-3	−0.0050	0.0135	−0.0072	0.0173	−0.0281	0.0032
	(0.2593)	(0.1834)	(0.2081)	(0.2271)	(0.8033)	(0.0409)
Ether return t-4	0.0287	−0.0166	−0.0192	−0.0029	−0.0267	0.0000
	(1.4527)	(0.2217)	(0.5486)	(0.0373)	(0.7481)	(0.0004)
Exogenous Controls: VIX return t-1	0.0037	0.0147	0.0092	0.0185	−0.0433	0.0219
	(0.1427)	(0.1497)	(0.2017)	(0.1842)	(0.9078)	(0.2049)
Gold return t-1	−0.2884 **	−0.6605	−0.3151	−0.7557	0.1009	−0.3971
	(1.9685)	(1.1886)	(1.2265)	(1.3294)	(0.3981)	(0.7001)
S&P 500 return t-1	0.0787	0.1536	0.0033	0.2078	−0.1986	0.1819
	(0.4857)	(0.2498)	(0.0116)	(0.3313)	(0.7087)	(0.2900)
ΔEthereum attention t-1	−0.1333 ***	−0.1152	0.3334 ***	−0.1137	0.0239	−0.1033
	(2.6990)	(0.6149)	(3.8449)	(0.5923)	(0.2823)	(0.5457)
NFT return t-1			−0.1129	−0.1201	−0.0057	0.0130
			(1.0393)	(0.4997)	(0.7523)	(0.7693)
Constant	0.1340	0.7301	0.5101	0.8031	0.0644	1.3120
	(0.4745)	(0.6818)	(1.0325)	(0.7345)	(0.1303)	(1.1872)
Observations	189	189	187	187	178	178
R2	0.2095	0.0499	0.18	0.0273	0.1212	0.0477
H0: Ether return does not Granger-cause NFT attention	7.5409		2.1153		4.8831	
Prob > chi2	0.11		0.715		0.3	
H0: NFT attention does not Granger-cause Ether return	6.5483		1.4026		6.1733	
Prob > chi2	0.162		0.844		0.187	

Note: This table presents the parameter estimates from vector autoregressive (VAR) models for Ether returns and NFT attention. The key independent variable is the first differences (Δ) of NTF attention from Google search activity for the keywords "NFT + non-fungible token", "Cryptopunk", "Decentraland". t values are in parentheses. All variables are defined in Appendix A. ***, **, and * indicate that the coefficient is significantly different from zero at the 1%, 5%, and 10% levels, respectively.

We now turn to our set of results based on a wavelet coherence approach. Figure 1 illustrates the co-movement and phase difference between Bitcoin returns and attention to NFT. Figure 2 shows the results for the co-movement and phase difference between Ether returns and attention to NFT. The horizontal axis depicts time, and the vertical axis shows frequency in all the figures (the lower the frequency, the higher the period). The warmer end of the color spectrum (red) stands for regions with significant interrelation, with the cooler end (blue) signifying lower dependence between the series. Cold regions beyond the significant areas represent time and frequencies without any dependence in the series. The arrows in the wavelet coherence plots represent the lead/lag phase relations between the examined series. Arrows pointing to the right (left) indicate time series that are in-phase (out of phase) or positively (negatively) correlated. An upward-pointing arrow suggests that the first time series leads the second. If it points downward, it indicates the reverse in that the second one leads the first.

Figure 1 confirms the co-movement for Bitcoin returns and NFT attention. In panel A of Figure 1, we see much co-movement between Bitcoin returns and search queries for the topic "non-fungible token" together with the term "NFT". This co-movement is evident at the 1–4-week cycle at the end of 2020 and early 2021. Panel B of Figure 1 shows the co-movement and phase difference between Bitcoin returns and search queries for the term "Cryptopunk". There is also consistent evidence of short-term (1–8 week) positive correlation cycles for Bitcoin returns and attention to the CryptoPunk collection of NFTs. When we consider search queries for the term "Decentraland", panel C of Figure 1 shows clear evidence of co-movement with Bitcoin returns across our sample period at the 1–4-week cycle and at the larger 8–16-week cycle as well. Figure 1 also suggests a positive correlation between Bitcoin returns and NFT attention, which is the most common arrow direction. Regarding the lead/lag relation between variables, the evidence depicted in the charts is inconclusive.

In contrast with the results obtained using VAR models, the wavelet coherence analysis depicted in Figure 2 illustrates the existence of co-movement between Ether returns and NFT attention. This co-movement is particularly evident across the period at the 1–4-week cycle and a larger 8–16-week cycle that dominates the chart of co-movement between Ether and Decentraland. Panel C of Figure 2 shows several red regions with significant interrelation, and the arrows pointing to the right indicate a positive correlation between Ether returns and Decentraland attention.

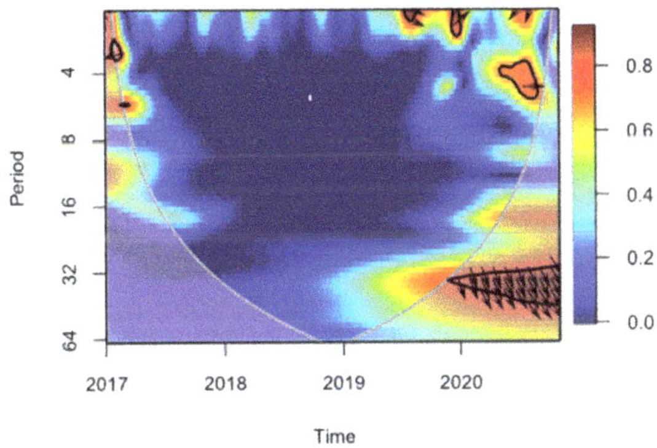

Panel **A**. Wavelet coherence: NFT attention and Bitcoin returns

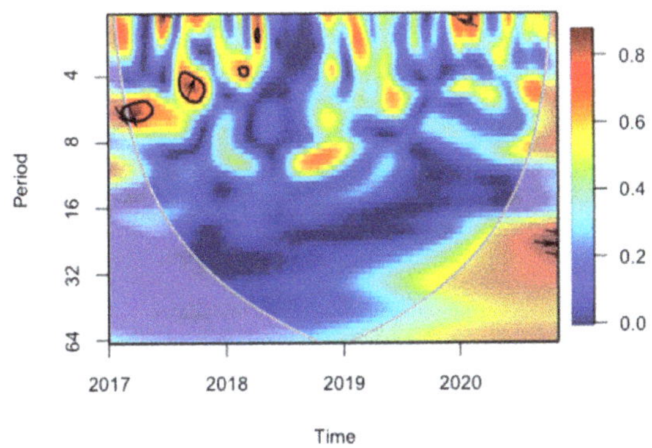

Panel **B**. Wavelet coherence: CryptoPunk attention and Bitcoin returns

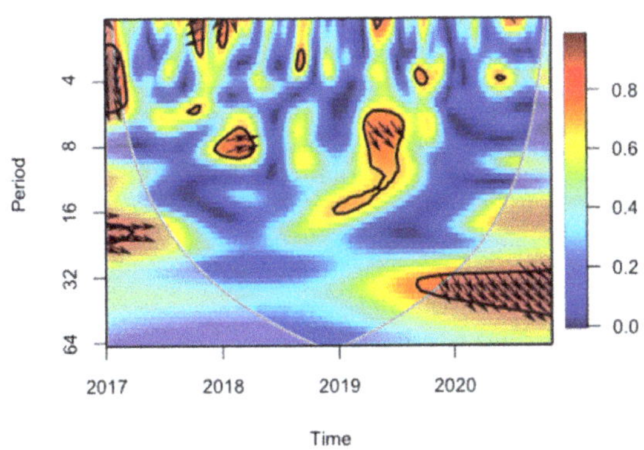

Panel **C**. Wavelet coherence: Decentraland attention and Bitcoin returns

Figure 1. This figure represents the wavelet coherence analysis for Bitcoin returns and NFT levels of attention (Panel **A**), Bitcoin returns and CryptoPunk attention (Panel **B**), and Bitcoin returns and Decentraland attention (Panel **C**). Correlation is shown by the colour—hotter colours (cool blue to hot red) indicate higher absolute correlations. For the arrows, $\rightarrow$ shows positive correlation, $\leftarrow$ shows negative correlation, $\nearrow$ and $\swarrow$ show Bitcoin leads the NFT, and $\searrow$ and $\nwarrow$ show the NFT leads Bitcoin. We use weekly Bitcoin returns and Google search activity between 1 December 2017 and 30 July 2021.

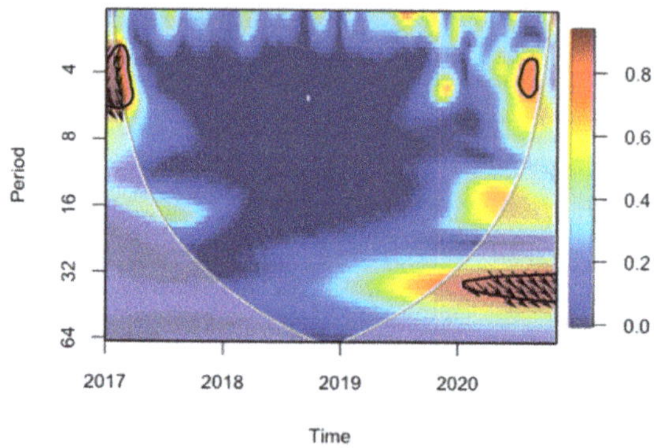

Panel **A**. Wavelet coherence: NFT attention and Ether returns

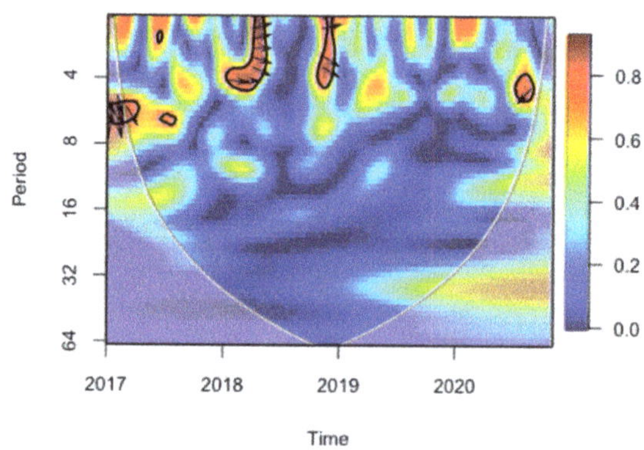

Panel **B**. Wavelet coherence: CryptoPunk attention and Ether returns

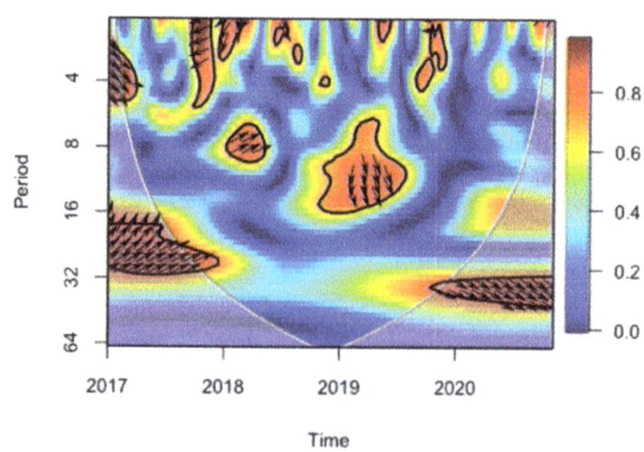

Panel **C**. Wavelet coherence: Decentraland attention and Ether returns

Figure 2. This figure represents the wavelet coherence analysis for Ether returns and NFT levels of attention (Panel **A**), Ether returns and CryptoPunk attention (Panel **B**), and Ether returns and Decentraland attention (Panel **C**). Correlation is shown by the colour—hotter colours (cool blue to hot red) indicate higher absolute correlations. For the arrows, $\rightarrow$ shows positive correlation, $\leftarrow$ shows negative correlation, $\nearrow$ and $\swarrow$ show Ether leads the NFT, and $\searrow$ and $\nwarrow$ show the NFT leads Ether. We use weekly Ether returns and Google search activity between 1 December 2017 and 30 July 2021.

4. Discussion and Concluding Remarks

This paper utilizes Google search queries to analyze the drivers of attention to non-fungible tokens (NFTs). We use weekly data between 2017 and 2021 to show that Google search activity for the topic "non-fungible token" and "NFT" is positively associated with major cryptocurrency returns. We arrive at similar conclusions when using Google search activities for specific NFT collections, such as "Cryptopunk" and "Decentraland". Using vector autoregressive (VAR) models, we find that the previous week's Bitcoin returns are significant attention drivers to NFTs. Furthermore, when we use wavelet coherence analysis, we find that investors are more attracted to NFTs after increases in both Bitcoin and Ether returns. Our findings are consistent with the notion that the excitement around cryptocurrencies induced by record-high prices in 2021 could explain the NFT growth in popularity during the same period.

Our paper contributes to the academic literature on NFTs that focuses on the factors that explain the sudden attention of investors in the NFT market. Furthermore, we extend the understanding of the effects of the leading cryptocurrencies on new blockchain developments, such as the NFT market.

The results of this study have practical implications for investors, institutions and governments that are called to understand this burgeoning industry as part of this new digital economy where the crypto markets are the protagonists.

Future research directions need to address the continued evolution of the NFT ecosystem, the effect of the transaction and environmental costs, and the legal framework associated with the use of the crypto technology.

Author Contributions: Conceptualization, C.P.-G. and S.G.; methodology, C.P.-G. and S.G.; software, C.P.-G. and S.G.; validation, C.P.-G., S.G., D.J. and S.V.; formal analysis, C.P.-G., S.G., D.J. and S.V.; investigation, C.P.-G., S.G., D.J. and S.V.; resources, C.P.-G., S.G., D.J. and S.V.; data curation, C.P.-G., S.G., D.J. and S.V.; writing—original draft preparation, C.P.-G. and S.G.; writing—review and editing, C.P.-G. and S.G. All authors have read and agreed to the published version of the manuscript.

Funding: This research received no external funding.

Institutional Review Board Statement: Not applicable.

Informed Consent Statement: Not applicable.

Data Availability Statement: The data presented in this study are available on request from the corresponding author.

Conflicts of Interest: The authors declare no conflict of interest.

Appendix A

Table A1 defines all the variables we use in this study.

Table A1. Definitions of variables.

Variable Name	Definition
Bitcoin return (%)	Weekly Bitcoin return in percentage is defined as $\left[\ln\left(\frac{bitcoin\ price_t}{bitcoin\ price_{t-1}}\right)\right] * 100$. Bitcoin price on week t is taken from coinmarketcap.com (accessed on 9 August 2021).
Ether return (%)	Weekly Ether return in percentage is defined as $\left[\ln\left(\frac{ether\ price_t}{ether\ price_{t-1}}\right)\right] * 100$. Ether price on week t is taken from coinmarketcap.com (accessed on 9 August 2021).
VIX return (%)	Weekly VIX index return in percentage is defined as $\left[\ln\left(\frac{VIX\ index_t}{VIX\ Index_{t-1}}\right)\right] * 100$. VIX index on week t is taken from Yahoo Finance (accessed on 9 August 2021).
Gold return (%)	Weekly gold return in percentage is defined as $\left[\ln\left(\frac{gold\ price_t}{gold\ price_{t-1}}\right)\right] * 100$. Gold price on week t is taken from Yahoo Finance (accessed on 9 August 2021).

Table A1. *Cont.*

Variable Name	Definition
S&P 500 return (%)	Weekly S&P 500 index return in percentage is defined as $\left[\ln\left(\frac{S\&P500\ index_t}{S\&P500\ index_{t-1}}\right)\right] * 100$. S&P 500 index on week t is taken from Yahoo Finance (accessed on 9 August 2021).
NFT attention	Weekly time series measuring the frequency of Google search volumes for the topics "NFT" and "Non-Fungible Token" at the worldwide level. The Google search index ranges between 0 and 100. Data is taken from Google Trends (accessed on 9 August 2021).
CryptoPunk attention	Weekly time series measuring the frequency of Google search volumes for the topic "CryptoPunk" at the worldwide level. The Google search index ranges between 0 and 100. Data is taken from Google Trends (accessed on 9 August 2021).
Decentraland attention	Weekly time series measuring the frequency of Google search volumes for the topic "Decentraland" at the worldwide level. The Google search index ranges between 0 and 100. Data is taken from Google Trends (accessed on 9 August 2021).
NFT return (%)	Weekly NFT return in percentage is defined as $\left[\ln\left(\frac{NFT\ price_t}{NFT\ price_{t-1}}\right)\right] * 100$. NFT price on week t is either the price of CryptoPunk or Decentraland, depending on the model. Prices are taken from nonfungible.com (accessed on 9 August 2021).
Bitcoin attention	Weekly time series measuring the frequency of Google search volumes for the topic "Bitcoin" at the worldwide level. The Google search index ranges between 0 and 100. Data is taken from Google Trends (accessed on 9 August 2021).
Ethereum attention	Weekly time series measuring the frequency of Google search volumes for the topic "Ethereum" at the worldwide level. The Google search index ranges between 0 and 100. Data is taken from Google Trends (accessed on 9 August 2021).

References

1. Wang, Q.; Li, R.; Wang, Q.; Chen, S. Non-Fungible Token (NFT): Overview, Evaluation, Opportunities and Challenges. *arXiv* **2021**, arXiv:2105.07447.
2. Dowling, M. Is non-fungible token pricing driven by cryptocurrencies? *Financ. Res. Lett.* **2021**, *44*, 102097. [CrossRef]
3. Ante, L. The non-fungible token (NFT) market and its relationship with Bitcoin and Ethereum. **2021**. [CrossRef]
4. Dowling, M. Fertile LAND: Pricing non-fungible tokens. *Financ. Res. Lett.* **2021**, *44*, 102096. [CrossRef]
5. Chohan, U.W. Non-Fungible Tokens: Blockchains, Scarcity, and Value. **2021**. [CrossRef]
6. Serada, A.; Sihvonen, T.; Harviainen, J.T. CryptoKitties and the New Ludic Economy: How Blockchain Introduces Value, Ownership, and Scarcity in Digital Gaming. *Games Cult.* **2020**, *16*, 457–480. [CrossRef]
7. Nadini, M.; Alessandretti, L.; Di Giacinto, F.; Martino, M.; Aiello, L.M.; Baronchelli, A. Mapping the NFT revolution: Market trends, trade networks, and visual features. *Sci. Rep.* **2021**, *11*, 20902. [CrossRef] [PubMed]
8. Urquhart, A. What causes the attention of Bitcoin? *Econ. Lett.* **2018**, *166*, 40–44. [CrossRef]
9. Al Guindy, M. Cryptocurrency price volatility and investor attention. *Int. Rev. Econ. Financ.* **2021**, *76*, 556–570. [CrossRef]
10. Lin, Z.-Y. Investor attention and cryptocurrency performance. *Financ. Res. Lett.* **2021**, *40*, 101702. [CrossRef]
11. Sabah, N. Cryptocurrency accepting venues, investor attention, and volatility. *Financ. Res. Lett.* **2020**, *36*, 101339. [CrossRef]
12. Zhu, P.; Zhang, X.; Wu, Y.; Zheng, H.; Zhang, Y. Investor attention and cryptocurrency: Evidence from the Bitcoin market. *PLoS ONE* **2021**, *16*, e0246331. [CrossRef] [PubMed]
13. Goodell, J.W.; Goutte, S. Co-movement of COVID-19 and Bitcoin: Evidence from wavelet coherence analysis. *Financ. Res. Lett.* **2021**, *38*, 101625. [CrossRef]
14. Qiao, X.; Zhu, H.; Hau, L. Time-frequency co-movement of cryptocurrency return and volatility: Evidence from wavelet coherence analysis. *Int. Rev. Financ. Anal.* **2020**, *71*, 101541. [CrossRef]
15. Phillips, R.; Gorse, D. Cryptocurrency price drivers: Wavelet coherence analysis revisited. *PLoS ONE* **2018**, *13*, e0195200. [CrossRef]
16. Kang, S.H.; McIver, R.P.; Hernandez, J.A. Co-movements between Bitcoin and Gold: A wavelet coherence analysis. *Phys. A Stat. Mech. Its Appl.* **2019**, *536*, 120888. [CrossRef]
17. Choi, D.; Gao, Z.; Jiang, W. Attention to Global Warming. *Rev. Financ. Stud.* **2020**, *33*, 1112–1145. [CrossRef]
18. Torrence, C.; Compo, G.P. A Practical Guide to Wavelet Analysis. *Bull. Am. Meteorol. Soc.* **1998**, *79*, 61–78. [CrossRef]
19. Torrence, C.; Webster, P.J. Interdecadal Changes in the ENSO-Monsoon System. *J. Clim.* **1999**, *12*, 2679–2690. [CrossRef]

20. Bouri, E.; Keung, C.; Lau, M.; Lucey, B.; Roubaud, D. Trading volume and the predictability of return and volatility in the cryptocurrency market. *Financ. Res. Lett.* **2019**, *29*, 340–346. [CrossRef]
21. Bouri, E.; Shahzad, S.; Roubaud, D. Co-explosivity in the cryptocurrency market. *Financ. Res. Lett.* **2019**, *29*, 178–183. [CrossRef]
22. Gandal, N.; Hamrick, J.T.; Moore, T.; Oberman, T. Price manipulation in the Bitcoin ecosystem. *J. Monet. Econ.* **2018**, *95*, 86–96. [CrossRef]

mathematics

Article

A Dual Incentive Value-Based Paradigm for Improving the Business Market Profitability in Blockchain Token Economy

Chaopeng Guo, Pengyi Zhang, Bangyao Lin and Jie Song *

Software College, Northeastern University, Shenyang 110000, China; guochaopeng@swc.neu.edu.cn (C.G.); 20185152@stu.neu.edu.cn (P.Z.); 2071292@stu.neu.edu.cn (B.L.)
* Correspondence: songjie@mail.neu.edu.cn

Abstract: Blockchain solves the problem of mutual trust and consensus in the business market of the token economy. In the existing paradigm of blockchain token economy, there are disadvantages of lacking the incentive mechanism, business applications and virtual token value. These shortcomings reduce consumers' willingness to consume and the profits of the merchants. In this paper, we propose a novel "Dual incentive value-based" paradigm to improve the business market profitability in blockchain token economy. To evaluate our proposed paradigm, we propose a business study case for improving merchants' environment state. In this case, we set up two economic models and make simulations to validate the profitability. The result shows that merchants with the novel paradigm have 32% more profit compared with those without the paradigm and at most 10% more profitable than those in existing paradigms.

Keywords: blockchain; token economy; incentive mechanism; effects in business market; economic model

Citation: Guo, C.; Zhang, P.; Lin, B.; Song, J. A Dual Incentive Value-Based Paradigm for Improving the Business Market Profitability in Blockchain Token Economy. *Mathematics* **2022**, *10*, 439. https://doi.org/10.3390/math10030439

Academic Editors: José Luis Miralles-Quirós and María Mar Miralles-Quirós

Received: 26 December 2021
Accepted: 28 January 2022
Published: 29 January 2022

1. Introduction

A token economy is a complex system of reinforcement, and it offers some medium of exchange (i.e., a token) for the participants to purchase various goods, services, or privileges [1]. The token economy could make the business market more active and profitable than before [2]. Traditional token economy has not fully reflected the characteristics of co-governance and mutual trust [3]. With the development of blockchain technology, many studies believe that the blockchain token economy is a crucial grasp to achieve this goal based on the consensus mechanism and autonomy of the blockchain [4].

Blockchain can be referred as a distributed ledger. Its data and transactions are not under the control of any third party [5]. Each node in the blockchain is equal. The blockchain is considered as persistence, anonymity and auditability by the academia and the industry [6]. In 2008, Satoshi Nakamoto proposed the definition of Bitcoin, where the concept blockchain was firstly proposed. After that, the blockchain experienced three development stages. Blockchain 1.0 resolves Double-spend with distributed transfer in the cryptocurrency transactions such as the Bitcoin. Blockchain 2.0 realized the programmable finance in the financial fields such as the Ethereum. Blockchain 3.0 focuses on using blockchain for various applications in industries other than finance [7]. Currently, Blockchain 3.0 can be well applied in many fields, such as healthcare [8], education [9] and the token economy introduced in this paper. In the blockchain, the token (i.e., Bitcoin) is a medium to stimulate nodes to work for the community more. The incentive mechanism is the approach to offer tokens. The incentive mechanism is a common approach to stimulate roles to work in different scenarios. It is widely used in different fields, such as network communications [10] and IoT [11]. The design of the incentive mechanism is the critical challenge of decentralized token design [12]. Moreover, it increases the blockchain nodes' interests in the token [13]. In the business market, the blockchain token economy can enforce a mutually beneficial business environment [14]. In this environment, the values of the token and the incentive mechanism are two essential factors [15].

Existing studies on the blockchain token economy mainly focus on three aspects: new incentive mechanism design, new economic scenario design and new business schema design

- For the first aspect, researchers concentrate on designing new incentive mechanism on the token to stimulate nodes to join in the activities of the community. Barreiro-gomez et al. [16] designed a game theory-based incentive mechanism on the token to research the risks in the token's circulation. Kim et al. [12] introduced the details in a Swiss blockchain's token, including the design of the incentive mechanism. Drasch et al. [17] modeled the associated incentives in a multi-sided blockchain-enabled platform for token value development.
- For the second aspect, researchers import particular economic scenarios in the blockchain token economy. The definitions of novel economies and management methods are necessary. Narayan et al. [18] proposed a tokenizing coopetition in the circular token economy to show how competition could be operationalized and optimized using tokens in a blockchain. Kim et al. [19] proposed a process for building a desirable model of a sustainable growth token economy.
- For the last aspect, researchers introduces the application of tokens in the actual business schema, such as the joint application of Initial Coin Offering (ICO) [20] and tokens. Tonnissen et al. [21] introduced the cluster-analysis of 195 ICOs and identified three different archetypes on ICO tokens.

At present, there is a lack of systematic research on the token economy paradigm. Therefore, we divide the current researches into three categories according to their research directions: the incentive-based paradigm, the new scenario-based paradigm, and the business schema-based paradigm.

However, the three paradigms all have disadvantages. First, the incentive-based paradigm's token cannot be used as a real currency [12,16]. Meanwhile, the current incentive-based paradigm focuses on the single incentive mechanism, leading to limited influence in their scenario. Second, the new scenario-based paradigm lacks applications in the business scenario. It also lacks regulation and control effects to the business market economy. Finally, the business schema-based paradigm lacks the incentive mechanism. It takes terrible effects, such as the virtual tokens scam.

Token economy strengthens the market profit and helps to build mutual trust and co-government [22]. The incentive mechanism and the liquidity of tokens are most essential parts. To increase market profitability, we combine the features of token value, business applications and incentive mechanisms in one paradigm to propose a novel paradigm "dual incentive value-based paradigm" as the fourth paradigm in the business blockchain token economy. Different with the previous paradigms, the novel paradigm achieves dual incentive effects on different types of nodes by only one token to expend the usage scenario. Meanwhile, it contains token value design and the liquidation design. Therefore, the token can be used as real currency and the novel paradigm can be used in the business market economy.

To prove the applicability in the business scenario, we propose a study case for improving merchants' environment state in the business scenario. In this case, the government, the alliance, the merchant and the customer are four roles, and the voucher is the token. Then we set up two economic models to prove that the novel paradigm can be more profitable than the existing paradigms. After that, we make simulations to compare the expected profitability of merchants in non-paradigm, existing paradigm and novel paradigm scenarios. The result shows that merchants in the novel paradigm can obtain at most 10% more profit than those in the existing paradigm and at most 32% more profit than those without paradigms. The contributions of our study are as follows:

- We conclude three existing paradigms of the blockchain token economy novelly and analyze the shortcomings of each paradigm.

- We propose a novel dual incentive value-based paradigm in the blockchain token economy. It can make dual incentive effects and enhance the entity value of the token in the business blockchain economy.
- We propose a study case and set up two economic models to prove the novel paradigm's profitability.
- We compare our novel paradigm with other paradigms in the study case to prove its effectiveness.

Our following sections are structured as follows: Section 2 summarizes existing paradigms of blockchain token economy; Section 3 proposes the novel "dual incentive value-based paradigm"; Section 4 proposes a business study case, a hierarchical alliance structure model to set the level for merchants and a new "newsvendor proble" profit model to evaluate the profit; Section 5 makes experiments to prove that the new paradigm is more profitable than the existing three paradigms and makes discussion and suggestions based on experiment results; Section 6 concludes our paper.

2. Literature Review

Blockchain token is originated from Bitcoin. At the early age of the blockchain development, the studies of the tokens are about the transcations of ICOs, such as the Bitcoin and the Ethereum. The ICO is a method of generating tokens and raising funds. It can be traded and liquidated as the currency. In February 2018, the Swiss Financial Market Supervisory Authority (FINMA) released ICO guidelines [23]. However, with the development of the ICO, more and more financial and economic problems are appearing, such as the scams and the fraud. As a consequence, the design of the Bitcoin is only used to stimulate nodes. Therefore, researchers design new tokens with incentive mechanisms in their customized business blockchain. This is the origin of the blockchain token economy.

Currently, researchers conduct blockchain token economy studies on three aspects: (1) the design of token's incentive mechanisms; (2) the design of particular economic scenarios; and (3) the relationship analysis between the ICO and the tokens.

The first aspect is the design of token's mechanisms. These studies on the blockchain token economy concentrate on how to design a token in detail and how to make token valuable. Since the incentive mechanism determines the rule of obtaining the tokens in the blockchain, some studies focus on designing novel incentive mechanisms. In these studies, a well-designed incentive mechanism can make nodes obtain tokens equally. It should also be able to control the circulation and balance the value of the token. Jung et al. [24] set up three roles in the healthcare blockchain and two real-world business scenarios of healthcare companies recruiting. In the scenarios, two economic models are set up by the game theory to explain the novel incentive mechanism for controlling the token's reward and the recruitment costs. The result shows the novel incentive mechanism can control them effectively. Drasch et al. [17] modeled a novel associated incentives on the token in a business blockchain platform. Drasch et al. proposed a two-stage incentive at the stage of platform development and platform operation. They use economic theory to analyze that tokens can help to overcome the "chicken and egg" problem and lead to contradictory incentives for platform participants. Takemiya [25] proposed a self-regulating token-based economic system and a dual-token system with a novel incentive mechanism. The self-regulating system is implemented through allocating votes in a Sybil-resistant manner. The dual-token system is designed in economic theories. In the incentive mechanism, each token's users can obtain the other token by storing and servicing their tokens. This could guarantee the users' and the system's benefit.

The second aspect is the design of particular economy scenarios. Generally, the economy contains sub-classifications, such as the circular economy, the market economy, and the government economy. In the blockchain token economy, different economies increase the variety of token value. In the service of different blockchains, different tokens can take different methods for nodes to obtain tokens. Therefore, researchers made studies on new economic scenarios to increase token variety in recent years. Kim et al. [19]

proposed a process for building a desirable model of a token economy. It can make a sustainable growth. The sustainable growth of the token economy is implemented by voluntary activities of participants and well defined economic models. It can increase the participants' interests and obtain sustainable profit growth. Kim et al. set up the economic model by strategic managements and set up incentive mechanisms to support the economic model on the token for a sustainable growing token economy. Narayan et al. [18] proposed a tokenizing coopetition in the circular token economy. The circular economy offers a way for businesses to conceptualize sustainable economic activity with a concern for environmental and societal wellbeing. Narayan et al. set up circular models by using competition to operationalize and optimize using tokens.

The third aspect is the relationship analysis between the ICO and the tokens. Except the well-defined tokens in different business scenarios, ICO is also a type of token in the blockchain. Therefore, a small number of researchers study the relationship between ICO and the token. Tonnissen et al. [21] analyzed 195 ICOs and performed cluster-analysis in order to identify three different archetypes. The archetypes are the pioneering model, the expansion model and the authority model. They can offer research concerns on token-based business models.

After analyzing the studies, the research of three aspects can be summarized into three well-designed types: First, most of the studies on **designing the incentive mechanism** set up economic models or theories to design a new incentive mechanism in the business scenario; Second, most of the studies on **the novel economic sub-classifications** explain the sub-classification. They use non-economic methods to model the sub-classification, and use economic model to design the token in non-business scenario. Third, most of the studies on **the relationship between the ICO and the token** introduce the combination of ICOs and tokens without incentive mechanisms in the business scenario. Based on this, we summarize the existing blockchain token economy literature into three paradigms. The paradigm characteristics and disadvantages are as follows:

(1) Incentive-based paradigm:

The incentive-based paradigm concentrates on the design of the incentive mechanism of the token and how to attain the best situation of maximum incentive effect:

- **Incentive Mechanism**: It aims to make the platform obtain maximum benefits or make consumers cost minimum;
- **Token Design**: It includes guidelines for the issuance, trading and functioning of tokens;
- **Token Visualization**: It contains a flow chart or a sequence diagram to explain how the token works;
- **Mechanism Feasibility Validation**: It includes theoretical and experimental verification.
- **Practical Application**: A healthcare blockchain system [24]. It models an incentive mechanism of blockchain based on game theory and a mechanism design that recruits participants through a health care blockchain platform in game theory. It proposes three roles: participants, data recipients (companies) and data providers (health care organizations). It also defines rules how roles can obtain tokens and represents a figure to show the token visualization. Finally, it sets simulations to estimate the benefit which the incentive mechanism can provide for users and the cost for the company. Results show that the incentive mechanism can minimize the cost of the company and stimulate users to join.

However, two disadvantages exist in this paradigm:

- **Disadvantage 1:** Few literature defines multiply roles. The current paradigm only includes two roles such as the community and the participates (nodes). Therefore, only the single incentive mechanism exist between the community and the participates.
- **Disadvantage 2:** No literature introduces the relationship between its token and ICO or the currency. Therefore, the value of the token is virtual and can only be expressed in their design.

(2) New scenario-based paradigm:

The new scenario-based paradigm concentrates on how the token economy works in a particular blockchain economic scenario, such as the circular economy and sustainable economy:

- **Scenario Explanation**: It explains the new scenario and the potential advantages of token economy use in non-traditional scenarios;
- **Token Design**: It includes the effect of the token in their new scenario.
- **Theoretical model**: Models for the new scenario that comes from any research field, such as the collaborative, crypto-economic, and management models;
- **Research framework/flow**: It includes two types: one does not contain the experiment based on the theories; the other contains the experiment with the research flow same as the incentive-based one.
- **Practical Application**: A blogging and social networking website "Steemit". It proposes a sustainable growing token economy [19]. It sets up a strategic model using cryptoeconomics and strategic management theories, which contains eight processes to define the token. It shows the research flow by a sequence diagram and theoretical analysis.

The disadvantage for the paradigm is shown as follows:

- **Disadvantage:** No literature applies the paradigm in the business scenario, and no literature defines roles. In a business scenario, multiple roles can be existing at the same time. Therefore, the paradigm lacks the regulation and control effect on the business market economy.

(3) Business schema-based paradigm:

The business schema-based paradigm introduces the application of tokens in the actual business schema, such as the joint application of ICO and tokens. It also optimizes the existing token economy system from the perspective of business economics and strengthens the value of its token. Moreover, the relationship between suppliers and consumers in the blockchain token economy is essential and needs to be considered:

- **Supplier analysis**: Supplier is the most critical role. It defines token issuing rules and using rules. This part contains the token's design and value and basic information of the supplier;
- **Roles in the business schema**;
- **Practical Application**: A blockchain-based token business start-up ecosystem [21]. It contains three roles: supplier, the network and participant. Suppliers work together in order to define the value proposition for each participant. The ecosystem uses theoretical analysis to show token visualization and mechanism feasibility.

Token visualization and **Mechanism Feasibility Validation** are the same with the incentive-based paradigm. Business schema-based paradigm's disadvantage is shown as follow.

- **Disadvantage:** Although the tokens in the paradigm can be circulated as a currency, no literature introduces the incentive mechanism. The value of the token in the paradigm may gradually bubble, such as virtual token fraud.

In summary, existing paradigms lack multiple incentive mechanisms, business applications and the liquidity of tokens. The design of incentive mechanisms and the valuable token determines consumers' consumer willingness and the profitability of the entire business market. Therefore, a novel paradigm with the multiple incentive mechanisms of a valuable token is essential to improve the business market profit in the blockchain token economy.

3. Dual Incentive Value-Based Paradigm

In this paper, we propose a novel blockchain token economy paradigm called "**D**ual **I**ncentive **V**alue-based paradigm"(DIV for short). To solve the disadvantages in the existing paradigms and improve the profitability of the paradigm, the following parts are novelly designed in DIV.

(1) Dual incentive effects by a token: Among different roles of the market, there are dual incentive mechanisms. For example, the community stimulates suppliers, and suppliers stimulate consumers by offering tokens in different periods.

(2) Entity value of the token: The token has strong liquidity and can be traded with other real currency, such as the dollar.

(3) Liquidation of token: The token has a service period. The community will liquidate unused tokens at the end of each period.

(4) Hierarchical roles: Roles are hierarchical in DIV. Each role hierarchy can set up multiple roles, and roles in the same hierarchy have the same functions and permission.

(5) Business study case: DIV should contain a suitable business case, and the case needs to prove the profitability of DIV.

Thus DIV consists of four parts: Roles, token design, incentive mechanism design and paradigm execution flow.

Roles:

(1) Initiator: The initiator is the creator of the blockchain token economy applied in the paradigm. It is an authoritative organization or individual. It offers the authorization of the alliance to stimulate suppliers to join in.

(2) Alliance: The alliance is similar to the "league" in the business scenario. It accepts suppliers to join in. It also offers and liquidates the tokens to the members at each period. The alliance obtains members' membership fees at the beginning of each period and liquidates members' unused tokens at the end of each period. Moreover, an alliance can exist with more than one type of supplier simultaneously. For example, a shopping market league can hold different shops, such as snack shops and fruit shops.

(3) Supplier (Member): The supplier is similar to the "merchant" in the business scenario. If the supplier joins the alliance, it becomes a **Member** of the alliance and obtains tokens from it at beginning of each period. Suppliers cannot obtain tokens from the alliance if they do not join the alliance. Each member has a level that determines the number of tokens they can obtain from the alliance. The level is based on some pre-defined rules. Members offer their tokens to consumers to obtain more profits and consumers. Moreover, members should pay the membership fee regularly to the alliance.

(4) Consumer: The consumer is similar to the "participant" in the blockchain. It can obtain benefits from using tokens and taking part in members' activities more. Moreover, a supplier/member can hold more than one type of consumer simultaneously.

Token Design is as follows.

(1) Overview of the token: In the business market scenario, the token is similar to the "voucher". Members obtain tokens and offer tokens to consumers. Members should bear the discount of consumers' tokens, small profits but quick turnover. Moreover, members can obtain profit from token liquidation. The authority of the token is from the initiator, and the transactions of tokens are recorded on the blockchain.

(2) Token liquidation: In the business market scenario, to increase the liquidity of the token, the alliance liquidates the unused tokens of members and gives compensation to them based on their unused tokens numbers at the end of each period. In the blockchain, the liquidation of tokens means a signal block with unused tokens information, which is created and recorded on the blockchain.

(3) The representation of token's value: The token can be used directly as a currency. Therefore, it has strong liquidity and entity value than other tokens in the blockchain. Moreover, the token can benefit all the roles in the paradigm. Consumers obtain discounts from tokens. Members obtain more profit from offering tokens. The alliance obtains profit

by obtaining membership fees from suppliers of the alliance. The circulation of tokens is shown in Figure 1.

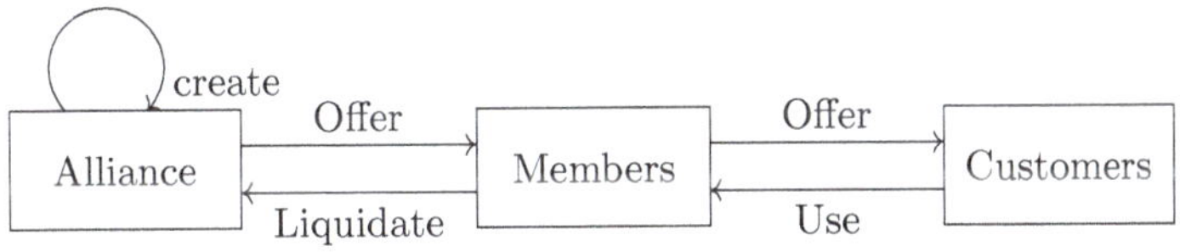

Figure 1. Circulation of tokens in the business-based paradigm. Tokens flow among the alliance, the members and the customers.

Incentive mechanism design:

In the paradigm, two types of incentive mechanisms coexist, and both use only one token.

- The incentive between the alliance and the members: The alliance sets levels and offers tokens to members. The profit of members increases by more consumers and liquidating from the alliance. The profit of members increases by more consumers and liquidating from the alliance.
- The incentive between the members and the consumers: Members offer tokens to consumers. Consumers obtain tokens and obtain discounts. Members need to bear the discounts of consumers, acquiring small profits but quick turnover.

Execution flow:

The total execution flow of the paradigm is shown in Figure 2.

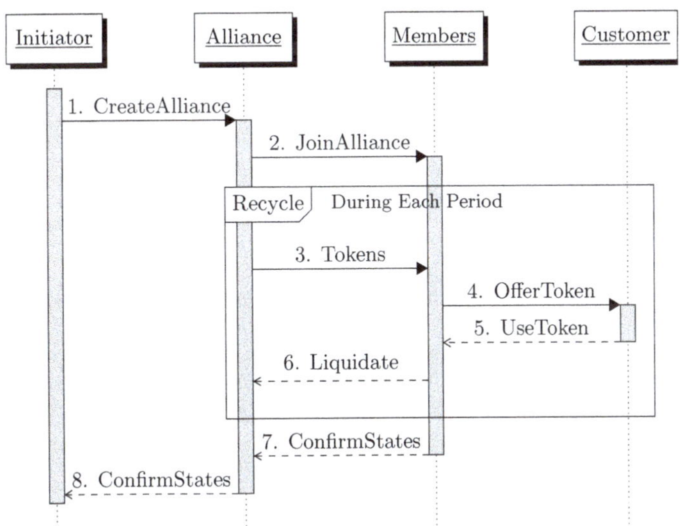

Figure 2. Total execution flow of the dual incentive value-based paradigm. The initiator creates the alliance. The alliance creates tokens and offers tokens to members at the beginning of a period. Members join in the alliance and offer tokens to customers. Customer can use tokens in members. When the period is over, the alliance liquidate all the unused token from members.

4. Study Case: A Business Blockchain Alliance for Improving Environment and Profitability

In this section, we propose a business blockchain alliance study case for improving **environment** and **profitability** (Env-profit for short) of DIV firstly. Then, we propose a theoretical analysis method to evaluate the profit of the roles in Env-profit. The route map is shown as Figure 3.

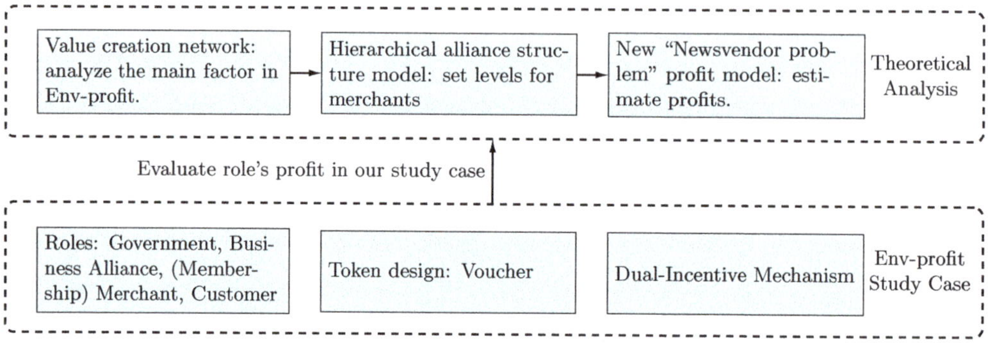

Figure 3. Route Map of the Study Case Env-Profit.

4.1. *Details of Env-Profit*

The corresponding relationships between **Env-alliance** and DIV are shown in Table 1.

Table 1. Corresponding relationships between the case and the paradigm.

	DIV Paradigm	**Env-Profit Case**
Roles	Initiator	Government
	Alliance	Business Alliance
	Supplier/Member	Merchant/Membership Merchant
	Consumer	Customer
Design	Token's real value	Use as a currency and can be liquidated
	Multiple incentive effects	(1) Business alliance offers vouchers to membership merchants. (2) Membership merchants offer vouchers to customers.
Token	Token	Voucher

In Env-profitt, the government builds up a blockchain-based business alliance to stimulate merchants to improve air quality consciously. The business alliance is a decentralized and autonomous organization. It provides a membership system that each merchant can join the alliance. Each membership merchant has a level, which depends on the average air quality of a period. The membership merchant can obtain vouchers from the alliance as incentives based on its level. Moreover, each membership merchant should pay the membership fee to the alliance regularly.

The voucher is the token of the blockchain alliance. It has a use period, such as a month. It can be used as a currency for customers to obtain discounts. In Env-profit, the merchant can choose whether to join the alliance or not. If it joins, it can become a membership merchant. Moreover, only the membership merchant can obtain vouchers, and it should afford the discount of vouchers. Despite this, the alliance also offers a liquidation system to repurchase membership merchants' unused vouchers at the end of each period. Moreover, because of the authority of the alliance, customers can visit more membership merchants. In this manner, membership merchants obtain more customers and obtain more profits.

Customers are the users of vouchers, and they obtain vouchers from membership merchants. Moreover, the alliance gathers many high-air quality merchants so that customers will consume more in the league, which improves the profitability of the entire business market. The summary relationship of roles in Env-profit is shown in Figure 4.

Finally, dual incentive effects exist in the Env-profit. The first incentive effect is that the alliance offers vouchers to membership merchants to improve air quality. The better air quality the membership merchants obtains, the higher the level they can be. The more vouchers they can have, the higher the profits they can have. The second incentive effect is that the membership merchants give out vouchers to customers to consume more, then membership merchants and the alliance can obtain more profits. Moreover, the voucher makes the token more valuable. It can be used as money, and its value and liquidity are shown.

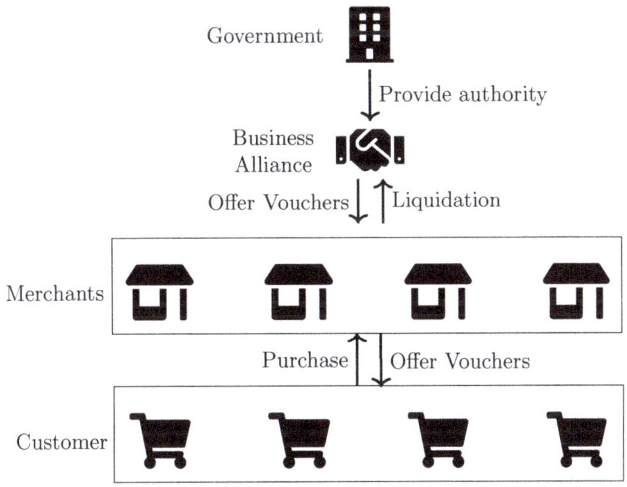

Figure 4. Summary relationship of roles in the case. Customers, merchants, the business alliance and the government are roles. The government provides the authority for the business alliance. The business alliance offer vouchers to merchants, and merchants offer vouchers to customers. Customers can purchase in merchants' by vouchers, and at the end of the period, the business alliance liquidates all unused vouchers from merchants.

4.2. Theoretical Analysis

In this section, we propose a theoretical analysis method to evaluate membership merchants' profit in Env-profit case. Firstly we set up a value creation network to analyze the main factor. Then, we propose two economic models: one is a hierarchical alliance structure model to set levels for merchants, and the other is a new "Newsvendor problem" profit model to evaluate membership merchants' profit.

4.2.1. Value Creation Network

We draw on the value net model concept, combine the value co-creation theory [26] and conclude a novel value creation network [27]. It consists of six creation modules: participants, external demand, value proposition, key business, core source and profit schema. The relationship among the modules is shown in the Figure 5. The corresponding relationships of the case is shown in the Table 2.

In Table 2, the **level system** effects the value proposition, key business and the core source modules, which mainly controls the entire paradigm. Therefore, we conclude that the **level system** is a significant model of the alliance; thus, we first set up the hierarchical alliance structure model to set levels of membership merchants.

Table 2. Corresponding relationship of the case in the value creation model.

Value Creation Model Modules	Modules in the Case
Participants	Merchants
Value proposition	Stimulate merchants by the level system and improve the authority of external demand
Key business	Set levels of merchants' air quality, give out and liquidate vouchers
Core source	Voucher and authorize level system
Profit schema	Collect membership fees

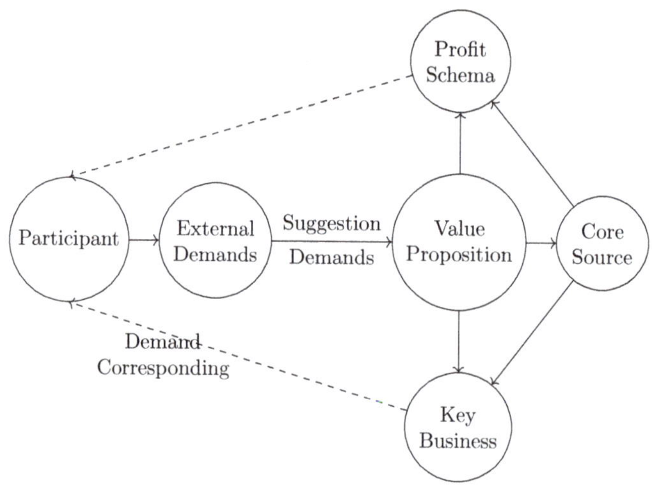

Figure 5. The relationship among value creation network model modules. The participant wants to create value. It has external demands. External demands can be exchanged into value proposition with receiving suggestions and demands. The value proposition is shown by the profit schema, the key business and the core source. The profit schema and the key business with demand correspondingly affect the participant's value, and the core source determines the profit schema and the business effect.

4.2.2. Hierarchical Alliance Structure Model

The effect of the merchant's level is shown in Figure 6, in which the membership merchant's score is transformed to the level. Three significant profit factors, namely the membership fee, the traffic and the number of vouchers, are affected by the level. This model sets up a rule to calculate membership merchants' scores and determine their levels in the alliance. The main steps are shown as follow:

1. We firstly need to find out all the corresponding qualitative and quantitative indicators;
2. Then, we set weights for each indicator;
3. Next, we calculate the scores based on the indicators' weights;
4. Later, we can set levels for membership merchants based on the score;
5. At last, we define other interactive functions in the Env-profit.

(1) Set indicators: We set qualitative and quantitative indicators of membership merchants that influence the level and is shown in Table 3. The quantitative factors are more important than qualitative factors. Therefore, we set the weight of quantitative indicators as 80% and the weight of qualitative indicators as 20%.

(2) Set weights: We use the "Analytic Hierarchy Process" (AHP) [28] to confirm the weight of every single indicator.

a. Construct the judgment matrix of indicators: The judgment matrix is denoted as $X_{Level} \in R^{n\times n}(n \in r)$, and $n = 8$ in our case. $X^{i,j}_{Level}$ indicates the degree of importance between indicator i and indicator j. The degree is shown in Table 4. Elements should follow rule $X^{i,j}_{Level} \times X^{j,i}_{Level} = 1$. The final judgment matrix X_{Level} is shown as Equation (1).

$$X_{Level} = \begin{pmatrix} 1 & 1 & 2 & 2 & 4 & 4 & 3 & 5 \\ 1 & 1 & 2 & 2 & 4 & 4 & 3 & 5 \\ \frac{1}{2} & \frac{1}{2} & 1 & 1 & 2 & 2 & 2 & 3 \\ \frac{1}{2} & \frac{1}{2} & 1 & 1 & 2 & 2 & 2 & 3 \\ \frac{1}{4} & \frac{1}{4} & \frac{1}{2} & \frac{1}{2} & 1 & 1 & 1 & 2 \\ \frac{1}{4} & \frac{1}{4} & \frac{1}{2} & \frac{1}{2} & 1 & 1 & 1 & 2 \\ \frac{1}{3} & \frac{1}{3} & \frac{1}{2} & \frac{1}{2} & 1 & 1 & 1 & 2 \\ \frac{1}{5} & \frac{1}{5} & \frac{1}{3} & \frac{1}{3} & \frac{1}{2} & \frac{1}{2} & \frac{1}{2} & 1 \end{pmatrix} \quad (1)$$

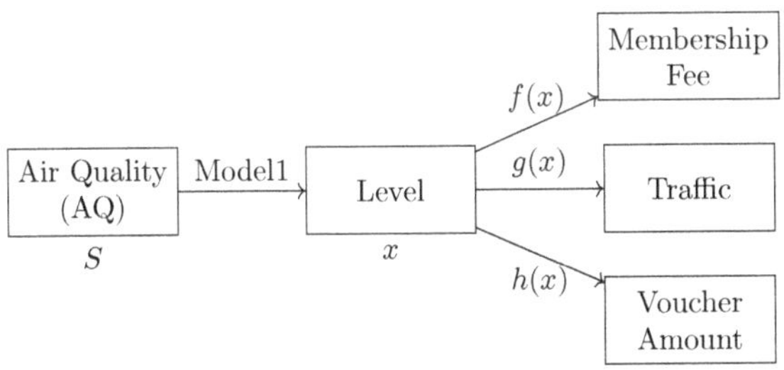

Figure 6. Importance of the merchant's level. The membership merchants' air quality(shorten as AQ) S can be exchanged into a level x by the hierarchical alliance structure model. Level x can be exchanged to three key factors: the membership fee, the traffic of the membership merchant and the voucher amount of the membership. The corresponding functions between the level and three factors are defined as $f(x)$, $g(x)$ and $h(x)$.

Table 3. Quantitative and qualitative indicators in the model.

Indicator Type	Indicator Name	Symbol
Qualitative	Average number of used vouchers	x_1
	Average air quality	x_2
	Average number of customers	x_3
	Average number of obtained vouchers	x_4
	Average number of membership merchants' store visits	x_5
Quantitative	Type of membership merchant	x_6
	Merchant awareness	x_7
	Reviews of membership merchant	x_8

b. Use root method to calculate indicator weight: We use the root method to calculate each indicator's weight as $\overline{w_i} = \sqrt[n]{\sum_{j=1}^{n} x^{i,j}_{Level}}$. Then, we normalize the element in $W = (\overline{w_1}, \overline{w_2}, \overline{w_3}, \cdots, \overline{w_8})$ as $w_i = \frac{\overline{w_j}}{\sum_{j=1}^{8} \overline{w_j}}$ and obtain the indicator weight vector W_{Level} of X_{Level} as Equation (2).

$$\begin{aligned} W_{Level} &= (w_1, w_2, w_3, \cdots, w_8) \\ &= (0.246, 0.246, 0.13, 0.13, 0.067, 0.067, 0.073, 0.041) \end{aligned} \quad (2)$$

Table 4. Degree explanation of the elements.

Degree of $X_{i,j}$	Explanation
1	The ith indicator is the same important with the jth indicator.
3	The ith indicator is more important than the jth indicator.
5	The ith indicator is strongly more important than the jth indicator.
7	The ith indicator is absolutely more important than the jth indicator.
2, 4, 6	Judgment median

c. **Consistency test:** We define the consistency indicator as $C(I)$, the average random indicator as $R(I)$ and the consistency ratio as $C(R)$. The corresponding relationship between n and $R(I)$ is shown in Table 5, and Equation (3) shows the calculation of $C(R)$. If $C(R) \leq 0.1$, the judgment matrix X_{Level} passes the consistency test. $C(I) = 0.05$, $R(I)_{n=8} = 1.41$, $C(R) = 0.035 < 0.1$ and W_{Level} pass the test. Thus, the weight of indicators is W_{Level}.

$$C(R) = \frac{C(I)}{R(I)} = \frac{\left| \frac{1}{n} \sum_{i=1}^{n} \frac{\sum_{j=1}^{n} W_{Level}^{i,j} \cdot w_j}{w_i} - n \right|}{(n-1) \cdot R(I)} \tag{3}$$

Table 5. Relationship between indicator amount and R.I.

n	1	2	3	4	5	6	7	8	9	10
R.I.	0	0	0.52	0.89	1.12	1.26	1.36	1.41	1.46	1.49

(3) Calculate scores: This step contains a quantitative judgment model and a qualitative model to calculate the final score for membership merchants and set the level. In the quantitative judgment model, three parts are needed:

a. **Confirm the quantitative indicators and judgment set:** The quantitative indicators set is $Set_{Quan} = \{x_1, x_2, x_3, x_4, x_5\}$. We define the quantitative judgment set as $Y = \{Excellent, Good, Medium, Pass, Fail\}$, and the max rating score is 100. Based on the 80% weighting, the reference table between the score and the quantitative judgment set is in the Table 6.

$$r_{ij} = \begin{cases} 0 & (U_i < u_{i,j-1}, U_i < u_{i,j+1}) \\ \frac{U_i - u_{i,j-1}}{u_{i,j-1} - u_{ij}} & (u_{i,j-1} < U_i < u_{ij}) \\ \frac{u_{i,j} - U_i}{u_{ij} - u_{i,j+1}} & (u_{ij} < U_i < u_{i,j+1}) \end{cases} \tag{4}$$

Table 6. Judgment-Score reference table.

Judgment	Excellent	Good	Medium	Pass	Fail
Score	(65, 80)	(49, 64)	(33, 48)	(17, 32)	(1, 16)

b. **Confirm the indicator fuzzy judgment matrix:** The judgment-indicator table is shown in Table 7, and each quantitative indicator owns a judgment score p_i. We define the indicator scoring vector $P_{Quan} = \{p_1, p_2, p_3, p_4, p_5\}^T$ and the indicator fuzzy judgment matrix $R_{Quan} = (r_{i,j})_{5\times5}$. r_{ij} means the membership degree of grade jth judgment for the ith indicator. Then, we define U_i as the real value of each indicator, and u_{ij} as the value border of each judgment for each indicator. The relationship among r_{ij}, u_{ij} and U_i is in

Equation (4). For example, the real value of indicator x_1 is 450; thus, the U_i of x_1 is 450, according to the Table 7; the score p_1 is 64; and u_{11} is 500, u_{12} is 300, r_{11} is 0.25 and r_{12} is 0.75. Each merchant has an indicator judgment fuzzy matrix R_{Quan} according to its situation.

Table 7. Judgment-indicator table.

Indicator	Excellent (65, 80)	Good (49, 64)	Medium (33, 48)	Pass (17, 32)	Fail (0, 16)
x_1(amount)	>500	[300,500]	[150,300]	[50,150]	<50
x_2(AQI)	<40	[40,60]	[60,90]	[90,150]	>150
x_3(amount)	>1000	[500,1000]	[200,500]	[50,200]	<50
x_4(amount)	>750	[450,750]	[200,450]	[75,200]	<75
x_5(amount)	>3000	[1500,3000]	[500,1500]	[100,500]	<100

c. Calculate the quantitative score with quantitative indicators weight: With the combination of W_{Quan} , R_{Quan} and P_{Quan} , the final quantitative score $Score_{Quan}$ is as follows.

$$\begin{aligned} Score_{Quan} &= W_{Quan} \times R_{Quan} \times P_{Quan} \\ &= (0.246, 0.246, \cdots, 0.067) \begin{pmatrix} r_{11} & r_{12} & r_{13} & r_{14} & r_{15} \\ r_{21} & r_{22} & r_{23} & r_{24} & r_{25} \\ r_{31} & r_{32} & r_{33} & r_{34} & r_{35} \\ r_{41} & r_{42} & r_{43} & r_{44} & r_{45} \\ r_{51} & r_{52} & r_{53} & r_{54} & r_{55} \end{pmatrix} (p_1, p_2, p_3, p_4, p_5)^T \end{aligned} \quad (5)$$

In the qualitative judgment model, due to the uncertain value of qualitative indicators, the judgment of qualitative indicators should be signed manually. Each customer can give each merchant a score in x_7, x_8 and x_9 indicators and the total score of each indicator is 100. Due to the extreme scores, we calculate the average top 25% to 75% customers' scores of each indicator and obtain a customer score vector $C_{Qual} = (C_{x_7}, C_{x_8}, C_{x_9})^T$. If a membership merchant has less than 50 customers' ratings, its qualitative score would be $Score_{Qual} = 0.25Score_{Quan}$. Based on the weights in W_{Level}, the weight vector of qualitative indicators W_{Qual} is $(0.067, 0.073, 0.041)$, and the qualitative score is $Score_{Qual} = C_{Qual} \times W_{Qual}$. Thus, the total score of a membership merchant is $Score_{Final} = 0.2Score_{Qual} + 0.8Score_{Quan}$.

(4) Set levels: In Env-profit, we set that only the merchant's air quality is better than 70, and the merchant can enter the alliance. We set a score ranking-level table for membership merchants in Table 8. The hierarchical alliance structure model offers researchers reference on setting levels for an alliance.

Table 8. Ranking-Level table.

Ranking	Top 5%	Top 5% to 15%	Top 15% to 35%	Top 35% to 65%	Bottom 35%
Level	5	4	3	2	1

(5) Definitions of othe the interactive functions in the Env-profit: We define some basic functions of the Env-profit. Based on Figure 6, we define the membership fee of merchants as $Fee_{Mer}(Level_{Mer})$, the traffic of merchants as $Traff_{Mer}(Level_{Mer})$ and the number of vouchers for merchants as $Voucher_{Mer}(Level_{Mer})$.

The traffic of merchants in the case is affected by merchants' levels and the incentive of vouchers. Agarwal and Qian [29] propose a study that MPC (Marginal Propensity to Consume) [30] of giving vouchers can rise 15% to 40%. In Env-profit, we set that membership merchants of Level 1 can obtain a 15% increase and membership merchants of Level 5 can obtain a 40% increase in traffic based on [29]. In addition, merchants cannot increase the traffic. We make a logarithmic fit on the function of Level-Traffic increase, and it is shown in Equation (6). We obtain the traffic increase rate of each level in Env-profit in Table 9.

$$Traff_{Mer}(Level_{Mer}) = 0.236ln(Level_{Mer} + 1.129) + 0.971 \quad Level_{Mer} = 0,1,2,3,4,5 \tag{6}$$

Table 9. Relationship between traffic increase rate and level.

Level	0	1	2	3	4	5
Traffic increase rate (new traffic/old traffic)	1	1.15	1.24	1.306	1.357	1.4

4.2.3. New "Newsvendor Problem" Profit Model

We introduce an alliance and the level system in the DIV to promote customers' consumption and increase profits of membership merchants. Therefore, we need to propose a novel profit model to reasonably estimate profits of membership merchants. "Newsvendor problem" [31] is a typical single-cycle storage problem in operations research. In Env-profit, membership merchants are similar to the newsvendors, and vouchers are similar to the newspapers. Therefore, we propose a new "newsvendor problem" profit model based on Env-profit to calculate the membership merchants' profits. In the DIV, the number of the customers is uncontrolled and essential to the membership merchants' profits, and other factors such as the discount and repurchase rate are controllable. Therefore, the objective of the model is to find the number of customers when a merchant can make the most profit.

Problem Description: A membership merchant has Q vouchers at the beginning of the period. During the period, r customers have used the voucher in the membership merchant. At the end of the period, the alliance repurchased the unused vouchers as u dollars per voucher.

Problem Denotation: We have the following denotations in this problem:

- The possible value of r is denoted as $r_j, (j = 1, 2, \ldots, n)$;
- The membership merchant's average cost is denoted as c;
- The average selling price is denoted as $p, (u < c < p)$;
- The membership fee of membership merchant is denoted as $f(x)$;
- the discount of a voucher is denoted as $d\%$, and it is given;
- The probability of r is satisfied with $P(r_j)$: $0 < P(r_j) < 1, \sum_{r>r_n} P(r) = 1$.

Problem Objective: The objective of the problem is to obtain the best value of Q when the membership merchant can obtain the most profit.

Solving: We firstly calculate the expectation of membership merchant's normal profit without repurchasing $E(R(r))$ and the profit of repurchasing $E(R_u(r))$. Then, we calculate the accounting profit expectation of a membership merchant $W(Q)$. Next, we divide $W(Q)$ into a constant and a new function $F(Q)$, and we use the differential to find the extreme of $F(Q)$. After our analysis, the extreme of $F(Q)$ is the best value of Q.

Set membership merchant's normal profit without repurchasing $R(r)$ as follows.

$$R(r) = \begin{cases} r > Q : p \cdot a\% \cdot Q + (r - Q)p \\ r \le Q : p \cdot d\% \cdot Q \end{cases} \tag{7}$$

The expectation of membership merchant's normal profit without repurchasing $E(R(r))$ is the following.

$$E(R(r)) = \sum R(r)P(r) = p \cdot \sum_{r>Q} [r + Q(d\% - 1)]P(r) + p \cdot d\% \sum_{r \le Q} rP(r) \tag{8}$$

Set the profit of repurchasing $R_u(r)$ as follows.

$$R_u = \begin{cases} r > Q: & 0 \\ r \leq Q: & (Q-r)u \end{cases} \tag{9}$$

Moreover, the expectation of the profit of repurchasing $E(R_u(r))$ is $E(R_u(r)) = \sum R_u(r)P(r) = u \cdot \sum_{r \leq Q}(Q-r)P(r)$; thus, the total profit expectation for a membership merchant in a period is as follows.

$$\sum[R(r) + R_u(r)]P(r) = \sum R(r)P(r) + \sum R_u(r)P(r) \tag{10}$$

The explicit cost expectation of the membership merchant at each period is $cr + f(x)$; thus, the accounting profit expectation of a membership merchant $W(Q)$ is as follows.

$$\begin{aligned} W(Q) =& \sum[R(r) + R_u(r)]P(r) - cr - f(x) \\ =& p \cdot \sum_{r>Q}[r + Q \cdot (d\% - 1)]P(r) + p \cdot d\% \cdot \sum_{r \leq Q} rP(r) + u \cdot \sum_{r \leq Q}(Q-r)P(r) \\ =& [p \cdot d\% \cdot \sum rP(r) - f(x) - cr] - (Q-r)[p(1-d\%)\sum_{r>Q} P(r) - u \cdot \sum_{r \leq Q} P(r)] \end{aligned} \tag{11}$$

Set $F(Q) = (Q-r)[p(1-d\%) \cdot \sum_{r>Q} P(r) - u \cdot P(r)]$, because $\sum rP(r)$ is the expectation of r, and $p, d\%, f(x), c$ and r are all constant values. We set $Cons = p \cdot d\% \cdot \sum rP(r) - f(x) - cr$; then, we obtain $W(Q) = Cons - F(Q)$. The goal of the model is to find the maximum value of $W(Q)$, and because of the finite number of values for r and Q, the maximum of $W(Q)$ and the minimum of $F(Q)$ must be existing. $Cons$ is a constant value; thus, the maximum value of $W(Q)$ is in the situation that $F(Q)$ is at the minimum value. To find the minimum of $F(Q)$, we set $F(r_m) = \min\{F(r_j) \mid j = 1, 2, \cdots, n\}(1 \leq m \leq n)$ and consider the differences of $\Delta F(Q)$ of $F(r_m) = F(Q)$. We set $r_{n+2} > r_{n+1} > r_n$; thus, the following is the case.

$$\begin{aligned} \Delta F(Q) =& \Delta F(r_j) = F(r_{j+1} - r_j) \\ =& (r_{j+1} - r_j)[p \cdot (1-d\%) \cdot \sum_{r>r_{j+1}} P(r) - u \cdot \sum_{r \leq r_j} P(r)] \end{aligned} \tag{12}$$

Using $\sum_{r>r_{j+1}} P(r) = 1 - \sum_{r \leq r_j} P(r)$, $\Delta F(Q) = (r_{j+1} - r_j)[p \cdot (1-d\%) + u]$ $(\sum_{r>r_{j+1}} P(r) - \frac{u}{p \cdot (1-d\%)+u})$. Since $r_{j+1} > r_j, [p \cdot (1-d\%) + u] > 0$, when $\sum_{r>r_{j+1}} P(r) < \frac{u}{p \cdot (1-d\%)+u}$, $\Delta F(Q) < 0$, $F(Q)$ is decreasing, and when $\sum_{r>r_{j+1}} P(r) > \frac{u}{p \cdot (1-d\%)+u}$, $\Delta F(Q) > 0$, $F(Q)$ is increasing. Thus, when $\sum_{r>r_{j+1}} P(r) = \frac{u}{p \cdot (1-d\%)+u}$, $F(Q)$ has a minimum. Thus, the best value of Q that can make the most profit is the following.

$$Q = \{r \mid \sum_{r>r_{m+1}} P(r) = \frac{u}{p \cdot (1-d\%) + u}\} \tag{13}$$

The final profit of membership merchant $Profit_{Mer}$ is the following.

$$Profit_{Mer} = p \cdot d\% \cdot \sum rP(r) - cr - f(x) \tag{14}$$

As long as the profit at Q for membership merchants is more than the merchant's, the paradigm is usable and profitable. Thus, we make simulations to show the results of the model more accurately in Section 5.

5. Experiment

In this section, we make simulations to prove the profitability of DIV. Our codes for all experiments are available at https://github.com/NEUSoftGreenAI/DIVEconomicBlockchain accessed on 28 January 2022.

5.1. Setup

Environment: The hardware environment contains: an Intel Core i7-8750H CPU, 8G memory and a 240G hard disk. The software environment is as follows: Windows 10 and Jupyter Notebook under Python 3.8.

Simulations: We set up two simulations based on the Env-profit:

1. The first simulation proves membership merchants can obtain more profits than merchants.
2. The second simulation proves DIV is more profitable than the incentive-based, new scenario-based and business schema-based paradigm. The new scenario-based paradigm lacks business application, and Env-profit has solved the disadvantage. The business schema-based paradigm lacks the incentive mechanism; thus, it has no incentive. The incentive-based and the new scenario-based paradigms have a single incentive. Therefore, we compare merchants' profits among dual, single and no incentive scenarios. In the second simulation, we set up two single incentive scenarios based on the dual incentive paradigm:
    - **A**ir **Q**uality **E**valuation incentive (AQE for short): In the AQE scenario, the government directly offers tokens to stimulate merchants based on their air quality. No customers in the scenario. The government and the alliance are the same role. Merchants can obtain tokens to exchange money from the government.
    - **M**erchants' **V**oucher incentive (MV for short) scenario: In the MV scenario, merchants directly offers vouchers to stimulate customers to consume more. No government and alliance in the scenario. Merchants need to bear the discount of vouchers and small profits, but it has quick turnover.

Assumptions: We have following assumptions in the experiments:

- Each period of Env-profit is a month. The merchants who are not in the alliance can obtain 1000 customers per month. The average sale price is 100$ and the average cost is 50$.
- The number of merchants' customers r obeys standard normal distribution and the expectation is 1000 for merchants not in the alliance. For membership merchants, the expectation of r is based on the level of merchants. The relationship between merchants' expectations and the level is shown in Figure 7.
- The discount of a voucher is a fixed rate to the selling price as $d\%$, and the repurchase money of each unused voucher is also a fixed rate to the selling price as $rp\%$. In the first simulation, we set $d\% = 2.5\%$, 5% and 10% as a precondition.
- The variance of r is σ, the expected number of customers for a merchant is $Customer_{Exp}$, the z-score for r is z and the amount of voucher $Voucher_{Mer}$ that a membership merchant obtains is $Voucher_{Mer}(Level_{Mer}) = Customer_{Exp} + \sigma \cdot z$.

Baseline The situation of merchants in the no incentive and dual incentive scenarios is the baseline. The baseline number of customers is 1000, the baseline profit of the alliance is 0$ and the baseline profit of a merchant is 50,000$.

Test Case Design: In the two simulations, we set up seven test cases as follows, and the result of each test case is analyzed from Sections 5.2.1–5.2.7:

Test Case 1: In the first simulation, when $d\% = 5\%$, we compare the profit in different σ and $rp\%$ to analyze the impact of the number of customers on membership merchants' profits.

Test Case 2: In the first simulation, when $d\% = 5\%$, we analyze the relationship between $rp\%$ and σ to obtain a suitable range of σ.

Test Case 3: In the first simulation, when $d\% = 5\%$, we estimate profit comparison for merchants of different levels and r to prove that the profitability of DIV can increase as the level and r increase.

Test Case 4: In the first simulation, when $d\% = 5\%$, we evaluate the expected profits for alliance and membership merchants to prove that both the alliance and the membership merchants can obtain more profits than the baseline.

Test Case 5: In the first simulation, when $d\% = 5\%$, we estimate the expected profit of membership merchants in different levels and $rp\%$ to validate that the DIV's profitability is more than the baseline's roundly.

Test Case 6: In the first simulation, we compare the value of σ when $rp\% = 2.5\%, 5\%$, 10% to explain that the suitable value of $d\%$ is 5%.

Test Case 7: In the second simulation, we compare alliance and merchant's expected profit at the same $d\%$ and $rp\%$ under four scenarios (no incentive mechanism, AQE, MV and Dual). We change the level of merchant to prove that the profitability of dual incentive scenario is better than other scenarios'.

Metrics: In the first simulation, based on the assumptions and baseline, if a customer uses the voucher, a membership merchant can earn 50–100$\cdot d\%$\$. If a voucher is repurchased, the merchant can obtain $100 \cdot rp\%$\$ profit. We set the actual number of customers for a merchant as $Customer_{real}$, and the actual profit of a merchant in the alliance $Profit_{real}$ is the following.

$$Profit_{real} = \begin{cases} Voucher_{Mer} > Customer_{real} : (50 - 100 \cdot d\%)Customer_{real} + 100(Voucher_{Mer} - Customer_{real}) \cdot rp\% \\ Voucher_{Mer} \leq Customer_{real} : (50 - 100 \cdot d\%)Voucher_{Mer} + 50(Customer_{real} - Voucher_{Mer}) \end{cases} \tag{15}$$

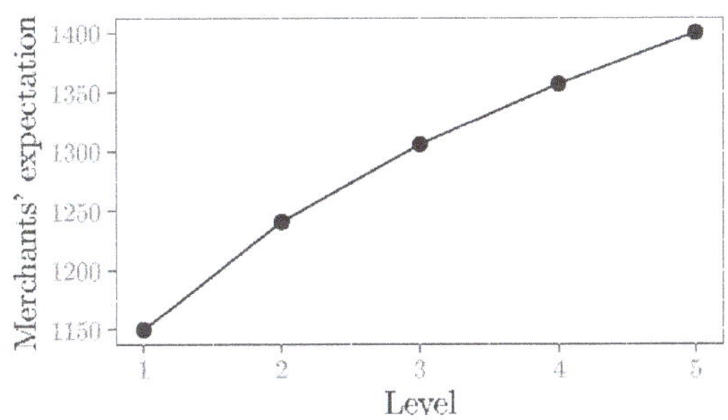

Figure 7. The relationship of merchants' expectation and level. The corresponding merchants' expectations from Level1 to Level5 are 1150, 1241, 1306, 1357 and 1400.

In Section 3, we experience the situation in which the merchant can obtain the maximum profit in Equation (13), as we assumed that the repurchased money u is $100 \cdot rp\%$, and p is 100. Therefore, the formula can be simplified as follows.

$$Q = \{r \mid \sum_{r > r_{m+1}} P(r) = \frac{100 \cdot rp\%}{100 \cdot (1 - d\%) + 100 \cdot rp\%} = \frac{rp\%}{1 - d\% + rp\%}\} \tag{16}$$

Since $\sum_{r>r_{m+1}} P(r) + \sum_{r \leq r_{m+1}} P(r) = 1$, $\sum_{r \leq r_{m+1}} P(r) = \frac{1-d\%}{1-d\%+rp\%}$, the z-score z of r can be obtained from the standard normal distribution table. The variance σ of r is calculated by the baseline situation.

$$\sigma = \frac{\frac{50000 - Customer_{real} \cdot (50 - 100 \cdot d\%)}{100 \cdot rp\%} - Customer_{Exp}}{z} \tag{17}$$

In addition, the profit of the alliance is denoted as $Profit_{Al}$. It is the sum of the membership fees and minus the cost of repurchasing the vouchers. We set the membership fee as $Fee_{Mer}(Level_{Mer}) = 0.5 \cdot r \cdot Level \quad (Level = 1, 2, 3, 4, 5)$.

In the second simulation, we set the profit and the number of merchant's vouchers in the AQE scenario as $Profit_{AQE}$ and $Voucher_{AQE}$, and those in the MV scenario as $Profit_{MV}$ and $Voucher_{MV}$. In the AQE scenario, we assume that the profit of tokens for merchants is $Profit_{AQE} = 50{,}000 + d\% \times Voucher_{AQE} \times 100$. We define $Voucher_{AQE} = 200 Level (Level = 1, 2, 3, 4, 5)$. In the MV scenario, we set that the number of vouchers of a merchant obeys all assumptions. Therefore, the equation of $Profit_{MV}$ is as follows.

$$Profit_{MV} = \begin{cases} Voucher_{MV} > Customer_{real} : (50 - 100 \cdot d\%) \cdot Customer_{real} \\ Voucher_{MV} \leq Customer_{real} : (50 - 100 \cdot d\%) \cdot Voucher_{MV} + 50(Customer_{real} - Voucher_{MV}) \end{cases} \quad (18)$$

5.2. Results

In this section, we show the experiment results of the seven test cases above.

5.2.1. Test Case 1: Result

In the first situation, we set the default level as **Level 1**. When $d\% = 5\%$, Figure 8 shows the membership merchants' expected profit comparison when σ is from 50 to 800 and $rp\%$ = 10% ,15% and 20%. It shows that when σ increases, the membership merchant's profit also increases. Moreover, with the increase in $rp\%$, the membership merchant can reach the baseline at a minor σ. The larger σ indicates that the number of customers is more unstable. The larger $rp\%$ indicates the profit of the alliance reduces. Therefore, a suitable σ and $rp\%$ is critical for both alliance and membership merchants.

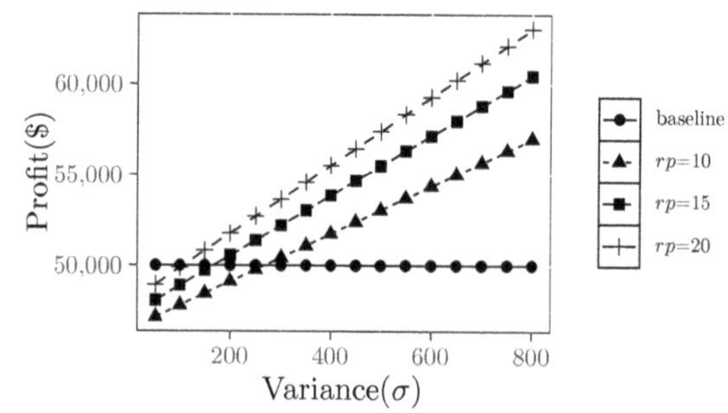

Figure 8. Profits comparison for different σ and $rp\%$.

5.2.2. Test Case 2: Result

Figure 9 shows the relationship between $rp\%$ and σ when $rp\%$ is from 5% to 20%. It shows that when $rp\%$ rises, σ decreases slower and slower. The expectation of r for membership merchants in Level 1 is 1150. The membership merchant should ensure that the maximum fluctuation is not more than half of our expectations. It means $2\sigma < \frac{1150}{2} = 575$, $\sigma < 287.5$; thus, $rp\% < 10\%$ is unsuitable. We set $rp\%$ as 10% to 20% in the following analysis.

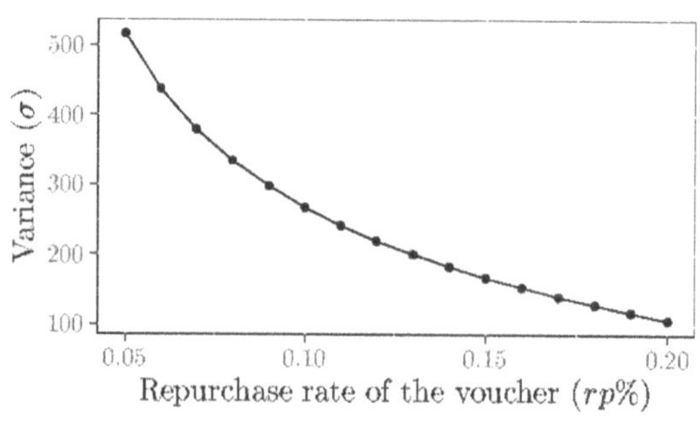

Figure 9. Relationship between $rp\%$ and σ.

5.2.3. Test Case 3: Result

Figure 10 shows the membership merchants' expected profit in different levels when $rp\%$ is from 10% to 20%. When the level rises, the profit of the same $rp\%$ also increases. Moreover, when the number of customers is the same as the baseline, membership merchants are also more profitable than the baseline. Figure 11 shows the relationship between r and membership merchant's profit when $rp\%$ is 10%, 15% and 20%. It shows that the profit increases in different $rp\%$ when r increases. When $r > 1000$, the profit is higher than the baseline in any $rp\%$. Moreover, we can conclude that each line in Figure 11 has a turning point. The bigger $rp\%$ is, the fewer vouchers merchant can obtain. The fewer profit merchants get, the earlier the turning point appears. Figures 10 and 11 validate the expected result that DIV is more profitable than the baseline when parameters are fixed at level-profit and r-profit.

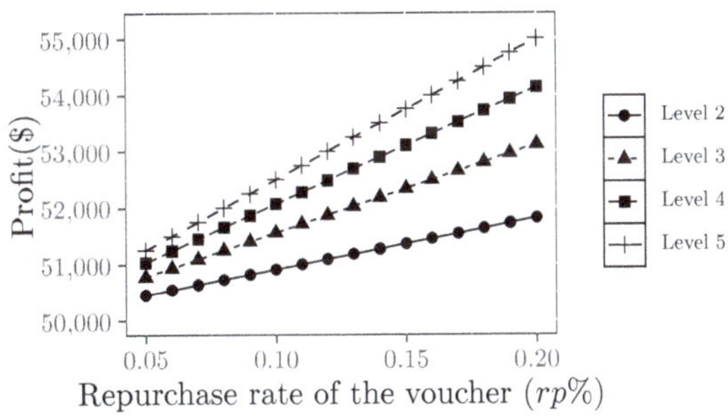

Figure 10. Merchants' profits comparison in levels and $rp\%$.

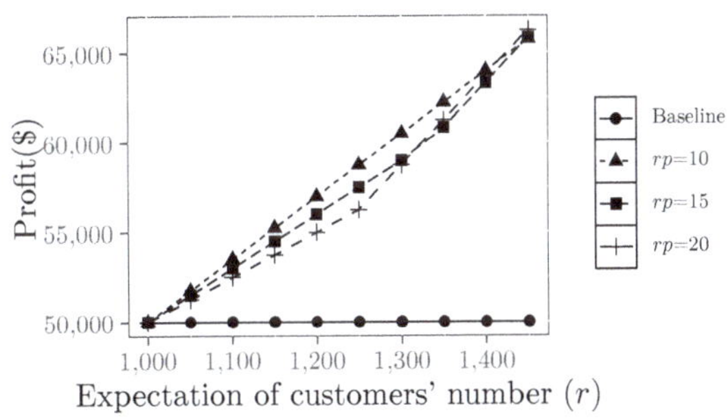

Figure 11. Profits comparison for merchants in r and $rp\%$.

5.2.4. Test Case 4: Result

Figure 12 considers the alliance's profit and shows the expected profits for the alliance and membership merchants. The membership merchant's profit here is below the baseline of 50,000, and the alliance's baseline profit is 0. We can conclude that membership merchants and the alliance can all obtain more profits than the baseline in expected situations. The higher the membership merchant's level is, the more profit the membership merchant and the alliance can obtain.

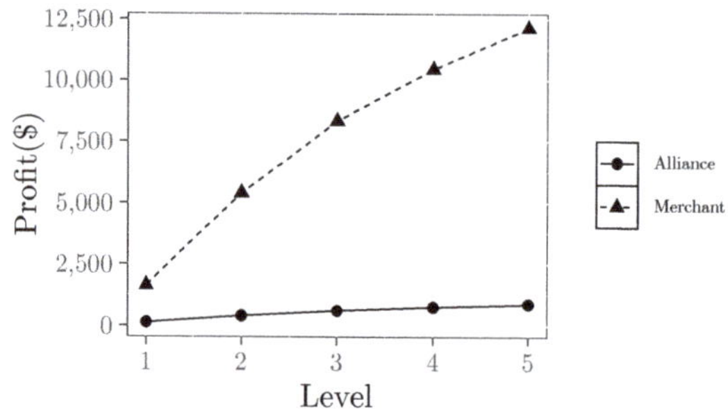

Figure 12. Expected profits for alliance and merchants.

5.2.5. Test Case 5: Result

Figure 13 shows the expected profit of merchants in each level (we set the baseline as Level 0) and expected r. It shows that the profit of membership merchants can be improved from 51,612.5 to 66,000. It is 3.2% to 32% more than merchants who are not in the alliance. In our case, all membership merchants can earn more profit. Therefore, the novel paradigm is more profitable than the baseline.

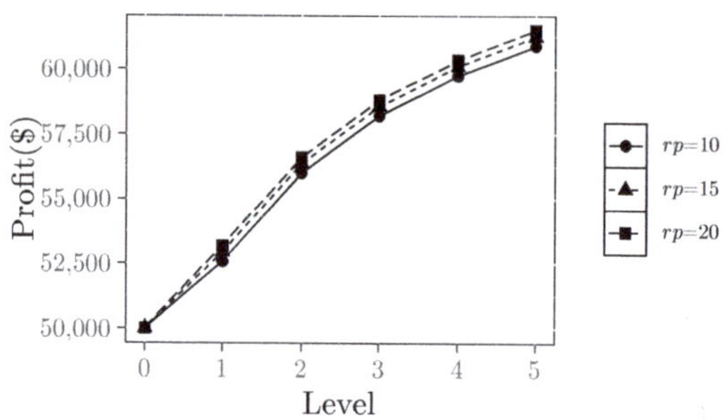

Figure 13. Expected profits of merchants in levels and $rp\%$.

5.2.6. Test Case 6: Result

Figure 14 represents the value of σ when $rp\%$ is from 10% to 20% and $d\%$ is 2.5%, 5% and 10%. It shows that when $d\%$ is too tiny($d\% = 2.5\%$), σ is very small even negative, which means that the discount of the voucher is too small and membership merchants do not use enough vouchers and even do not need vouchers to obtain the baseline profit. Therefore, we conclude that when σ is too small, and the incentive mechanism is useless. Moreover, σ is very large when $d\%$ is too large($d\% = 10\%$). It means that the discount of the voucher is so big that membership merchants need many vouchers to reach the baseline, and the fluctuation in the number of customers is large as well. However, we have analyzed that σ is less than 287.5 in Section 5.2.2. When $d\% = 10\%$ and $rp\% = 20\%$, σ is still more than 287.5. Therefore, the situation of $d\% = 5\%$ is more suitable than $d\% = 2.5\%$ and $d\% = 10\%$. A suitable $d\%$ is needed in DIV.

5.2.7. Test Case 7: Result

In the second simulation. We calculate the expected profit of each merchant and the alliance of four scenarios in different levels. Based on the first simulation, we set $d\% = 5\%$, $rp\% = 10\%$, and the value of r is the expectation of different levels.

Figure 15 shows the alliance's profit from one merchant in four scenarios. As mentioned, there is no alliance in the MV scenario and no incentive scenario. Therefore, their alliance's profit is zero. The alliance's profit in the AQE scenario is negative. It decreases as the level increases, because the token profits of merchants in the AQE scenario is from the alliance. Therefore, the AQE scenario is not profitable for the alliance. It is not suitable in the business market either. The profit in the dual incentive scenario is positive. It increases as the level increases. Therefore, only the dual incentive scenario can make profits for the alliance. The dual incentive paradigm is friendly relative to large alliances and governments in the business market.

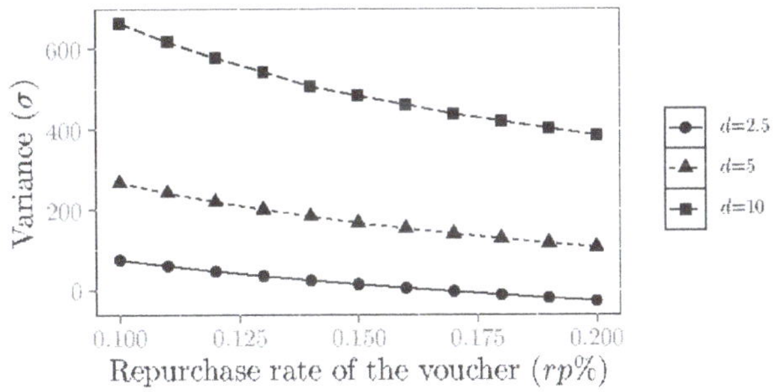

Figure 14. The value of σ in different $rp\%$ and $d\%$.

Figure 16 shows the merchant's profit comparison of four scenarios in five levels. We can conclude that the profit of the AQE, MV and dual incentive scenario can increase as the level increases. Moreover, the profit of the dual incentive scenario is the highest in each level. The result is in line with our expectations.

To sum up, DIV is more profitable than the baseline and all existing blockchain token economy paradigms. DIV is the most suitable paradigm in business blockchain token economy scenario at present.

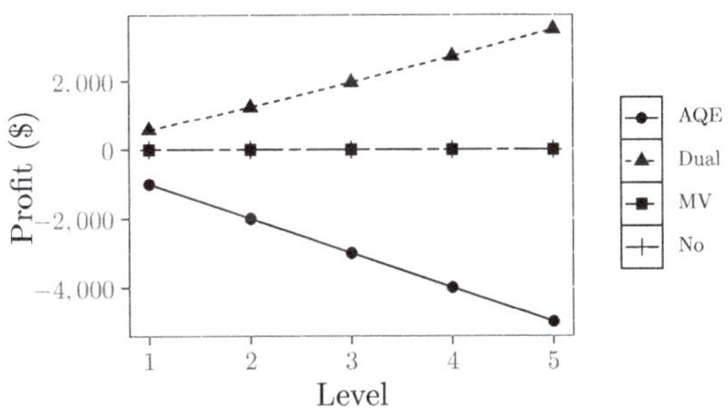

Figure 15. Alliance's profit comparison of four scenarios.

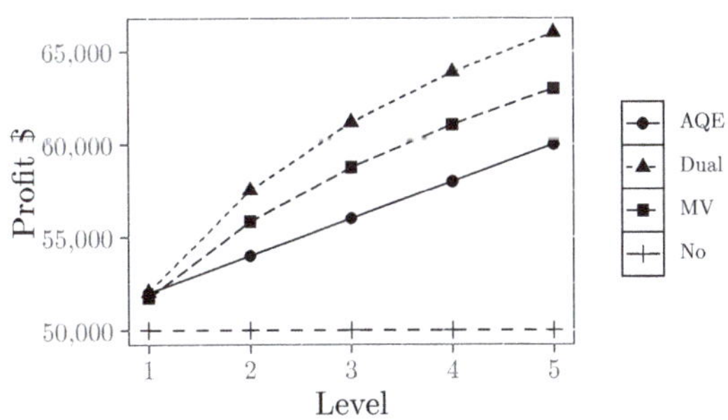

Figure 16. Merchant's profit comparison of four scenarios.

5.3. Discussion and Suggestions

Based on the experiments, we can conclude that the DIV paradigm can be more profitable than other paradigms in the Env-profit case. In our analysis, the alliance and the customers are the two essential roles in the DIV paradigm. The alliance offers the second incentive mechanism to the merchants. The merchants receive the second incentive mechanism and offer more tokens to customers. Therefore, the customers can obtain more tokens and consume more and increase market profitability. There are two reasons why existing paradigms are less profitable than the DIV paradigm: (1) The business schema-based paradigms and the incentive-based incentive lack the role of alliance, which lack the second incentive mechanism. (2) The new scenario-based paradigm lacks business applications, which lacks dual incentive mechanisms in the business scenario. Overall, the DIV paradigm is the most profitable paradigm in our case. It implements the exchange between the currency and the token by suitable incentive mechanisms in the business scenarios. Moreover, it increases the liquidity and the value of the token.

Currently, people's enthusiasm on ICOs increased, but the value of ICOs is being criticized. We suggest that the ICO market can be applied the DIV in future. DIV can provide a complete set of ICO acquisition, ICO repurchase and the ICO transaction process. Therefore the value of the ICO is guaranteed and supervised by the DIV paradigm. The authority, liquidity and credibility of the ICO are also guaranteed. Moreover, we set up a business alliance in the Env-profit, and the business alliance can hold different merchants. We suggest that a blockchain token league can be founded in the real blockchain economy. Different tokens and ICOs can be traded and exchanged as currencies in the league. Moreover, the league can design novel cross-chain tokens and implement the cross-chain transactions of the tokens. However, the transformation rules of different ICOs and tokens and the suitable incentive mechanism to obtain different ICOs and tokens should be well designed.

6. Conclusions

The blockchain token economy has played an essential role in the business market. It increases the economy's security and strengthens the marketization of resource allocation. The incentive-based paradigm, the new scenario-based and the business schema-based paradigm are existing blockchain token economy paradigms. They lack the incentive mechanism, the business application and the token's liquidity. They can maximize the consumers' willingness to consume, but they can also decrease the profitability of the entire business market. In this paper, we propose a "Dual incentive value-based" paradigm (DIV), including roles, token design, incentive mechanism design and execution flow. Then, we propose a business study case called "Env-profit" based on the DIV paradigm. We propose a hierarchical alliance structure model and a new "newsvendor problem" profit model in Env-profit and set up two simulations to prove the profitability of DIV. The results show that the alliance of the DIV paradigm can make all the members be more profitable than those not in the alliance, and the DIV paradigm can be more profitable than other three existing paradigms. Based on the results, we analyze that the alliance provides the second incentive mechanism in order to stimulate customers to consume and profitability increases. Existing paradigms all lack the role of alliance so that profitability is less than the DIV paradigm without the second incentive mechanism. Overall, the DIV paradigm set the incentive mechanism to obtain tokens. The tokens can be liquidated, used and traded as real currencies. It increases the value of the token and market profitability. Moreover, the DIV paradigm will be widely used in the business blockchain, which can offers new research directions for researchers. For example, the ICO market can be applied the DIV, and a blockchain token league containing different tokens and ICOs can be founded in the real blockchain economy.

In addition to profitability, risk assessment is also an essential part of economic theory. In this paper, we focus on dual incentive mechanism research and do not consider the risk control mechanisms. In the future, if there are risks in the DIV environment, the methods for strengthening the risk avoidance ability of the DIV paradigm will be our novel research priorities. We believe that the DIV paradigm can be the leader in blockchain token economy study, and the blockchain token economy will be the mainstream in the token economy.

Author Contributions: Conceptualization, C.G., P.Z., B.L. and J.S.; data curation, C.G. and P.Z.; formal analysis, C.G., P.Z., B.L. and J.S.; investigation, B.L.; methodology, C.G., P.Z. and J.S.; project administration, C.G.; resources, C.G. and B.L.; validation, P.Z.; visualization, C.G., P.Z. and B.L.; writing—original draft, C.G. and P.Z.; writing—review and editing, C.G. and J.S. All authors have read and agreed to the published version of the manuscript.

Funding: This research was funded by the Natural Science Foundation of Liaoning Province (2020-BS-054), the Fundamental Research Funds for the Central Universities (N2017005) and the National Natural Science Foundation of China (62162050).

Institutional Review Board Statement: Not applicable.

Informed Consent Statement: Not applicable.

Data Availability Statement: Data are contained within the article.

Conflicts of Interest: The authors declare no conflict of interest.

Abbreviations

The following abbreviations are used in this manuscript:

DIV	Dual Incentive Value-based paradigm;
Env-profit	a business blockchain alliance case for improving the environment and profitability;
AQE	Air Quality Evaluation incentive scenario;
MV	Merchants' Voucher incentive scenario.

References

1. Letychevsky, O.; Peschanenko, V.; Radchenko, V.; Poltoratzkyi, M.; Kovalenko, P.; Mogylko, S. Formal Verification of Token Economy Models. In Proceedings of the 2019 IEEE International Conference on Blockchain and Cryptocurrency (ICBC), Seoul, Korea, 14–17 May 2019; pp. 201–204. [CrossRef]
2. Wittek, K.; Lazzati, L.; Bothe, D.; Sinnaeve, A.J.; Pohlmann, N. An SSI Based System for Incentivized and SelfDetermined Customer-to-Business Data Sharing in a Local Economy Context. In Proceedings of the 2020 IEEE European Technology and Engineering Management Summit (E-TEMS), Dortmund, Germany, 5–7 March 2020; pp. 1–5. [CrossRef]
3. Jorgenson, D.W. Production and welfare: Progress in economic measurement. *J. Econ. Lit.* **2018**, *56*, 867–919. [CrossRef]
4. Aziz, N.A.A.; Yasin, M.H.M. Token Economy to Improve Concentration among Students with Learning Disabilities in Primary School. *J. ICSAR* **2018**, *2*, 32–36. [CrossRef]
5. Song, J.; Zhang, P.; Alkubati, M.; Bao, Y.; Yu, G. Research advances on blockchain-as-a-service: Architectures, applications and challenges. *Digit. Commun. Netw.* **2021**. [CrossRef]
6. Zhang, P.; Song, J. Research Advance on Efficiency Optimization of Blockchain Consensus Algorithms. *Comput. Sci.* **2020**, *47*, 296–303.
7. Nanayakkara, S.; Rodrigo, M.; Perera, S.; Weerasuriya, G.; Hijazi, A.A. A methodology for selection of a Blockchain platform to develop an enterprise system. *J. Ind. Inf. Integr.* **2021**, *23*, 100215. [CrossRef]
8. Khan, A.A.; Shaikh, Z.A.; Baitenova, L.; Mutaliyeva, L.; Moiseev, N.; Mikhaylov, A.; Laghari, A.A.; Idris, S.A.; Alshazly, H. QoS-Ledger: Smart Contracts and Metaheuristic for Secure Quality-of-Service and Cost-Efficient Scheduling of Medical-Data Processing. *Electronicsweek* **2021**, *10*, 3083. [CrossRef]
9. Ayub Khan, A.; Laghari, A.A.; Shaikh, A.A.; Bourouis, S.; Mamlouk, A.M.; Alshazly, H. Educational Blockchain: A Secure Degree Attestation and Verification Traceability Architecture for Higher Education Commission. *Appl. Sci.* **2021**, *11*, 10917. [CrossRef]
10. Cao, B.; Xia, S.; Li, Y.; Li, B. An incentive-based workload assignment with power allocation in ad hoc cloud. In Proceedings of the 2017 IEEE International Conference on Communications (ICC), Paris, France, 21–25 May 2017; pp. 1–6. [CrossRef]
11. Xia, S.; Yao, Z.; Li, Y.; Mao, S. Online Distributed Offloading and Computing Resource Management with Energy Harvesting for Heterogeneous MEC-Enabled IoT. *IEEE Trans. Wirel. Commun.* **2021**, *20*, 6743–6757. [CrossRef]
12. Kim, H.M.; Laskowski, M.; Zargham, M.; Turesson, H.; Barlin, M.; Kabanov, D. Token Economics in Real Life: Cryptocurrency and Incentives Design for Insolar's Blockchain Network. *Computer* **2021**, *54*, 70–80. [CrossRef]
13. Lee, J.Y. A decentralized token economy: How blockchain and cryptocurrency can revolutionize business. *Bus. Horizons* **2019**, *62*, 773–784. [CrossRef]
14. Ivy, J.W.; Meindl, J.N.; Overley, E.; Robson, K.M. Token Economy: A Systematic Review of Procedural Descriptions. *Behav. Modif.* **2017**, *41*, 708–737. [CrossRef]

15. Dalphonse, A. Token Economy: Examples and Applications in ABA. 2021. Available online: https://masteraba.com/token-economy-2/ (accessed on 25 December 2021).
16. Barreiro-Gomez, J.; Tembine, H. Blockchain Token Economics: A Mean-Field-Type Game Perspective. *IEEE Access* **2019**, *7*, 64603–64613. [CrossRef]
17. Drasch, B.J.; Fridgen, G.; Manner-Romberg, T.; Nolting, F.M.; Radszuwill, S. The token's secret: The two-faced financial incentive of the token economy. *Electron. Mark.* **2020**, *30*, 557–567. [CrossRef]
18. Narayan, R.; Tidström, A. Tokenizing coopetition in a blockchain for a transition to circular economy. *J. Clean. Prod.* **2020**, *263*, 1–9. [CrossRef]
19. Kim, M.; Chung, J. Sustainable Growth and Token Economy Design: The Case of Steemit. *Sustainability* **2018**, *11*, 167. [CrossRef]
20. Fisch, C.; Masiak, C.; Vismara, S.; Block, J. Motives and profiles of ICO investors. *J. Bus. Res.* **2021**, *125*, 564–576. [CrossRef]
21. Tönnissen, S.; Beinke, J.H.; Teuteberg, F. Understanding token-based ecosystems—A taxonomy of blockchain-based business models of start-ups. *Electron. Mark.* **2020**, *30*, 307–323. [CrossRef]
22. Zhao, H.; Cui, W.; Li, S.; Xu, R. Token Economy: A New Form Economy with Decentralized Mutual Trust and Collective Governance. In Proceedings of the IEEE International Symposium on Autonomous Decentralized System, Utrecht, The Netherlands, 8–10 April 2019; pp. 1–7. [CrossRef]
23. FINMA. *FINMA Publishes ICO Guidelines*; FINMA: Bern, Switzerland, 2018. Available online: https://www.finma.ch/en/news/2018/02/20180216-mm-ico-wegleitung (accessed on 25 December 2021).
24. Jung, S.Y.; Kim, T.; Hwang, H.J.; Hong, K. Mechanism Design of Health Care Blockchain System Token Economy: Development Study Based on Simulated Real-World Scenarios. *J. Med. Internet Res.* **2021**, *23*, e26802. [CrossRef]
25. Takemiya, M. Sora: A Decentralized Autonomous Economy. In Proceedings of the IEEE International Conference on Blockchain and Cryptocurrency, Seoul, Korea, 14–17 May 2019; pp. 95–98. [CrossRef]
26. Galvagno, M.; Dalli, D. Theory of value co-creation. A systematic literature review. *Manag. Serv. Qual.* **2014**, *24*, 643–683. [CrossRef]
27. Krenz, P.; Basmer-Birkenfeld, S.V.; Buxbaum-Conradi, S.; Redlich, T.; Wulfsberg, J. Facing the conflict of transparency and non-disclosure of knowledge within value creation networks. In Proceedings of the 2015 Second International Conference on eDemocracy & eGovernment (ICEDEG), Quito, Ecuador, 8–10 April 2015; pp. 26–33. [CrossRef]
28. Tyagi, S.; Chambers, T.; Yang, K. Enhanced fuzzy-analytic hierarchy process. *Soft Comput.* **2018**, *22*, 4431–4443. [CrossRef]
29. Agarwal, S.; Qian, W. Consumption and Debt Response to Unanticipated Income Shocks: Evidence from a Natural Experiment in Singapore. *SSRN Electron. J.* **2014**, *104*, 4205–4230. [CrossRef]
30. Wikepedia. Marginal Propensity to Consume. 2022. Available online: https://en.wikipedia.org/wiki/Marginal_propensity_to_consume (accessed on 25 December 2021).
31. DeYong, G.D. The price-setting newsvendor: Review and extensions. *Int. J. Prod. Res.* **2020**, *58*, 1776–1804. [CrossRef]

mathematics

Article

Is There an Asymmetric Relationship between Economic Policy Uncertainty, Cryptocurrencies, and Global Green Bonds? Evidence from the United States of America

Aamir Aijaz Syed [1], Farhan Ahmed [2], Muhammad Abdul Kamal [3], Assad Ullah [4] and Jose Pedro Ramos-Requena [5,*]

1 Institute of Management, Commerce and Economics, Shri Ramswaroop Memorial University, Lucknow 226016, India; aamirank@gmail.com
2 Department of Economics and Management Sciences, NED University of Engineering & Technology, Karachi 75270, Pakistan; fahmed@neduet.edu.pk
3 Department of Economics, Abdul Wali Khan University, Mardan 23200, Pakistan; kamal@awkum.edu.pk
4 Department of Economics, Henan University, Kaifeng 475001, China; assad@henu.edu.cn
5 Department of Economics and Business, University of Almeria, 04120 Almería, Spain
* Correspondence: jpramosre@ual.es

Abstract: The environmental degradation and the concern for sustainable development have garnered extensive attention from researchers to evaluate the prospects of green bonds over other traditional assets. Against this backdrop, the current study measures the asymmetric relationship between green bonds, U.S. economic policy uncertainty (EPU), and bitcoins by employing the Nonlinear Autoregressive Distribution Lag (NARDL) estimation technique recently developed by Shin et al. The outcome of the empirical analysis confirms an asymmetric cointegration between EPU, bitcoins, the clean energy index, oil prices, and green bonds. The NARDL estimation substantiates that positive shock in EPU exerts a negative impact on green bonds, whereas a negative shock in EPU increases the performance of green bonds. It implies, in the long run, a 1 percent increase (decrease) in EPU decreases (increases) the performance of green bonds by 0.22 percent and 0.11 percent, respectively. Likewise, the study also confirms a bidirectional relationship between bitcoins and green bonds. A positive shock in bitcoin increases the performance of green bonds and vice versa. In addition, our study also reveals a direct co-movement between clean energy, oil prices, and green bonds. This outcome implies that green bonds are not a different asset class, and they mirror the performance of other asset classes, such as clean energy, oil prices, and bitcoins. The findings offer several implications to understand the hedging and diversification properties of bitcoins, and assist in understanding the role of U.S. economic policy uncertainty on green bonds.

Keywords: green bonds; environmental sustainability; asymmetric analysis; EPU; clean energy

Citation: Syed, A.A.; Ahmed, F.; Kamal, M.A.; Ullah, A.; Ramos-Requena, J.P. Is There an Asymmetric Relationship between Economic Policy Uncertainty, Cryptocurrencies, and Global Green Bonds? Evidence from the United States of America. *Mathematics* **2022**, *10*, 720. https://doi.org/10.3390/math10050720

Academic Editors: José Luis Miralles-Quirós and Anatoliy Swishchuk

Received: 20 January 2022
Accepted: 23 February 2022
Published: 24 February 2022

1. Introduction

The rapid environmental degradation and climate change over the past several years have garnered the attention of policymakers to take suitable actions to lower the emission of harmful gases, and evade devastating consequences on human life and the ecosystem. The innovation in cleaner sources of energy is considered a revolutionary move toward decarbonization and environmental sustainability. Previous studies highlighted that massive investment is needed to convert from a high carbon economy to a low carbon economy [1]. For instance, according to the United Nations' Intergovernmental Panel on climate change, $3 trillion investments are required every year until 2050 to limit the temperature increase by two centigrade [2]. In context to the above investment concern, Baker et al., 2018, advocated that green bonds could play a prominent role in channelizing funds toward such environmentally friendly projects. Green bonds are similar to fixed income securities, but the only difference is that the proceeds of green bonds are employed to fund sustainable projects. In 2007, the first green bond was issued; in the initial years, the price of green bonds recorded a slow growth, but later on, due to the Paris Agreement and the Sustainable Development Goals, green bond prices witnessed exponential growth. It is estimated by the Climate Bonds initiative that the value of the green bond market will reach $ I trillion by 2023 [3].

Furthermore, since the global financial crisis in 2008, economic uncertainty prompted investors to search for alternative investments tools to diversify risk, and provide hedging facilities. Due to the above benefits globally, the green bond has also emerged as a potential risk-diversifying and hedging investment option for investors. Green bonds are becoming more popular among investors than other conventional assets, since they address the issue of financial resources and environmental sustainability [4]. As the green bond complements government plans for environmental sustainability, they are considered a more stable investment tool. In addition, the formation of Green Bond Principles (GBP) by the International Capital Markets Association in 2014 also instilled confidence to invest in green bonds among the investors. Thus, due to the benefit of diversification, and the growing interest in environmental projects, green bonds are an ideal investment avenue among investors [5]. Similar to green bonds, cryptocurrencies have also emerged as an alternative investment option. Cryptocurrencies are an ideal choice for risky investors, given the likelihood of high profits in a short period of time, and a shift away from conventional assets. Cryptocurrencies are binary data used for digital exchange. Since 2009, cryptocurrencies have captured a sizeable market share. According to the world bank, the market share of cryptocurrencies has reached US$364.5 billion in 2020. Previous studies show that since the last decade, cryptocurrencies (bitcoins) have witnessed exponential growth. The value of one bitcoin has increased from $1 in 2009 to around $60,000 in 2021 [6]. Despite high volatility and return, the future of cryptocurrencies is still unclear. A strand of literature described cryptocurrencies more as a speculative tool, bubble event, or a technologically driven product rather than a medium of exchange [7,8]. In the recent past, a vast body of literature advocated that cryptocurrencies have a spillover effect on the conventional stock market performance. A few studies reported a positive relationship between cryptocurrencies and stock market performance, whereas others concluded a negative relationship between the two variables [9,10]. In addition, there is another strand of literature that highlights cryptocurrencies and the stock market are unrelated [11]. Based on these interrelation and transmission effects of investment products, the current study attempts to explore the probable relationship between cryptocurrencies, preferable bitcoins, and green bond markets. The above variables are incorporated, since they are new financial investment products that provide diversification and hedging benefits. Besides, both of them have also captured a sizable market share in a quick span of time. Past literature reveals that there are sufficient studies on the relationship between the conventional financial market and green bonds [12,13]. However, there are limited studies that have examined the above relationship. In addition, the studies have only explored the symmetric impact of cryptocurrencies on green bond markets [14,15]. The literature, on the other hand, suggests that the relationship between explanatory and outcome variables can be both symmetric and asymmetric [16]. Thus, against this backdrop, we have explored the asymmetric impact of bitcoins on the green bond market.

In addition to the above analysis, we have also explored the impact of the U.S. economic policy uncertainty (EPU) on the green bond. EPU is an independent risk associated with the interaction of the financial system, fiscal policy, monetary policy, and other regulatory policies. Previous studies have highlighted that it is easier to diversify security-specific risk, but it is difficult to avoid systematic risk such as EPU. Global financial integration and several financial crises over the years, such as the global financial crisis and the eurozone crisis, had a transmission effect on the economic policy uncertainty. These economic disturbances have a magnified impact on the functioning of varied industries; the finance and investment industries are no exception. During the recent pandemic, we have again witnessed similar economic uncertainty. As previously stated, green bonds are considered stable investment options due to their environmental goals and government support. Therefore, it is worth investigating whether high and low EPU has a symmetric and asymmetric impact on the performance of green bonds in the U.S., or if green bonds are immune to the EPU. The clean energy index and oil prices, which are relevant to the study, are also included for empirical analysis. The clean energy index is included because the production of clean energy complements sustainable goals. Therefore, improvement in the clean energy stock can also enhance the performance of the green bond and vice versa. Furthermore, we have included oil prices in our empirical analysis to re-establish the theoretical assumption that an increase in oil prices surges the purchase of green bonds. An increase in oil prices necessitates the diversification of energy sources, especially for oil-importing economies. Likewise, a decrease in oil prices might have a decreasing influence on the issuance of green bonds, as there is less pressure to encourage renewable energy resources [17].

The current study contributes to the extant literature in the following ways. Initially, this is the first study that explores the asymmetric long-run and short-run relationship between EPU, bitcoins, and green bonds. There are a few studies that have explored the above relationship; however, the previous studies have only explored the one side movement of time-series analysis, but the present study examines how the negative and positive shocks of explanatory variables (bitcoins and U.S. EPU) influence the outcome variables (green bonds), thus adding to the literature void. The question we try to address is whether uncertainty in the U.S. EPU helps to explain risk spillover on green bonds, and likewise, whether bitcoin volatility drives the movement of green bonds, and if the clean energy index or oil prices have any association with green bond volatility. Analyzing the empirical interrelationship between the green bond and other investment options over a different period is important for the various economic agents. From the viewpoint of investors, it is also worthwhile to know the suitability of green bonds as a hedging or diversifying instrument over other asset classes. Besides, the study also explores whether green bonds are resilient to financial market shocks and economic volatility due to their involvement in the sustainable financial system that increases the effectiveness of governments' climate policies. Second, in the present study, we have also explored the consequences of structural breaks on the robustness of the results by employing a Brock, Dechert, and Scheinkman (BDS) test. Thus, identifying structural breaks induced by financial crisis and pandemics will also add to the methodological novelty of the study. Third, the sample country also adds to the existing literature. We have included the United States in our empirical analysis because it is one of the fastest developed economies in the world. Due to the tag of a developed country, the U.S. economy act as the growth engine of the world economy. The United States has a trading or economic tie with every country across the globe. Therefore, any disturbance in its economic policies has a transmitting effect on the world economy, which we have already witnessed during the global financial recession. Another justification for including the U.S. in our empirical analysis originates from the fact that the United States accounts for the highest value of the investment in the green bond market globally, amounting to 36.7 billion dollars. Therefore, empirically analyzing how these explanatory variables influence the U.S. green bond market will give significant policy-oriented recommendations for emerging and developing economies. In addition, due to the negative consequences of COVID-19, the US GDP shrank by 1.22 percent in the first quarter of 2020. As a corollary, examining how economic policy uncertainty in the United States affects green bond markets will considerably contribute to the existing literature on the relationship between EPU and sustainable indices. Finally, we included energy stocks, such as the clean energy index and oil prices, in our empirical analysis to assess the relationship between green bond performance, oil price volatility, and the clean energy index.

The rest of the paper proceeds as follows. Section 2 discusses the previous literature, Section 3 highlights the data and methodology, Section 4 reports empirical findings, and the last section focus on the concluding remarks.

2. Literature Review

Over the years, the environmental crisis, and the need for generating investment for sustainable development, have attracted the interest of investors toward green bonds. Since the world bank issue in 2008, the green bond market has grown significantly, from $11 billion in 2013 to $167 billion in 2018 [18]. Regardless of the rapid growth in the green bond market, only a few studies have estimated the transmission effect of other modern financial assets on green bonds [19]. A few recent studies projected that the interdependency between green bonds and other financial and energy stocks might vary due to the heterogeneity of the magnitude of investors who interact in these indices [1]. Investors deal in different time frames, ranging from a day to several years, because of their varied needs, risk appetite, preferences, information asymmetry, and monetary constraints. Such diverse alternatives and information asymmetry lead to abrupt responses to the market news, and economic uncertainty. In this reference, Berger and Czudaj [20] advocated that negative news and economic environments compel short-term investors to sell, and creates an opportunity to buy for long-term investors. Likewise, Park et al. [21], while exploring green bonds' asymmetric volatility, revealed that green bonds have a unique character whose volatility is sensitive to positive shocks, unlike other financial assets. Importantly, they also affirmed that the green bond and financial markets have several spillover effects, and neither of them responds remarkably to markets' negative shock. Drawing inferences from these conceptual arguments, we can predict that economic and financial shocks can be transmitted asymmetrically across financial markets; the green bond market is not an exception. Thus, studying the short-run and long-run asymmetric connectedness between green bonds, cryptocurrencies (bitcoin), and economic policy uncertainty will assist in answering the unanswered questions, and contribute to the existing literature void. The subsequent section delves into the specifics of the existing literature on the above interrelationship between green bonds and other economic and financial agents.

Chiappini et al. [22] conducted one of the recent studies on the interaction of sustainable indexes with COVID-19 lockdown. The study intends to examine how the sustainable indexes react to market distress. They conclude that sustainable indexes in the US and Europe are susceptible to COVID-19-induced lockdown and uncertainty. However, the sustainable indexes are less volatile compared to the other traditional assets. Likewise, Huynh et al. [4] examined the role of artificial intelligence, green bonds, bitcoins, and robotics stocks on portfolio diversification during policy uncertainty. The authors report that the probability of joint losses is high during high economic uncertainty. In addition, the author also reveals that although the above classes of the asset are a good source of return, these assets are shock senders, and fluctuation and volatility are remarkably high in these assets. Considering the relationship between traditional assets and green bonds, Hung [19] empirically investigates the influence of commodity and energy indexes on the green bond market performance. Using the Quantile and Quantile method, the author reveals a positive interaction between the performance of the explanatory and the outcome variables. Likewise, Park et al. [21] explored the volatility dynamics and spillovers between green bonds and equity markets. The author advocated that similar to conventional assets, the green bond also shows asymmetric responses. The volatility of green bonds is more sensitive toward positive market shocks than negative market shocks.

Nguyen et al. [23] added to the existing literature by exploring the relationship between green bonds and other asset classes, such as stock, commodities, and conventional bonds. The authors concluded a strong correlation between the asset classes, which peaked during the global financial recession. The authors also highlighted the diversification properties of green bonds, due to their low correlation with conventional stock markets. Pham and Nguyen [24] also strengthen the above findings by highlighting the hedging properties of green bonds. They investigated the influence of oil volatility, EPU, and stock returns on green bonds, and concluded that the impact of policy uncertainty on the green bond is time-varying and state-dependent. Furthermore, the author also suggested that as EPU and green bonds are weakly related, green bonds can be used as a perfect hedging tool during such uncertainty. In another study on the interaction between green bonds and stock markets, Baulkaran [25] concluded that the issue of green bonds at a higher coupon rate exerts a negative response on the conventional stock market performances. In context to the influence of traditional and fixed-income markets on green bonds, Reboredo [13] advocated that the transmission influence of the fixed-income market is high on green bonds, and green bonds are less sensitive to energy and stock market fundamentals. Contrary to the above findings, Liu et al. [26], while examining the spillover relationship between green bonds and clean energy stock, commented that there is a positive tail dependence between clean energy stocks and green bonds. Hammoudeh et al. [27] and Jin et al. [28] also strengthen the above findings, and conclude a direct and significant association between carbon emission stocks and green bonds. Further, they also added that green bonds are the perfect substitute for carbon futures, and they perform well even during crisis periods. Other studies which reported similar findings are Zerbib [29] and Nguyen et al. [23].

We can infer that, considering the importance of green bonds, there are still limited studies conducted on this topic. Few empirical studies have examined the relationship of green bonds with conventional stocks markets (for example, Pham et al. [30], Broadstock et al. [31], Reboredo et al. [32]). Another strand of literature has examined the interaction of green bonds with commodities, cryptocurrencies, and the traditional bond market (for example, Naeem et al. [33], Bouri et al. [34]). In addition, a more recent strand of literature has also highlighted the hedging and diversification properties of green bonds over other conventional assets (for instance, Guo and Zhau [35], Arif et al. [36]). In the previous literature, although the behavior of green bonds relative to other financial assets has been analyzed from multiple angles, there is a literature void in context to the asymmetric relationship between the green bond market, economic policy uncertainty, and other innovative financial assets such as bitcoins. Against this backdrop, the current study examines the asymmetric influence of the U.S. EPU, and bitcoins, in addition to measuring the impact of the clean energy index and oil prices on the Standard and Poor (S&P) green bonds.

3. Data Description and Empirical Model

We have included the following proxies to empirically investigate the influence of economic policy uncertainty, cryptocurrencies, clean energy, and oil prices on green bonds. We have taken the green bond select index released by S&P to measure green bonds. It is a composite index representing the relevant green bond stocks. We have used the S&P global clean energy index for measuring clean energy. We have taken the daily oil prices to measure the influence of oil price volatilities on green bonds. In addition, to estimate the impact of cryptocurrencies on green bonds, we have used the daily prices of bitcoin. We have included only bitcoin because it represents the highest proportion of the global cryptocurrency market. Finally, to estimate the influence of policy uncertainty on the green bond market, U.S. daily economic policy uncertainty data is extracted. To understand the time-varying properties of the explanatory and outcome variables, and to consider the lack of data availability, we have included the daily time-series data from December 2016 to October 2021. Moreover, we have considered the following sources for data extraction: policyuncertainty.com, datastream.com, as well as the S&P green index website, and the S&P global clean energy index.

In the present paper, to estimate the asymmetric relationship between the explanatory and outcome variables, we have employed the recently developed Nonlinear Autoregressive Distribution Lag (NARDL) estimation technique proposed by Shin et al. [37]. We have used the above estimation technique because this technique provides a robust estimate in the presence of nonlinearity and structural breaks. Previous studies highlight that economic and financial distress augments structural breaks in time series data. Therefore, to avoid the complexity of structural breaks, and to provide a robust estimate, the NARDL estimation technique is employed. Furthermore, we have also used the NARDL estimation technique due to the following benefits: first, this technique is suitable for small sample data. Second, it is also appropriate for the mixed level of integration. In addition, this technique also confirms cointegration and hidden asymmetries. Considering the above benefits, the ARDL symmetric takes the following form:

$$\Delta GB_t = \varnothing_{EPU} EPU_{t-1} + \varnothing_{BIT} BIT_{t-1} + \varnothing_{CII} CII_{t-1} + \varnothing_{OIL} OIL_{t-1} + \sum_{j=1}^{r} \varphi_{GB} \Delta GB_{t-j} + \sum_{j=1}^{s} \varphi_{EPU} \Delta EPU_{t-j} + \sum_{j=1}^{s} \varphi_{BIT} \Delta BIT_{t-j} + \sum_{j=1}^{s} \varphi_{CII} \Delta CII_{t-j} + \sum_{j=1}^{s} \varphi_{OIL} \Delta OIL_{t-j} + \mu_t \quad (1)$$

In Equation (1), GB represents green bonds, EPU denotes economic policy uncertainty, CII represents the clean energy index, BIT shows daily bitcoin prices, OIL denotes daily oil prices, μ_t is the error term, r and s are the lead and lag order based on SIC criteria, and Δ is the first-order difference. Furthermore, based on Shin et al. [37], Equation (1) is reframed after including the short and long run asymmetries:

$$\Delta GB_t = \phi_0 + \omega_1 GB_{t-1} + \phi_2^+ EPU_{t-1}^+ + \phi_3^- EPU_{t-1}^- + \phi_4^+ BIT_{t-1}^+ + \phi_5^- BIT_{t-1}^- + \phi_6 CII_{t-1} + \phi_7 OIL_{t-1} + \sum_{j=1}^{r} \varphi_{1j} \Delta GB_{t-j} + \sum_{j=1}^{s} \varphi_{2j}^+ \Delta EPU_{t-j}^+ + \sum_{j=0}^{s} \varphi_{3j}^- \Delta EPU_{t-j}^- + \sum_{j=0}^{s} \varphi_{4j}^+ \Delta BIT_{t-j}^+ + \sum_{j=0}^{s} \varphi_{5j}^- \Delta BIT_{t-j}^- + \sum_{j=0}^{s} \varphi_{6j} \Delta CII_{t-j} + \sum_{j=0}^{s} \varphi_{7j} \Delta OIL_{t-j} + \mu_t \quad (2)$$

where ϕ and φ represent the short-long-run coefficients; EPU_{t-1}^+, EPU_{t-1}^-, BIT_{t-1}^+, BIT_{t-1}^- denote positive and negative shocks in economic policy uncertainty and bitcoins, respectively. Under NARDL estimation, short-run parameters measure the response of the outcome variable to the independent variables, whereas long-run parameters quantify the speed of adjustments. The positive and negative variation in the economic policy uncertainty and bitcoins can be further derived as follows:

$$EPU_t^+ = \sum_j^t \Delta EPU_j^+ = \sum_{j=1}^t \max(\Delta EPU_j, 0) \quad (3)$$

$$EPU_t^- = \sum_{j=1}^t \Delta EPU_j^- = \sum_{j=1}^t \min(\Delta EPU_j, 0) \quad (4)$$

$$BIT_t^+ = \sum_{j=1}^t \Delta BIT_j^+ = \sum_{j=1}^t \max(\Delta BIT_j, 0) \quad (5)$$

$$BIT_t^- = \sum_{j=1}^t \Delta BIT_j^- = \sum_{j=1}^t \min(\Delta BIT_j, 0) \quad (6)$$

In addition, the long-run positive and negative coefficient of economic policy uncertainty and bitcoins are further ascertained as: $\phi_{EPU}^+ = -\phi_2^+/\omega_1$, $\phi_{EPU}^- = -\phi_3^-/\omega_1$ and $\phi_{BIT}^+ = -\phi_4^+/\omega_1$, $\phi_{BIT}^- = -\phi_5^-/\omega_1$ respectively. Likewise, the short-run positive and negative shocks are estimated as follows: $\sum_{i=1}^j \varphi_{2j}^+$, $\sum_{i=1}^j \varphi_{3j}^+$ and $\sum_{i=1}^j \varphi_{4j}^+$, $\sum_{i=1}^j \varphi_{5j}^+$.

Previous studies highlight that it is mandatory to confirm the presence of unit root before applying the linear or nonlinear ARDL model. Furthermore, the linear and nonlinear model also mandate that none of the variables be of the second order of integration. Therefore, to confirm the presence of unit root, we have employed the Augmented Dicky–Fuller (ADF) unit root test. Most of the earlier studies suggest that a conventional unit root test does not provide robust estimates in the presence of structural breaks [38]. To provide an unbiased estimate in the presence of structural breaks, we have used the Zivot and Andrews unit root test. The presence of a structural break in the data also entails the use of a structural break test, and, therefore, we have also included the BDS (Broock, Scheinkman, Dechert, and LeBaron [39]) structural break test in our empirical analysis. The BDS test permits us to confirm the presence of nonlinearity in the series. After implementing all of the above tests, we proceed with the NARDL estimation. We have used the bound test approach to figure out the asymmetric cointegration among the variables, and for optimum lag selection, we have used SIC criteria. We have referred to the F-statistic, and compared its lower and upper bound values to estimate the presence of cointegration. If the F-statistic value is more than the upper and lower bound value, we can infer an asymmetric cointegration among the variables. Finally, the Wald test is employed to confirm the asymmetric relationship between EPU, bitcoin, and green bonds.

4. Result and Discussion

Table 1 exhibits the stochastic properties of all of the explanatory and outcome variables. The descriptive statistic shows that most of the variables are negatively skewed. We can observe that the standard deviation of the green bond (0.06%) is less than the standard deviation of the rest of the variables, for instance, bitcoin (1.85%). Thus, we can infer that green bonds are less risky compared to other variables. In addition, based on the probability value of the Jarque–Bera test, we can reject the claim of normality, and conclude that the data are not normal. The claim of non-normality further encourages to proceed with the asymmetric estimation [40].

Table 1. Descriptive Statistics.

Measures	EPU	GB	OIL	CII	BIT
Mean	4.2379	4.1474	3.9900	6.0567	9.0180
Median	4.5744	4.9354	4.0244	6.4686	9.1419
Minimum	1.3987	4.8159	2.1871	6.2101	8.0857
Maximum	6.7582	5.0688	4.4501	7.6511	11.120
Skewness	0.4262	−0.1748	−1.9700	0.9294	−0.6327
Kurtosis	4.7451	7.1587	9.9080	6.3282	2.1426
Jarque–Bera	196.62 ***	43.262 ***	327.70 ***	203.64 ***	121.79 ***
Std. Dev	0.9651	0.0632	1.7261	0.0824	1.8575

Note: *** represents the rejection of the null hypothesis at a 1 percent level of significance.

After discussing the stochastic properties of the variables, we proceed with the unit root estimation. Confirming the level of integration is a pre-condition for the NARDL analysis, and hence, we have used the Augmented Dicky–Fuller (ADF) unit root test. The resulting outcome attached in Table 2 reveals that green bond and clean energy are stationary at a level, whereas economic policy uncertainty, oil prices, and bitcoins are first-difference stationary at a 5 percent significance level. The result also indicates that none of the variables are of the second order of integrations. The outcome of mix integration further permits us to proceed with the asymmetric investigation.

Table 2. Augmented Dicky–Fuller unit root test.

Variables	Level		First Difference	
	Constant	Constant and Trends	Constant	Constant and Trends
EPU	−2.56 (−2.085)	−2.78 (−3.091)	−4.18 (−2.812) *	−3.76 (−3.182)
GB	−0.19 (−2.182) *	−1.08 (−2.813)	−3.04 (−2.670)	−3.98 (−2.053)
OIL	−3.07 (−2.271)	−3.17 (−3.114)	−2.78 (−1.009) *	−2.74 (−2.198)
CII	2.17 (−1.191)	−1.04 (−2.031) *	−3.09 (−2.765)	−2.92 (−3.513)
BIT	−1.12 (−2.610)	−2.18 (−2.964)	−2.18 (−2.228)	−2.05 (−3.782) *

Note: * refers to a 5 percent level of significance.

Previous studies confront that conventional unit root tests are not equipped to handle the issue of time break, which may result in biased estimates [41]. In the presence of structural breaks, the Zivot and Andrews (ZA) test is an appropriate choice among the researchers. Therefore, as financial data are more susceptible to structural breaks, we have included the ZA test in our empirical analysis. In addition, the above test also reconfirms the order of integration in our sample series. The outcome of the ZA test attached in Table 3 depicts the presence of a structural break in our sample, and also reinstates that the variable is integrated at I(0) and I(1), and that none of the variables are of the I(2) order of integration. The structural break in the explanatory and outcome variable is experienced during 2020–2021. We can relate the probable reason for the structural break in the data series to the COVID-19 outbreak. The study conducted by Taghizadeh-Hesary et al. [42] also strengthens the above justification for the structural break in the data series. They reiterated that COVID-19-induced recession reduced the investments in green bonds globally, and thus, the exorbitant growth in green bond markets recorded a sudden fall.

Table 3. Zivot and Andrews test.

Variables	Level		First Difference	
	t-Statistic	Time Break	t-Statistic	Time Break
EPU	−3.1941 ***	2020	−6.7140 *	2020
GB	−5.0674 *	2019	−4.9302 **	2021
OIL	−4.7123	2020	−3.2815 *	2020
CII	3.1980 *	2020	−5.1817 **	2020
BIT	−6.1853 **	2020	−5.4461 **	2021

Note: *, **, and *** refer to 10, 5, and 1 percent levels of significance.

The presence of time breaks in the data series further entails the usage of the BDS test, which examines the nonlinear dependence. The result of the Broock et al., 1996 test attached in Table 4 confirms the presence of non-linearity among the various dimensions of the variables, by rejecting the null hypothesis of identical distribution. The confirmation of non-linearity re-affirms the reason for employing the NARDL approach.

Table 4. BDS test results.

	m = 2	m = 3	m = 4	m = 5	m = 6
EPU	0.2418 ***	0.1183 ***	0.2189 ***	0.3131 ***	0.3182 ***
GB	0.0854 **	0.2491 ***	0.3531 ***	−0.0124 ***	0.1983 **
OIL	0.1134 ***	0.1874 **	0.2815 **	0.2109 ***	0.4171 **
CII	0.0381 ***	0.2980 *	0.3817 ***	0.4763 **	0.0167 **
BIT	0.1721 **	0.1617 **	0.0198 **	0.4246 **	0.3184 **

Note: *, **, and *** refer to 10, 5, and 1 percent levels of significance.

Previous studies depict that it is mandatory to choose the optimal lag length before estimating cointegration between the variables. Following the Schwarz and Akaike information criteria, we have taken lag 2 in our empirical model. Furthermore, earlier studies advocate that we need to run the various diagnostic tests before estimating NARDL cointegration. Therefore, we have included the following diagnostic test, which is similar to the Ramsey RESET test to confirm misspecification, the Lagrange multiplier, and the Brush Pagan test to ascertain serial correlation and heteroskedasticity. The resulting outcome of all the diagnostic tests validates the stability and specification of the model. The result further confirms no heteroskedasticity and serial correlation in the data. After validating the diagnostic test, we proceed with the NARDL cointegration. The result showcased in Table 5 highlights that the F-statistic value is greater than the critical value in all three cases. This suggests that on the basis of the F-value, we can reject the null hypothesis of no-cointegration among the variables, and conclude the existence of long-run cointegration among the variables.

Table 5. Bound test cointegration.

F-Statistic (7.24) *	Lower Bound I(0)	Upper Bound 1(1)
10%	2.04	3.97
5%	2.43	4.02
1%	2.91	4.53

Note: * Critical value at 5 percent level of significance; SIC criteria are used for optimum lag selection.

The long-run cointegration relationship between the variables encourages us to proceed with the estimation of the asymmetric relationship between EPU, bitcoin, and green bonds. Tables 6 and 7 present the proceedings of the short-run and long-run NARDL approaches. The short-run result exhibits a short-run asymmetric relationship between U.S. economic policy uncertainty, bitcoins, and green bonds. The result unveils that an increase in policy uncertainty reduces the performance of green bonds, whereas a decrease in policy uncertainty enhances the performance of green bonds. A 1 percent increase (decrease) in EPU decreases (increases) green bond performances by 0.07 and 0.15 percent. The short-run NARDL result further reveals that positive shocks in bitcoin performances create a positive impact on green bonds and vice versa. The coefficient value reveals that the impact of bitcoins on green bonds is minimal (0.0092, 0.0103). In addition, in context to control variables, the short-run outcome suggests that fluctuation in oil prices are insignificant in determining the performances of green bonds, whereas in the short-run, clean energy has a positive impact on the performance of green bonds. This indicates that with the increase in the performance of clean energy, the performance of green bonds also increases. The coefficient value shows that the performance of green bonds increases by 0.10 percent with a 1 percent increase in the clean energy index. The difference in the magnitude and the outcome of the Wald test also confirms the asymmetric relationship between bitcoins, EPU, and green bonds in the short run.

Table 6. NARDL short-run estimates.

Dependent Variables: GB	Coefficient	St. Error	t-Statistics
$\Delta EPU_t{}^+$	−0.0701	0.1629	2.1012 ***
$\Delta EPU_t{}^-$	0.1583	0.2810	3.3854 **
$\Delta BIT_t{}^+$	0.0092	0.1683	2.4190 **
$\Delta BIT_t{}^-$	0.0103	0.4910	3.0119 ***
ΔOIL_t	0.0812	0.1843	4.1890
ΔCII_t	0.1019	0.0441	3.4014 **
Wald Test (Section B)	**F-Value**	**Probability Value**	
EPU_{SR}	14.321	0.000	
BIT_{SR}	16.041	0.000	

Note: **, and *** refer to 5 and 1 percent levels of significance. H_0 denotes no short-run asymmetric relationship.

After confirming the short-run NARDL estimates, we proceed with the long run NARDL estimation. The resulting outcome of the long-run NARDL estimates presented in Table 7 confirms an asymmetric relationship between economic policy uncertainty and green bonds. The coefficient value reveals that positive shocks in EPU reduce the performance of green bonds, whereas negative shocks increase the performance of green bonds. In addition, the outcome also depicts that the long-run coefficient is much more powerful than the short-run estimates. The economic policy uncertainty long-run estimate shows that a 1 percent increase in EPU reduces the performance of green bonds by 0.22 percent. The probable reason for such an outcome is because higher uncertainty curtails the free flow of investments required for sustainable projects, which eventually hampers the market potential of industries associated with green products; hence, the performance of green bonds falls. Based on the findings, we can also infer that green bonds are not an appropriate hedging tool in the case of U.S. EPU. The empirical outcome is in line with the study performed by Pham et al. [24], and contradicts the findings of Haq et al. [43]. The work performed by Pham et al. [24] advocates that green bonds are severely affected by high economic uncertainty. During high economic uncertainty, green bonds cannot be used as a risk-hedging instrument; however, during a period of low economic uncertainty, they can be considered as a risk-hedging option.

Table 7. NARDL long-run estimates.

Dependent Variables: GB	Coefficient	St. Error	t-Statistics
ΔEPU_t^{+}	−0.2201	0.1732	3.2198 **
ΔEPU_t^{-}	0.1135	0.2298	2.0140 **
ΔBIT_t^{+}	0.0201	0.3610	2.2139 ***
ΔBIT_t^{-}	0.0110	0.2917	4.1781 **
ΔOIL_t	0.0541	0.1253	3.2853 *
ΔCII_t	0.1310	0.0951	2.2109 **
Wald Test (Section B)	**F-Value**	**Probability Value**	
EPU_{LR}	11.031	0.000	
BIT_{LR}	12.261	0.010	
Diagnostic Test (Section C)			
RAMSEY RESET	**LM Test**	**Brush–Pagan Test**	**CUSUM Test**
1.88 (0.510)	1.391 (0.833)	0.741 (0.419)	Stable parameters

Note: *, **, and *** refer to 10, 5, and 1 percent levels of significance. H_0 denotes no short-run asymmetric relationship.

In context to the long-term asymmetric relation between green bonds and bitcoins, the study highlights a bi-directional asymmetric relationship. It implies that positive shocks in bitcoins increase the performance of green bonds and vice versa. A 1 percent increase in bitcoins increases the performance of green bonds by 0.02 percent, and a 1 percent decrease in bitcoins prices decreases green bonds by 0.01 percent. The coefficient value reveals the minimum transmission effect between green bonds and bitcoins. The resulting outcome reiterates the connectedness between modern financial investment instruments and sustainable financial products. A reasonable justification for such a relationship exists because both asset classes are the latest innovations in financial markets. Investors prefer these investments options over conventional assets due to the higher returns and future prospects. Therefore, based on such optimistic attitudes of investors, these instruments refer to similar co-movements. We can also infer that in the case of bitcoins, the green bond is not an appropriate hedging instrument. Besides, we can consider green bonds as a risk-diversifying instrument. The resulting outcome is consistent with the study carried out by Le et al. [15]. Our empirical findings also collaborate with the previous studies that project a medium-risk transmission between innovative financial assets, and recommend careful investment strategies for risk diversification and hedging [3].

The changes in the magnitudes and the probability values of the Wald test further substantiate the long-run asymmetric relationship between EPU, bitcoins, and green bonds.

In addition, in reference to the energy-related variables, we can conclude that oil prices and the clean energy index have a positive influence on green bond performance. The result shows that a 1 percent increase (decrease) in oil prices increases (decreases) the performance of green bonds by 0.05 percent. Likewise, a 1 percent increase (decrease) in the clean energy index increases (decreases) green bond performance by 0.13 percent. In addition, the coefficient value indicates that the influence of the clean energy index is more on green bonds as compared to the oil prices in the long run. The time series plot of green bonds, the clean energy index, and oil prices reported in Figure 1 also reports a similar association. One plausible reason for a similar movement between clean energy and green bonds can be attributed to the fact that both of the assets' class belongs to the same category of investors, who are risk-averse and have a conservative profile. Thus, similar investor profiles and risk aversion play a prominent role in the strong linkage between green bonds and the clean energy index. The findings recommend that green bonds offer noteworthy diversification benefits for investors both in energy stocks and oil-related assets regardless of their investment horizon. Overall, our results suggest that although green bonds represent a different asset class, they closely replicate the performance of oil prices and clean energy stock. The empirical outcome of a positive linkage between green bonds and oil prices also strengthens the theoretical viewpoint that an increase in oil prices should increase the issuance of green bonds, as it necessitates the diversification of energy sources, especially for oil-importing economies. Likewise, a decrease in oil prices might have a decreasing influence on the issuance of green bonds, as there is less pressure to encourage renewable energy resources, and a continued reliance on the available fossil fuels. Lastly, we can infer that the study highlights a complementary relationship between green bonds, oil prices, and the clean energy index. Our result outcome is in line with the study conducted by Azhgaliyeva et al. [44], Lee et al. [45], and Ahmed et al. [46] who projected that oil, the clean energy index, and green bond prices mutually affect each other in such a way that any movements in oil prices and the clean energy index will lead to changes in green bond prices and vice versa. Therefore, investors and portfolio managers should consider this causal transmission mechanism when making portfolio and hedging decisions. Furthermore, the diagnostic test also confirms the stability and reliability of the long-run NARDL model.

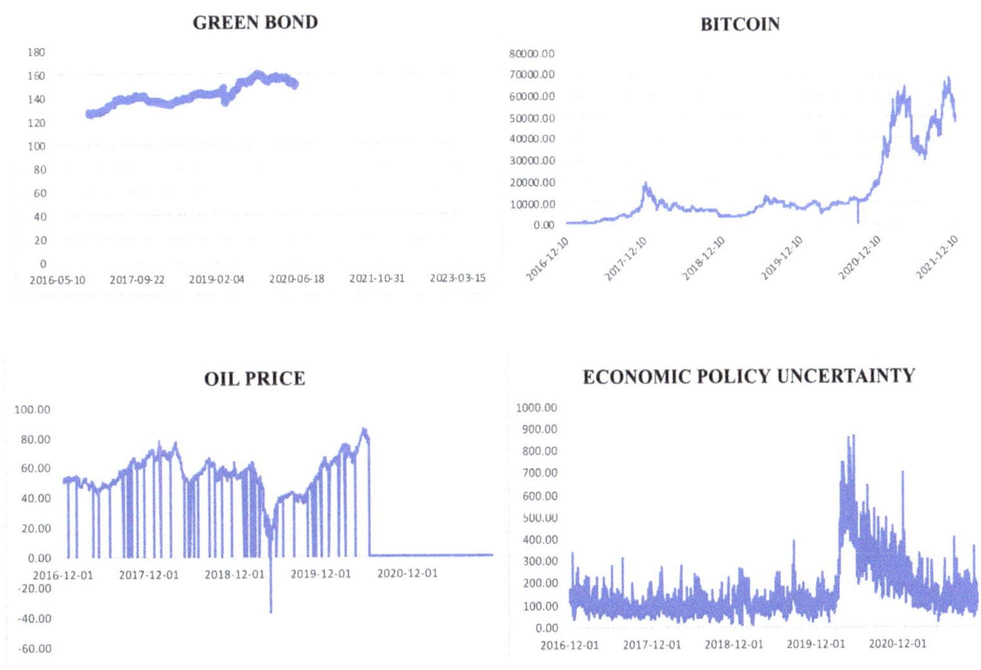

Figure 1. *Cont.*

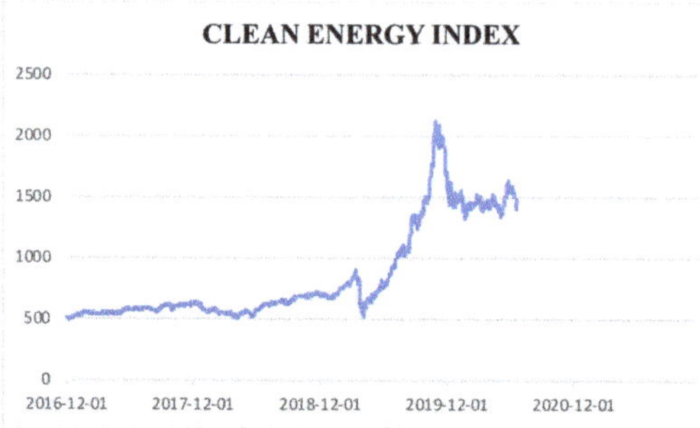

Figure 1. Time series plot of explanatory and outcome variables.

5. Conclusions and Policy Recommendations

The concern for environmental sustainability, and the urge to generate adequate investments to finance sustainable environment goals, have attracted the interest of investors towards green bonds. The growing investor interest in green bonds has motivated us to examine how modern financial assets, policy uncertainty, oil prices, and the clean energy index influence green bond performances. In the present study, we tried to answer whether green bonds are a hedging tool or a risk-diversifying instrument among investors. Furthermore, we also evaluated the bidirectional relationship between green bonds, U.S. economic policy uncertainty, and bitcoins from 1st December 2016 to 31st October 2021. To this end, we utilized the Baker et al. [47] EPU index, S&P clean energy index, S&P green bond index, daily oil prices, bitcoin prices, and nonlinear autoregressive distribution lag approach recently developed by Shin et al. [37]. Another major contribution of this research is the inclusion of structural break and nonlinearity tests to estimate the presence of nonlinearity and structural breaks in the time series. Our empirical outcome confirms an asymmetric relationship between green bonds, bitcoins, and U.S. economic policy uncertainty. According to our findings, a positive shock in the U.S. EPU creates a negative influence on green bonds. On the other side, a negative shock in the U.S. EPU helps to increase the performance of green bonds. This implies that, similar to other conventional assets, green bonds are also not immune to economic policy uncertainty. Fluctuations in monetary, fiscal, and other economic policies have a consequential impact on green bonds. Hence, during high economic policy uncertainty, green bonds cannot be considered as a hedging tool; moreover, they account as risk-diversifying instruments. In addition to the above results, the study also concludes an asymmetric relationship between bitcoins and green bonds. The positive shocks of bitcoins exert a positive influence on green bonds and vice versa. These results reiterate that green bonds are similar to other modern financial instruments, and report similar movement. Thus, investors can use them as a risk-diversifying instrument, and not as a hedging tool. In addition to the above results, our study also highlights a positive relationship between oil prices, the clean energy index, and green bonds. It implies that green bond performance increases with an increase in the clean energy index and oil prices. Our findings support the theoretical explanation that an increase in oil prices necessitates the expansion in the purchase of green bonds, as it necessitates the diversification of energy sources, especially for oil-importing economies. Thus, based on these outcomes, we can infer that we cannot consider green bonds as a different asset class, and they work more as a substitute to conventional assets. Investors must include these shares in their portfolios as risk-diversifying instruments.

Our empirical analysis offers several policy implications highlighting the diversification and hedging properties of green bonds vis-à-vis bitcoins, clean energy, and economic policy uncertainty. The asymmetric dynamic connectedness provides instructive suggestions from a portfolio diversification standpoint. Based on the empirical outcome, we can recommend that investors include green bonds in their portfolios as a risk-diversifying instrument. Aside from the environmental benefits, they offer significant diversification benefits to investors against conventional stocks, cryptocurrencies, oil, and clean energy stock in the long run. It is highlighted in the study that during high policy uncertainty, investors should be more cautious when investing in green bonds, as in the long run, the negative influence of EPU on green bonds is much more severe. Therefore, on the basis of environmental benefits, investors should not presume that green bonds are immune to economic policy uncertainty. Our study also recommends that investors looking to contribute toward sustainable development include green bonds in their portfolios, as green bonds are viable alternatives to clean energy or renewable energy stocks. In addition, based on the findings, we can recommend that, similar to bitcoins, green bonds also offer attractive returns. Green bonds are also more stable than bitcoins due to their long-term goal of sustainability. Therefore, investors looking for moderate returns and long-term growth can switch to green bonds over bitcoins. Likewise, in the short-run, investors can hedge the volatility of oil prices by investing in green bonds, as in the short-run, there is no significant linkage between oil prices and green bonds. To sum up, we can conclude that over the years, green bonds have emerged as a powerful tool to combat climate change by attracting funds required for sustainable projects. The diversification properties against conventional and innovative market instruments also make green bonds an attractive investment avenue, provided investors consider the vulnerability of green bonds to policy uncertainty.

Our study provides insights into green bonds, an innovative financial asset that not only enhances the transition to a low-carbon economy, but also generates the attention of policymakers and investors to reduce risk and innovative transmission across different markets. The diversification benefit of green bonds develops policymakers' confidence to scale up the green bond market for environmental responsibility. Furthermore, understanding the relationship between green bonds and other asset classes is of paramount importance to global investors, especially ethical investors, since this information helps gain superior risk-adjusted returns across the allocation of conventional assets to a portfolio. Finally, the above empirical outcomes will also assist in understanding the long-run influence of explanatory variables on green bonds, especially for emerging and developing countries. Emerging countries, such as the BRICS countries, are the largest emitters of carbon emissions. Therefore, to meet their ESG goals, these countries are resorting to environmentally friendly measures; green bond financing is no exception. However, the green bond market of these countries is in a transition process (except for China), and thus, considering the immense investment and financing opportunities to meet the sustainable goal, the above outcome will assist the investor in understanding how green bonds react to financial assets and policy uncertainties. These outcomes will assist them in devising appropriate long-run investment strategies.

6. Limitation and Future Direction of the Study

Despite the novelty and extensiveness, the current study only explores the asymmetric relationship between green bonds, bitcoins, and U.S. economic policy uncertainty; hence, it will be more beneficial for future studies to explore the connectiveness of green bonds with other conventional financial indices. In addition, future studies can also investigate the influence of economic policy uncertainty in European countries on green bond markets, as these countries are more inclined toward sustainable development goals. The inclusion of a wider sample of countries and variables will give a clearer picture to understand the future of green bonds as risk-diversifying and hedging instruments.

Author Contributions: Conceptualization, A.A.S. and F.A.; methodology, A.A.S. and M.A.K.; formal analysis, A.U. and M.A.K.; investigation, F.A. and M.A.K.; data curation, A.A.S. and A.U.; writing—original draft preparation, J.P.R.-R. and A.A.S.; writing—review and editing, A.U. and J.P.R.-R.; funding, F.A. and J.P.R.-R. All authors have read and agreed to the published version of the manuscript.

Funding: This research received no external funding.

Institutional Review Board Statement: Not applicable.

Informed Consent Statement: Not applicable.

Data Availability Statement: Publicly available datasets were analyzed in this study. The data can be found here: S&Pgreenbond.com, policyuncertainty.com (accessed on 14 November 2021).

Conflicts of Interest: The authors declare no conflict of interest.

References

1. Ferrer, R.; Shahzad, S.J.H.; Soriano, P. Are green bonds a different asset class? Evidence from time-frequency connectedness analysis. *J. Clean. Prod.* **2021**, *292*, 125988. [CrossRef]
2. Gielen, D.; Boshell, F.; Saygin, D.; Bazilian, M.D.; Wagner, N.; Gorini, R. The role of renewable energy in the global energy transformation. *Energy Strategy Rev.* **2019**, *24*, 38–50. [CrossRef]
3. Bachelet, M.J.; Becchetti, L.; Manfredonia, S. The green bonds premium puzzle: The role of issuer characteristics and third-party verification. *Sustainability* **2019**, *11*, 1098. [CrossRef]
4. Huynh, T.L.D.; Hille, E.; Nasir, M.A. Diversification in the age of the 4th industrial revolution: The role of artificial intelligence, green bonds and cryptocurrencies. *Technol. Forecast. Soc. Change* **2020**, *159*, 120188. [CrossRef]
5. Reboredo, J.C.; Ugolini, A. Price connectedness between green bond and financial markets. *Econ. Model.* **2019**, *88*, 25–38. [CrossRef]
6. MacAskill, S.; Roca, E.; Liu, B.; Stewart, R.; Sahin, O. Is there a green premium in the green bond market? Systematic literature review revealing premium determinants. *J. Clean. Prod.* **2020**, *280*, 124491. [CrossRef]
7. Katsiampa, P.; Corbet, S.; Lucey, B. High frequency volatility co-movements in cryptocurrency markets. *J. Int. Financ. Mark. Inst. Money* **2019**, *62*, 35–52. [CrossRef]
8. Gronwald, M. Is Bitcoin a Commodity? On price jumps, demand shocks, and certainty of supply. *J. Int. Money Financ.* **2019**, *97*, 86–92. [CrossRef]
9. White, R.; Marinakis, Y.; Islam, N.; Walsh, S. Is Bitcoin a currency, a technology-based product, or something else? *Technol. Forecast. Soc. Change* **2020**, *151*, 119877. [CrossRef]
10. Demiralay, S.; Gencer, H.G.; Bayraci, S. How do Artificial Intelligence and Robotics Stocks co-move with traditional and alternative assets in the age of the 4th industrial revolution? Implications and Insights for the COVID-19 period. *Technol. Forecast. Soc. Chang.* **2021**, *171*, 120989. [CrossRef]
11. Umar, M.; Su, C.-W.; Rizvi, S.K.A.; Shao, X.-F. Bitcoin: A safe haven asset and a winner amid political and economic uncertainties in the US? *Technol. Forecast. Soc. Chang.* **2021**, *167*, 120680. [CrossRef]
12. Tang, D.Y.; Zhang, Y. Do shareholders benefit from green bonds? *J. Corp. Financ.* **2018**, *61*, 101427. [CrossRef]
13. Reboredo, J.C. Green bond and financial markets: Co-movement, diversification and price spillover effects. *Energy Econ.* **2018**, *74*, 38–50. [CrossRef]
14. Karim, S.; Naeem, M.A.; Mirza, N.; Paule-Vianez, J. Quantifying the hedge and safe-haven properties of bond markets for cryptocurrency indices. *J. Risk Financ.* **2022**. [CrossRef]
15. Le, T.-L.; Abakah, E.J.A.; Tiwari, A.K. Time and frequency domain connectedness and spill-over among fintech, green bonds and cryptocurrencies in the age of the fourth industrial revolution. *Technol. Forecast. Soc. Chang.* **2020**, *162*, 120382. [CrossRef] [PubMed]
16. Syed, A.A.; Kamal, M.A.; Tripathi, R. An empirical investigation of nuclear energy and environmental pollution nexus in India: Fresh evidence using NARDL approach. *Environ. Sci. Pollut. Res.* **2021**, *28*, 54744–54755. [CrossRef] [PubMed]
17. Grobys, K.; Ahmed, S.; Sapkota, N. Technical trading rules in the cryptocurrency market. *Financ. Res. Lett.* **2019**, *32*, 101396. [CrossRef]
18. Azhgaliyeva, D.; Kapoor, A.; Liu, Y. Green bonds for financing renewable energy and energy efficiency in South-East Asia: A review of policies. *J. Sustain. Financ. Investig.* **2019**, *10*, 113–140. [CrossRef]
19. Hung, N.T. Green Bonds and Asset Classes: New Evidence from Time-varying Copula and Transfer Entropy Models. *Glob. Bus. Rev.* **2021**. [CrossRef]
20. Berger, T.; Czudaj, R.L. Commodity futures and a wavelet-based risk assessment. *Phys. A Stat. Mech. Its Appl.* **2020**, *554*, 124339. [CrossRef]
21. Park, D.; Park, J.; Ryu, D. Volatility Spillovers between Equity and Green Bond Markets. *Sustainability* **2020**, *12*, 3722. [CrossRef]
22. Chiappini, H. Sustainable Finance and COVID-19 Pandemic: Weathering the Storm and Preventing a New One. In *Contemporary Issues in Sustainable Finance: Financial Products and Financial Institutions*; Palgrave Macmillan: Cham, Switzerland, 2021; p. 285.
23. Naeem, M.A.; Nguyen, T.T.H.; Nepal, R.; Ngo, Q.T.; Taghizadeh–Hesary, F. Asymmetric relationship between green bonds and commodities: Evidence from extreme quantile approach. *Financ. Res. Lett.* **2021**, *43*, 101983. [CrossRef]
24. Pham, L.; Nguyen, C.P. Asymmetric tail dependence between green bonds and other asset classes. *Glob. Financ. J.* **2021**, *50*, 100669. [CrossRef]
25. Baulkaran, V. Stock market reaction to green bond issuance. *J. Asset Manag.* **2019**, *20*, 331–340. [CrossRef]

26. Liu, N.; Liu, C.; Da, B.; Zhang, T.; Guan, F. Dependence and risk spillovers between green bonds and clean energy markets. *J. Clean. Prod.* **2021**, *279*, 123595. [CrossRef]
27. Hammoudeh, S.; Ajmi, A.N.; Mokni, K. Relationship between green bonds and financial and environmental variables: A novel time-varying causality. *Energy Econ.* **2020**, *92*, 104941. [CrossRef]
28. Jin, J.; Han, L.; Wu, L.; Zeng, H. The hedging effect of green bonds on carbon market risk. *Int. Rev. Financ. Anal.* **2020**, *71*, 101509. [CrossRef]
29. Zerbib, O.D. The effect of pro-environmental preferences on bond prices: Evidence from green bonds. *J. Bank. Financ.* **2018**, *98*, 39–60. [CrossRef]
30. Pham, L. Is it risky to go green? A volatility analysis of the green bond market. *J. Sustain. Financ. Investig.* **2016**, *6*, 263–291. [CrossRef]
31. Broadstock, D.C.; Cheng, L.T. Time-varying relation between black and green bond price benchmarks: Macroeconomic determinants for the first decade. *Financ. Res. Lett.* **2019**, *29*, 17–22. [CrossRef]
32. Reboredo, J.C.; Ugolini, A.; Aiube, F.A.L. Network connectedness of green bonds and asset classes. *Energy Econ.* **2020**, *86*, 104629. [CrossRef]
33. Naeem, M.A.; Adekoya, O.B.; Oliyide, J.A. Asymmetric spillovers between green bonds and commodities. *J. Clean. Prod.* **2021**, *314*, 128100. [CrossRef]
34. Dutta, A.; Bouri, E.; Noor, H. Climate bond, stock, gold, and oil markets: Dynamic correlations and hedging analyses during the COVID-19 outbreak. *Resour. Policy* **2021**, *74*, 102265. [CrossRef] [PubMed]
35. Guo, D.; Zhou, P. Green bonds as hedging assets before and after COVID: A comparative study between the US and China. *Energy Econ.* **2021**, *104*, 105696. [CrossRef]
36. Arif, M.; Naeem, M.A.; Farid, S.; Nepal, R.; Jamasb, T. Diversifier or More? Hedge and Safe Haven Properties of Green Bonds during COVID-19. (February 8, 2021). CAMA Working Paper No 20/2021. Available online: http://dx.doi.org/10.2139/ssrn.3782126 (accessed on 14 November 2021).
37. Shin, Y.; Yu, B.; Greenwood-Nimmo, M. Modelling asymmetric cointegration and dynamic multipliers in a non-linear ARDL framework. In *Festschrift in Honor of Peter Schmidt*; Springer: New York, NY, USA, 2014; pp. 281–314.
38. Ullah, A.; Zhao, X.; Kamal, M.A.; Zheng, J. Environmental regulations and inward FDI in China: Fresh evidence from the asymmetric autoregressive distributed lag approach. *Int. J. Financ. Econ.* **2020**, *27*, 1340–1356. [CrossRef]
39. Souto, F.; Calado, V.; Pereira, N., Jr. Lignin-based carbon fiber: A current overview. *Mater. Res. Exp.* **2018**, *5*, 072001. [CrossRef]
40. Hashmi, S.H.; Fan, H.; Fareed, Z.; Shahzad, F. Asymmetric nexus between urban agglomerations and environmental pollution in top ten urban agglomerated countries using quantile methods. *Environ. Sci. Pollut. Res.* **2021**, *28*, 13404–13424. [CrossRef]
41. Shahbaz, M.; Zakaria, M.; Shahzad, S.J.H.; Mahalik, M.K. The energy consumption and economic growth nexus in top ten energy-consuming countries: Fresh evidence from using the quantile-on-quantile approach. *Energy Econ.* **2018**, *71*, 282–301. [CrossRef]
42. Taghizadeh-Hesary, F.; Yoshino, N.; Phoumin, H. Analyzing the characteristics of green bond markets to facilitate green finance in the post-COVID-19 world. *Sustainability* **2021**, *13*, 5719. [CrossRef]
43. Haq, I.U.; Chupradit, S.; Huo, C. Do green bonds act as a hedge or a safe haven against economic policy uncertainty? Evidence from the USA and China. *Int. J. Financ. Stud.* **2021**, *9*, 40. [CrossRef]
44. Azhgaliyeva, D.; Mishra, R.; Kapsalyamova, Z. *Oil Price Shocks and Green Bonds: A Longitudinal Multilevel Model*; Asian Development Bank Institute: Tokyo, Japan, 2021.
45. Lee, C.-C.; Lee, C.-C.; Li, Y.-Y. Oil price shocks, geopolitical risks, and green bond market dynamics. *N. Am. J. Econ. Financ.* **2021**, *55*, 101309. [CrossRef]
46. Ahmed, F.; Syed, A.A.; Kamal, M.A.; de las Nieves López-García, M.; Ramos-Requena, J.P.; Gupta, S. Assessing the Impact of COVID-19 Pandemic on the Stock and Commodity Markets Performance and Sustainability: A Comparative Analysis of South Asian Countries. *Sustainability* **2021**, *13*, 5669. [CrossRef]
47. Baker, S.R.; Bloom, N.; Davis, S.J. Measuring Economic Policy Uncertainty. *Q. J. Econ.* **2016**, *131*, 1593–1636. [CrossRef]

mathematics

Article

Do Not Rug on Me: Leveraging Machine Learning Techniques for Automated Scam Detection

Bruno Mazorra [1,†], Victor Adan [2,†] and Vanesa Daza [1,*]

[1] Department of Information and Communications Technology, Pompeu Fabra University, Tanger Building, 08018 Barcelona, Spain; brunomazorra@gmail.com
[2] Faculty of Economics and Business, Universitat de Barcelona, 08034 Barcelona, Spain; victor8adan@gmail.com
* Correspondence: vanesa.daza@upf.edu
† These authors contributed equally to this work.

Abstract: Uniswap, as with other DEXs, has gained much attention this year because it is a non-custodial and publicly verifiable exchange that allows users to trade digital assets without trusted third parties. However, its simplicity and lack of regulation also make it easy to execute initial coin offering scams by listing non-valuable tokens. This method of performing scams is known as rug pull, a phenomenon that already exists in traditional finance but has become more relevant in DeFi. Various projects have contributed to detecting rug pulls in EVM compatible chains. However, the first longitudinal and academic step to detecting and characterizing scam tokens on Uniswap was made. The authors collected all the transactions related to the Uniswap V2 exchange and proposed a machine learning algorithm to label tokens as scams. However, the algorithm is only valuable for detecting scams accurately after they have been executed. This paper increases their dataset by 20K tokens and proposes a new methodology to label tokens as scams. After manually analyzing the data, we devised a theoretical classification of different malicious maneuvers in the Uniswap protocol. We propose various machine-learning-based algorithms with new, relevant features related to the token propagation and smart contract heuristics to detect potential rug pulls before they occur. In general, the models proposed achieved similar results. The best model obtained accuracy of 0.9936, recall of 0.9540, and precision of 0.9838 in distinguishing non-malicious tokens from scams prior to the malicious maneuver.

Keywords: ethereum; DeFi; Dex; scam detection

MSC: 91-08; 91G50

Citation: Mazorra, B.; Adan, V.; Daza, V. Do Not Rug on Me: Leveraging Machine Learning Techniques for Automated Scam Detection. *Mathematics* **2022**, *10*, 949. https://doi.org/10.3390/math10060949

Academic Editors: Jose Luis Miralles-Quiros, David Carfi and María Mar Miralles-Quirós

Received: 4 February 2022
Accepted: 12 March 2022
Published: 16 March 2022

1. Introduction

Blockchain technology has proven to be enormously disruptive and empowering in both the public and private sectors of computing applications. Blockchains are permissionless and immutable digital ledgers that can be implemented and audited without a trusted third party or central authority. At their basic level, they enable participants to record transactions in a shared public ledger such that, under the regular operation of the blockchain network, no transaction can be changed once committed. In 2008 [1], the blockchain idea was combined with several other technologies to create Bitcoin: a peer-to-peer electronic cash system protected through cryptographic mechanisms without needing a central repository or authority. However, users and developers perceived that Bitcoin had a limited use case due to the lack of complete programmability of the Bitcoin Virtual Machine. For this reason, many developers worked on the launch of other chains such as Ethereum, a Turing-complete blockchain that has evolved to include a wide range of decentralized applications. Often, a decentralized application (DApp) will use one or more "smart contracts" deployed on top of the blockchain.

A smart contract is an executable code that runs on the blockchain to facilitate, execute, and enforce the terms of an agreement between untrusted parties. The most popular and exciting area where smart contracts have been crucial is decentralized finance (DeFi), which makes financial products available on a publicly decentralized blockchain network. DeFi could potentially offer a new pseudo-anonymous, non-custodial, and permissionless financial architecture that allows open audit [2]. However, the Turing-complete blockchain technology is not a silver bullet; the pseudo-anonymous and permissionless nature of the blockchain allows attackers, scammers, and money launderers to act with impunity. In parallel to the work carried out in [3], in this paper, we will focus on the thefts and scams in the most popular tool of DeFi, the decentralized exchanges (DEX), the DeFi version of market exchanges. The most common way in which scammers and malicious agents execute a theft is through a rug pull. A rug pull of a project is a malicious operation or set of operations in the cryptocurrency industry where the developers abandon the project and take the investors' funds as profits. As mentioned in [3], rug pulls are a popular maneuver that usually happens in DEXs, particularly in Uniswap, where malicious agents develop an ERC-20 token (Ethereum Request for Comments 20) and list it on a DEX and pair it with a leading cryptocurrency such as USD or Ether. Once some uninformed investors swap their leading coin for the token, the developers then remove all the currencies from the liquidity pool, making the token untradable and with zero economic value. In order to make the attack more profitable, the creators usually use different marketing tools such as a fake website, telegram groups, and Discord chat rooms to cultivate confidence among potential investors.

Our contribution: In this paper, we expand the rug pull dataset of the paper [3] to 27,588 tokens. To do this, we collected all Uniswap data until 3 September 2021 by directly interacting with the Ethereum blockchain. Then, we labelled different tokens as *scam*, *malicious*, and *non-malicious* tokens using various relevant features of the smart contract and the liquidity pool state (see Sections 3.4 and 6). We manually observed different ways of executing the rug pull, proposed a rug pull classification, and observed new, complex forms of performing the theft. Moreover, we have observed a further usage of the Uniswap protocol to send ETH (ETH is the native cryptocurrency of the Ethereum network) unnoticed for most common tracking protocols. Finally, as we detail in Section 7, we propose new features of tokens, liquidity pools, and the transaction graphs, and a new framework to predict the probability of a liquidity pool becoming a rug pull or a scam in the future.

In summary, in this work, we make the following contributions:

- We provide the most extensive labelled dataset of Uniswap rug pulls to date, including the source code, the liquidity, the prices, the mint/burn, and transfer events. The dataset includes all tokens from 4 May 2020 to 3 September 2021. In total, we labelled 26,957 tokens as scams/rug pulls and 631 tokens as non-malicious.
- We provide a theoretical classification of three different types of rug pulls, simple, sell, and trap-door rug pulls, and provide tools to identify them.
- To the best of our knowledge, we are the first to design an accurate automated rug pull detection to predict future rug pulls and scams using relevant features of the pool's state and the token distribution among the users. More specifically, we used the Herfindahl–Hirschman Index and clustering transaction coefficient as heuristics to measure the distribution of the token among the investors.
- We prove that the use of lock contracts such as Unicrypt by other scam detectors [4,5] provides misleading data about the economic security of the token. More precisely, we show that 90% of tokens using locking contracts tend to become a rug pull or a malicious token eventually.
- We define two methods that use machine learning models to discriminate between malicious and non-malicious tokens in different scenarios. In the first scenario, tokens can be evaluated at any block prior to the malicious maneuver. In the second scenario, all tokens are evaluated at a certain time after the creation of their respective pools.

Specifically, we use a new machine learning algorithm based on attention mechanisms for tabular data called FT-Transformer [6]. Our best model obtains accuracy of 0.9936, recall of 0.9540, and precision of 0.9838 in distinguishing non-malicious tokens from scams in the first scenario and accuracy of 0.992, recall of 0.784, and precision of 0.869 in the second scenario.

All these results can be replicated using the code and the pipeline in [7]. To use it, we highly recommend access to a full or an archive Ethereum node.

Organization of the paper: In Section 2, we describe the state of the art of scam detection in smart-contract-based blockchains. Section 3 gives an overview of DeFi and DEXs and the main features needed for our analysis. Section 4 introduces a classification of malicious Uniswap maneuvers, emphasizing the theoretical methodology behind different rug pulls. In Section 5, we explain the methodology used to obtain all the data needed to train our models and obtain our results. In Section 6, we explain the methodology used to label the tokens listed in the Uniswap protocol as malicious and non-malicious and give an overview of the results obtained by applying this methodology. Finally, Section 7 explains the model used to detect future rug pulls in the early stages. We explain the two different methodologies used and describe the accuracy, sensitivity, and F1 score of the models used.

2. Related Work

Due to the role of smart contracts in Blockchain Technology, some studies have analyzed the security and the automatic vulnerability detection within such contracts. Some have focused on finding anomalies in the transaction graph [8–11] and clustering malicious addresses [12–14]. For example, paper [8] uses the transaction graph to predict relevant market price changes and [14] uses the transaction graph and fingerprints in the gas price (https://ethereum.org/en/developers/docs/gas/, accessed on 15 February 2022) in order to detect the addresses of the same user.

Other studies have focused on the vulnerabilities of smart contracts [15–18]; for example, [16] is a static analysis framework for smart contracts that detects potential vulnerabilities. In a similar direction, other research [19–23] examines the vulnerabilities of DeFi protocols when interacting with rational agents.

Regarding blockchain scams, many studies have investigated phishing scams [24–27], Ponzi Schemes [28–30], and automated scam detection [31–33].

More related to our work, various studies or projects [3–5] have addressed the detection of rug pulls or frauds working on top of DEX protocols. Two projects [4,5] use the simple heuristics of holders, liquidity, and an automatic smart contract analysis, to give a risk score of the token. Both projects share two major problems: the lack of longitudinal studies to check their results, and the failure to detect non-malicious tokens accurately. On the other hand, ref. [3] provided the only longitudinal and cross-sectional study to date. The study provides a good introduction and overview of different rug pulls, as well as a dataset of more than 10K scam tokens listed in Uniswap. However, the major flaw of the paper is that the algorithm is trained to classify tokens and detect rug pulls only after they have occurred; that is, the machine learning algorithm is trained in order to classify tokens, but is not able to detect future rug pulls.

3. Preliminaries

3.1. Ethereum and Smart Contracts

Ethereum is a blockchain with a quasi-Turing-complete programming virtual machine that compiles different programming languages such as Solidity [34]. One relevant goal of Ethereum is for any party to develop arbitrary applications and scripts that execute in blockchain through transactions, using the blockchain to synchronize their state in a manner that is fully verifiable by any system participant. These scripts are usually referred to as smart contracts. Participants and smart contracts in the Ethereum network transact with the base currency known as Ether. Ether is the coin used to transact and to pay the fees to the miners to transfer Ether or to interact with smart contracts. Accounts on the

Ethereum network can be linked to programs in a virtual machine-based language called the Ethereum Virtual Machine (EVM). More specifically, smart contracts are programs that are deployed on the blockchain public ledger and are executed in transactions, which, similarly to ACID-style database transactions [19], alter the state of the ledger atomically (that is, either all the operations of the transaction are executed or all the operations are reverted). In the moment of deploying a smart contract, a byte-code is sent in a transaction to the ledger, and this contract is assigned a unique address of 42 hexadecimal characters and its code is uploaded to the ledger. Once successfully created, a smart contract consists of a contract address of 42 hexadecimal characters, a balance, a code defined in the contract creation, and a state. Different users and parties can then change the state of a specific contract by sending transactions invoking particular functions to a known contract address. If the transaction holds the constraints hard-coded in the smart contract, this transaction will trigger a set of actions established in the smart contract code as a result, such as reading and modifying the contract state, interacting and executing other contracts, or transferring Ether or tokens to other addresses. These actions can be coded to produce events, a transaction log of the relevant information produced by the actions triggered. These events are useful for developers and users to track the state of the smart contract.

The most popular and significant smart contracts of Ethereum are known as ERC-20 tokens, and emerged in 2015 as the technical standard used for all smart contracts on the Ethereum blockchain for fungible token implementations. A token is fungible if any token is exactly equal to any other token; no tokens have special rights or behavior associated with them. This makes ERC-20 tokens useful for currency exchange, voting rights, staking, and more. ERC-20 defines a common set of functions, of which only the signatures, but not the implementations, are specified. Table 1 lists the common rules of ERC-20, including the global variables and functions.

Table 1. ERC-20 standard signatures.

Requirements	Type	Signature
Required	Method	`totalSupply()`
		`balanceOf(address)`
		`transfer(address,uint256)`
		`approve(address,uint256)`
		`allowance(address,address)`
		`transferFrom(address,address,uint256)`
	Event	`Transfer(address,address,uint256)`
		`Approval(address,address,uint256)`
Optional	Method	`name()`
		`symbol()`
		`decimals()`

In addition to the base ERC-20 functionality, many tokens provide other functionalities [17]. For instance, it is quite common to find contracts that can freeze accounts, transfer ownership, pause contracts, or make complex interactions with other DeFi protocols. In this study, we focused on three functionalities that involve the manipulation of tokens: minting, pausable, and complex buy/sell operations in which tokens can be obtained from or exchanged to Ether. Token minting corresponds to the creation of tokens, increasing the total supply of tokens, and associating the newly minted tokens with a specific address. Token burning is the reverse operation: tokens can be erased from an account and their total supply decreases. Token sale works in terms of operations that allow an account to buy tokens using Ether, or obtain Ether by selling tokens.

In order to obtain those features, one can use compilers such as Slither [16], a static analysis framework designed to provide human-readable information and insights into smart contracts written in the Solidity programming language. Slither allows the application of commonly used program analysis techniques such as dataflow and taint tracking. Moreover, Slither detects various important features and vulnerabilities, such as minting, reentrancy vulnerability, and pausable smart contracts.

3.2. Decentralized Exchanges

Decentralized exchanges (DEXs) [2] are a category of Decentralized Finance (DeFi) protocol that allow the non-custodial exchange of digital assets. All trades are executed on-chain and are, thus, publicly verifiable. The policy that matches buyers and sellers (or traders and liquidity providers) is hard-coded in a smart contract. DEXs have different mechanisms for price discovery: order book DEXs and automated market makers (AMM). While order book exchanges have been broadly studied [35,36] and used in traditional finance (TradFi), AMMs have been proven to be more useful in blockchain environments due to their computational efficiency and simplicity [2]. In general, in an automated market maker, each asset pair comprises a distinct pool or market. Liquidity providers supply liquidity by adding both assets in proportion to the existing pool size. Traders exchange assets by adding one asset to the pool and removing the other. The ratio of the two traded assets is the average price paid, which is calculated according to a downward sloping, convex relationship called *constant function* (CF). The convexity implies that the AMM is liquidity-sensitive; that is, larger orders have a larger price impact. DEXs and, particularly AMM, have become very popular in DeFi for several reasons:

1. they permit easy provision of liquidity for minor assets, i.e., any assets can be listed in a DEX;
2. they allow any party to become a market maker;
3. they are censorship-resilient in highly volatile periods;
4. they can be audited by anyone.

However, these properties also have their drawbacks:

1. blockchain transactions are publicly visible in the mempool, which means that miners or users can front-run trading transactions in DEXs [21,23], consistently leading to a worse price for users;
2. every token can be listed to trade in AMM protocols, making uninformed users fall into different scams or suboptimally performing projects [3].

With an AMM, the price of an asset is determined by the state (number of reserves) and the number of assets that users are willing to trade. The most popular AMMs, such as Uniswap (https://uniswap.org/whitepaper.pdf), Sushiswap (https://sushi.com/), Curve (https://curve.fi/whitepaper), and Balancer (https://balancer.fi/whitepaper.pdf), all accessed on 15 February 2022, use different variations of the constant product formula; see Section 3.3.

3.3. Uniswap

Uniswap, the most relevant decentralized exchange, was launched in November 2018 and, to date, more than 40,000 ERC-20 tokens are locked and tradable in the Uniswap protocol, adding a total value of 7 billion USD. In this section, we will provide an overview of the Uniswap V2 protocol; for more details, see [37,38].

Providing Liquidity: Each pair pool comprises a pair of tokens. Most frequently, as we will show in Section 5, one of the currencies is wrapped Eth (Weth), the ERC-20 equivalent version of Ether. We will typically use Eth or Weth as the numéraire and will denote it by $\mathcal{E}$, and we will refer to the other ERC-20 tokens as token, denoted by $\mathcal{C}$. A party wishing to provide liquidity to a specific pool deposits both $\mathcal{E}$ and $\mathcal{C}$ into the pool. If the pair pool has no tokens deposited yet, the deposit ratio can be arbitrarily chosen by the liquidity provider. Otherwise, the deposit ratio of Eth to token is determined by the existing ratio in the pool, which implicitly defines the infinitesimal price of the token $\mathcal{C}$ with respect to Eth $\mathcal{E}$. A liquidity provider who makes such a deposit receives a proportional amount of a liquidity provider token (LP-token). This third token is specific for each pool listed in Uniswap and represents the share of the liquidity provided by the agent of the total liquidity pool. As the users swap tokens in the pool, the value of the liquidity pool may rise or fall in value. Liquidity providers can redeem their liquidity tokens at any time and have their share of the liquidity pool paid out in equal value of Eth and tokens. Providing liquidity is potentially profitable because each trade incurs a transaction fee of 0.3%, which is redeposited into the pool. However, providing liquidity also has its own risks, leading in some situations to temporary losses [39].

Price formula: The pricing protocol for tokens listed on Uniswap is given by a constant product formula [38]. Suppose that a trader wants to buy an amount of Δ_y tokens, and the current reserves of the pair pool of Eth and tokens are x and y, respectively. Then, the amount Δ_x of Eth that they have to deposit is the unique solution to the following equation:

$$(x + (1 - f)\Delta_x)(y - \Delta_y) = xy,$$

where f is the fee of the protocol, currently sett to $f = 0.3\%$. After the trade, the reserves of the pair pool are updated in the following way: $x \leftarrow x + \Delta_x$, $y \leftarrow y - \Delta_y$. Analogously, a trader may want to sell tokens for Eth. The name *constant product market* comes from the fact that when the fee is set to zero, any trade must change in such a way that the reserves lie in the curve $xy = k$ for some positive real number k.

Uniswap Architecture: Uniswap V2 contracts are divided into two types of contracts, the *core* and the *periphery*. This division allows the core contracts, which hold the assets and therefore have to be secure, to be audited more easily. All the extra functionality required by traders can then be provided by periphery contracts. The most relevant periphery contract is the UniswapV2Router (https://etherscan.io/address/0x7a250d5630b4cf539739df2c5dacb4c659f2488d, accessed on 15 February 2022). This contract allows the user to easily interact with other core contracts in order to quote prices, create pair pools, swap tokens, and add/remove liquidity. Two of the most fundamental core contracts are the UniswapV2Factory (https://etherscan.io/address/0x5c69bee701ef814a2b6a3edd4b1652cb9cc5aa6f, accessed on 15 February 2022) and UniswapV2Pair (https://github.com/Uniswap/v2-core/blob/master/contracts/UniswapV2Pair.sol, accessed on 15 February 2022). The UniswapV2Factory is responsible for creating new pool pairs and recording all the pairs created. The UniswapV2Pair contract is responsible for recording the current state of the pool, i.e., the balance of Eth $\mathcal{E}$ (or any other token $\mathcal{C}'$) and the token $\mathcal{C}$, computing the price for trading and the number of tokens needed to add liquidity. Moreover, the UniswapV2Pair contract has an ERC-20 structure and records the ownership of the liquidity provided to the pool.

Uniswap Events: As we mentioned in Section 3.1, events track the state of different variables of a smart contract. The Uniswap protocol contains five important events.

1. `PairCreated`: It is an event in the UniswapV2 Factory contract. This event emits each time a new pair is created, and outputs the tuple (`token0,token1, pair, block_creation`) of a new pool created.
2. `Sync`: It is an event in the UniswapV2 PairPool contract. This event emits each time the reserves of the pool change. Every time the balance of the pool updates, the smart contract outputs the tuple (`reserves0,reserves1`), which is the reserves of the `token0` and `token1` after the update.
3. `Mint,Burn & Transfer`: These are events in the UniswapV2 PairPool contract that tracks the state of the ERC-20 LP-token.

Locking contracts: The locking contracts are protocols that run on top of the Uniswap protocol to provide a partial solution to rug pulls. These protocols are not part of the main Uniswap protocol. In general, in the first phase of developing a token or project, the liquidity provided to Uniswap is mostly added by the developers or creators of the project. It is for this reason that, initially, the distribution of the LP tokens is managed by a small number of addresses, making potential investors less confident in the project. In order to provide some trust to new investors, the developers lock the liquidity in a smart contract (Unicrypt is the most popular DEX LP lock) or burn the LP token, making it unfeasible for the developer to remove the liquidity for some time or indefinitely.

3.4. Token Propagation

We refer to token propagation as the set of metrics and tools to study the token distribution and circulation of the token during its activity period. As we mentioned previously, tokens are transferable. To send a token from an address A to an address B, the sender A can either call the function `transfer` of the token's smart contract or call other smart contracts that inherit the functions `approve` and `transferFrom`. Either way, an ERC-20 token emits the event `transfer` that contains the tuple (`sender,receiver,amount`). The first means of transferring tokens is usually cheaper and is used to directly transfer the tokens from one external ownable account (EOA) to another. The most common approach is to deposit or withdraw tokens from centralized exchanges. The second method tends to be used by different DeFi protocols such as DEXs, lending protocols, or voting systems to allow smart contracts to exchange tokens on behalf of an EOA address.

3.4.1. Token Distribution

The set of transfers and transactions allows us to compute the balance of each address for any snapshot. In order to study the distribution of the tokens, we propose using the Herfindahl–Hirschman Index (HHI).

In a nutshell, the HHI is a popular measure of market concentration and is used to calculate market competitiveness. The closer a market is to a monopoly, the higher the market's concentration (and the lower its competition). As we will explain later, this measure will be useful in order to detect some potential rug pulls in Uniswap. Below, we provide a mathematical definition of the HHI (Figure 1).

Definition 1. *Let T be a token, $\mathcal{A}$ be the set of addresses, and $B_t : \mathcal{A} \to \mathbb{R}_{\geq 0}$ be the balance mapping in some time frame t. The Herfindahl–Hirschman Index of the token T in time t is defined as*

$$HHI_t := \frac{\sum_{a \in \mathcal{A}} B_t(a)^2}{(\sum_{a \in \mathcal{A}} B_t(a))^2}.$$

The HHI curve is defined as $HHI : [t_{init}, t_{end}] \to [0,1]$.

In the cryptocurrency ecosystem, decentralization and the proper distribution of resources are important features. A smoother distribution of power implies less risk of breakdowns or malfunctioning produced by some participants misbehaving. In exchanges, a similar pattern occurs. In general, the more centralized the capital or funds, the higher the risk of market manipulations or liquidity removal, implying a loss of funds by retail investors.

From a game theory perspective, the more uniformly distributed the tokens and the liquidity, the less likely it is that agents can manipulate the market or remove funds in a short time period. For this reason, the lower the HHI, the better for the investors. Clearly, one of the problems of the HHI is that it is easy to manipulate and is sensitive to Sibyl attacks, since any adversary can create an arbitrary number of addresses and transfer an arbitrary amount of tokens among the addresses on his control. However, these manipulations incur some costs for the malicious agent, reducing the net profits of the attack.

To mitigate some of the problems mentioned, we propose using deeper network analysis tools. Recent studies used token transactions as a tool to forecast prices [40], detect price anomalies [8], and detect possible malicious activities [9,11,24]. Each period will be considered as a set of blocks with a separation of approximately one day between them.

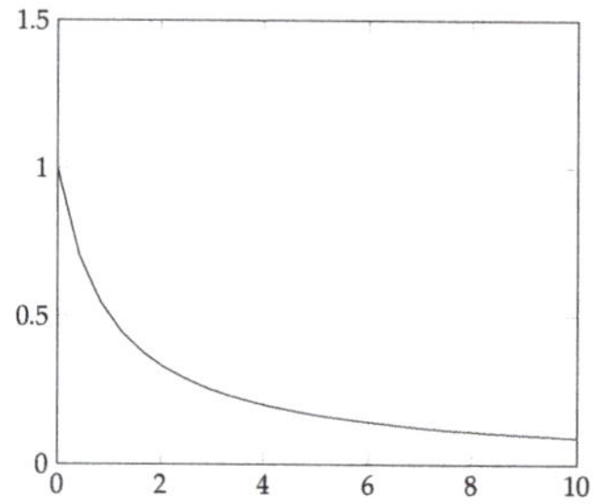

Figure 1. Ideal Herfindahl–Hirschman curve.

3.4.2. Transaction Graph Analysis

The set of transactions and transfers provides insightful information; however, this set can be better studied by giving it the natural graph structure, interpreting each address as a node and each transaction as a weighted edge.

Definition 2 (Transaction graph). *Let $G = (V, E, w)$ be a directed and weighted graph where V is the set of unique addresses, $E \subseteq V \times V$ the transfers from one address to another, and $w(\mathtt{tx})$ the amount transacted by the transfer $\mathtt{tx}$. Then, $G = (G_1, G_2, \ldots, G_n)$, $i = 1, \ldots, n+1$ is the time series for which G_i represents the transaction graph generated during period $i, i+1$.*

This time series captures the relationship between the users at each period. This allows us to study the circulation of the token between the different addresses.

Now, for each $G_i = (V_i, E_i)$, we define the number of transactions $N_{tx} = \#E_i$, the number of unique addresses $N_{addr} = \#V_i$, and the volume transacted as $\sum_{e\in E} w(e)$. Finally, the average clustering coefficient is defined as $ACC_i = \frac{1}{n}\sum_{u\in V_i} c_u$, where c_u is the geometric average of the subgraph edge weights [10], computed as follows:

$$c_u = \frac{1}{deg(u)(deg(u)-1)} \sum_{vw\in E} (\hat{w}_{uv}\hat{w}_{vw}\hat{w}_{wu})^{1/3}$$

and $\hat{w}_{uv}$ are normalized by the maximum weight in the network, i.e., $\hat{w}_{uv} = w_{uv} / \max_{uv\in E} (w(uv))$.

The average clustering coefficient is a measure of network segregation that captures the connections of individual nodes and their neighbors. In our scenario, this calculation allows us to quantify the interaction of each of the addresses with their neighboring addresses in a given period of time.

In general, the lower the use case of the token, the lower the average cluster coefficient. The main reason behind this heuristic is that a low diameter and use case usually imply that the transaction graph is close to a star graph (Figure 2) with `Pool` being the center node. Therefore, the average cluster coefficient is close to zero. However, users use non-malicious tokens in a large range of protocols, causing the nodes of these protocols to have a non-trivial cluster coefficient. Moreover, the daily average cluster coefficient is more prone to bias due to the constant need to make transactions between *Sybil* nodes and the impossibility of using `batchTransfer` operations, a type of operation that allows assets to be transfered to different addresses in one transaction.

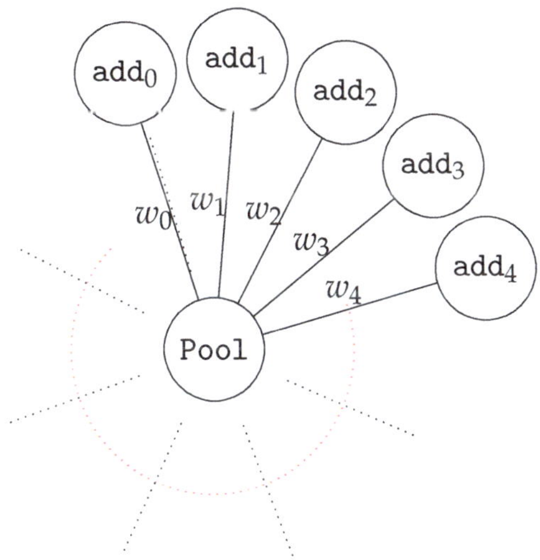

Figure 2. Transaction graph of centralized token, with average clustering coefficient 0.

4. Malicious Uniswap Maneuvers

As we have mentioned before, a rug pull is one of the most popular means of scamming in decentralized exchanges combined with a phishing attack. Different techniques are used to trick new investors into buying malicious tokens. To understand the malicious tokens traded in UniswapV2, we introduce a comprehensive classification by manually classifying both malicious and non-malicious tokens. While this classification will provide a clear overview of the tokens in Uniswap, it depends on non-observable variables, such as intentionality and profits. Therefore, we will use a weaker classification for our machine learning model. In this section, we will propose an ideal classification that will provide insights into different rug pulls. Figure 3 provides an overview of the classification.

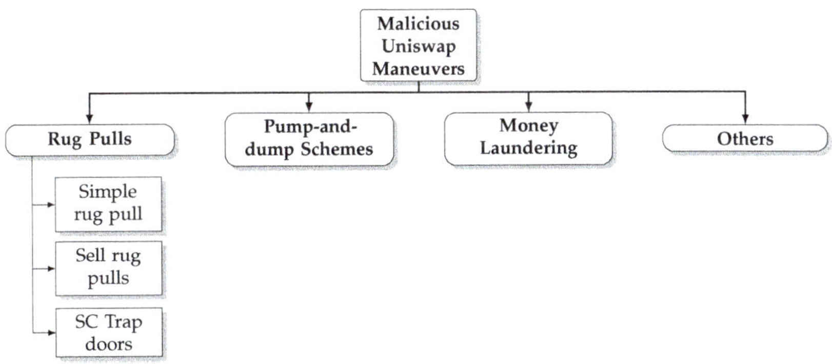

Figure 3. Malicious Uniswap maneuver classification.

The terms scam and malicious token are not being used identically by all researchers. For example, papers such as [3] use the terms scam and under-performing token indistinguishably, leading to inaccurate results and classifications. In the current paper, we define a *malicious token* as one released by a developer or a group of developers with no intrinsic value or use case. This definition is similar to that used in paper [30]. Clearly, this definition is ambiguous unless the value and use case are properly defined. In general, this is a complex issue to address. For example, it is not clear that cryptocurrencies such as Doge (https://dogecoin.com/, accessed on 15 February 2022) or Shiba (https://www.shibatoken.com/, accessed on 15 February 2022) have any use case or intrinsic value, but they are among the most popular meme-coins. In our framework, we say that a token has no intrinsic value or use case if the developer knows that the trading price with respect to USD will eventually be zero. In other words, a tradable malicious token in Uniswap induces a zero-sum game between the users and the developers, i.e., the incentives for the investors are not aligned with those of the token creators. Therefore, the main difference between malicious and non-malicious tokens is the developer's intentionality towards the token. One of the main problems of these definitions is that it is unfeasible to distinguish between scam tokens and under-performing or abandoned projects without accurate off-chain data. However, in general, the two terms do coincide. For these reasons, in the following section, rather than trying to identify whether a token is malicious or not, we will give a methodology for classifying and predicting under-performing and inactive tokens.

Simple rug pulls are the most common and easy to identify rug pulls. Essentially, simple rug pulls consist of three steps. The developer creates an ERC-20 token $\mathcal{C}$ and interacts with UniswapV2 Factory to create a new trading pair with wETH or any other relevant token, fixing the reserves to (x, y). Then, the investors execute the swap transaction on the trading pair, exchanging ETH for $\mathcal{C}$, and the reserves update to $(x + \Delta_x, y - \Delta_y)$. Afterwards, the developer activates the function `removeLiquidity`, obtaining $x + \Delta_x$ Ether and $y - \Delta_y$ of $\mathcal{C}$. Since the coin $\mathcal{C}$ has no intrinsic value, the net profit of the attacker is $x + \Delta_x -$ fees.

Sell rug pulls are also prevalent. However, they are not easy to identify and compute the total gains of the attack. A simplification of the attack would be as follows. The developer creates an ERC-20 token $\mathcal{C}$, with total supply S, and a new trading pair with a relevant token $\mathcal{E}$. The developer adds a fraction $f < S$ of the total supply of the $\mathcal{C}$ to the pool, having complete control of the remaining coins $S - f$. Then, they wait for a sufficient number of investors to execute the swap transaction on the trading pair. Afterwards, the developer swaps f coins $\mathcal{C}$ for $\mathcal{E}$. While this kind of rug pull is theoretically less profitable for the attacker, if combined with more features, it can be even more profitable than the first one. For example, in order to build confidence in investors, the attackers lock the liquidity in a smart contract or burn it. This makes investors think that a simple rug pull cannot happen, and that therefore it is a potentially profitable investment. In other words, the fact that the liquidity is locked makes the market volume increase. Moreover, if the token is mintable, the attacker can recover all the funds, minting as many coins as needed to recover nearly all the tokens $\mathcal{E}$ in the trading pool.

Smart Contract Trap Door rug pulls are the most difficult to identify and prevent. There are several reasons for this. The first is that the EVM is Turing-complete, and therefore it is highly complex to identify all vector attacks; the second is that smart contracts do not exist in isolation, i.e., smart contracts can work on top of other smart contracts. This means that the economic security of some smart contracts depends on other smart contracts [19]. In the following section, we will explain some of the most popular examples of these trap doors.

- `Mintable` is a property shared by many tokens, including non-malicious ones such as USDT (https://tether.to/, accessed on 15 February 2022). In general, we say that a token is mintable if it has a function that allows it to increase the supply of the token with some pre-defined conditions. Usually, mintable tokens give rights to mint new tokens to the developers to a fixed set of addresses. While this functionality can be a useful feature in some contexts, it can also be used by malicious users to subtract all the liquidity of the pull by minting as many tokens as needed.
- `TransferFrom/Approve` bad design is a property shared by some malicious tokens. `TransferFrom` is the function that allows a smart contract to transfer assets on behalf of an externally owned account. In the context of Uniswap, a proper design of this function allows tokens to be sold. In other words, arbitrarily changing the `TransferFrom` function makes the Uniswap Pool behave as a honeypot [18]. There are different means of making this smart contract; however, the most popular example

of this kind of scam is the use of tokens that contain the line code `require(from == owner |||| to == owner |||| from == UNI)` in the `TransferFrom` function.

- Composability vulnerabilities are the least common ones and the hardest to find. In general, this type of rug pull is not made by the developers but by malicious agents external to the project, who take advantage of the bad design of the smart contract token interacting with Uniswap or other DEXs. Those that we have been able to identify are the tokens with a price oracle vulnerability. Usually, we observed that these tokens have Uniswap integrated in the source code of the smart contract in order to reward holders. However, these rewards depend on the price. The higher the price, the higher the reward. The fundamental problem of this mechanism is that the price is defined through an oracle that, as shown in [22], is easy to manipulate with enough funds or using a flash loan.

In general, these rug pulls are not exclusive and, in reality, different techniques are applied in order to execute a rug pull. Moreover, these techniques are usually combined with phishing attacks and pump-and-dump schemes.

Money laundering: In traditional finance, money laundering is the processing of money obtained from illicit activities, to make it appear that it originated from a legitimate source. In the Ethereum environment or cryptospace in general, we will define money laundering as the process of sending some coins obtained from heists, honeypots, or hacks from an address $\texttt{addr}_1$ to another address $\texttt{addr}_2$ privately. That is, observers cannot link these two addresses through the transaction graph (Figure 4). In Ethereum, the most common technique to obtain privacy is through mixers [14]. The most popular mixer is TornadoCash (https://tornado.cash/, accessed on 15 February 2022), which implements a smart contract that accepts transactions in Ether so that the amount can later be withdrawn with no reference to the original transaction by means of using zero-knowledge proofs. Analyzing rug pulls in the Uniswap protocol, we have found some users that use the Uniswap protocol to send Ether to other addresses without being noticed by most common address clustering algorithms. The operation consists of three main steps. First, the address $\texttt{addr}_2$ creates an unsellable token C and lists it in Uniswap with an arbitrary amount of liquidity. Then, the address $\texttt{addr}_1$ changes the Ether for C in the Uniswap pool. Finally, the address $\texttt{addr}_2$ removes all the liquidity from the pool.

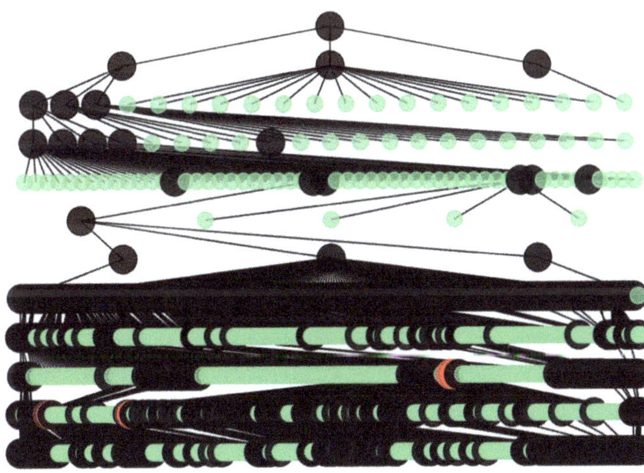

Figure 4. Transaction graph with depth = 10, of scammer addr = 0x775744... (https://etherscan.io/address/0x775744a529f73a754164e4fE740e44C7c5aa5942, accessed on 15 February 2022), where black nodes are addresses directly connected, green nodes are transactions of type rug pull/money laundering, and red nodes are centralized exchanges, such as Binance, Coinbase, and Huobi.

A good example of this is given by the user that controls the address 0x775744... (https://etherscan.io/address/0x775744a529f73a754164e4fE740e44C7c5aa5942, accessed on 15 February 2022), in charge of creating more than 500 tokens in order to money launder, pump prices, and obtain profits via executing trap door rug pulls.

Pump-and-dump schemes: In traditional finance, a pump-and-dump scheme is a malicious maneuver that manipulates the market price of a stock, in which the executors first purchase a financial asset at a certain price. They then persuade other speculative non-informed investors to purchase, within a short period of time, thereby causing the price to rise artificially (pump), and executors sell their assets at a profit. This typically leads to a rapid price drop (dump), leaving the victims with a loss. In traditional markets, pump-and-dump schemes have generally been illegal around the globe. However, in cryptocurrencies, the lack of regulations and the nature of cryptospace allow these maneuvers to happen easily and avoid sanctions. While these maneuvers have some intersection points with the rug pull maneuver, the fundamental difference is that, in pump-and-dump schemes, the targeted asset is not necessarily malicious, while, in rug pulls, it is.

Others: While malicious maneuvers are usually a combination of the ones mentioned before, all of them have a characteristic in common: the victims are uninformed users. However, there are other maneuvers in EVM-compatible blockchains that try to attack the weaknesses of maximal extractable value (MEV) bots. A good example of this is Salmonella (https://github.com/Defi-Cartel/salmonella, accessed on 15 February 2022), a bot that tries to trick sandwich traders [23]. Salmonella creates a token with an `approve/transferFrom` bad design. Afterwards, it creates a swap transaction that tricks MEV bots to sandwich it with a buy and sell operation. At the moment that the transactions are executed, by design of the Salmonella smart contract, the buy is accepted, but the sell transaction is reverted, leaving a lot of cash in the pool for the Salmonella developer.

5. Data Collection

To download all the data needed to perform the labelling and the analysis, we used an Infura archive node (https://infura.io/, accessed on 15 February 2022) and the Etherscan API (https://etherscan.io/apis, accessed on 15 February 2022.) To obtain the state of the Uniswap exchange and the tokens, we used the events produced by their respective smart contracts. Any node connected to Ethereum JSON-RPC API can observe these events and act accordingly. Events can also be indexed, so that the event history is searchable later.

1. *Tokens listed*: We obtained the history of all tokens listed in the Uniswap V2 from its creation to 3 September 2021, asking for all events of the `PairCreated` type in the UniswapV2Factory contract.
2. *Smart contract and features*: After obtaining all listed tokens in Uniswap, with the help of Etherscan, we downloaded the transactions in which they were created, their smart contract, their decimals, and their symbol. In order to speed up these calls, we used the multicall contract (https://etherscan.io/address/0xb1f8e55c7f64d203c1400b9d8555d050f94adf39, accessed on 15 February 2022) to batch these calls to the blockchain in a single call. Afterwards, we used Slither [16] to obtain different features of the smart contract, such as `pausable` and `mintable`.
3. *Events*: From all the pools of Uniswap obtained in *Tokens listed*, we collected all events of type `Sync, Mint, Burn` and `Transfer` for each of the PairPools obtained. Finally, we downloaded all `Transfer` events from each of the tokens.

There are several attributes that we could not download via API, such as the transaction creation of a contract and full market cap of a token; however, they are available on certain block explorers such as Etherscan. In these cases, we have used scrapping techniques to obtain this information. For example, some of the data that we have not been able to find via the Etherscan API and Infura include the hash of the transaction in which tokens were created and tokens that have had some type of external audit.

6. Token Labelling

In this section, we provide the set of tools and the methodology we used in order to label the tokens listed in the Uniswap protocol as malicious and non-malicious, and provide the results obtained using this methodology. First, we define the maximum drop and the recovery of token prices and liquidity time series. Then, we explain the distribution of tokens that eventually became inactive or that became a rug pull. Finally, we explain which methodology we used to accurately label tokens as non-malicious.

6.1. Ground Truth Labelling

One of the final goals of this study is to create an ML algorithm capable of detecting malicious tokens. To do this, we have built a list of tokens tagged as malicious and non-malicious. In this case, the label of the malicious tokens has been deduced from a series of calculations defined below:

Definition 3. *Let $X = \{X_t \mid t \in \{0, \dots, S\}\}$, be the time series representing the price or liquidity in all the token activity up to the last sync event S. The maximum drop is defined as*

$$MD = \left| \frac{X_l - X_h}{X_h} \right|,$$

where $X_h = max\{X_\tau \mid \tau \in \{0, \dots, S\}\}$, $h = argmax\{X_\tau \mid \tau \in \{0, \dots, S\}\}$, and $X_l = min\{X_\tau \mid \tau \in \{h, \dots, S\}\}$.

The maximum drop is usually known in the literature as maximum drawdown and is often used as a risk measure of portfolios (Figure 5). Informally, the maximum drop is the largest drop from a peak to a trough. In our context, the maximum drop measures a fall in the price or liquidity of the Uniswap-listed pools. In Section 4, we have seen that the last step in a simple rug pull is the removal of all liquidity from the pool. Therefore, by definition, in a simple rug pull, the MD of the liquidity or time series of a rug pull tends to be approximately 1. However, the opposite implication is not true in general. While the price maximum drawdown being close to 1 implies that the token is malicious, the MD of liquidity being 1 does not necessarily imply some malicious behavior. For example, the developer could have moved the funds to another pool or another DEX project. Moreover, it could be possible that the market maker just wants to retire their funds and does not have any more interest in providing liquidity. In general, if the token has a use case and a market value, other agents will have incentives to take over as market makers. For this reason, we introduce the recovery.

Definition 4. *Let $h, l \in [0, S]$ be the elements defined previously. Then, the recovery from X_τ to X_S is computed as*

$$RC = \frac{X_S - X_l}{X_h - X_l}.$$

Informally, the recovery is the largest pump from the bottom. This measure makes it possible to check if the liquidity position and the price of a token have recovered after the drop. Next, we will show how the data split, taking into account the maximum drawdown and the recovery.

Figure 6a shows two examples of different rug pulls with no recovery and a maximum drop of one in liquidity and price, respectively. Moreover, one can deduce that the rug pull (a) is a simple rug pull while the rug pull (b) is a sell rug pull.

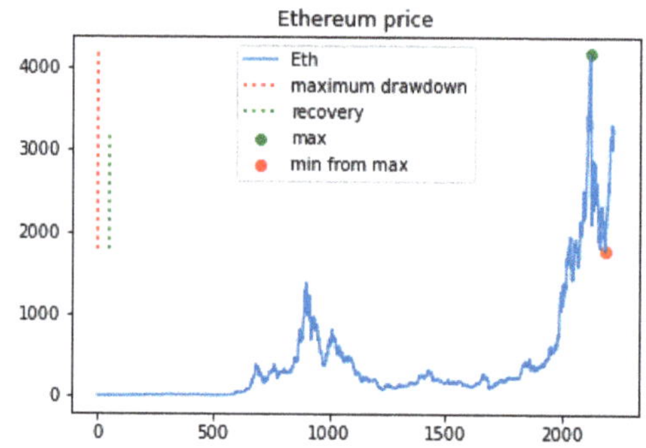

Figure 5. Maximum drawdown and recovery of ETH price.

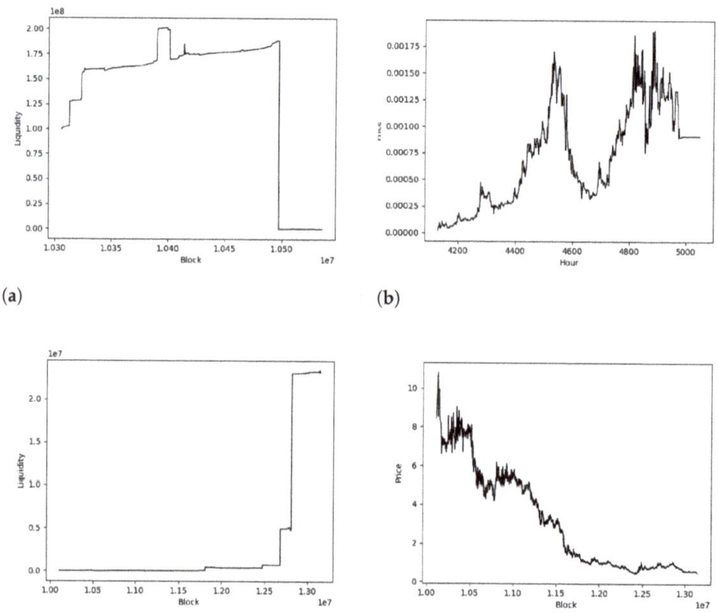

(a) (b) (c) (d)

Figure 6. This figure shows the price and liquidity time series of two different types of rug pulls. The two first pictures are associated with a simple rug pull with token 0x896a07e3788983ec52eaf0F9C6F6E031464Ee2CC, while the second pair of pictures is associated with a sell rug pull with token 0x0A7e4D70e10b63FeF9F8dD19FbA3818d15154d2Fa. (**a**) Liquidity Fast Rug Pull; (**b**) Price Fast Rug Pull; (**c**) Liquidity Rug Pull without Burn Events; (**d**) Price Rug Pull without Burn Events.

6.1.1. Malicious Token Labelling

Various features were computed, taking into account two properties: fluctuations in price or liquidity, and activity. As explained above, the maximum drop computes the greatest drop, either in liquidity or price, during the activity of the tokens.

Most malicious tokens, at some point, lose all their liquidity or their price drops to zero. However, this does not necessarily indicate malicious behavior, as it may be due to a simple fluctuation. Thus, we also computed the recovery. If a token loses all its liquidity or its price drops to zero and these levels are never recovered, then the probability that the falls are due to malicious intent increases.

In addition, to ensure that these fluctuations are not due to simple market movement, we compute the time elapsed since the last movement of the pool or token transfer to 13 September 2021. If more than one month has passed between the last movement or transaction of the token so far, we consider that the token is inactive. Finally, we obtain a list of inactive tokens, which have drops in price or liquidity of almost one hundred percent and which do not recover. Our initial list contained 46,499 tokens. We discarded those that did not have decimals defined in their contract (169). We then selected those that had a pool connected to wETH (44,685) and downloaded their `Sync`, `Mint`, `Burn` and `Transfer` events. The final list contains 37,891 tokens that have at least one pool connected with wETH and more than 5 Sync events in all their activity. This last property is necessary to be able to compute the heuristics used to label the tokens (Figure 7).

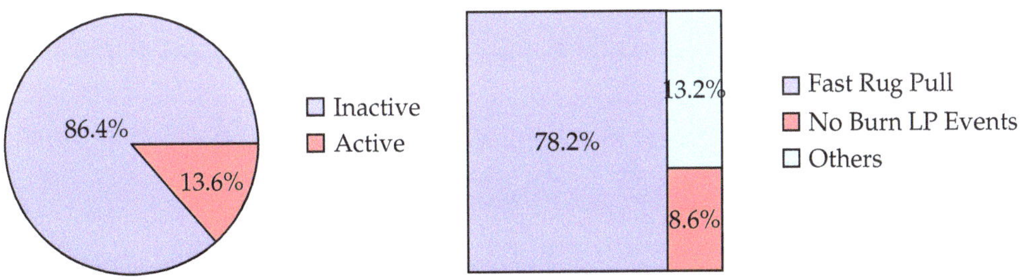

(a) Tokens activity

(b) Inactive tokens overview

Figure 7. Pie charts of features activity (**a**) and maximum drop (**b**) for the final list of 37,891 tokens.

As explained above, we first checked if the tokens were inactive, i.e, if they had not registered `Transfer` or `Sync` events for more than 30 days (86.4% of the total). We also computed the maximum liquidity drop and saw that the liquidity of 78.2% of the inactive pools had been completely withdrawn at some point. Finally, we noticed that only 0.4% of pools that at some point had lost all their liquidity recovered in all subsequent activity. This made a total of 24,870 tokens that could be tagged as malicious since they were inactive tokens that had, at some point, lost all their liquidity and had not recovered it again.

On the other hand, as shown in Figure 8, 8.6% of the inactive tokens did not have any Burn LP events in all their activity period. However, 79.2% of this 8.6% had seen a price drop of more than 90% at some point, and only 1.9% recovered their value after the drop. This adds 2087 tokens that can be identified as malicious since they are inactive, with a price MD of at least 90% and no recovery.

6.1.2. Non-Malicious Token Labelling

Unlike malicious tokens, non-malicious tokens cannot be chosen from a liquidity, price, and activity analysis. Given a token, it may be considered malicious if there has been at least one rug pull at some point in its activity. However, a token that has not had any rug pull cannot be considered non malicious, since it could experience a rug pull later on. Therefore, we take advantage of audits carried out by external companies (Certik, Quantstamp, Hacken, etc.). It is important to highlight that non-malicious tokens can have drops in price and liquidity, too. Nevertheless, none of them simultaneously fulfil all three properties that define malicious tokens, namely inactivity, a sharp drop in price or a sharp drop in liquidity, and no recovery. Thus, a list of 674 tokens labelled as non-malicious has been mined from different sources (https://coinmarketcap.com/view/defi/; https://www.coingecko.com/en/categories/dec entralized-finance-defi; https://etherscan.io/tokens, all accessed on 15 February 2022). We have also discarded those that are so large that it becomes computationally expensive to compute its features—for example, USDT or USDC. The final list contains 631 tokens labelled as non-malicious.

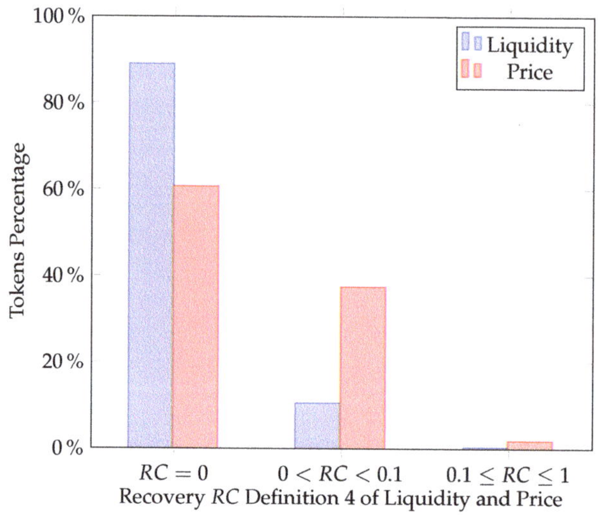

Figure 8. Price and liquidity recovery.

7. Scam Detection

We start from a list of tokens labelled as malicious or non-malicious, according to their features; therefore, it can be considered a binary classification problem. In this classification, we distinguish between the two types of tokens in the moments prior to the malicious activity. This means that models are capable of detecting malicious tokens in the activity prior to the rug pull. In this section, we present two methods: one considering all the activity of a token, and the other considering just the first 24 h. Moreover, we detail the different classifiers used in both methods and their hyperparameter optimization. Finally, we present the results of each method.

7.1. Activity-Based Method

Our goal is to detect malicious tokens at an early stage, i.e., before users lose their capital. Thus far, we have characterized two main types of rug pull: the ones that lose all liquidity at some point and the ones where the price drops to almost zero. In this way, for each token labelled as malicious, we have randomly chosen several evaluation points prior to the maximum drop. Non-malicious tokens have been evaluated throughout their activity. Then, for each evaluation point, we have calculated the token features up to that block and used them to train two ML algorithms in order to find those patterns related to malicious activity.

In this method, we choose n evaluation blocks at random. For example, Figure 9 shows the price and liquidity of one token labelled as malicious. In this token, liquidity suddenly drops to zero and does not recover again. Therefore, we consider it to be a fast rug pull. The three vertical lines leading up to the crash represent the three evaluation points for that particular token. This means that we have calculated the variables of that token up to those blocks. In this way, we have proceeded with each of the labelled tokens. As explained in Section 7.4, the final metrics have been computed taking five evaluation points on non-malicious tokens and one on malicious tokens. All evaluations are prior to the malicious act; this implies that this method can later be used as a tool to detect malicious tokens at any time. However, there are subtleties that can skew the ML algorithms used. For example, tokens labelled as non-malicious tend to have a much larger capitalization compared to malicious tokens; therefore, the algorithm could end up differentiating between "small" tokens and "large" tokens instead of malicious and non-malicious. Although this differentiation is not a bad approach to this task, we think that there may be other situations that require different approaches. In the next method, we evaluate all tokens at the same temporal evaluation points in order to identify these possible biases.

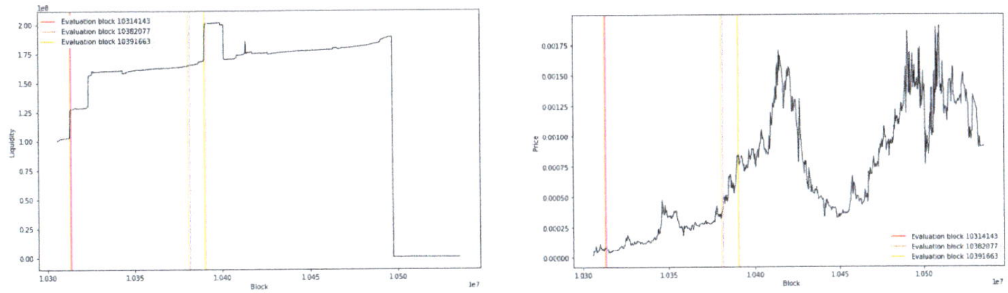

(a) (b)

Figure 9. Evaluation points in liquidity (**a**) and price (**b**) chosen for token 0x896a07e3788983ec52eaf0F9C6F6E031464Ee2CC labeled as malicious.

7.2. 24-Hour Early Method

Rug pulls are profitable if their malicious act is done before they are discovered. Therefore, most rug pulls (93%) occur in the first 24 h after the pool is created. This encourages us to build a tool to detect malicious tokens at startup. For each labelled token, we have computed its features in each of the 24 h after its pool creation. Then, we create a different dataset for each hour in which the tokens are evaluated.

Note that, in this case, we are training the models for each hour; therefore, we only have one evaluation point for each dataset. This also implies that we will have a smaller dataset compared to the other method. In Appendix C, we present the different metrics obtained for each of the hours. Moreover, we can measure the evolution of the predictive power of the algorithm in the first hours of the token's life. The fact that this method requires a certain history to be able to give a prediction implies that the more history we obtain, the better the prediction. This intuition is confirmed in Section 7.4.

7.3. Machine Learning and Hyperparameter Optimization

Gradient Boosting Decision Tree (GBDT) [41] models offer high performance in classification tasks with tabular data since they allow the definition of different cost functions, do not require preprocessing for categorical features, and can handle missing data. Thus, it seems clear to apply a GBDT model to our problem. In particular, we have used the *XGBoost* [42] algorithm.

On the other hand, algorithms with Transformer architecture [43] are obtaining high results in fields such as natural language processing [44,45], computer vision [46], etc. In this work, we have used a model based on attention mechanisms called FT-Transformer [6] in order to test a tabular algorithm with Transformer architecture in our problem.

Hyperparameters cannot be learned during the training process. Furthermore, they have a significant impact on the performance of the model being trained. Thus, optimizing them is crucial for better efficiency, faster convergence, and overall better results. In this work, we have used Optuna [47], a software framework designed primarily for hyperparameter optimization in ML algorithms.

Finally, in order to evaluate the impact of each variable, we have used the SHAP (SHapley Additive exPlanations) Values [48]. SHAP uses game theory to explain the results obtained in ML algorithms. In particular, it uses the classical Shapley values of game theory and their related extensions.

7.4. Results

The final list contains 27,588 labelled tokens, 631 labelled as non-malicious tokens and 26,957 labelled as malicious. Within the malicious, 24,870 are fast rug pulls and 2087 do not contain LP Burn events. We see that there are far fewer non-malicious tokens than malicious ones. There are many techniques (https://imbalanced-learn.org/stable/references/index.html, accessed on 15 February 2022) to deal with this problem; however, none of them have been applied in order to make the results more understandable. Instead, our data augmentation technique consists of choosing more evaluation points for non-malicious tokens than for malicious tokens. Now, given this dataset, we want to increase the performance in predicting non-malicious tokens since it would be enough to label all of them as malicious to achieve an accuracy rate of 97.7%. Therefore, we label the non-malicious tokens as 1 and the malicious tokens as 0.

We have used the cross-validation method to validate both ML algorithms. Cross-validation is a resampling method that uses different parts of the data to test and train a model in different iterations. In particular, we have used the stratified version, in which the partitions are selected so that the mean response value is approximately the same in all partitions. In the case of binary classification, this means that each partition contains roughly the same proportions of the two types of class labels. In the first method, we have five evaluation points on non-malicious tokens and one on malicious tokens. Thus, in each of the iterations, the tokens of the training and validation set are separated in a stratified way with all their corresponding evaluations. This implies that the same token will never have evaluations in the training and validation set at the same time, and all folds will have roughly the same number of malicious tokens. Finally, we used five-fold cross-validation; therefore, all the results will be presented as the mean and standard deviation of all folds.

We have used the `xgboost` (https://xgboost.readthedocs.io/en/stable/, accessed on 15 February 2022) Python library to apply the XGBoost model to each method. Specifically, in each of the five folds, we have used the training partition to perform a hyperparameter optimization (see Appendix B) to later predict the test of the corresponding fold. In the case of FT-Transformer, we have used the default parameters of the `rtdl` (https://yandex-research.github.io/rtdl/stable, accessed on 15 February 2022) Python library, since training this model is too expensive to perform hyperparameter optimization.

7.4.1. Activity-Based Method Results

Both XGBoost and FT-Transformer obtain high metrics for accuracy, recall, precision, and F1 score. However, XGBoost outperforms FT-Transformer in all metrics. As we previously mentioned, unlike XGBoost, FT-Transformer hyperparameters have not been optimized due to the high computational complexity required to train the model (Table 2).

Table 2. Accuracy, recall, precision and F1 score obtained in a 5-fold cross-validation for first method.

(a) XGBoost metrics.

XGBoost	Mean	Std
Accuracy	0.9936	0.0029
Recall	0.9540	0.0297
Precision	0.9838	0.0056
F1 score	0.9684	0.0151

(b) FT-Transformer metrics.

FT-Transformer	Mean	Std
Accuracy	0.9890	0.0036
Recall	0.9180	0.0363
Precision	0.9752	0.0109
F1 score	0.9454	0.0187

To understand the impact of each feature in both models, we have computed the SHAP values. In this work, we only focus on XGBoost; however, the process would be the same for FT-Transformer. The SHAP values assign the importance of each feature for each prediction. In general, the greater the impact of features on a prediction, the greater the SHAP value in absolute values.

In Figure 10, we show, on the left side, the feature importance in terms of the SHAP value applied in the first method, and, on the right, the impact on the final output. As previously noted, most malicious tokens die in the first 24 h after the pool is created; by contrast, non-malicious tokens have a longer life. This explains why features such as the number of transactions or number of unique addresses have so much weight in the model. Another important feature is the difference in blocks between the creation of the token and the pool. We notice that a smaller block difference between token and pool creation implies negative SHAP values, and negative SHAP values should correspond to malicious tokens. This conclusion coincides with [3] since several of the malicious tokens take advantage of social trends by copying the name of official tokens and take money from investors who become confused. This technique implies speed in the creation of the token and the pool, since otherwise the trend may be lost.

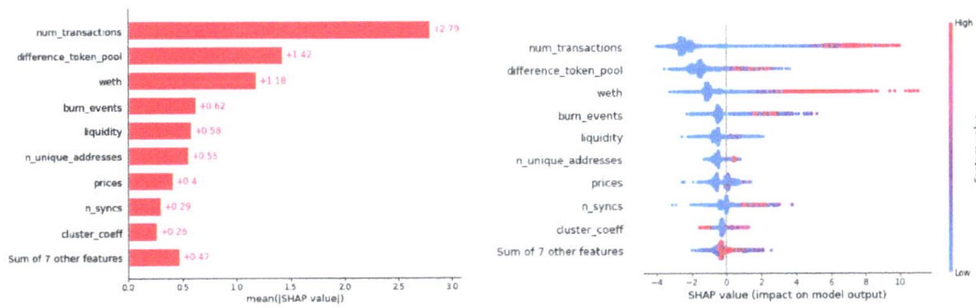

Figure 10. Impact of the variables in the XGBoost model applied to the first method. Mean of SHAP values on the left and global impact of the features on the right. Images generated from the Python SHAP library.

7.4.2. 24-Hour Early Method Results

The results of the second method must be understood from another perspective, since the problem posed is not the same. As we said, the difference with respect to the first method lies in the fact that, we evaluate all the tokens at a certain time after the creation of their respective pools.

Figure 11 shows the evolution of the metrics for each of the ML algorithms used. XGBoost obtains better metrics, except precision in some cases. We also notice that the metrics of the first hour are lower than those of the last. This confirms the intuition that our methods require a certain token history in order to work correctly and that models improve as this history grows. Our algorithm obtains very high accuracy (see Appendix C) even in the first few hours. However, the precision, recall and F1 score are lower than in the activity-based method. In the best of cases, i.e., 20 h after the creation of the pool, our best algorithm obtains a recall score of 0.789. This could indicate that while malicious tokens are easily detectable in the first few hours, non-malicious tokens require more time. On the other hand, the precision remains quite high compared to the recall. This implies that, although the algorithms do not have a strong ability to detect non-malicious tokens, once they predict that one of them is non-malicious, it is very likely to be the case.

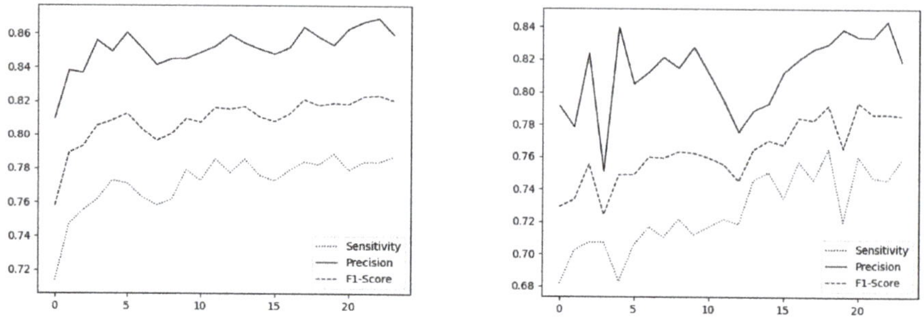

(a) (b)

Figure 11. Evolution of recall, precision, and F1 score for the XBGoost and FT-Transformer model in the first 24 h after the creation of the token. (**a**) XGBoost; (**b**) FT-Transformer.

7.4.3. Unicrypt Results

As explained in Section 3.3, Unicrypt is a protocol that runs on top of the Uniswap protocol with the purpose of being a partial solution to rug pulls. In this work, we have empirically demonstrated that most of the tokens that use Unicrypt are malicious. First, from our list of labelled tokens, 745 use Unicrypt, 725 are labelled as malicious, and 20 as non-malicious. Then, from the unlabelled tokens, we compute their features up to the present time and use the activity-based method with the XGBoost algorithm to evaluate them. Based on these predictions, of the 2544 of the non-labelled tokens using Unicrypt, 2211 are predicted to be malicious and 333 non-malicious.

8. Conclusions

In summary, first, we increased the dataset provided in [3] by 18K scam tokens, finding new ways of actively executing the rug pulls. Then, we provided a theoretical classification to understand the different ways of executing the scam, and through the process of identifying rug pulls, we found new token smart contract vulnerabilities (composability attacks) and new ways of money laundering. Based on this theoretical foundation, we provided a methodology to find rug pulls that had already been executed. Not surprisingly, we found that more than the 97.7% of the tokens labelled were rug pulls. Finally, we defined two methods that use ML models to distinguish non-malicious tokens from malicious ones. We also verified the high effectiveness of these models in both scenarios. This implies that new malicious tokens can be detected prior to the malicious act, and, on the other hand, tokens supported by a strong project can also be detected at an early stage. The software to replicate the numerical results obtained is provided in (https://github.com/T2Project/RugPullDetection, accessed on 15 February 2022).

9. Future Work

While our study has produced high precision and accuracy in detecting scams listed in Uniswap, it carries some limitations. First, we believe that transferring learning techniques will not obtain the same quality of results in DEXs of other chains such as PancakeSwap (https://pancakeswap.finance, accessed on 15 February 2022) and QuickSwap (https://quickswap.exchange, accessed on 15 February 2022). Since the `gasPrice` is much lower, the economic cost of simulating volume and transfers is almost negligible. Therefore, in order to obtain similar results in other chains, we should repeat the same longitudinal work and compute new features. In addition, as market trends may change, these algorithms will have to be retrained in order to keep adding new information.

Second, even though our approach for studying the source code of the tokens with Slither [16] was efficient and reliable for our purpose, it was not completely accurate, since it is a static analysis tool of the code and does not take into account complex composability problems among other protocols. Therefore, to have more insights for a particular token, we suggest using stronger testing tools and formal verification tools, such as the ones provided in [19].

Third, even though the clustering coefficient proved to be useful, computing this feature is highly time-consuming. Therefore, we propose using other graph analysis methods, such as topology data analysis, to have a more efficient scam detection algorithm and obtain even more reliable insights into the transaction graph.

Author Contributions: Data curation, V.D.; Investigation, B.M. and V.A. All authors have read and agreed to the published version of the manuscript.

Funding: This paper is part of a project that has received funding from the European Union's Horizon 2020 research and innovation programme under grant agreement number 814284.

Institutional Review Board Statement: Not applicable.

Informed Consent Statement: Not applicable.

Conflicts of Interest: The authors declare no conflict of interest.

Appendix A. Table of Features

Table A1. This table describes each feature used in the XGBoost and FT-Transformer classifiers. Note that apart from the *Token* group, all features are defined as time series.

Group	Name	Description
HHI index	liq_curve	HHI applied to LP tokens.
	tx_curve	HHI applied to each token.
Pool	n_pool_syncs	Total sync events.
	weth	Total weth.
	price	Price of token.
	liquidity	Total liquidity.
LP-Token	lp_transfer	Total number of LP token transfers.
	mints	Total number of mint events.
	burns	Total number of burn events.
Token transfers	n_transfers	Total number of transfers.
	n_unique_addresses	Total number of unique addresses.
	clus_coeff	Clustering coefficient.
Token	difference_token_pool	Number of blocks between token and pool creation.
	lock	This feature is 1 if part of the liquidity is locked and 0 otherwise.
	yield	This feature is 1 if there is yield farming involved and 0 otherwise.
	burn	This feature is 1 if part of the liquidity has been burned and 0 otherwise.

Appendix B. Hyperparameters

Table A2. List of hyperparameters optimized using the Optuna Python library.

Model	Parameter	Type	Distribution	Range
XGBoost	max_depth	Int	Uniform	[3, 10]
	subsample	Float	Uniform	[0.5, 1]
	learning_rate	Float	Uniform	$[1 \times 10^{-5}, 1]$
	gamma	Float	Log-Uniform	$[1 \times 10^{-8}, 1 \times 10^{2}]$
	lambda	Float	Log-Uniform	$[1 \times 10^{-8}, 1 \times 10^{2}]$
	alpha	Float	Log-Uniform	$[1 \times 10^{-8}, 1 \times 10^{2}]$

Appendix C. Second Method Results

XGBoost 24 h					FT-Transformer 24 h				
Hour	Accuracy	Sensitivity	Precision	F1_Score	Hour	Accuracy	Sensitivity	Precision	F1_Score
1	0.990	0.714	0.810	0.758	1	0.989	0.682	0.791	0.729
2	0.991	0.747	0.838	0.789	2	0.988	0.702	0.778	0.734
3	0.991	0.755	0.837	0.793	3	0.990	0.707	0.824	0.755
4	0.992	0.762	0.856	0.806	4	0.987	0.707	0.751	0.724
5	0.992	0.773	0.849	0.809	5	0.990	0.683	0.840	0.749
6	0.992	0.771	0.860	0.813	6	0.989	0.706	0.805	0.749
7	0.992	0.763	0.851	0.804	7	0.990	0.717	0.812	0.760
8	0.991	0.758	0.841	0.797	8	0.990	0.710	0.821	0.759
9	0.991	0.762	0.845	0.801	9	0.990	0.722	0.815	0.763
10	0.992	0.779	0.845	0.810	10	0.990	0.712	0.828	0.762
11	0.992	0.773	0.849	0.808	11	0.990	0.717	0.811	0.759
12	0.992	0.786	0.852	0.816	12	0.989	0.722	0.795	0.755
13	0.992	0.778	0.859	0.815	13	0.989	0.718	0.775	0.745
14	0.992	0.786	0.854	0.817	14	0.989	0.746	0.789	0.764
15	0.992	0.776	0.851	0.811	15	0.990	0.750	0.793	0.770
16	0.992	0.773	0.848	0.808	16	0.990	0.734	0.812	0.767
17	0.992	0.779	0.852	0.813	17	0.991	0.757	0.820	0.784
18	0.992	0.784	0.864	0.821	18	0.991	0.746	0.826	0.782
19	0.992	0.782	0.858	0.818	19	0.991	0.765	0.829	0.792
20	0.992	0.789	0.853	0.819	20	0.990	0.720	0.838	0.765
21	0.992	0.779	0.863	0.818	21	0.991	0.760	0.834	0.793
22	0.992	0.784	0.867	0.823	22	0.991	0.747	0.834	0.786
23	0.992	0.784	0.869	0.824	23	0.991	0.746	0.843	0.786
24	0.992	0.787	0.860	0.821	24	0.991	0.758	0.819	0.785

References

1. Nakamoto, S. *Bitcoin: A Peer-to-Peer Electronic Cash System*; Technical Report; SSRN: Rochester, NY, USA, 2019.
2. Werner, S.M.; Perez, D.; Gudgeon, L.; Klages-Mundt, A.; Harz, D.; Knottenbelt, W.J. Sok: Decentralized finance (defi). *arXiv* **2021**, arXiv:2101.08778.
3. Xia, P.; Gao, B.; Su, W.; Yu, Z.; Luo, X.; Zhang, C.; Xiao, X.; Xu, G. Demystifying Scam Tokens on Uniswap Decentralized Exchange. *arXiv* **2021**, arXiv:2109.00229.
4. Rug Pull Detector. Available online: http://rugpulldetector.com/ (accessed on 30 September 2021).
5. Token Sniffer. Available online: https://tokensniffer.com/ (accessed on 30 September 2021).
6. Gorishniy, Y.; Rubachev, I.; Khrulkov, V.; Babenko, A. Revisiting Deep Learning Models for Tabular Data. 2021; Available online: http://xxx.lanl.gov/abs/2106.11959 (accessed on 15 February 2022).
7. Zero-Dimensional Scam Detection. Available online: https://github.com/T2Project/RugPullDetection (accessed on 12 December 2021).

8. Li, Y.; Islambekov, U.; Akcora, C.; Smirnova, E.; Gel, Y.R.; Kantarcioglu, M. Dissecting ethereum blockchain analytics: What we learn from topology and geometry of the ethereum graph? In Proceedings of the 2020 SIAM International Conference on Data Mining, SIAM, Cincinnati, OH, USA, 7–9 May 2020; pp. 523–531.
9. Ofori-Boateng, D.; Dominguez, I.S.; Kantarcioglu, M.; Akcora, C.G.; Gel, Y.R. Topological Anomaly Detection in Dynamic Multilayer Blockchain Networks. 2021. Available online: http://xxx.lanl.gov/abs/2106.01806 (accessed on 15 February 2022).
10. Onnela, J.P.; Saramäki, J.; Kertész, J.; Kaski, K. Intensity and coherence of motifs in weighted complex networks. *Phys. Rev. E* **2005**, *71*, 065103. [CrossRef] [PubMed]
11. Patel, V.; Pan, L.; Rajasegarar, S. Graph Deep Learning Based Anomaly Detection in Ethereum Blockchain Network. In *Proceedings of the International Conference on Network and System Security*; Springer: Berlin, Germany, 2020; pp. 132–148.
12. Phillips, R.; Wilder, H. Tracing Cryptocurrency Scams: Clustering Replicated Advance-Fee and Phishing Websites. In Proceedings of the 2020 IEEE International Conference on Blockchain and Cryptocurrency (ICBC), Toronto, ON, Canada, 2–6 May 2020; pp. 1–8. [CrossRef]
13. Poursafaei, F.; Hamad, G.B.; Zilic, Z. Detecting Malicious Ethereum Entities via Application of Machine Learning Classification. In Proceedings of the 2020 2nd Conference on Blockchain Research Applications for Innovative Networks and Services (BRAINS), Paris, France, 28–30 September 2020; pp. 120–127. [CrossRef]
14. Seres, I.A.; Nagy, D.A.; Buckland, C.; Burcsi, P. Mixeth: Efficient, trustless coin mixing service for ethereum. In Proceedings of the International Conference on Blockchain Economics, Security and Protocols (Tokenomics 2019), Schloss Dagstuhl-Leibniz-Zentrum fuer Informatik, Paris, France, 6–7 May 2019.
15. Dika, A.; Nowostawski, M. Security vulnerabilities in ethereum smart contracts. In Proceedings of the 2018 IEEE International Conference on Internet of Things (iThings) and IEEE Green Computing and Communications (GreenCom) and IEEE Cyber, Physical and Social Computing (CPSCom) and IEEE Smart Data (SmartData) IEEE, Yogyakarta, Indonesia, 19–21 November 2018; pp. 955–962.
16. Feist, J.; Grieco, G.; Groce, A. Slither: A static analysis framework for smart contracts. In Proceedings of the 2019 IEEE/ACM 2nd International Workshop on Emerging Trends in Software Engineering for Blockchain (WETSEB), IEEE, Montreal, QC, Canada, 27–27 May 2019; pp. 8–15.
17. Oliva, G.A.; Hassan, A.E.; Jiang, Z.M.J. An exploratory study of smart contracts in the Ethereum blockchain platform. *Empir. Softw. Eng.* **2020**, *25*, 1864–1904. [CrossRef]
18. Torres, C.F.; Steichen, M. The art of the scam: Demystifying honeypots in ethereum smart contracts. In Proceedings of the 28th {USENIX} Security Symposium ({USENIX} Security 19), Santa Clara, CA, USA, 14–16 August 2019; pp. 1591–1607.
19. Babel, K.; Daian, P.; Kelkar, M.; Juels, A. Clockwork Finance: Automated Analysis of Economic Security in Smart Contracts. *arXiv* **2021**, arXiv:2109.04347.
20. Caldarelli, G.; Ellul, J. The Blockchain Oracle Problem in Decentralized Finance—A Multivocal Approach. *Appl. Sci.* **2021**, *11*, 7572. [CrossRef]
21. Daian, P.; Goldfeder, S.; Kell, T.; Li, Y.; Zhao, X.; Bentov, I.; Breidenbach, L.; Juels, A. Flash boys 2.0: Frontrunning in decentralized exchanges, miner extractable value, and consensus instability. In Proceedings of the 2020 IEEE Symposium on Security and Privacy (SP) IEEE, San Francisco, CA, USA, 18–21 May 2020; pp. 910–927.
22. Eskandari, S.; Salehi, M.; Gu, W.C.; Clark, J. SoK: Oracles from the Ground Truth to Market Manipulation. *arXiv* **2021**, arXiv:2106.00667.
23. Zhou, L.; Qin, K.; Torres, C.F.; Le, D.V.; Gervais, A. High-frequency trading on decentralized on-chain exchanges. In Proceedings of the 2021 IEEE Symposium on Security and Privacy (SP) IEEE, San Francisco, CA, USA, 24–27 May 2021; pp. 428–445.
24. Chen, W.; Guo, X.; Chen, Z.; Zheng, Z.; Lu, Y. Phishing Scam Detection on Ethereum: Towards Financial Security for Blockchain Ecosystem. In Proceedings of the Twenty-Ninth International Joint Conference on Artificial Intelligence, IJCAI-20, International Joint Conferences on Artificial Intelligence Organization, Special Track on AI in FinTech, Yokohama, Japan, 11–17 July 2020; Bessiere, C., Ed.; pp. 4506–4512.
25. Wu, J.; Yuan, Q.; Lin, D.; You, W.; Chen, W.; Chen, C.; Zheng, Z. Who Are the Phishers? Phishing Scam Detection on Ethereum via Network Embedding. *IEEE Trans. Syst. Man Cybern. Syst.* **2020**, *52*, 1156–1166. [CrossRef]
26. Xia, P.; Wang, H.; Luo, X.; Wu, L.; Zhou, Y.; Bai, G.; Xu, G.; Huang, G.; Liu, X. Don't Fish in Troubled Waters! Characterizing Coronavirus-themed Cryptocurrency Scams. In Proceedings of the 2020 APWG Symposium on Electronic Crime Research (eCrime), Boston, MA, USA, 16–19 November 2020; pp. 1–14. [CrossRef]
27. Yuan, Q.; Huang, B.; Zhang, J.; Wu, J.; Zhang, H.; Zhang, X. Detecting Phishing Scams on Ethereum Based on Transaction Records. In Proceedings of the 2020 IEEE International Symposium on Circuits and Systems (ISCAS), Seville, Spain, 12–14 October 2020; pp. 1–5. [CrossRef]
28. Bartoletti, M.; Carta, S.; Cimoli, T.; Saia, R. Dissecting Ponzi schemes on Ethereum: Identification, analysis, and impact. *Future Gener. Comput. Syst.* **2020**, *102*, 259–277. [CrossRef]
29. Chen, W.; Zheng, Z.; Ngai, E.C.H.; Zheng, P.; Zhou, Y. Exploiting Blockchain Data to Detect Smart Ponzi Schemes on Ethereum. *IEEE Access* **2019**, *7*, 37575–37586. [CrossRef]
30. Liebau, D.; Schueffel, P. *Crypto-Currencies and Icos: Are They Scams? An Empirical Study*; Elsevier: Amsterdam, The Netherlands, 2019.

31. Badawi, E.; Jourdan, G.V.; Bochmann, G.; Onut, I.V. An Automatic Detection and Analysis of the Bitcoin Generator Scam. In Proceedings of the 2020 IEEE European Symposium on Security and Privacy Workshops (EuroS PW), Genoa, Italy, 7–11 September 2020; pp. 407–416. [CrossRef]
32. Bian, L.; Zhang, L.; Zhao, K.; Wang, H.; Gong, S. Image-Based Scam Detection Method Using an Attention Capsule Network. *IEEE Access* **2021**, *9*, 33654–33665. [CrossRef]
33. Sureshbhai, P.N.; Bhattacharya, P.; Tanwar, S. KaRuNa: A Blockchain-Based Sentiment Analysis Framework for Fraud Cryptocurrency Schemes. In Proceedings of the 2020 IEEE International Conference on Communications Workshops (ICC Workshops), Dublin, Ireland, 7–11 June 2020; pp. 1–6. [CrossRef]
34. Dannen, C. *Introducing Ethereum and Solidity*; Springer: Berlin, Germany, 2017; Volume 318.
35. Puljiz, M.; Begušic, S.; Kostanjcar, Z. Market microstructure and order book dynamics in cryptocurrency exchanges. In Proceedings of the Crypto Valley Conference on Blockchain Technology, Rotkreuz, Switzerland, 24–26 June 2019.
36. Warren, W.; Bandeali, A. 0x: An Open Protocol for Decentralized Exchange on the Ethereum Blockchain. 2017; pp. 4–18. Available online: https://github.com/0xProject/whitepaper (accessed on 15 February 2022).
37. Adams, H.; Zinsmeister, N.; Robinson, D. Uniswap v2 Core Whitepaper. *Retrieved Oct.* **2020**, *12*, 36.
38. Angeris, G.; Kao, H.T.; Chiang, R.; Noyes, C.; Chitra, T. An analysis of Uniswap markets. *arXiv* **2019**, arXiv:1911.03380.
39. Aigner, A.A.; Dhaliwal, G. UNISWAP: Impermanent Loss and Risk Profile of a Liquidity Provider. *arXiv* **2021**, arXiv:2106.14404.
40. Van Vliet, B. An alternative model of Metcalfe's Law for valuing Bitcoin. *Econ. Lett.* **2018**, *165*, 70–72. [CrossRef]
41. Friedman, J. Greedy Function Approximation: A Gradient Boosting Machine. *Ann. Stat.* **2000**, *29*, 1189–1232. [CrossRef]
42. Chen, T.; Guestrin, C. XGBoost. In *Proceedings of the 22nd ACM SIGKDD International Conference on Knowledge Discovery and Data Mining*; ACM: New York, NY, USA, 2016. [CrossRef]
43. Vaswani, A.; Shazeer, N.; Parmar, N.; Uszkoreit, J.; Jones, L.; Gomez, A.N.; Kaiser, L.; Polosukhin, I. Attention Is All You Need. 2017. Available online: http://xxx.lanl.gov/abs/1706.03762 (accessed on 15 February 2022).
44. Devlin, J.; Chang, M.W.; Lee, K.; Toutanova, K. BERT: Pre-Training of Deep Bidirectional Transformers for Language Understanding. 2019. Available online: http://xxx.lanl.gov/abs/1810.04805 (accessed on 15 February 2022).
45. Liu, Y.; Ott, M.; Goyal, N.; Du, J.; Joshi, M.; Chen, D.; Levy, O.; Lewis, M.; Zettlemoyer, L.; Stoyanov, V. RoBERTa: A Robustly Optimized BERT Pretraining Approach. 2019. Available online: http://xxx.lanl.gov/abs/1907.11692 (accessed on 15 February 2022).
46. Dosovitskiy, A.; Beyer, L.; Kolesnikov, A.; Weissenborn, D.; Zhai, X.; Unterthiner, T.; Dehghani, M.; Minderer, M.; Heigold, G.; Gelly, S.; et al. An Image is Worth 16x16 Words: Transformers for Image Recognition at Scale. 2021. Available online: http://xxx.lanl.gov/abs/2010.11929 (accessed on 15 February 2022).
47. Akiba, T.; Sano, S.; Yanase, T.; Ohta, T.; Koyama, M. Optuna: A next-generation hyperparameter optimization framework. In Proceedings of the 25th ACM SIGKDD International Conference on Knowledge Discovery & Data Mining, Anchorage, AK, USA, 4–8 August 2019; pp. 2623–2631.
48. Lundberg, S.; Lee, S.I. A Unified Approach to Interpreting Model Predictions. 2017. Available online: http://xxx.lanl.gov/abs/1705.07874 (accessed on 15 February 2022).

Σ mathematics MDPI

Article

A Stacking Ensemble Deep Learning Model for Bitcoin Price Prediction Using Twitter Comments on Bitcoin

Zi Ye †, Yinxu Wu †, Hui Chen, Yi Pan, Qingshan Jiang *

Shenzhen Institute of Advanced Technology, Chinese Academy of Sciences, Shenzhen 518055, China; zi.ye@siat.ac.cn (Z.Y.); wyx83coria@hotmail.com (Y.W.); hui.chen1@siat.ac.cn (H.C.); yi.pan@siat.ac.cn (Y.P.)
* Correspondence: qs.jiang@siat.ac.cn
† These authors contributed equally to this work.

Abstract: Cryptocurrencies can be considered as mathematical money. As the most famous cryptocurrency, the Bitcoin price forecasting model is one of the popular mathematical models in financial technology because of its large price fluctuations and complexity. This paper proposes a novel ensemble deep learning model to predict Bitcoin's next 30 min prices by using price data, technical indicators and sentiment indexes, which integrates two kinds of neural networks, long short-term memory (LSTM) and gate recurrent unit (GRU), with stacking ensemble technique to improve the accuracy of decision. Because of the real-time updates of comments on social media, this paper uses social media texts instead of news websites as the source data of public opinion. It is processed by linguistic statistical method to form the sentiment indexes. Meanwhile, as a financial market forecasting model, the model selects the technical indicators as input as well. Real data from September 2017 to January 2021 is used to train and evaluate the model. The experimental results show that the near-real time prediction has a better performance, with a mean absolute error (MAE) 88.74% better than the daily prediction. The purpose of this work is to explain our solution and show that the ensemble method has better performance and can better help investors in making the right investment decision than other traditional models.

Keywords: cryptocurrencies; forecasting model; financial technology; ensemble learning; Bitcoin price prediction

MSC: 68Uxx; 68U35

Citation: Ye, Z.; Wu, Y.; Chen, H.; Pan, Y.; Jiang, Q. A Stacking Ensemble Deep Learning Model for Bitcoin Price Prediction Using Twitter Comments on Bitcoin. *Mathematics* **2022**, *10*, 1307. https://doi.org/10.3390/math10081307

Academic Editors: María Mar Miralles-Quirós and José Luis Miralles-Quirós

Received: 27 February 2022
Accepted: 10 April 2022
Published: 14 April 2022

1. Introduction

Bitcoin is the first and the most important cryptocurrency. It is a ledger application based on blockchain, cryptography and peer-to-peer technology. In the field of financial technology, many mathematical models are developed to forecast Bitcoin's future price. These models can provide investment advice for quantitative investors.

Similar to other assets, such as stocks [1,2] and commodities, Bitcoin price forecasts are a series of continuous predictions because Bitcoin prices also change over time. One major difference between Bitcoin and a stock is that stocks trade only at certain times on weekdays, but the Bitcoin market typically operates around the clock, and investors can buy or sell Bitcoin all day, which may result in Bitcoin price fluctuations at unpredictable times. We can learn the stock price prediction method and use it to predict the price of Bitcoin. To address the time series problem of Bitcoin prices, two types of models have mainly been used in previous works: traditional time series models, such as autoregressive comprehensive moving average (ARIMA) [3] and generalized autoregressive conditional heterovariance (GARCH) [4]. Another is machine learning models, such as random forest (RF), and deep learning networks, such as recurrent neural networks (RNN), long short-term memory (LSTM), and gated recurrent units (GRU) [5].

According to a study by the American Institute of Economic Research (AIER), globally influential news and sentiment can drive large fluctuations in the price of Bitcoin [6]. Some research uses sentiment analysis based on Twitter data to predict the price of Bitcoin [5,7]. It is effective to explore people's reactions to Bitcoin from tweets since Twitter is an incredibly rich source of information about how people are feeling about a given topic. Previous research methods of sentiment analysis based on Bitcoin-related comments can be divided into two types: dictionary-based methods, such as valence aware dictionary and sentiment reasoner (VADER) [8], and machine learning-based methods, such as RF [7], hard voting classifiers [5], deep learning-based classifiers [9], and other specific analyzers [10].

However, the current research still has some limitations: Firstly, in most previous works, only historical data are used as the input data of the prediction model, which ignores that prices are also affected by unexpected factors in price data. Secondly, sentiment analysis simply categorizes every tweet or comment as positive, neutral or negative and then creates a simple statistic, which loses much emotional detail and is not conducive to learning how different levels of sentiment affect prices. Thirdly, a single model such as ARIMA, LSTM, or GRU, is employed by most previous methods. To solve the existing limitations, this paper proposed following aspects: Firstly, considering the financial nature of Bitcoin, we added the most commonly used technical indicators in traditional finance as predicting input. Secondly, instead of using a simple statistical method to categorize the mood trend of tweets, we used a linguistic method to process tweets about Bitcoin, which proved it brought a higher accuracy. Thirdly, to improve the prediction results, a stacking ensemble Deep Learning, combining LSTM and GRU, was trained to forecast the price of the next time interval. The major steps are as follows. We proposed to use linguistic sentiment analysis to categorize tweets and a stacking ensemble deep learning model to forecast the price of the next time interval based on sentiment trend of tweets and technical indicators. It combines multiple models to add a bias to the final prediction result, which will be offset by the variance of the neural network, making the prediction of the model less sensitive to the details of training data.

The rest of this paper is organized as follows: Section 2 shows the previous related work; Section 3 shows the whole methodology of this paper, including the data acquisition step, data preprocessing step and stacking ensemble prediction model; Section 4 lists all the experimental results and compares our method with common methods; Section 5 draws the conclusion of this paper.

2. Related Work

Many previous studies can mainly be divided into three main models and three main data categories. The three models include: (1) statistical methods; (2) machine learning; (3) ensemble learning. The three main data types are as follows: (1) price data, including opening, highest, lowest, closing, trading volume, number of trades, quote asst volume and other data; (2) technical indicators based on price data and indicators derived from market technical statistics, such as moving average convergence divergence (MACD) and relative strength index on balance volume (RSI OBV) statistics; (3) sentiment indicators refer to the indicators calculated after natural language processing of text data from social media during a certain time period; (4) other related data, such as blcokchain hashrate, number of online nodes, active address, Google trends and other financial indexes.

Early research into the price prediction of bitcoin were mostly based on the statistical method. P. Katsiampa et al. [11] used price data, and certain types of GARCH models have been used to calculate the daily closing prices between 18 July 2010 and 1 October 2016. As a result of the paper, AR-CGARCH is the best model. S. Roy et al. [4] used price data and performed ARIMA, autoregressive (AR), and moving average (MA) models on the time series dataset. The results of this paper used the ARIMA model to predict the price of Bitcoin with an accuracy rate of 90.31%. Therefore, it can be said that the best results are obtained using ARIMA. Ayaz et al. [12] used price data and only used the ARIMA algorithm to predict the price of Bitcoin. To find the lowest mean square error (MSE), the researchers used different fitting functions in the ARIMA algorithm and found that the lowest MSE = 170,962.195. Because it avoids the use of scaling functions, this result is different from those of other studies. In a recent paper [13], it proposed a general method of user behavior analysis and knowledge pattern extraction based on social network analysis. This method extracts relevant information from the blockchain transaction data in a specified period, carries out statistics and builds an ego network, and extracts important information such as active transaction addresses and different user groups. Using Ethereum blockchain data from 2017–2018, the method was proved to be able to identify bubble speculators. In 2021, R. K. Jana et al. [14] proposed a regression framework based on differential evolution to predict bitcoin. They first decomposed the original sequence into granular linear and nonlinear components using maximum overlapping discrete wavelet transform, and then fitted polynomial regression with interaction (PRI) and support vector regression (SVR) on both linear and nonlinear components to obtain the component-wise projections.Apart from the previously introduced statistical methods, Jong-Min Kim et al. [15] proposed to use linear and nonlinear error correction models to predict bitcoin log returns, and compared with neural network, ARIMA and other methods. The experiment was verified with the price data from 1 January 2019 to 27 August 2021. The results showed that the error correction model was the best in all evaluation indexes, and MAE was as low as 1.84, while other comparison models were all above 3.2. They also ran a Granger causality test on 14 cryptocurrencies.

Over the past few decades, major advances in machine learning have allowed more accurate methods to spread across the field of quantitative finance. A Bayesian neural network model that uses blockchain information to predict the price of Bitcoin was proposed by Jang et al. in 2017 [16]. Specifically, they use price data, blockchain data, economic indices, currency exchange rates and more. Four methods were trained for price prediction using price data, including logistic regression, support vector machine, RNN and ARIMA models in [17]. As far as the prediction accuracy of these four methods is concerned, ARIMA only has a 53% return on the next day's price prediction, and the long-term performance is poor, such as using the price prediction of the last few days to predict the price of the next 5–7 days. The RNN consistently obtains an approximate accuracy of 50% for up to 6 days. It does not violate the assumptions of the logistic regression-based model; it can accurately classify only when there is a separable hyperplane with 47% accuracy. The support vector machine has an accuracy rate of 48%. Shen et al. [18] used price data for training the GARCH, simple moving average (SMA) and RNN (GRU) models. The GRU model performs better than the SMA model with the lowest root MSE (RMSE) and mean absolute error (MAE) ratios. Some researchers used price data, technical indicators and a complex neural network called CNN-LSTM [19]. Compared with a single CNN and a single LSTM model, the results are slightly improved, with the MAE reaching 209.89 and the RMSE reaching 258.31. The stochastic neural network model has also been used to predict the price of cryptocurrency [20]. The model introduces layer-wise randomness into the observed neural network feature activation to simulate market fluctuations. It used market transaction data, blockchain data, and Twitter and Google Trends data. A latest research on cryptocurrencies by Wołk [21] used Google Trends and Twitter to predict the price of cryptocurrencies by distinctive multimodal scheme. However, they used textual data mechanically, unlike our article, which considers linguistic approaches to textual data. In 2021, Jagannath et al. [22] proposed a Bitcoin price prediction method using data features of users, miners, and exchanges. They also propose jSO adaptive deep neural network optimization algorithm to speed up the training process. The model uses Bitcoin data from 2016 to 2020 for training and testing. The MAE value of LSTM is 2.90, while the MAE value of this method is 1.89, thus effectively reducing the MAE value. A novel price prediction model WT-CATCN was proposed in 2021 by Haizhou Guo et al. [23]. It utilizes Wavelet Transform (WT) and Casual Multi-Head Attention (CA) Temporal Convolutional Network (TCN) to predict cryptocurrency prices. The data input of the model is divided into three categories: blockchain transaction information, exchange information, and Google Trends.

Considering how widespread cryptocurrency information has become, Loginova proposed a bitcoin price direction prediction method in 2021 that combined the sentiment analysis model JST and TS-LDA [24]. They used market trading data as well as text data from Reddit, CryptoCompare and Bitcointalk. The model was verified by using the data from 20 February 2017 to 6 April 2019. The accuracy of the model using JST and TS-LDA was 57%, which was improved compared with the same model that was not used. For Dogecoin, which has a huge market cap, Sashank Sridhar et al. proposed a multi-head attention-based encoder–decoder model for a transformer model to predict its price [25]. It is verified using real DOGE hourly transaction data from 5 July 2019 to 28 April 2021, with an R-squared value of 0.8616 for the model. A more complex hybrid framework, DL-GuesS, was proposed by Raj Parekh et al. for cryptocurrency price prediction [26]. This framework takes into account its interdependence with other cryptocurrencies and market sentiment. The model uses transaction data from different cryptocurrencies as input, along with Twitter text. The model was validated using Bitcoin Cash data from March 2021 to April 2021, and the model MSE value was as low as 0.0011.

Ensemble learning is also a popular method for forecasting. Using this approach, researchers have been able to improve the accuracy and stability of predictions. Ahmed Ibrahim [27] used price and sentiment data to predict Bitcoin prices by constructing an XGBoost-Composite integrated model. A paper using price data to compare different ensemble models, including averaging, bagging, and stacking was written in 2020 [28]. Among them, stacking has the best performance, but the blending ensemble was not used in the paper. Other researchers used price data and integrated LSTM models after training for different lengths of time (days, hours, and minutes) to obtain an integrated model that was superior to each individual model [29].

Mainly inspired by Li and Pan [1], whose workflow is shown in Figure 1, this paper designs a series of methods to avoid these current limitations: (1) more data sources are used as input; (2) linguistic methods are used for sentiment analysis to replace the simple statistical methods used in most papers; (3) one kind of ensemble model is used for training and prediction.

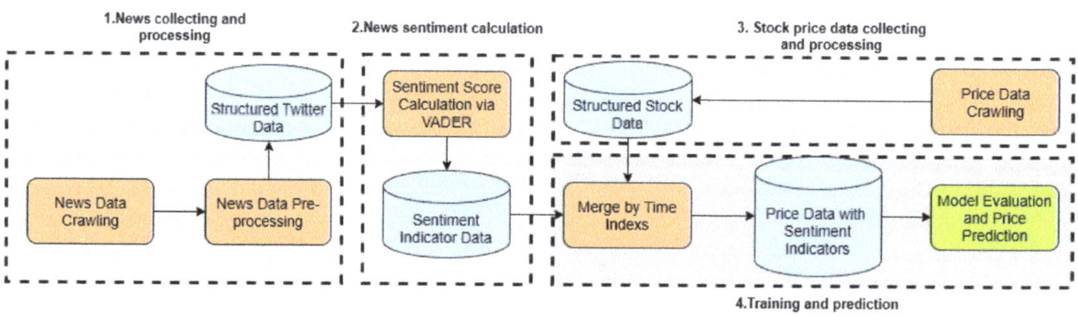

Figure 1. The workflow for forecasting stock using news data in Li [1].

However, due to different data sources, the methods proposed in this paper are somewhat different from those proposed in Li [1]. The differences of specific data sources are as follows:

1. There is less news about digital currency than stocks, which means there are not many reports about digital currency in the news, which is not enough to support our real-time prediction, so we chose social media.
2. Digital currencies are traded 24 h a day and comments on Twitter are live 24 h a day, so real-time comments on Twitter can be very effective for price forecasting.

3. Li's work uses two data sources, price and news, to predict price. Considering the financial properties of digital currency, we use price, comments on Twitter and technical indicators to predict price.
4. Data preprocessing methods are also different: The text data used in Li [1], namely news data, does not need to be cleaned and can be scored directly by VADER. Moreover, the Twitter data we obtain from crawlers is very dirty, such as pictures, links, etc., which need to be cleaned.

3. Methodology

In this paper, sentiment indicators are combined with Bitcoin price data to predict the future price. The proposed model workflow is shown in Figure 2. In step 1, Twitter data are collected and processed to form a structured Twitter date, which is in CSV format. In step 2, the structured Twitter date is sent to the sentiment calculation program. The SGSBI and SGSDI are calculated and attached to the market sentiment indicator data. In step 3, Bitcoin price data are collected and processed with TA-LIB to generate price data with technical indicators. In step 4, two parts of the data are merged by time indexes to evaluate the models.

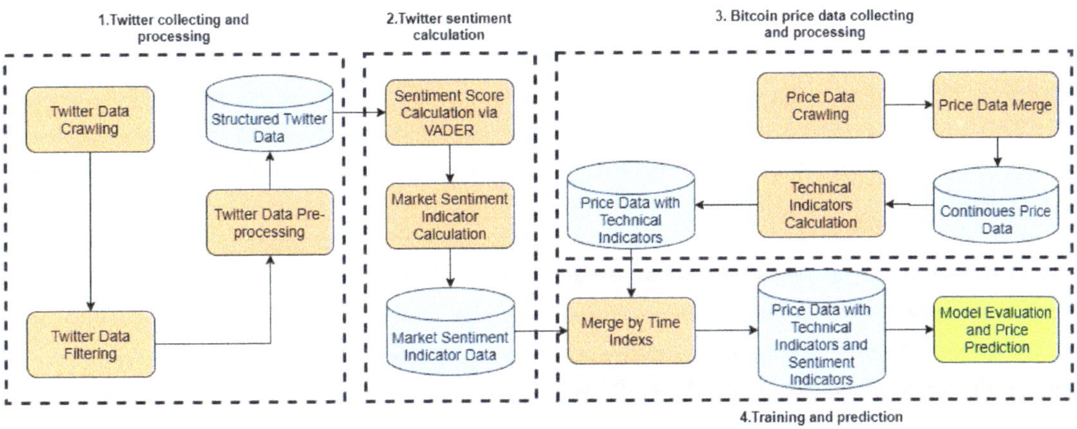

Figure 2. The proposed model workflow for Bitcoin price prediction using tweets.

3.1. Bitcoin Price Data

Bitcoin price data is provided by Binance.com. To help Bitcoin researchers, Binance collects and processes all their trading data and provides them at http://data.binance.vision/, accessed on 2 November 2021. The data is stored in CSV format. In this paper, the data from September 2017 to January 2021 are selected as the data for model learning and prediction in most cases.

3.2. Twitter Data

3.2.1. Data Collection

Twint is used to collect tweets from Twitter in this paper. Twint, which is the abbreviation for the Twitter Intelligence Tool, is an open source Twitter scraper that searches and scrapes tweets; it is different from the Twitter Search API. Since no authentication is needed, Twint is an out-of-the-box tool for anyone who needs to scrape tweets. Additionally, Twint has no rate limitations, while the Twitter Search API limits a search to the last 3200 tweets. Certainly, Twint supports almost all the functions of the Twitter Search API, which allows users to request specific queries and allows filtering based on language, region, geographic location, and time range. CSV, JSON, and txt are supported output file formats.

BTC and Bitcoin are the keywords to search for in the related tweets. Instead of #, $ is used for the hashtag symbol to avoid a very large number of unwanted tweets. From September 2017 to January 2021, more than 7 million tweets were collected.

3.2.2. Sentiment Score Calculation

This paper uses VADER for the basic sentiment score calculation. VADER is an open source Python library for sentiment analysis based on dictionaries and rules. The library is used out-of-the-box and does not need to use text data for training. Compared with traditional sentiment analysis methods, VADER has many advantages: (1) it is suitable for multiple text types, such as social media; (2) training data are not required; and (3) due to fast speeds and streaming data, it can be used online.

VADER not only calculates the positive, neutral and negative scores about the input statement but also provides a compound score, which is a numeric value between -1 and $+1$. In general, a compound score from -1 to -0.05 is considered negative, a score from 0.05 to 1 is considered positive, and the rest is considered neural. However, in this way, information of the numeric score is filtered out. For example, the compound scores 0.12 and 0.86 are both considered positive emotions, but the degree of positive emotion expressed is not the same.

3.2.3. Small Granularity Sentiment Indicators

According to previous work [30], the sentiment indexes constructed by Antweiler and Frank have been revised. Specifically, this work took advantage of VADER and the work of Antweiler and Frank and then proposed small granular sentiment indicators, as shown in Equations (1)–(3).

$$SGSBI_t = \frac{\sum C_t^{Pos} - \sum C_t^{Neg}}{\sum C_t^{Pos} + \sum C_t^{Neg}} \tag{1}$$

$$SGSDI_t = \frac{\sum_{i \in D(t)} (C_i - SGSBI_t)^2}{\sum C_t^{Pos} + \sum C_t^{Neg}} \tag{2}$$

$$Comt_t = M_t^{Pos} + M_t^{Neu} + M_t^{Neg} \tag{3}$$

3.3. *Technical Indicator Calculation*

The technical indicators in Table 1, including MACD, SMA, OBV, RSI and MFI, are calculated based on the raw price data through a Python library called TA-Lib. The input data to the TA-Lib function are transferred to the ndarray type by numpy in advance. These technical indicators are chosen because of their popularity in the field of traditional financial market price forecasting.

The simple moving average (SMA) is a simple technical analysis tool that smooths out price data by creating a constantly updated average price. A simple moving average helps cut down the amount of noise on a price chart. The stop and reverse (SAR) indicator is used by traders to determine trend direction and potential reversals in price. Moving average convergence divergence (MACD) is a trend-following momentum indicator that shows the relationship between two moving averages of a security's price. The MACD is calculated by subtracting the 26-period exponential moving average (EMA) from the 12-period EMA. The relative strength index (RSI) is a momentum indicator used in technical analysis that measures the magnitude of recent price changes to evaluate overbought or oversold conditions in the price of a stock or other asset. The Money Flow Index (MFI) is a technical oscillator that uses price and volume data for identifying overbought or oversold signals in an asset. On-balance volume (OBV) is a technical trading momentum indicator that uses volume flow to predict changes in stock price.

Table 1. Technical indicators.

Technical Indicators	Type	Description
MACD: Moving Average Convergence/Divergence	Momentum Indicator Functions	$\text{MACD} = EMA_{12\text{-}period} - EMA_{26\text{-}period}$
SMA: Simple Moving Average	Overlap Studies Functions	$\text{SMA} = \frac{P_1+P_2+\ldots+P_n}{n}$ P_n = the price of asset at period n n = the number of total periods
SAR: Stop And Reverse	Overlap Studies Functions	$\text{SAR}_{up} = SAR_{prior} + AF_{prior}(EP_{prior} - SAR_{prior})$ $\text{SAR}_{down} = SAR_{prior} - AF_{prior}(SAR_{prior} - EP_{prior})$
OBV: On Balance Volume	Volume Indicators	$if\ price_t^{close} > price_{t-1}^{close}$: $\text{OBV} = OBV_{prior} + Day's\ Volume_{Current}$ $if\ price_t^{close} = price_{t-1}^{close}$: $\text{OBV} = OBV_{prior}(+0)$ $if\ price_t^{close} < price_{t-1}^{close}$: $\text{OBV} = OBV_{prior} - Day's\ Volume_{Current}$
RSI: Relative Strength Index	Momentum Indicator Functions	$\text{RSI} = 100 - \frac{100}{1+RS}$ $RS = \frac{Average\ gain}{Average\ loss}$
MFI: Money Flow Index	Momentum Indicator Functions	$\text{MFI} = 100 - \frac{100}{1+Money\ Ratio}$ $MoneyRatio = \frac{Money\ flow_{14\text{-}period}^{positive}}{Money\ flow_{14\text{-}period}^{negative}}$

3.4. Stacking Ensemble Neural Network

3.4.1. Long Short-Term Memory

Long short-term memory (LSTM) is a neural network with the ability to remember long-term and short-term information. It was first proposed by Hochreiter and Schmidhub [31] in 1997 and then led to the rise of deep learning in 2012. After undergoing several generations of development, a relatively systematic and complete framework has been formed for the LSTM model.

LSTM is a special kind of RNN model that is designed to solve the problem of gradient dispersion of the RNN model. In traditional RNNs, back propagation through time (BPTT) is used in the training algorithm. When the training time is relatively long, the residual error that needs to be returned will decrease exponentially, which leads to slow network weight updating; hence, it cannot reflect the long-term memory effect of RNNs [32]. Therefore, a storage unit is needed to store memory, and the architecture of the LSTM model prevents the problem of long-term dependence.

In an ordinary RNN, which is shown in Figure 3, the structure of the repeating module is very simple; for example, there is only one tanh layer. LSTM also has a kind of chain structure, which is shown in Figure 4, but its repeating module structure is different. There are four neural network layers in the repeating module of LSTM, and the interactions between them are very special.

The LSTM model can store important past information into the cell state and forget unimportant information. Its memory cell consists of three parts: the forget gate, the input gate, and the output gate.

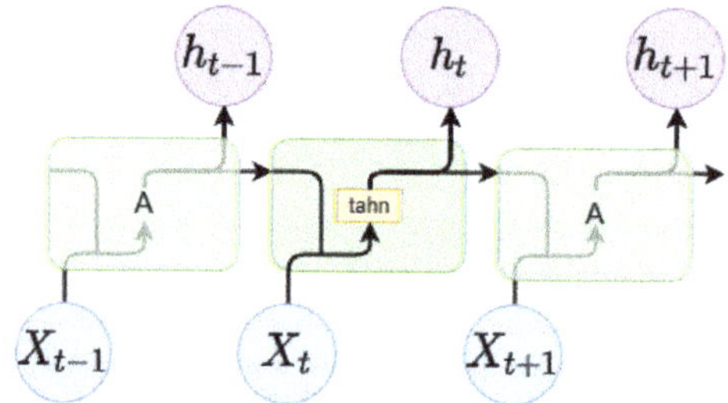

Figure 3. RNN basic architecture [33].

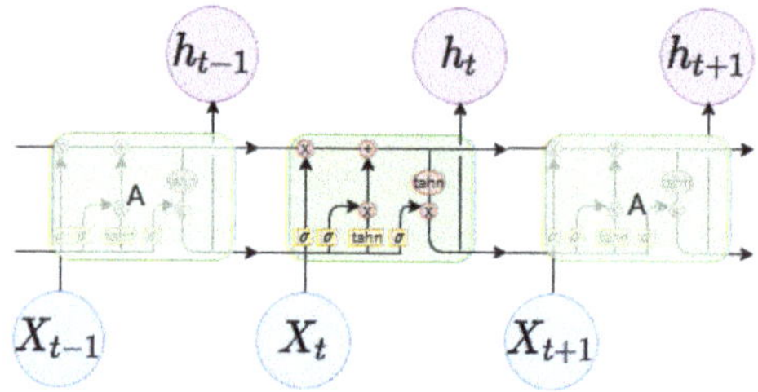

Figure 4. LSTM basic architecture [33].

The first step of LSTM is to decide what information will be abandoned from the cell state. The decision is controlled by a sigmoid layer called the "forget gate". f_t (the forget gate) observes h_{t-1} (the output vector) and x_t (the input vector) and outputs a number between 0∼1 for each element in the cell state C_{t-1}, where 1 means "keep this information completely" and 0 means "discard this information completely".

$$f_t = \sigma(W_{fx}X_t + W_{fh}h_{t-1} + b_f) \tag{4}$$

The next step is to decide which new information will be stored in the cell state. First, there is a sigmoid layer called the "input gate" i_t that determines what information should be updated. Next, a tanh layer creates a new candidate value $\widetilde{c_t}$, which may be added to the cell state.

$$i_t = \sigma(W_{ix}x_t + W_{ih}h_{t-1} + b_i) \tag{5}$$

$$\widetilde{c_t} = \sigma(W_{cx}x_t + W_{ch}h_{t-1} + b_c) \tag{6}$$

Then, the old cell state C_{t-1} updates to the new state c_t.

$$c_t = f_t c_{t-1} + i_t\widetilde{c_t} \tag{7}$$

In the end, the final output o_t is supposed to be decided, and it is based on the current cell state after some filtering. Initially, an output gate in the sigmoid layer is established to determine which parts of the cell will be output. Then, the cell state is multiplied by the output gate after passing through the tanh layer, and the output value is between −1∼1.

$$o_t = \sigma(W_{ox}x_t + W_{oh}h_{t-1} + b_o) \tag{8}$$

$$h_t = o_t tanh(c_t) \tag{9}$$

3.4.2. Gate Recurrent Unit

Proposed by Cho et al. in 2014 [34], Gate recurrent unit (GRU), another special kind of RNN, was proposed to solve the vanishing gradient problem of RNNs through an update gate and a reset gate. In addition to eliminating the RNN vanishing gradient problem, the two gates can store relevant information in the memory cell and pass the values to the next steps of the network. The performances of LSTM and GRU are equally matched under different test conditions. However, there are some differences between GRU and LSTM: first, GRU does not have a separate memory cell; computationally, GRU is more efficient than LSTM because of the lack of memory units; and when dealing with small datasets, GRU is more suitable.

3.4.3. Stacking Ensemble

As a primary paradigm of machine learning, ensemble learning has achieved notable success in a vast range of real-world applications. One model that fits an entire training dataset may not be enough to meet all expectations. Many previous studies have shown that ensemble learning, which combines multiple individual learning algorithms, outperforms a single learning algorithm in both accuracy and robustness [35].

Thomas G. Dietterich pointed out the reasons for the better performance of ensemble learning from statistical, computational, and representational aspects [36]. There are various types of ensemble learning models, such as bagging, boosting, stacking, and blending [36]. A deep learning network, a special kind of artificial neural network, consists of multiple processing layers. With the ability to mine information from the plethora of historical data and effectively use that data for future predictions, deep learning has become a popular choice for problem solving [37]. However, deep learning methods have one obvious disadvantage: deep learning models are very sensitive to initial conditions. According to [38], it is computationally expensive to train deep learning neural networks, and even if a vast amount of time is spent to train a model, the trained network with the best performance on validation sets may not perform best on new test data. Generally, we could regard deep learning neural networks as models with low bias but high variances. Combining the advantages of both deep learning and ensemble learning, ensemble deep models have been proposed [39]. Specifically, ensemble deep models combine the predictions from multiple good but different deep learning models. Good means that the performance of each deep learning neural network used is relatively good. Different means that each of the deep learning neural networks has different prediction errors. As stated in [40], different models usually have different errors on a test set, and this has resulted in studies on model averaging. The combination of ensemble models and deep learning models adds bias that in turn cancels out the variance in a single training neural network model. The bias–variance tradeoff is illustrated in the graph in Figure 5.

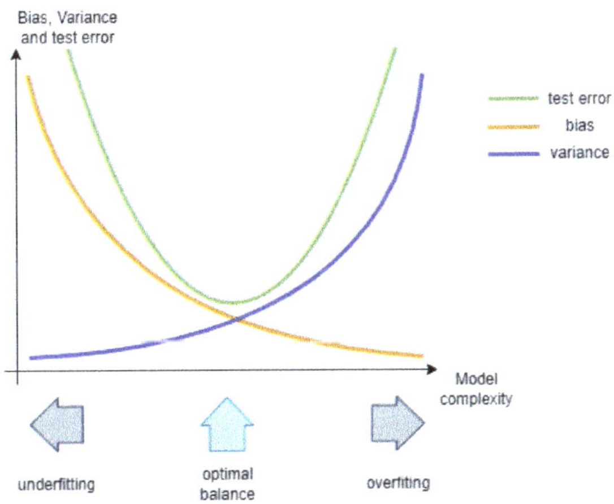

Figure 5. The bias–variance tradeoff [41].

In addition to reducing the variance in the prediction, an ensemble deep model can also produce better predictions than any single best model according to the ensemble model properties described above.

Our model consists of two levels, shown in Figure 6: level 1 contains five LSTM and five GRU, which are called sub-models; and level 2 is a single-layer model called the meta-model. We choose LSTM and GRU as sub-models due to their good performance in the field of price prediction. Based on a large number of experiments, we set the number of sub-models in the first layer to five in order to achieve a balance between accuracy and computation. The steps of the model are as follows:

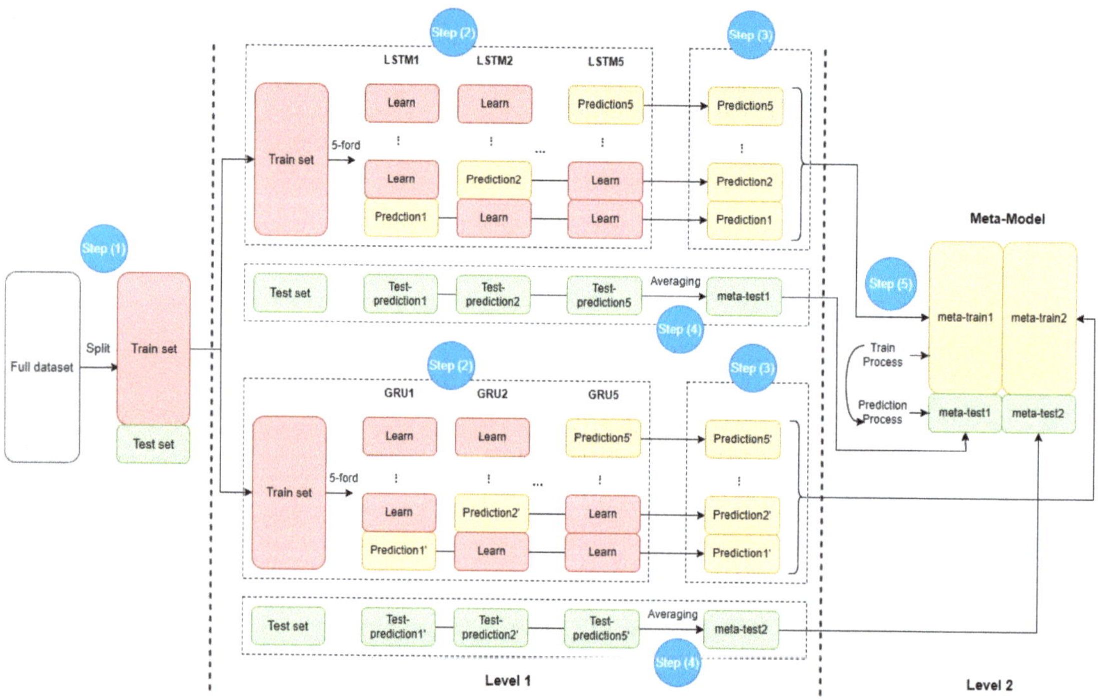

Figure 6. Stacking ensemble architecture.

1. Data split: Divide the data used into training set and test set as shown in the step (1).
2. Sub-model training: Further divide the training set into five subsets, defined as train1 to train5. Then define the five LSTM instances as LSTM1 to LSTM5, and the five GRU instances as GRU1 to GRU5.
    - Train sub models: Train LSTM1 on train1 to train4, and then predict the result as Prediction1 on data subset train5. Train LSTM2 on train1, train3 to train5, and then predict the result as Prediction2 on data subset train4, and so on. The same action was repeated in the five instances of GRU as shown in the step (2);
    - Generate training features for meta-model: Combine prediction1-5 of LSTM successively and therefore obtain the feature meta-train1 for training meta-model. The same action was repeated on GRU to obtain the feature meta-train2 for training meta-model as shown in the step (3);
    - Create new prediction features for layer two: Make predictions respectively on LSTM1-5 to obtain five prediction results by using the test set. Average these results to yield a feature meta-test1 for prediction. The same operation was repeated on GRU to obtain another feature for prediction as shown in the step (4).

3. Meta-model training and predicting: Concatenate meta-train1 and meta-train2 for training the meta-model. Predict the result by using meta-model through the merging of meta-test1 and meta-test2 as shown in the step (5).

Let n be sequence length and d be representation Dimension, and the LSTM/GRU of this model is a single layer. The time complexity of the stacking ensemble is estimated to be $O(n \cdot d^2)$.

3.5. Evaluation Metrics

Many metrics have been used to compare the performance of price trend and price movement direction predictions of different models. To comprehensively evaluate the performance of the models, four widely used indicators are adopted in the experiments: the MSE, the MAE, the mean absolute percentage error (MAPE), and the symmetric MAPE (sMAPE).

$$\text{MAE} = \frac{1}{N}\sum_{i=1}^{N}|y_i - \hat{y}_i| \tag{10}$$

$$\text{MSE} = \frac{1}{N}\sum_{i=1}^{N}(y_i - \hat{y}_i)^2 \tag{11}$$

$$\text{MAPE} = \frac{100\%}{N}\sum_{i=1}^{N}\left|\frac{y_i - \hat{y}_i}{y_i}\right| \tag{12}$$

$$\text{sMAPE} = \frac{200\%}{N}\sum_{i=1}^{N}\frac{|y_i - \hat{y}_i|}{|y_i| + |\hat{y}_i|} \tag{13}$$

where N is the number of predictions, y is the actual value and $\hat{y}$ is the predicted value of the model.

The movement direction accuracy (MDA) is an evaluation metric of price movement direction.

$$\text{MDA} = \frac{Number\ of\ Correct\ Movement\ Predictions}{Total\ Number\ of\ Movement\ Predictions} \tag{14}$$

4. Result Evaluation

In this section, the proposed method is used to forecast the Bitcoin closing price. We implement the proposed method using the TensorFlow deep learning framework on TITAN RTXs through the Python programming language. Many trials of simulation experiments are conducted to determine the parameters of the model.

The comparative experiments in this paper are divided into two categories: the first is to compare the performance of different models; the other is to compare the performance of different categories of data combinations in the forecast.

As shown in Figure 7, the whole data is divided into two parts: training data, and testing data. The training data is from 24 September 2017 to 11 April 2020, which is used to train the weak learners in level 1; the testing data is from 12 April 2020 to 30 November 2020, which is used to make the final prediction.

A rolling window with 5 steps is used in these financial time series data, as shown in Figure 8. In addition, technical indicators and sentiment indicators are calculated as data sources. Table 2 lists the input features for Bitcoin price prediction from the price data sector, technical indicator sector, and sentiment indicator sector.

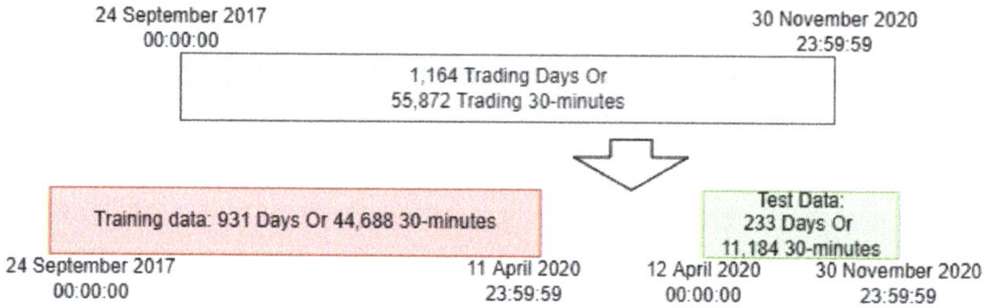

Figure 7. Schematic diagram of the split dataset.

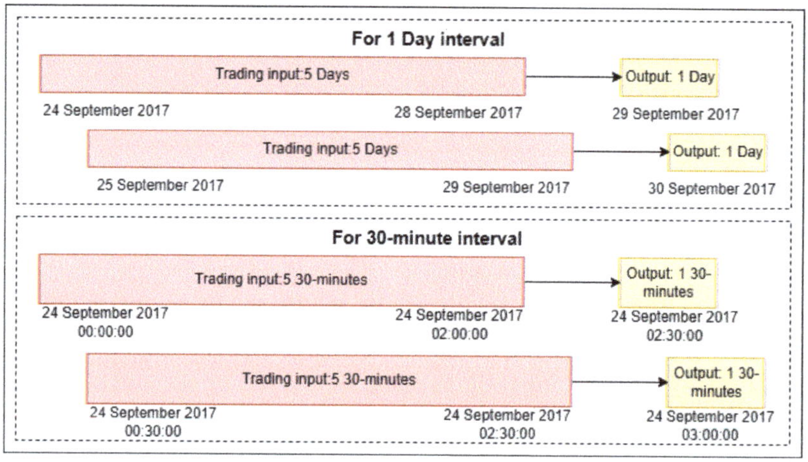

Figure 8. Schematic diagram of the time step window.

Table 2. Features and indicators used in the model.

Price Data	Technical Indicators	Sentiment Indicators
Open	MACD	CA
High	RSI	SGSBI
Low	MFI	SGSDI
Close	OBV	
Volume	SMA	
Quote Asset Volume		
Number of Trades		
Taker Buy Base Asset Volume		
Taker Buy Quote Asset Volume		

The training duration of models are show in Table 3. Stacking ensemble model training on 30 min interval data only costs about 27 min because of the GPU.

Table 3. Time complexity and training duration of models.

Model	Training Duration (Unit Second) (30-min Interval)	Training Duration (Unit Second) (1-Day Interval)
LSTM	169	26
GRU	154	16
AE	266	33
BE	322	48
SE	1576	99

The first part is the experiments that compare the different models. The compared models include not only neural network models, such as LSTM and GRU, but also average ensemble (AE) and blending ensemble (BE). Both LSTM and GRU are single models that can be used for prediction. They are essential components of our ensemble models. The average ensemble model takes the average of the sum of the LSTM and GRU results as the final result. The MAE, MSE, MAPE, sMAPE, and MDA are used to evaluate the performance results of the proposed method and other models. All our results are shown in the Tables 4 and 5.

Table 4. Results of the 30 min intervals.

Metric	Model	Price Data	Price Data Technical Indicators	Price Data Sentiment Indicators	Price Data Technical Indicators Sentiment Indicators
MAE	LSTM	312.011825	374.999918	330.661338	412.554188
	GRU	268.728793	415.652382	419.355862	389.918484
	AE	168.247519	262.082363	172.195087	271.482766
	SE	155.933634	130.200637	107.650458	88.740831
	BE	156.373369	210.544757	103.320151	188.535888
MSE	LSTM	108,823.7765	153,829.8002	121,815.3616	184,271.5385
	GRU	105,638.9155	186,314.9489	190,762.1637	165,616.467
	AE	48,081.01116	88,879.84332	50,461.551	97,194.7086
	SE	60,092.71839	36,440.18042	27,892.31183	30,067.70409
	BE	43,270.7287	59,769.57549	31,385.89856	58,818.47366
MAPE	LSTM	2.969864	3.592678	3.151563	3.966612
	GRU	2.361411	4.008615	4.0305	3.740284
	AE	1.483315	2.387113	1.533826	2.457365
	SE	1.341431	1.103336	0.951954	0.69763
	BE	1.376177	1.932841	0.849297	1.651553
sMAPE	LSTM	2.922733	3.524576	3.098525	3.884225
	GRU	2.393608	3.924512	3.945382	3.666772
	AE	1.497166	2.418689	1.548865	2.490969
	SE	1.356031	1.101221	0.958526	0.70038
	BE	1.388322	1.954286	0.855509	1.66841
MDA	LSTM	51.591618	51.618368	51.654035	51.645118
	GRU	48.773963	51.627285	51.716451	51.618368
	AE	49.166295	48.72938	49.121712	48.747214
	SE	49.478377	51.457869	50.325457	52.144449
	BE	49.193045	48.952296	50.50379	48.970129

As shown in Table 6, the proposed stacking ensemble model has amazing performance in the MAE, MSE, and MDA evaluation categories. In MAPE evaluation, the proposed stacking ensemble model is the best compared with the other models on the 30 min time interval, but on the 1-day time interval, the blending ensemble obtains the best MDA score. In general, the proposed stacking ensemble model outperforms other models in most cases.

Figure 9 shows the results of the different models on the testing data. Figure 10 is part of Figure 9, the result of stacking ensemble model is marked 'X' and the actual value is marked '+' to illustrate performance of models. The graph visually illustrates that the prediction results of the stacking ensemble model are closer to the actual closing price, and the shape of the prediction line is more identical to the shape of the actual line.

Table 5. Results of 1-day intervals.

Metric	Model	Price Data	Price Data Technical Indicators	Price Data Sentiment Indicators	Price Data Technical Indicators Sentiment Indicators
MAE	LSTM	848.14	886.21	710.44	724.19
	GRU	853.15	547.62	612.19	854.11
	AE	446.10	489.68	454.78	902.65
	SE	396.47	382.03	443.76	492.90
	BE	395.78	359.08	461.73	521.10
MSE	LSTM	1,269,660.00	1,295,847.00	1,019,135.00	1,047,841.00
	GRU	1,118,205.00	428,177.66	525,815.54	911,621.13
	AE	439,481.27	514,340.94	421,803.11	1,010,587.00
	SE	432,656.06	253,018.37	412,734.49	392,582.15
	BE	334,694.01	276,185.43	357,483.50	430,310.16
MAPE	LSTM	7.05	7.45	5.81	5.92
	GRU	7.27	5.26	5.87	8.34
	AE	3.73	4.09	3.91	8.82
	SE	3.25	3.53	3.73	4.49
	BE	3.37	3.18	4.25	4.89
sMAPE	LSTM	7.42	7.83	6.06	6.17
	GRU	7.62	5.10	5.67	7.93
	AE	3.80	4.19	3.91	8.36
	SE	3.29	3.46	3.75	4.40
	BE	3.44	3.16	4.16	4.74
MDA	LSTM	47.21	46.35	48.50	48.93
	GRU	42.49	57.94	59.23	57.51
	AE	54.51	49.36	57.08	58.37
	SE	54.08	59.23	56.65	57.51
	BE	52.79	57.08	59.66	59.23

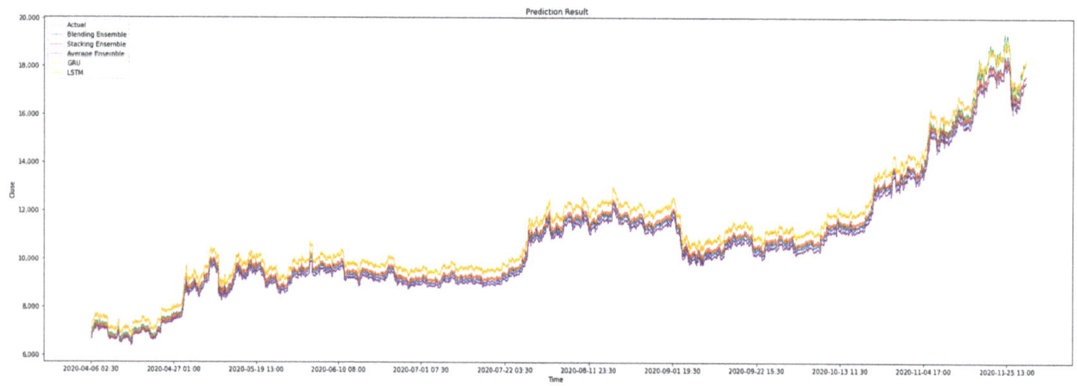

Figure 9. Price + technical indicator + sentiment indicator prediction results of the models.

Table 6. Comparison of the metrics obtained by the models.

Interval		30 min	1 Day
Metric	**Model**	**Price Data Technical Indicators Sentiment Indicators**	**Price Data Technical Indicators Sentiment Indicators**
MAE	LSTM	412.554188	724.19
	GRU	389.918484	854.11
	AE	271.482766	902.65
	SE	88.740831	492.90
	BE	188.535888	521.10
MSE	LSTM	184,271.5385	1,047,841.00
	GRU	165,616.467	911,621.13
	AE	97,194.7086	1,010,587.00
	SE	30,067.70409	392,582.15
	BE	58,818.47366	430,310.16
MAPE	LSTM	3.966612	5.92
	GRU	3.740284	8.34
	AE	2.457365	8.82
	SE	0.69763	4.49
	BE	1.651553	4.89
sMAPE	LSTM	3.884225	6.17
	GRU	3.666772	7.93
	AE	2.490969	8.36
	SE	0.70038	4.40
	BE	1.66841	4.74
MDA	LSTM	51.645118	48.93
	GRU	51.618368	57.51
	AE	48.747214	58.37
	SE	52.144449	57.51
	BE	48.970129	59.23

Note: the underlined numbers indicate the best performance out of the different models.

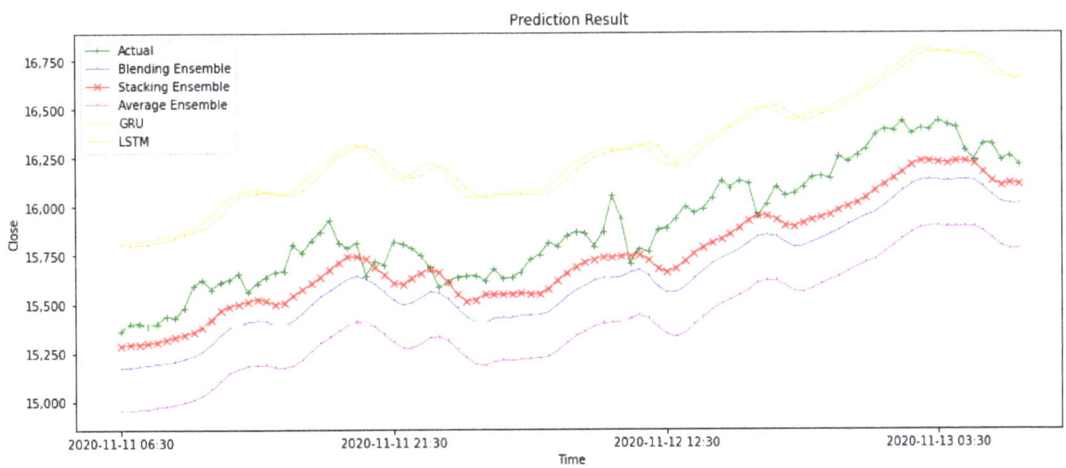

Figure 10. Price + technical indicator + sentiment indicator prediction results of the models from 11 November 2020 to 13 November 2020.

The second part is the comparative experiments with different data combinations. It is shown in Table 7 that, for different time intervals, the data combinations that produce optimal performance are not necessarily the same. Specifically, when the data interval is one day, the combination of price data and technical indicators has better prediction performance than other data combinations since it obtains the best value of 492.90 among all the 1-day interval data combinations. The combination of price data, technical indicators, and sentiment indicators outperforms the other combinations for time intervals of 30 min, since it obtains the best value of 88.74 among all data combinations for 30-min intervals.

Table 7. Comparison of the MAE obtained by the stacking ensemble with different intervals.

Interval	Price Data	Price Data Technical Indicators	Price Data Sentiment Indicators	Price Data Technical Indicators Sentiment Indicators
1 day	396.47	382.03	443.76	492.90
30 min	155.933634	130.200637	107.650458	88.740831

Note: The underlined numbers indicate the best performance out of the different data combinations.

Experiments show that, in most cases, the combination of price data, technical indicators and sentiment indicators outperforms the data combination in previous articles. We can conclude that the richness of the input data used in the prediction can improve the accuracy of the prediction.

Furthermore, other metrics are shown in Figure 11. The better the prediction obtained with the data combination, the redder the values are; the worse the prediction obtained with the data combination, the whiter its values are. The combination of price data and technical indicators achieves the best performance for 1-day intervals, and the combination of price data, technical indicators and sentiment indicators achieves the best performance for 30 min intervals. From our experiments, we found that price data with technical indicators are better for short-term predictions, such as predicting the next-day prices; however, price data with sentiment indicators are better for extra-short-term predictions, such as predicting the prices in the next 30 min.

Metric	Interval	Price Data	Price Data Technical Indicators	Price Data Sentiment Indicators	Price Data Technical Indicators Sentiment Indicators
MAE	1 DAY	396.47	382.03	443.76	492.90
	30 MIN	155.93	130.20	107.65	88.74
MSE	1 DAY	432,656.06	253,018.37	412,734.49	392,582.15
	30 MIN	60,092.72	36,440.18	27,892.31	30,067.70
MAPE(%)	1 DAY	3.25	3.53	3.73	4.49
	30 MIN	1.34	1.10	0.95	0.70
sMAPE(%)	1 DAY	3.29	3.46	3.78	4.40
	30 MIN	1.36	1.10	0.96	0.70
MDA	1 DAY	54.08	59.23	56.65	57.51
	30 MIN	49.48	51.46	50.33	52.14

Good / Bad

Figure 11. Stacking ensemble model prediction results of the data combinations.

Figure 12 shows the testing data with different data combinations. Figure 13 is part of Figure 12, the result of using all data is marked 'X' and the actual value is marked '+' to illustrate performance of data combinations. The graph visually illustrates that, for the stacking ensemble model, the accuracy of the prediction results depends on whether it is used for short-term prediction or long-term prediction. Generally, the combination of price data and technical indicators is better for short-term prediction, and the combination of price data, technical indicators and sentiment indicators is better for extra short-term prediction.

At present, in the research field of Bitcoin price prediction, there are several difficulties limiting the fair comparison of the new proposed method and previous methods: (1) the data format is diverse and difficult to unify; (2) the data acquisition methods are different, and the versions are different; (3) some implementation details are not mentioned in the theses of previous studies; (4) the source code is hard to obtain and run in new environments. Therefore, we briefly compare the results of previous related work with our newly proposed method in Table 8.

Figure 12. Stacking ensemble model prediction result for different data combinations.

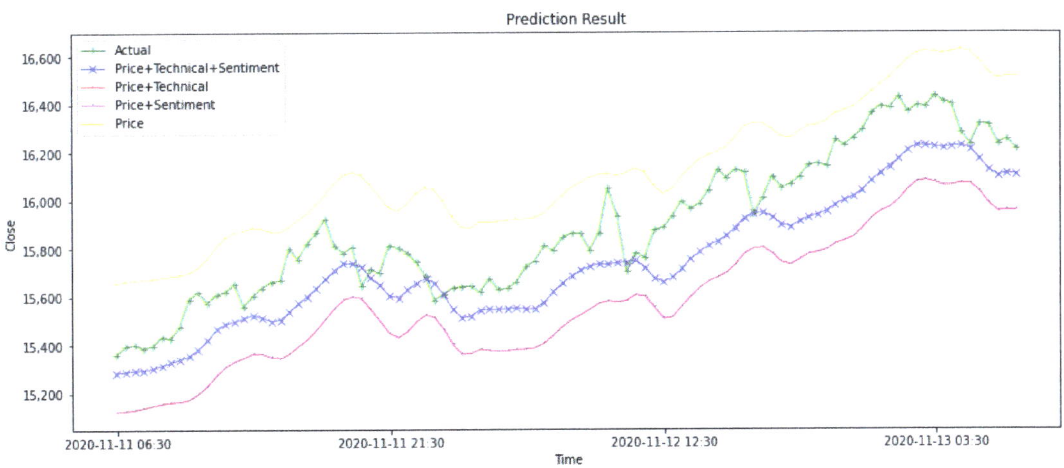

Figure 13. Stacking ensemble model prediction result for different data combinations from 11 November 2020 to 13 November 2020.

Specially, the data combination of price and sentiment indicators under the 1-day time internal can be considered as the variant of Li and Pan's proposed method [1] in our experiments. By this way, it is shown that our proposed method has got the improvement from Li and Pan's proposed method.

Bitcoin price data and social media text data are presented in different formats due to different providers or acquisition tools. Most of the methods in this paper only read data in one of the formats. For data formats other than the specified format, additional processing work is required.

As there are no standard open data for Bitcoin price prediction, all researchers collect data on their own. At present, there are several major trading platforms that provide their own transaction data for Bitcoin price data. The version differences among Bitcoin's social media texts, such as those on Twitter or Reddit, are even more serious because the collection tools are different and the collection times are different. For example, a tweet that was published yesterday may be deleted by the author today. Then, the data version collected today is not the same as the data version collected yesterday.

Table 8. Comparison of the proposed method and previous methods in Bitcoin price prediction.

Author & Reference No.	Year	Method	Dataset	Metric
S, Ji [42]	2019	Deep neural network (DNN)	Daily Bitcoin price data and blockchain infomation from 29 November 2011 to 31 December 2018	MAPE: 3.61%
S, Raju [43]	2020	LSTM (LSTM)	634 daily Bitcoin English tweets and transaction data from 2017 to 2018	RMSE: 197.515
M, Shin [29]	2021	Ensemble Minute + Hour + Day LSTM	Transaction data from December 2017 to November 2018 per 3 min	RMSE: 31.60 (weighted price)
Proposed work (ensemble deep model)	2021	Stacking ensemble deep model of 2 base models: LSTM & GRU	Tweets, transaction data, technical data from September 2017 to January 2021 per 30 min	MAE: 88.740831 RMSE: 173.400415 MAPE: 0.69763%

There are many parameters and implementation details in modeling and model training. In a deep neural network, the structure of each layer has many parameters. However, these parameters are not all written in the original theses for good reasons. Moreover, there are many details in modeling, such as the split of training and test data and some shuffle operations to prevent overfitting of the model. These details can also be missing due to the lengths of the theses and the focus of the topics. The lack of this information makes it difficult to reproduce previous methods solely by the theses themselves.

If one is fortunate enough to obtain the source code with the author's consent, there will still be environmental and operational difficulties. We know that many machine learning and statistical toolkits are updated very frequently. A piece of code can run under the package version used by the author at the time, but it may not be able to run smoothly under a new version. In addition, it is also possible that the running result is different from the author's result due to the inability to obtain the same running environment as the author.

5. Conclusions

The price of Bitcoin often fluctuates wildly, inspired by the work of Li and Pan [1], we propose an ensemble deep method, which combines two RNNs, to predict the future price and price movement of Bitcoin based on the combination of historical transaction data, tweet sentiment indicators and technical indicators. It is worth noting that we crawled two datasets at different time intervals: 1 day and 30 min. Because of the financial attribute of cryptocurrency, four evaluation indicators, the MSE, the MAE, the MAPE, and the sMAPE, are used to measure the price prediction performance, and the movement direction accuracy (MDA) is used to measure the price movement prediction. Two types of comparative experiments are conducted in this research: experiments that compare different models and experiments that compare the impact of different data combinations on forecast prices. The results show that in the same situation, a stacking ensemble can help with fewer training resources and better performance, and social media sentiment analysis makes a greater contribution to extra short-term price prediction than to short-term price prediction.

Prediction models and input data sources have great room for improvement in the future. First, the model can be optimized from the three aspects of the model framework, model size and optimization process to improve prediction performance [44]. For the model framework, we can consider changing the model types and activation function. For the model size, the width and number of hidden layers are two potential values where we can make adjustments. For optimization, the proper setting of the hyperparameters is essential. Second, the inclusion of other data sources may improve the existing forecasting accuracy. In this research, we consider the historical transaction data, sentiment trends of Twitter, and technical indicators. However, there may be other potential factors, including regulatory and legal matters, competition between Bitcoin and other cryptocurrencies, and the supply and demand of Bitcoin. In addition, the microexpressions of cryptocurrency investors during trading can also be considered potential factors affecting cryptocurrency prices. Third, we can also dynamically change the size of the window according to different data types. For example, news is not published as quickly as social media comments, such as tweets. Therefore, we can set different window sizes for data with different update frequencies and study the long-term or short-term influences on prices. Experiments based on the proposed model can be extended to research on the price prediction of other cryptocurrencies. The new bitcoin price prediction model proposed by us provides a reference for practitioners to avoid their potential risks in trading. In addition, researchers can develop better regulatory measures and laws by studying the relationship 429 between opinion analysis on social media and price movements of cryptocurrencies.

Author Contributions: Conceptualization, Y.P. and Q.J.; Data curation, Z.Y. and Y.W.; Formal analysis, Z.Y. and Y.W.; Funding acquisition, Q.J.; Investigation, Y.P. and Q.J.; Methodology, Z.Y. and Y.P.; Project administration, H.C., Y.P. and Q.J.; Resources, Y.P. and Q.J.; Software, Z.Y. and Y.W.; Supervision, H.C., Y.P. and Q.J.; Validation, Z.Y. and Y.W.; Visualization, Y.W.; Writing—original draft, Z.Y. and Y.W.; Writing—review and editing, Z.Y., Y.W. and H.C. All authors have read and agreed to the published version of the manuscript.

Funding: This work is supported by the Hebei Academy of Sciences under research fund No. 22602 and the National Key Research and Development Program of China under fund No. 2021YFF1200104.

Data Availability Statement: The data used in this work is available at https://github.com/Coria/bitcoin_prediction_with_twitter, accessed on 26 February 2022.

Acknowledgments: The authors would like to thank all the anonymous reviewers for their insightful comments and constructive suggestions that have upgraded the quality of this manuscript.

Conflicts of Interest: The authors declare that they have no known competing financial interests or personal circumstances that could have appeared to influence the work reported in this manuscript.

References

1. Li, Y.; Pan, Y. A novel ensemble deep learning model for stock prediction based on stock prices and news. *Int. J. Data Sci. Anal.* **2021**, *13*, 139–149. [CrossRef] [PubMed]
2. Aslam, S.; Rasool, A.; Jiang, Q.; Qu, Q. LSTM based model for real-time stock market prediction on unexpected incidents. In Proceedings of the 2021 IEEE International Conference on Real-Time Computing and Robotics (RCAR), Xining, China, 15–19 July 2021; pp. 1149–1153. [CrossRef]
3. Sutiksno, D.U.; Ahmar, A.S.; Kurniasih, N.; Susanto, E.; Leiwakabessy, A. Forecasting historical data of bitcoin using ARIMA and α-Sutte indicator. *J. Phys. Conf. Ser.* **2018**, *1028*, 012194. [CrossRef]
4. Roy, S.; Nanjiba, S.; Chakrabarty, A. Bitcoin price forecasting using time series analysis. In Proceedings of the International Conference of Computer and Information Technology, Dhaka, Bangladesh, 21–23 December 2018; Volume 1, pp. 1–5. [CrossRef]
5. Pant, D.R.; Neupane, P.; Poudel, A.; Pokhrel, A.K.; Lama, B.K. Recurrent neural network based bitcoin price prediction by Twitter sentiment analysis. In Proceedings of the 2018 IEEE 3rd International Conference on Computing, Communication and Security (ICCCS), Kathmandu, Nepal, 25–27 October 2018; Volume 1, pp. 128–132. [CrossRef]
6. Gulker, M. Bitcoin's largest Price Changes Coincide with Major News Events about the Cryptocurrency. Available online: https://www.aier.org/article/bitcoins-largest-price-changes-coincide-with-major-news-events-about-the-cryptocurrency/ (accessed on 15 December 2021).
7. Li, T.R.; Chamrajnagar, A.S.; Fong, X.R.; Rizik, N.R.; Fu, F. Sentiment-based prediction of alternative cryptocurrency price fluctuations using gradient boosting tree model. *Front. Phys.* **2019**, *7*, 98. [CrossRef]
8. Ötürk, S.S.; Bilgiç, M.E. Twitter & Bitcoin: Are the most influential accounts really influential? *Appl. Econ. Lett.* **2021**, 1–4. [CrossRef]

9. Nasekin, S.; Chen, C.Y.-H. *Deep Learning-Based Cryptocurrency Sentiment Construction*; SSRN Scholarly Paper ID 3310784; Social Science Research Network: Rochester, NY, USA, 2019. [CrossRef]
10. Liu, W.; Jiang, Q.; Jiang, H.; Hu, J.; Qu, Q. A Sentiment Analysis Method Based on FinBERT-CNN for Guba Stock Forum. *J. Integr. Technol.* **2022**, *11*, 27–39. [CrossRef]
11. Katsiampa, P. Volatility estimation for Bitcoin: A comparison of GARCH models. *Econ. Lett.* **2017**, *158*, 3–6. [CrossRef]
12. Ayaz, Z.; Fiaidhi, J.; Sabah, A.; Anwer Ansari, M. Bitcoin price prediction using ARIMA model. *TechRxiv* **2020**. [CrossRef]
13. Bonifazi, G.; Corradini, E.; Ursino, D.; Virgili, L. A Social Network Analysis–based approach to investigate user behaviour during a cryptocurrency speculative bubble. *J. Inf. Sci.* **2021**.
14. Jana, R.K.; Ghosh, I.; Das, D. A differential evolution-based regression framework for forecasting Bitcoin price. *Ann. Oper. Res.* **2021**, *306*, 295–320.
15. Kim, J.M.; Cho, C.; Jun, C. Forecasting the Price of the Cryptocurrency Using Linear and Nonlinear Error Correction Model. *J. Risk Financ. Manag.* **2022**, *15*, 74.
16. Jang, H.; Lee, J. An Empirical Study on Modeling and Prediction of Bitcoin Prices With Bayesian Neural Networks Based on Blockchain Information. *IEEE Access* **2018**, *6*, 5427–5437. [CrossRef]
17. Mangla, N. Bitcoin price prediction using machine learning. *Int. J. Inf. Comput. Sci.* **2019**, *6*, 318–320.
18. Shen, Z.; Wan, Q.; Leatham, D.J. *Bitcoin Return Volatility Forecasting: A Comparative Study of GARCH Model and Machine Learning Model*; Technical Report 290696; Agricultural and Applied Economics Association: Washington, DC, USA, 2019. Available online: https://ideas.repec.org/p/ags/aaea19/290696.html (accessed on 15 December 2021).
19. Li, Y.; Dai, W. Bitcoin price forecasting method based on CNN-LSTM hybrid neural network model. *J. Eng.* **2020**, *2020*, 344–347. [CrossRef]
20. Jay, P.; Kalariya, V.; Parmar, P.; Tanwar, S.; Kumar, N. Stochastic Neural Networks for Cryptocurrency Price Prediction. *IEEE Access* **2020**, *8*, 82804–82818. [CrossRef]
21. Wołk, K. Advanced social media sentiment analysis for short-term cryptocurrency price prediction. *Expert Syst.* **2020**, *37*, e12493. [CrossRef]
22. Jagannath, N.; Barbulescu, T.; Sallam, K.M.; Elgendi, I. A Self-Adaptive Deep Learning-Based Algorithm for Predictive Analysis of Bitcoin Price. *IEEE Access* **2021**, *9*, 34054–34066. [CrossRef]
23. Guo, H.Z.; Zhang, D.; Liu, S.Y.; Wang, L. Bitcoin price forecasting: A perspective of underlying blockchain transactions. *Decis. Support Syst.* **2021**, *151*, 113650. [CrossRef]
24. Loginova, E.; Tsang, W.K.; van Heijningen, G.; Kerkhove, L.; Benoit, D.F. Forecasting directional bitcoin price returns using aspect-based sentiment analysis on online text data. *Mach. Learn.* **2021**.
25. Sridhar, S.; Sanagavarapu, S. Multi-Head Self-Attention Transformer for Dogecoin Price Prediction. In Proceedings of the 2021 14th International Conference on Human System Interaction (HSI), Gdansk, Poland, 8–10 July 2021.
26. Parekh, R.; Patel, N.P.; Thakkar, N.; Gupta, R.; Tanwar, S. DL-GuesS: Deep Learning and Sentiment Analysis-based Cryptocurrency Price Prediction. *IEEE Access* **2022**, *10*, 35398–35409.
27. Ibrahim, A.; Kashef, R.; Li, M.; Valencia, E.; Huang, E. Bitcoin network mechanics: Forecasting the btc closing price using vector auto-regression models based on endogenous and exogenous feature variables. *J. Risk Financ. Manag.* **2020**, *13*, 189. [CrossRef]
28. Livieris, I.E.; Pintelas, E.; Stavroyiannis, S.; Pintelas, P. Ensemble deep learning models for forecasting cryptocurrency time-series. *Algorithms* **2020**, *13*, 121. [CrossRef]
29. Shin, M.; Mohaisen, D.; Kim, J. Bitcoin price forecasting via ensemble-based LSTM deep learning networks. In Proceedings of the 2021 International Conference on Information Networking (ICOIN), Jeju Island, Korea, 13–16 January 2021; Volume 1, pp. 603–608. [CrossRef]
30. Ye, Z.; Liu, W.; Jiang, Q.; Pan, Y. A cryptocurrency price prediction model based on Twitter sentiment indicators. In Proceedings of the International Conference on Big Data and Security, Shenzhen, China, 26–28 November 2021. [CrossRef]
31. Hochreiter, S.; Schmidhuber, J. Long short-term memory. *Neural Comput.* **1997**, *9*, 1735–1780. [CrossRef] [PubMed]
32. Lipton, Z.C.; Berkowitz, J.; Elkan, C. A critical review of recurrent neural networks for sequence learning. *arXiv* **2015**, arXiv:1506.00019.
33. Colah Understanding LSTM Networks. 2015. Available online: http://colah.github.io/posts/2015-08-Understanding-LSTMs/ (accessed on 15 December 2021).
34. Cho, K.; van Merrienboer, B.; Bahdanau, D.; Bengio, Y. On the properties of neural machine translation: Encoder-decoder approaches. *arXiv* **2014**, arXiv:1409.1259.
35. Zhou, Z.-H. *Ensemble Methods: Foundations and Algorithms*; Chapman and Hall/CRC: London, UK, 2012. [CrossRef]
36. Dietterich, T.G. Ensemble methods in machine learning. In *Multiple Classifier Systems*; Springer: Berlin/Heidelberg, Germany, 2000; pp. 1–15. [CrossRef]
37. Zhang, D.; Jiang, Q.; Li, X. Application of neural networks in financial data mining. In Proceedings of the International Conference on Computational Intelligence, Xi'an, China, 15–19 December 2005; Volume 4.
38. Bishop, C.M. *Neural Networks for Pattern Recognition*; Oxford University Press: Oxford, UK, 1995.
39. Ganaie, M.A.; Hu, M.; Tanveer, M.; Suganthan, P.N. Ensemble deep learning: A review. *arXiv* **2021**, arXiv:2104.02395
40. Goodfellow, I.; Bengio, Y.; Courville, A. *Deep Learning*; The MIT Press: Cambridge, UK, 2016.

41. Rocca, J. Ensemble Methods: Bagging, Boosting and Stacking. Available online: https://towardsdatascience.com/ensemble-methods-bagging-boosting-and-stacking-c9214a10a205 (accessed on 15 December 2021).
42. Ji, S.; Kim, J.; Im, H. A comparative study of bitcoin price prediction using deep learning. *Mathematics* **2019**, *7*, 898. [CrossRef]
43. Raju, S.M.; Tarif, A.M. Real-time prediction of BITCOIN price using machine learning techniques and public sentiment analysis. *arXiv* **2020**, arXiv:2006.14473.
44. Hu, X.; Chu, L.; Pei, J.; Liu, W.; Bian, J. Model complexity of deep learning: A survey. *arXiv* **2021**, arXiv:2103.05127.

mathematics

MDPI

Article

The Macroeconomic Effects of an Interest-Bearing CBDC: A DSGE Model

Ferry Syarifuddin [1] and Toni Bakhtiar [2,*]

1 Bank Indonesia Institute, Jl. M.H. Thamrin No. 2, Jakarta 10350, Indonesia; ferry.s@bi.go.id
2 Department of Mathematics, Kampus IPB Dramaga, IPB University, Bogor 16680, Indonesia
* Correspondence: tbakhtiar@apps.ipb.ac.id

Abstract: We develop a medium size dynamic stochastic general equilibrium (DSGE) model to assess the macroeconomic consequences of introducing an interest-bearing central bank digital currency (CBDC), an electronic alternative of payment with public use properties of cash and that can furnish as bank settlement balances. The model consists of seven sectors, namely households, retail firms, wholesale firms, capital producing firms, commercial banks, central bank, and government, and offers rich features. The use of cash and CBDC is differentiated with respect to their prices and transaction costs. In particular, we quantify the effects of negative shock on CBDC transaction cost to evaluate the potential of CBDC as an alternate instrument in liquidity holding in addition to cash and bank deposits. We also examine the effects of productivity shock and monetary policy shock on CBDC interest rate and CBDC demand, and their interaction with other main variables of the model.

Keywords: DSGE model; interest-bearing CBDC; monetary policy; transaction costs

MSC: 91-10; 91B51

JEL Classification: D53; E42; E43; E58

Citation: Syarifuddin, F.; Bakhtiar, T. The Macroeconomic Effects of an Interest-Bearing CBDC: A DSGE Model. *Mathematics* **2022**, *10*, 1671. https://doi.org/10.3390/math10101671

Academic Editors: José Luis Miralles-Quirós, María Mar Miralles-Quirós and David Carfì

Received: 16 February 2022
Accepted: 10 May 2022
Published: 13 May 2022

1. Introduction

The rise of privately issued digital currencies supported by the advancement of transaction validation technology has raised concerns among central banks and other monetary authorities. The rapid innovation of the payment infrastructure offers new alternate payment platforms to compete with central bank paper money, i.e., cash as the only form of central bank money available for customers. Digital or virtual currencies, popularly known as crypto-currencies, have broadened the option of payment settlement and have automated contracts. Additionally, due to the invention of blockchain, which uses distributed ledger technology (DLT), crypto-currencies can function in an open and decentralized fashion independent of any controlling entity, while ensuring safety and anonymity [1].

The advent of crypto-currencies as payment solutions has posed challenges to central banks to consider upgrading the concept and provision of money. This payment diversity is, however, coincidence with the decline of the use of cash as a means of payment due to the COVID-19 pandemic. The wish to avoid coronavirus transmission through banknotes and coins has accelerated a shift from cash to digital transactions. As reported by Bank for International Settlements (BIS) [2], there was a decline in the total number of cash withdrawals by 23% and more than 10% in value. It is cited by Balz [3] that the worldwide transactions using PayPal have increased from about USD 3.26 billion in the first quarter of 2020 to around USD 3.74 billion in the second quarter. Additionally, the number of transactions using girocard in Germany in the first semester of 2020 was 21 percent up on the first two quarters of 2019, increasing the volume of transactions to USD 2.6 billion.

Cashless payments are expected to continue considering that consumers who had been conducting such payments prior to the pandemic have been even more likely to do so [4].

Recently, according to what BIS reported in [5], no less than eighty percent of central banks worldwide have begun studying the process and consequences of introducing their own version of a digital currency, namely a central bank digital currency (CBDC). Almost 50 percent of central banks have run CBDC-related experiments or released proofs-of-concept. Moreover, about 10 percent of the surveyed central banks project to establish a generally available (retail) CBDC in the short run (up to three years) and around 20 percent in the medium term (up to six years). In 2014, China's central bank (PBoC) starts focusing on the development of a CBDC by forming a special task force. In 2015, the Bank of England was pioneering a series of studies to assess the potential of CBDCs. In 2017, e-krona was proposed to study by Riksbank, the central bank of Sweden, in response to the weakening of the use of cash to the lowest level in the world. This initiative is then followed by Bahamas, the Eastern Caribbean Currency Union, and the Marshall Islands [6]. Some emerging economies including Tunisia, Lithuania, Venezuela, and Uruguay also implemented pilot programs to test CBDCs.

A CBDC can loosely be described as an electronic alternative of cash issued by a central bank. From the household's perspective, CBDCs can thus mimic the public use characteristics of cash and from commercial banks and other financial institutions with the payment system point of views, CBDCs can furnish as electronic central bank deposits, also known as reserves or settlement balances [7]. From a theoretical viewpoint, there are two important and long-standing questions regarding the issuance of a CBDC, namely the provision of public and private money, and the ability of the central bank to harness CBDC as a direct monetary policy tool to households. A central bank may consider introducing a CBDC with the following reasons: to ensure payment resilience, prevent private sector monopolies in the payment market, and strengthen monetary sovereignty [8].

Despite the luminous potential of CBDC, academicians and central banks have been in the combination of cautious and curious. They have recently started to examine merits and dangers of introducing CBDC. A series of CBDC-related studies and discussions were carried-out to address the aforementioned questions by focusing on the consequences of introducing a CBDC on commercial banks and monetary policy as well as financial stability and welfare implications [9]. To our knowledge, no study tries to examine the multiple roles of CBDC in their models. Particularly, there is no existing study that unifies the roles of CBDC in macroeconomics and monetary policy. Given the existing gaps, the objectives of this paper are to develop a medium size dynamic stochastic general equilibrium (DSGE) model in a closed economy, where a CBDC is introduced as an alternative liquidity asset as well as a monetary policy instrument, and to quantify the macroeconomic consequences in the presence of interest-bearing CBDCs in competing with cash and bank deposits as well as the implication for optimal monetary policy. In order to differentiate with other studies, we extent some models of money-in-utility function [10,11], cash presence [8], price setting [12], and interest rate [13]. DSGE model is a prominent tool for policy analysis of central banking and contributes a major strand of the modern macroeconomics literature. The ability of DSGE models to quantitatively reveal macroeconomic fluctuations are then strengthened after seminal works of Christiano et al. [14] on the inertia and persistence of inflation in aggregate quantities subject to a monetary policy shock and Smets & Wouters [15] on Bayesian estimation of monetary business cycle model with sticky wages and prices. Since then, DSGE models have extensively been adopted for various purposes in macroeconomics forecasting.

2. Related Works: Modeling CBDC

From a theoretical point of view, the introduction of central bank digital currency poses some challenging questions relating to the supply of public and private money and the ability of the central bank to utilize CBDC as a tool to increase the efficiency of monetary policy. Despite its potential, CBDCs could threaten the stability of banking and financial systems. Bank runs and disintermediation may occur when a substantial amount of bank deposits is converted into CBDCs. Deposit outflows decrease banks' funding ability and therefore, decline the volume of loan, investment, and economic activities in general [8]. Thus, the focus of theoretical literature in CBDC modeling lays in the effect of CBDC on commercial banks, monetary policy, financial stability, and welfare implications. Literature in this topic of research can be divided into three strands [16]: papers introducing a CBDC in general, papers presenting a CBDC in DSGE model, and those analyzing a CBDC in an open economy setting.

2.1. Non-DSGE Models

In the first strand, i.e., non-DSGE modeling of CBDC, many researchers utilize a stylized and often two-period model to assess the implication of CBDC in domestic economy. Agur et al. [17] discuss the optimal design of interest and non-interest bearing CBDCs. In this network effect induced environment, economic agents may choose cash, CBDC, and bank deposits based on their preferences over anonymity and security. Two-period model economy which consists of households, banks, firms, and a central bank is considered to maximize welfare. In the first period, the central bank decides whether and in what form to introduce a CBDC. Then, in the second period, households decide to use either cash, bank deposits, or CBDC (if introduced by central bank) in their transactions. Commercial banks extend loan to firms by using deposits from households. It is found that, when network effect matter, the interest bearing CBDC can be introduced by central bank to alleviate the trade-off between maintaining intermediation versus the diverse instruments of payment.

Andolfatto [18] develops an overlapping generation model as a combination of the Diamond government debt model and Klein-Monti monopoly bank model to study the impact of interest bearing CBDC on monopolistic banking sector. It is shown that CBDC has no damaging effect toward lending activity of banks. More precisely, if the CBDC interest rate is independently set of the interest of reserve, then the establishment of CBDC will not discourage the lending activities. Accordingly, if CBDC interest rate is fixed below the interest of reserve, then there is an incentive for the monopoly banks to match the CBDC rate for the purpose of retaining deposits. Thus, it is shown by the model that introduction of an interest-bearing CBDC does reduce bank monopoly profit, but does not necessarily lead to bank disintermediation.

The optimal monetary in an environment where cash and CBDC co-exist is studied by Davoodalhosseini [19]. By adapting Lagos–Wright model into two-period setting, i.e., a model with decentralized and centralized markets, an economy with only cash, only CBDC, or both of cash and CBDC can be analyzed. It is found that, under small carrying cost, the introduction of CBDC enables the central bank to acquire better allocations than with cash. By calibrating the model to the Canadian and US data, it is revealed that introducing CBDC can lead to an increase of up to 0.64 percent and 1.6 percent in consumption for Canada and for the US, respectively. The Lagos–Wright model with decentralized–centralized markets is also considered by [20]. Chiu et al. [21,22] develop a model of a banking system with imperfect competition to investigate the effect of general equilibrium of establishing CBDC. It is discovered that the introduction of CBDC as an outside option for households can still improve the efficiency of bank intermediation and increase lending and aggregate output, even if its usage is low. Furthermore, when the model is calibrated to the US economy, it is shown that CBDC can increase the volume of bank lending and investment by 6 percent under the proper interest rate. The output can also be increased by a maximum of 1 percent.

Keister & Monnet [23] study the effect of CBDC establishment on the financial stability under the condition of private information about the quality of assets held by the bank. In this work, the seminal model of Diamond–Dybvig on bank runs is modified in such a way that patient and impatient agents face two types of liquidity shocks. It is shown that, by observing the funds inflow into CBDC, the central bank can deduce the financial condition of bank more quickly and monitoring the flow of funds into this new asset. Diamond–Dybvig model on bank runs is also adapted by Fernandez-Villaverde et al. [24]

to study the impact of CBDC on financial stability and bank runs in which banks can offer nominal contracts. Other papers thematically most similar with this are [25–27].

2.2. DSGE Models

Studies in the second strand employ DSGE framework to model the consequences of CBDC on economy. It is well known that the dynamic stochastic general equilibrium (DSGE) models are widely used to explain and predict co-movements of aggregate time series over the business cycle. DSGE models can be viewed as an objectively good representation of a market economy mechanism. DSGE models can also be considered as the leading tool to evaluate the relative strength of interaction among agents [28]. However, the DSGE approach has also received criticism by economists. Among others, it is raised by [29] that DSGE failed to incorporate key aspects of economic behavior, especially in predicting or responding to a financial crisis (see for instance, [30]). Blanchard [31] lists many reasons to dislike current DSGE models: from its unappealing assumptions and unconvincing estimation method to its inability to communicate with other types of general equilibrium models and, of course, Lucas' critique on parameter instability due to changes in economic policy [32]. Criticism on DSGE is also boosted by the Austrian school of economic thought. The core of the school lies in the inability of DSGE models to adapt to economic changes, particularly in dealing with the diversity of agents, preferences, and information sets. Other concerns relate to the heterogeneity and multi-specification of capital stock and production function, which can lead to malinvestment and sensitive to policy shocks [33–35]. Regardless the flaws, DSGE still serves to guide debates about the direction of the economy [31], provides policy evaluation exercises [36], and offers simplification and flexibility to be used for many purposes [37]. Rebuilding Macroeconomic Theory, set up by the Oxford Review of Economic Policy, is a project to rebuild the benchmark New Keynesian model [30].

Compared to the use of the non-DSGE models, research on the effects of CBDC using the DSGE models is still rare. Gross & Schiller [8] build a DSGE model to evaluate the effects of interest and non-interest bearing CBDC, especially in the period of financial crises. A Gertler–Karadi model is adopted by focusing the household utility maximization, bank intermediation in lending, and the central bank role. In particular, households have three instruments of saving with remuneration, liquidity, and risk exposures, i.e., bank deposits, CBDC, and government bonds. It is found that the effect of bank deposits crowd out can be mitigated by assigning additional central bank funds or setting a low CBDC interest rates to disincentivize large-scale CBDC accumulation. Barrdear & Kumhof [38] propose a monetary-financial DSGE model and assess the steady state effects of an interest-bearing CBDC. Calibration of the model to pre-2008 US data shows that even if CBDC introduction of 30 percent of GDP would cause a bank deposits outflow, the output could still increase by three percent in the long run.

A New Keynesian DSGE model consisting of three economic sectors, namely households, commercial bank, and central bank, is examined by Luo et al. [39] to analyze the impact of electronic money (including CBDC) on monetary policy and, specifically, the impact of behavior changes on savings, loans, output, and interest rate. The simulation results suggest that electronic money exhibits asymmetric effects on savings and loans, but an irrational distortion on households, electronic money influences the interest rate in reverse manner leading to the management difficulties of the micro subjects and affecting the monetary policy effectiveness, and electronic money has the effect of restraining risk. Lim et al. [40] develop a DSGE model equipped with cash and digital currency to quantify the effect of loan prime rate (LPR) setting and CBDC introduction in China. Using Bayesian estimation, the optimal LPR can be designed to improve the stability property of post-CBDC economy.

2.3. Open Economy Models

Open economy means an economy open to trade and capital flows. The third strand of research topic extend the DSGE models into open economy context. This direction is more challenging compared to a standard closed economy as we now allow, for instance, the world demand and transmission channel through exchange rate. The results regarding CBDC effect through DSGE modeling in open economy are thin. George et al. [41] extend the Barrdear–Kumhof model to a small open economy by introducing foreign sector, where export–import activities and capital flows are possible. It is discovered that the introduction of CBDC with an adjustable interest rate may improve the welfare and increase the monetary policy effectiveness. Moreover, exchange rate and inflation exhibit more stable movements. Ferrari et al. [16] build a two-country open economy DSGE model to assess the international transmission of standard monetary policy and technology shocks in light of two scenarios, namely with and without CBDC, and to explore the monetary policy optimality and households' welfare in the economies. It is shown that the introduction of CBDC strengthen the international spillovers of shocks to a significant extent, thus reinforce international connections. A DSGE model proposed by Benigno et al. [42] discusses the two-country open economy nature of more globally issued crypto-currencies, which are different in safety and reputation with CBDC. The presence of a crypto-currency in a home and a foreign environment with two national currencies is analyzed in the framework of monetary policy autonomy.

3. The Model Economy

We follow the standard framework of DSGE modeling to assess the macroeconomic consequences of introducing an interest-bearing CBDC, especially we want to know how the cash will compete with CBDC with respect to their prices and transaction costs. In this section, we outline the economy of our model and expose the optimization problems solved by households and firms. We also describe the behavior of financial intermediaries by commercial bank and the monetary and fiscal authorities by the central bank and the government.

3.1. Assumptions

Our model economy is populated by seven classes of agents: a continuum of identical households of measure unity indexed by $h \in [0,1]$, a retail firm or final-good producing firm, a continuum of wholesale firms or intermediate-good producing firms indexed by $j \in [0,1]$, a capital-producing firm, commercial banks, the central bank as a monetary authority and the government as a fiscal authority. In a representative agent model, identical agents in household and firm sectors mean that all agents differ, but they act in such a way that the sum of their preferences is mathematically equivalent to the decision of one representative agent.

The basic structure of our DSGE model is depicted in Figure 1. The model is built according to the closed economy New Keynesian framework by [8,43,44]. Households consume and supply labor to wholesale firms, receive wages, choose the real levels of cash, deposits, and CBDC to hold at the beginning of the period, and pay lump-sum tax to the government. As the owners, households also receive dividends from firms and commercial banks. Retail firm aggregates imperfectly substitutable intermediate goods into a single final good, which is used for consumption, investment, or government spending. The final good is sold at a perfectly competitive price. Wholesale firms use the labor provided by households and capital to produce a unique good that is sold on the monopolistically competitive market. Wages are fully flexible and adjust to clear the market. Capital-producing firm purchases the final good for investment and combines it with existing capital stock to produce new capital goods. Commercial bank is owned by households. The bank supplies credit to wholesale firms to finance their short-term working capital needs, supplies credit to the capital-producing firm for investment financing, pays interest on household deposits and central bank loans, and holds minimum reserves against deposits at the central bank without remuneration. The central bank regulates the commercial bank and sets its policy interest rate using a Taylor-type rule and supplies all the credit demanded by the bank at the prevailing refinance rate. The government issues bonds, receives tax payments, and makes spending.

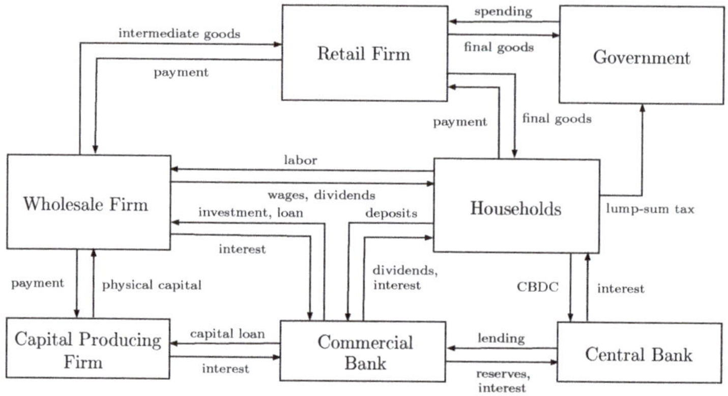

Figure 1. The model structure.

In some respects, we follow approaches developed in previous studies by others and in different standpoints we make few extensions. Our model has the following features:

1. We consider a money-in-utility (MIU) intertemporal welfare function to be maximized by households [10,11]. The presence of cash in addition to bank deposits and CBDC is slightly extend the one by Gross & Schiller [8]. The cash also appears in the budget constraint.
2. In the profit maximization of wholesale firms, we adopt the so-called Calvo price setting mechanism, where firms have a certain probability of either keeping the price fixed in the next period or optimally determining the price [12].
3. Similar to [8,13], the nominal interest rate on CBDC follows the interest rate of central bank funding considering the financial stress expressed as the percentage deviation of banks' equity from steady state. This rule is intended to disincentivize CBDC accumulation in a crisis.
4. Government bonds are held by banks and the central bank.
5. To quantify the effect of disruptions by economic shocks, our model is equipped with three shock generators, namely productivity shock, liquidity demand shock, and the monetary policy shock.

3.2. Households

In this model, the economy is populated by a continuum of households indexed by $h \in [0,1]$ whose problem is to maximize a particular intertemporal welfare function. To this end, a money-in-utility function proposed by Sidrauski [10] and in the form of the constant relative risk aversion (CRRA) utility function is adopted. The lifetime utility function U^H is additively separable into consumption of goods $C_{h,t}$, supply of working hours $L_{h,t}$, and saving in the form of bank deposits $D_{h,t}$, money holding in cash (real money balance) $M_{h,t}$, and digital money holding in CBDC $E_{h,t}$. Each household h wants to maximize the following expected utility:

$$U^H = \mathbb{E}_0 \sum_{i=0}^{\infty} \beta^i \left(\begin{array}{c} \frac{C_{h,i}^{1-\sigma}}{1-\sigma} + \frac{\alpha_e}{1-\eta_e}\left(\frac{E_{h,i}}{P_i}\right)^{1-\eta_e} + \frac{\alpha_m}{1-\eta_m}\left(\frac{M_{h,i}}{P_i}\right)^{1-\eta_m} \\ + \frac{\alpha_d}{1-\eta_d}\left(\frac{D_{h,i}}{P_i}\right)^{1-\eta_d} + \frac{\alpha_l L_{h,i}^{1+\varphi}}{1+\varphi} \end{array} \right), \tag{1}$$

where $\mathbb{E}_0$ stands for the rational expectation operator conditional on the information set at time zero. In (1), CBDC, cash, and deposits are expressed in nominal values as they are weighted by the price level P_i, $\beta \in (0,1)$ is the intertemporal discount factor, $\sigma \in (0,1)$ is the relative risk aversion coefficient, $\alpha_e, \alpha_m, \alpha_d > 0$ are relative utility weights or preference parameters of CBDC, cash, and bank deposits, respectively, φ is coefficient relates to Frisch elasticity of labor supply, and $\eta_e, \eta_m, \eta_d > 0$ are coefficients relate to elasticity of bank deposits, cash, and CBDC. Note that we may extend the form of household's utility function by introducing wealth in the form of government bonds $B^H_{h,i}$ as discussed by, for instance, Michaillat & Saez [45]. However, this extension modifies the properties of the New Keynesian IS curve, where the interest rate is now negatively related to output instead of being constant, equal to the time discount rate.

Households are assumed to consume goods, invest money, pay taxes, and receive wages for their labor supplied. Households also own the firms and the banks, and therefore receive dividends and profits sharing. Decisions made by households in maximizing (1) must satisfy the following budget constraint:

$$\begin{aligned} P_t(C_{h,t} + INV_{h,t}) + E_{h,t} + M_{h,t} + D_{h,t} + TAX_{h,t} &= W_t L_{h,t} + R^K_t K_{h,t} \\ &+ (1 + I^E_{t-1})E_{h,t-1} + M_{h,t-1} + (1 + I^D_{t-1})D_{h,t-1} + \Pi^{FB}_{h,t}. \end{aligned} \quad (2)$$

The terms on the left-hand side of (2) summarize the use of economic resources by households, and those on the right-hand side indicate the economic resources. $INV_{h,t}$ is level of investment, $TAX_{h,t}$ is the lump sum tax, W_t is the level of wages, $K_{h,t}$ is the capital stock, R^K_t is the return on capital, I^E_t is the nominal interest rate of CBDC, I^D_t is the nominal interest rate of bank deposits, and $\Pi^{FB}_{h,t}$ is the profit (dividend) from firms and banks. An additional equation represents the capital stock dynamics is:

$$K_{h,t+1} = INV_{h,t} + (1 - \delta)K_{h,t}, \quad (3)$$

where δ is the depreciation rate of physical capital.

Lifetime utility (1) maximization, with respect to $C_{h,t}$, $L_{h,t}$, $K_{h,t}$, $E_{h,t}$, $M_{h,t}$, and $D_{h,t}$, subject to budget constraint (2) and capital stock (3) yields the following first order conditions:

$$\alpha_l C^\sigma_t L^\varphi_t = \frac{W_t}{P_t}, \quad (4)$$

$$\left(\frac{\mathbb{E}_t C_{t+1}}{C_t}\right)^\sigma = \beta\left(1 - \delta + \mathbb{E}_t \frac{R^K_{t+1}}{P_{t+1}}\right), \quad (5)$$

$$\alpha_e \left(\frac{E_t}{P_t}\right)^{-\eta_e} = \frac{C^{-\sigma}_t}{P_t} - \beta(1 + I^E_t)\mathbb{E}_t \frac{C^{-\sigma}_{t+1}}{P_{t+1}}, \quad (6)$$

$$\alpha_m \left(\frac{M_t}{P_t}\right)^{-\eta_m} = \frac{C^{-\sigma}_t}{P_t} - \beta\mathbb{E}_t \frac{C^{-\sigma}_{t+1}}{P_{t+1}}, \quad (7)$$

$$\alpha_d \left(\frac{D_t}{P_t}\right)^{-\eta_d} = \frac{C^{-\sigma}_t}{P_t} - \beta(1 + I^D_t)\mathbb{E}_t \frac{C^{-\sigma}_{t+1}}{P_{t+1}}. \quad (8)$$

Note that derivation processes allow us to drop the index h from variables. The complete proofs for (4)–(8) can be found in Appendix B.

Under transaction costs of using cash and CBDC, the total consumption can be decomposed as follows:

$$C_t = C^M_t(1 + S(v^M_t)) + C^E_t(1 + S(v^E_t)), \quad (9)$$

where $S(v^M_t)$ and $S(v^E_t)$ are the transaction costs of using cash and CBDC, respectively, as functions of money velocities v^M_t and v^E_t, while C^M_t and C^E_t are the consumption levels using cash and CBDC. The money velocities with respect to cash and CBDC are, respectively, given by:

$$v^M_t = \frac{C^M_t}{M_t}, \quad (10)$$

$$v^E_t = \frac{C^E_t}{E_t}. \quad (11)$$

In this work, we adopt transaction cost functions proposed by Schmitt-Grohe & Uribe [46] as follows:

$$S(v_t) = av_t + \frac{b}{v_t} - 2\sqrt{ab}, \tag{12}$$

where a and b are all positive cost parameters. Cost function S has a satiation level of velocity $v^* = \sqrt{b/a}$. We can easily verify that S is decreasing when $v_t < v^*$ and increasing when $v_t > v^*$. The transaction cost functions for cash and CBDC are given by:

$$S_t^M = Z_t^M a_M \frac{C_t^M}{M_t} + b_M \frac{M_t}{C_t^M} - 2\sqrt{a_M b_M}, \tag{13}$$

$$S_t^E = Z_t^E a_E \frac{C_t^E}{E_t} + b_E \frac{E_t}{C_t^E} - 2\sqrt{a_E b_E}, \tag{14}$$

where we denote $S_t^M = S(v_t^M)$ and $S_t^E = S(v_t^E)$, while Z_t^M and Z_t^E are the shocks on the demand for total liquidities in term of cash and CBDC, respectively, which follow first order autoregressive processes:

$$\ln Z_t^M = \rho_M \ln Z_{t-1}^M + \varepsilon_t^M, \tag{15}$$

$$\ln Z_t^E = \rho_E \ln Z_{t-1}^E - \varepsilon_t^E, \tag{16}$$

where $\rho_M, \rho_E \in (0,1)$ are the degree of persistence in the cash and CBDC demands, and $\varepsilon_t^M \sim N(0, \sigma_M)$ and $\varepsilon_t^E \sim N(0, \sigma_E)$ are the errors. As pointed out by [38], an increase in S_t^M or S_t^E can be considered as a flight to safety, meaning a higher demand for liquid assets for a given volume of real economic transactions. CBDC that has cheaper transaction cost than cash will have smaller parameters values, i.e., $a_E \leq a_M$ and $b_E \leq b_M$.

Further, consumption levels by using cash and CBDC are given by:

$$C_t^M = \left(\frac{P_t^M}{P_t}\right)^{-\zeta} C_t, \tag{17}$$

$$C_t^E = \left(\frac{P_t^E}{P_t}\right)^{-\zeta} C_t, \tag{18}$$

where ζ is the elasticity of substitution between cash and CBDC payments for consumption, P_t^M and P_t^E are the prices of goods by using cash and CBDC, respectively, and they govern the general price:

$$P_t = ((P_t^M)^{1-\zeta} + (P_t^E)^{1-\zeta})^{\frac{1}{1-\zeta}}. \tag{19}$$

The proofs for (17)–(19) are provided in Appendix C.

3.3. Retail Firms

Suppose that at time t wholesale firm j produces $Y_{j,t}$ units of intermediate good and there are a continuum of intermediate goods over the unit interval $[0,1]$. These intermediate goods are CES aggregated by a retail firm (final good producer) to produce Y_t. The production technology for assembling intermediate goods to produce the final good is given by the standard Dixit-Stiglitz technology [47]:

$$Y_t = \left(\int_0^1 (Y_{j,t})^{\frac{\theta-1}{\theta}} dj\right)^{\frac{\theta}{\theta-1}}, \tag{20}$$

where $\theta > 1$ represents the elasticity of substitution between intermediate goods. With the nominal price of a final good being denoted by P_t and that of a intermediate good j denoted by $P_{j,t}$, the price of each intermediate good is taken as a given by retail firms. Therefore, the representative retail firm chooses the quantities of intermediate goods such that maximize its profits:

$$U^{RF} = P_t Y_t - \int_0^1 P_{j,t} Y_{j,t}\, dj, \tag{21}$$

where the first term in (21) is the total revenue from selling final goods and the second term is the total cost of buying intermediate goods. Substituting the aggregator technology (20) leads to the following first order condition of profit maximization:

$$Y_{j,t} = \left(\frac{P_{j,t}}{P_t}\right)^{-\theta} Y_t. \tag{22}$$

Equation (22) accounts the demand level of intermediate good j, which is directly proportional to aggregate demand Y_t and inversely proportional to its relative price level P_t.

3.4. Wholesale Firms

Each wholesale firm j produces a perishable intermediate good that is sold on a monopolistically competitive market. To produce these goods, each firm rents capital at the price R_t from the capital good producer and combines it with labor from households. To produce the output Y_t, each wholesale firm has a Cobb–Douglas production function:

$$Y_{j,t} = A_t K_{j,t}^{\alpha} L_{j,t}^{1-\alpha}, \tag{23}$$

where $K_{j,t}$ is the amount of capital rented by wholesale firm j from capital market, $L_{j,t}$ is the number of working hours supplied by households to firm j, $\alpha \in (0,1)$ is the elasticity of output with respect to capital, and A_t is the productivity shock, a variable that can be interpreted as the level of general knowledge about the arts of production available in an economy. It is assumed that productivity shocks follow a first-order autoregressive process, such that:

$$\ln A_t = \rho_A \ln A_{t-1} + \varepsilon_t^A, \tag{24}$$

where $\rho_A \in (-1,1)$ is the degree of persistence of the shock and $\varepsilon_t^A \sim N(0,\sigma_A)$ is the error.

Total wages should be transferred by wholesale firm j to household is $W_t L_{j,t}$. However, we assume that there is a possibility wholesale firm j can take a loan from commercial bank to pay some part of wages in advance. The amount of the loan for this purpose, denoted by $Q_{j,t}^{IF}$, is given by:

$$Q_{j,t}^{IF} = k_Q W_t L_{j,t}, \tag{25}$$

where $k_Q \in (0,1)$ is the portion of total wages borrowed from bank. In [44], k_Q represents the strength of the cost channel. As we may write $W_t L_{j,t} = Q_{j,t}^{IF} + (1-k_Q) W_t L_{j,t}$ and since it is assumed that short-term loans for working capital do not carry any risk and are therefore contracted at a rate that reflects only the marginal cost of borrowing from the central bank, I_t^{CB}, which is the refinance rate [44], then the wages claim faced by the wholesale firm is given by:

$$(1 + I_t^{CB}) Q_{j,t}^{IF} + (1-k_Q) W_t L_{j,t} = (1 + k_Q I_t^{CB}) W_t L_{j,t}. \tag{26}$$

3.4.1. The Cost Minimization Problem

The wholesale firm solves a two-stage optimization problem. First, the firm j takes the prices of the factors of production (return on capital R_t^K and wages W_t) as given and determines the amount of capital and labor that it will use to minimize its total production cost. The total cost $TC_{j,t}$ to be minimized by the firm consists of wages bill (26) and capital rent:

$$TC_{j,t} = (1 + k_Q R_t^L) W_t L_{j,t} + R_t^K K_{j,t}, \tag{27}$$

subject to production function (23). The corresponding Lagrange function for this problem is:

$$\mathcal{L}^{IF} = (1 + k_Q I_t^{CB}) W_t L_{j,t} + R_t^K K_{j,t} + \Lambda_t^{IF} (Y_{j,t} - A_t K_{j,t}^a L_{j,t}^{1-a}), \tag{28}$$

where Λ_t^{IF} is the Lagrange multiplier. The first order condition with respect to $L_{j,t}$ and $K_{j,t}$ are, respectively, as follow:

$$(1 + k_Q I_t^{CB}) W_t - (1 - \alpha) \Lambda_t^{IF} A_t K_{j,t}^{\alpha} L_{j,t}^{-\alpha} = 0,$$
$$R_t^K - \alpha \Lambda_t^{IF} A_t K_{j,t}^{\alpha-1} L_{j,t}^{1-\alpha} = 0.$$

From the second condition, we have:

$$\frac{R_t^K K_{j,t}}{\alpha L_{j,t}} = \Lambda_t^{IF} A_t K_{j,t}^{\alpha} L_{j,t}^{-\alpha},$$

and substitution to the first condition provides:

$$\frac{K_{j,t}}{L_{j,t}} = \frac{\alpha(1 + k_Q I_t^{CB})}{1 - \alpha} \frac{W_t}{R_t^K}. \tag{29}$$

Since none of the terms on the right hand side of (29) depend on j, then the capital-labor ratio will be the same across all firms.

From (29) we may express K_t as:

$$K_t = \frac{\alpha(1 + k_Q I_t^{CB})}{1 - \alpha} \frac{W_t}{R_t^K} L_t. \tag{30}$$

By substituting (30) into total cost (27) we obtain:

$$TC_t = \frac{1 + k_Q I_t^{CB}}{1 - \alpha} W_t L_t, \tag{31}$$

and by substituting (30) into production function (23) we get:

$$Y_t = A_t \left(\frac{\alpha(1 + k_Q I_t^{CB})}{1 - \alpha} \frac{W_t}{R_t^K} \right)^{\alpha} L_t,$$

or equivalently:

$$L_t = \frac{Y_t}{A_t} \left(\frac{\alpha(1 + k_Q I_t^{CB})}{1 - \alpha} \frac{W_t}{R_t^K} \right)^{-\alpha}. \tag{32}$$

Substitution (32) into the total optimal cost function (31) yields:

$$TC_t = \frac{Y_t}{A_t} \left(\frac{(1 + k_Q I_t^{CB}) W_t}{1 - \alpha} \right)^{1-\alpha} \left(\frac{R_t^K}{\alpha} \right)^{\alpha}. \tag{33}$$

Finally, the marginal cost function MC_t is the derivative of the total cost function (33) with respect to Y_t:

$$MC_t = \frac{1}{A_t} \left(\frac{(1 + k_Q I_t^{CB}) W_t}{1 - \alpha} \right)^{1-\alpha} \left(\frac{R_t^K}{\alpha} \right)^{\alpha}. \tag{34}$$

Subsequently, we can rewrite L_t in (32) and K_t in (30) in term of MC_t, respectively, as follow:

$$L_t = \frac{1 - \alpha}{1 + k_Q I_t^{CB}} MC_t \frac{Y_t}{W_t}, \tag{35}$$

$$K_t = \alpha MC_t \frac{Y_t}{R_t^K}. \tag{36}$$

3.4.2. The Profit Maximization Problem

In the second stage, wholesale firm wants to maximize the real profits it gives back to households. Since the real marginal cost is the optimal cost of producing one unit of goods, the firm's problem is to maximize:

$$\Pi_{j,t}^{IF} = P_{j,t}Y_{j,t} - MC_tY_{j,t}. \tag{37}$$

In addition to the stochastic discount factor β, firms will also discount their future profits by ϕ. We also impose that the wholesale firms face the constraint that they can only adjust prices following a Calvo-type rule. The wholesale firm has a ϕ probability of keeping the price fixed in the next period and a $1-\phi$ probability of optimally determining its price. Hence, a wholesale firm wants to maximize:

$$\Pi_{j,t}^{IF} = \mathbb{E}_t \sum_{s=0}^{\infty} (\beta\phi)^s (P_{j,t}Y_{j,t+s} - MC_{t+s}Y_{j,t+s}), \tag{38}$$

subject to production constraint (22), which is adjusted as:

$$Y_{j,t+s} = \left(\frac{P_{t+s}}{P_{j,t}}\right)^{\theta} Y_{t+s}. \tag{39}$$

Substitution the optimal production constraint (39) into profit function (38) gives:

$$\Pi_{j,t}^{IF} = \mathbb{E}_t \sum_{s=0}^{\infty} (\beta\phi)^s (P_{j,t}^{1-\theta}P_{t+s}^{\theta} - P_{j,t}^{-\theta}P_{t+s}^{\theta}MC_{t+s})Y_{t+s}. \tag{40}$$

The first order condition with respect to $P_{j,t}$ is then given by:

$$\mathbb{E}_t \sum_{s=0}^{\infty} (\beta\phi)^s ((1-\theta)P_{j,t}^{-\theta}P_{t+s}^{\theta-1} + \theta P_{j,t}^{-\theta-1}P_{t+s}^{\theta-1}MC_{t+s})Y_{t+s} = 0, \tag{41}$$

or equivalently:

$$\mathbb{E}_t \sum_{s=0}^{\infty} (\beta\phi)^s \left(1 + \frac{\theta}{1-\theta}\frac{MC_{t+s}}{P_{j,t}}\right) = 0. \tag{42}$$

We may proceed (42) to have:

$$\begin{aligned} \sum_{s=0}^{\infty} (\beta\phi)^s &= \frac{\theta}{1-\theta}\mathbb{E}_t \sum_{s=0}^{\infty} (\beta\phi)^s \frac{MC_{t+s}}{P_{j,t}} \\ \frac{P_{j,t}}{1-\beta\phi} &= \frac{\theta}{1-\theta}\mathbb{E}_t \sum_{s=0}^{\infty} (\beta\phi)^s MC_{t+s} \\ P_{j,t} &= \frac{\theta(1-\beta\phi)}{1-\theta}\mathbb{E}_t \sum_{s=0}^{\infty} (\beta\phi)^s MC_{t+s}. \end{aligned}$$

Instead, we follow the approach adopted by Fernandez-Villaverde et al. [24] to proceed (41) such that we obtain:

$$\mathbb{E}_t \sum_{s=0}^{\infty} (\beta\phi)^s \left(\frac{1-\theta}{P_{j,t}}\left(\frac{P_{j,t}}{P_{t+s}}\right)^{1-\theta} + \frac{\theta}{P_{j,t}}\left(\frac{P_{j,t}}{P_{t+s}}\right)^{-\theta}\frac{MC_{t+s}}{P_{t+s}}\right)Y_{t+s} = 0,$$

and then becomes:

$$\mathbb{E}_t \sum_{s=0}^{\infty} (\beta\phi)^s \left(\left(\frac{P_{j,t}}{P_{t+s}}\right)^{1-\theta} + \frac{\theta}{1-\theta}\left(\frac{P_{j,t}}{P_{t+s}}\right)^{-\theta}\frac{MC_{t+s}}{P_{t+s}}\right)Y_{t+s} = 0. \tag{43}$$

3.5. Capital Producing Firms

In the economy, all the capital is owned by the capital producing firm who adopts a linear production function to produce capital goods. At the beginning of the period, the capital producing firm buys INV_t of the final goods from the retail firm for investment purposes. Because payments for these final goods must be made in advance, the capital producing firms borrows Q_t^{CF} from the commercial bank to purchase the capital. Thus,

$$Q_t^{CF} = INV_t. \tag{44}$$

The loan in (44) must be paid in full plus interest with lending rate I_t^L. The capital producing firms then combines investment goods and the existing capital stock to create new capital goods K_{t+1}. The new capital stock is then rented to wholesale firms at the rate R_t^K. Recall that the dynamic of capital stocks is given in (3).

Taking the rental rate of capital R_t^K, the lending interest rate I_t^L, and the price of the final goods P_t as given, the capital producing firm chooses the level of the capital stock so as to maximize the profits to the household. The real profits of the capital producing firm can be denoted as:

$$\Pi_t^{CF} = R_t^K K_t - (1 + I_t^L) INV_t, \tag{45}$$

and the value of the discounted stream of dividend payments to the household to be maximized is then formulated as:

$$\Pi^{CF} = \mathbb{E}_t \sum_{t=0}^{\infty} \beta^t \Lambda_t^H \Pi_t^{CF}, \tag{46}$$

where it is assumed, as in [44,48], that the capital producing firm values future profits according to the household's intertemporal marginal rate of substitution in consumption Λ_t^H, i.e., the Lagrange multiplier of households' utility maximization given in (A35). This assumption is imposed because, in this model, the household and capital producing firm can be considered as a single unit with respect to housing choices.

From (3), we get $INV_i = K_{i+1} - (1-\delta)K_i$, and by substituting it into (46) together with (45), we have the real profits function to be maximized:

$$\Pi^{CF} = \mathbb{E}_t \sum_{i=0}^{\infty} \beta^i \Lambda_i^H (R_i^K K_i - (1 + I_i^L)(K_{i+1} - (1-\delta)K_i)).$$

By explicitly showing Π_t^{CF} at time t and $t+1$, we have:

$$\Pi^{CF} = \cdots + \beta^t \Lambda_t^H (R_t^K K_t - (1 + I_t^L)(K_{t+1} - (1-\delta)K_t))$$
$$\beta^{t+1} \Lambda_{t+1}^H (R_{t+1}^K K_{t+1} - (1 + I_{t+1}^L)(K_{t+2} - (1-\delta)K_{t+1})) + \cdots,$$

from which we obtain the first order condition with respect to K_{t+1} as follows:

$$-\Lambda_t^H (1 + I_t^L) + \beta \mathbb{E}_t \Lambda_{t+1}^H (R_{t+1}^K + (1-\delta)(1 + I_{t+1}^L)) = 0.$$

Since $\Lambda_t^H = -C_t^{-\sigma}/P_t$ from (A36), we then have:

$$\frac{C_t^{-\sigma}}{P_t}(1 + I_t^L) = -\beta \mathbb{E}_t \frac{C_{t+1}^{-\sigma}}{P_{t+1}} (R_{t+1}^K + (1-\delta)(1 + I_{t+1}^L)). \tag{47}$$

3.6. Banks

The commercial banks receive deposits D_t from households at the beginning of each period. These deposits are managed by the banks to finance loans to wholesale firms for paying wages claim, which for a representative firm j it is $Q_{j,t}^{IF}$ in (25), and to the capital producing firm for investment Q_t^{CF} in (44). Therefore, total lending Q_t^B provided by the bank is:

$$Q_t^B = Q_t^{IF} + Q_t^{CF} = k_Q W_t L_t + INV_t. \tag{48}$$

As refinancing via the central bank is more expensive than refinancing via deposits, i.e., $I_t^{CB} > I_t^D$, bank will only demand central bank funding to fill the gap between the supply of deposits D_t and the maximum amount of total external lending Q_t^B. If the total lending is bigger than deposits, i.e., there is a shortfall in funding, bank borrows from the central bank Q_t^{CB} with a net interest rate I_t^{CB}.

Bank's liabilities comprise of loans from the central bank Q_t^{CB}, bank deposits D_t, and bank's equity N_t, while bank's assets consist of central bank reserves TR_t, loans to firms Q_t^B, and bonds B_t^B as risk-free asset. Thus, the bank's balance sheet is provided by:

$$Q_t^B + TR_t + B_t^B = Q_t^{CB} + D_t + N_t. \tag{49}$$

As total reserves TR_t is a portion ψ of deposit, i.e., $TR_t = \psi D_t$, and by (48), bank's balance sheet (49) is then rewritten as:

$$Q_t^{IF} + Q_t^{CF} + B_t^B = Q_t^{CB} + (1-\psi)D_t + N_t. \tag{50}$$

Note that N_t captures the bank's equity, which is mainly driven by the interest rate premia. Since commercial bank lends their equity, households' deposits, and funds from the central bank to the production sector, then the bank's equity evolves according to the following equation:

$$N_{t+1} = (1+I_t^L)N_t + (I_t^L - I_t^D)D_t + (I_t^L - I_t^{CB})Q_t^{CB}. \tag{51}$$

In (51), $I_t^L - I_t^D$ and $I_t^L - I_t^{CB}$ denote the interest rate premia from deposits and central bank funds, respectively, by assuming that $I_t^L \geq I_t^D$ and $I_t^L \geq I_t^{CB}$.

The bank's revenues come from equity $(1+I_t^L)N_t$, loans to wholesale firms $(1+I_t^{CB})Q_t^{IF} = k_Q(1+I_t^{CB})W_tL_t$, loans to capital production firms $(1+I_t^L)Q_t^{CF} = (1+I_t^L)INV_t$, and bonds $(1+I_t^B)B_t^B$. Meanwhile, the bank's liabilities come from deposits $(1+I_t^D)D_t$ and central bank loans $(1+I_t^{CB})Q_t^{CB}$. Therefore, the bank's profit to be maximized is formulated as:

$$\begin{aligned}\Pi^B = {} & (1+I_t^L)N_t + (1+I_t^{CB})Q_t^{IF} + (1+I_t^L)Q_t^{CF} + (1+I_t^B)B_t^B \\ & - (1+I_t^D)D_t - (1+I_t^{CB})Q_t^{CB},\end{aligned} \tag{52}$$

subject to bank's balance sheet (50). From (50), we may substitute Q_t^{CB} as follows:

$$Q_t^{CB} = Q_t^{IF} + Q_t^{CF} + B_t^B - (1-\psi)D_t - N_t.$$

Thus, the bank's profit (52) becomes:

$$\begin{aligned}\Pi^B = {} & (1+I_t^L)N_t + (1+I_t^{CB})Q_t^{IF} + (1+I_t^L)Q_t^{CF} + (1+I_t^B)B_t^B \\ & - (1+I_t^D)D_t - (1+I_t^{CB})(Q_t^{IF} + Q_t^{CF} + B_t^B - (1-\psi)D_t - N_t).\end{aligned} \tag{53}$$

The banks aim to determine the loan interest rate I_t^L and the deposits interest rate I_t^D in order to maximize their profit (53). Instead of maximizing (53) with respect to I_t^L and I_t^L, it will be much easier differentiating (53) with respect to $(1+I_t^L)$ and $(1+I_t^D)$. Doing so, we respectively obtain:

$$N_t + Q_t^{CF} + (1+I_t^L)\frac{\partial Q_t^{CF}}{\partial(1+I_t^L)} - (1+I_t^{CB})\frac{\partial Q_t^{CF}}{\partial(1+I_t^L)} = 0, \tag{54}$$

$$-D_t - (1+I_t^D)\frac{\partial D_t}{\partial(1+I_t^D)} + (1-\psi)(1+I_t^{CB})\frac{\partial D_t}{\partial(1+I_t^D)} = 0. \tag{55}$$

We derive (54) and (55) by considering that Q_t^{CF} is a function of $(1+I_t^L)$ and D_t is a function of $(1+I_t^D)$. Next, we follow an approach in [44] by defining the coefficient of interest elasticity for loan supply to the wholesale firm ϕ_L and that for deposits supply to households ϕ_D as follows:

$$\phi_L = \frac{\partial Q_t^{CF}}{\partial(1+I_t^L)} \frac{1+I_t^L}{Q_t^{CF}}, \tag{56}$$

$$\phi_D = \frac{\partial D_t}{\partial(1+I_t^D)} \frac{1+I_t^D}{D_t}. \tag{57}$$

Thus, by reformulating (54) and (55) in terms of ϕ_L in (56) and ϕ_D in (57), we obtain the optimal rates of loan and deposits:

$$1+I_t^L = \frac{\phi_L(1+I_t^{CB})INV_t}{N_t+(1+\phi_L)INV_t}, \tag{58}$$

$$1+I_t^D = \frac{\phi_D(1-\psi)(1+I_t^{CB})}{1+\phi_D}. \tag{59}$$

It is shown in (58) and (59) that loan and deposit rates depend positively on refinance rate from the central bank I_t^{CB}. It is also known that I_t^L depends negatively on the ratio of bank's equity and investment N_t/INV_t.

3.7. The Central Bank

While the rate of government bonds I_t^B follows the interest rate on central bank funding I_t^{CB} in the way that:

$$I_t^B = I_t^{CB} + \Delta^B, \tag{60}$$

where $\Delta^B > 0$ is the fixed spread, the nominal interest rate on CBDC I_t^E is set by the central bank. In the case of a non-interest-bearing CBDC, the central bank sets $I_t^E = 0$. In order to use CBDC as a policy instrument, for an interest-bearing CBDC, the interest rate on CBDC strictly follows the interest rate on central bank funding with an individual rule-based determination, as suggested by Gross & Schiller [8]:

$$I_t^E = I_t^{CB} - \left(\Delta^E + k_N \frac{\bar{N}-N_t}{\bar{N}}\right). \tag{61}$$

The terms in brackets in (61) define the spread between the interest rates on central bank funding I_t^{CB} and that of CBDC I_t^E, where $\Delta^E > 0$ is the fixed spread, and N_t is the bank's equity with steady state value $\bar{N}$. If N_t is below its steady state value $\bar{N}$, then the spread increases, meaning that the CBDC rate is much lower than the central bank rate. In (61), the percentage deviation of banks' equity from steady state $(\bar{N}-N_t)/\bar{N}$ represents the financial stress with $k_N \in (0,1)$ denotes the reaction intensity.

The central bank sets the policy interest rate on central bank funding i_t^{CB} according to a Taylor-type rule. The policy rule is given in the following linear form:

$$I_t^{CB} = \rho_R I_{t-1}^{CB} + (1-\rho_R)(\bar{R}^B + \pi_t + \phi_\pi(\pi_t - \pi^T) + \phi_y(Y_t - \bar{Y}) + u_t, \tag{62}$$

where $\rho_R \in (0,1)$ is the interest rate smoothing parameter, $\bar{R}^B$ is the steady state value of the bonds interest rate, π_t is the current inflation rate, π^T is the central bank's inflation target, y_t is the output with steady state value $\bar{Y}$, ϕ_π and ϕ_y are, respectively, relative weights on inflation deviation and the output gap, and u_t is the shock of first-order autoregressive process:

$$u_t = \rho_u u_{t-1} + \varepsilon_t^u, \tag{63}$$

where $\rho_u \in (-1,1)$ is the degree of persistence of the shock and $\varepsilon_t^u \sim N(0,\sigma_u)$ is the error.

The central bank's assets consist of government bonds holding B_t^{CB}, tax payment TAX_t, and loans to the commercial banks Q_t^{CB}, whereas its liabilities comprise total reserves TR_t and currency supplied to households and firms in the forms of cash M_t^S and CBDC E_t^S. The central bank's balance sheet is thus formulated as:

$$(1 + I_t^B)B_t^{CB} + TAX_t + (1 + I_t^{CB})Q_t^{CB} = TR_t - TR_{t-1} + M_t^S + E_t^S. \quad (64)$$

Note that profits from bonds holding $I_t^B B_t^{CB}$ and from loan $I_t^{CB} Q_t^{CB}$ as well as lump sum tax TAX_t are then transferred to the government. Since $TR_t = \psi D_t$ and currencies supplies can be given by $M_t^S = M_t - \mu_m M_{t-1}$ and $E_t^S = E_t - \mu_e E_{t-1}$ for cash and CBDC, respectively, then (64) becomes:

$$(1 + I_t^B)B_t^{CB} + TAX_t + (1 + I_t^{CB})Q_t^{CB} = \psi(D_t - D_{t-1}) + (M_t - \mu_m M_{t-1}) + (E_t - \mu_e E_{t-1}), \quad (65)$$

where μ_m and μ_e are the measure of nominal rigidity in the money supply process.

3.8. The Government

In the economy, the government purchases the final good from retail firms G_t, collects taxes from households TAX_t, and issues one-period risk-free bonds B_t. The total bonds issued by government is given by:

$$B_t = B_t^B + B_t^{CB}, \quad (66)$$

where B_t^B are bonds held by commercial bank and B_t^{CB} are those held by the central bank. The government's budget constraint is formulated as:

$$P_t G_t + (1 + I_{t-1}^B)B_{t-1} = TAX_t + B_t + I_t^{CB} Q_t^{CB} + I_t^B B_t^{CB}, \quad (67)$$

where we assume that the profits earned by the central bank from loans and bonds holding are transferred to the government as fiscal authority. By (66), the budget constraint (67) becomes:

$$P_t G_t + (1 + I_{t-1}^B)B_{t-1}^B + B_{t-1}^{CB} = TAX_t + B_t^B + (1 + I_t^B)B_t^{CB} + I_t^{CB} Q_t^{CB}. \quad (68)$$

The government's spending can be a constant fraction $k_G \in (0, 1)$ of output of the final goods:

$$G_t = k_G Y_t, \quad (69)$$

and since output is divided into consumption, investment, and government spending, then the economy-wide budget constraint is expressed as:

$$Y_t = C_t + INV_t + G_t. \quad (70)$$

4. Log-Linearization

One easy and common approach to solve and analyze DSGE models is to approximate the nonlinear equations characterizing the equilibrium with the corresponding log-linearized equations. The principle is to employ a first order Taylor approximation around a particular point (usually a steady state value) to replace the nonlinear equations with their approximations, which are linear in the log-deviations of the variables. In this work, we follow a log-linearization method proposed by Uhlig [49].

Let X_t be the value of variable at time t and $\bar{X}$ be the steady state value of X_t. The log-linearized form of X_t, denoted by x_t, is defined as:

$$x_t = \ln X_t - \ln \bar{X} = \ln \frac{X_t}{\bar{X}}. \quad (71)$$

Since the first order Taylor approximation of function $h = h(x)$ around $x = a$ is given by $h(x) \approx h(a) + h'(a)(x - a)$, and thus for $h(X_t) = \ln(X_t/\bar{X})$ we have $h'(X_t) = 1/X_t$, then the approximation of X_t around its steady state value $\bar{X}$ in (71) is $x_t \approx (X_t - \bar{X})/\bar{X}$, from which we obtain the equivalency:

$$X_t \approx \bar{X}(1 + x_t). \quad (72)$$

Alternatively, as from (71) we get $\ln X_t = x_t + \ln \bar{X}$, then by taking the exponent of both sides, we obtain $X_t \approx \bar{X}e^{x_t}$. By fact that Taylor approximation provides $e^{x_t} \approx 1 + x_t$, then we again reclaim (72).

The nonlinear equations characterizing the equilibrium conditions of the model are presented in Section 3. The log-linearized version of these equations can be found in Appendix A.

5. Calibration

In this section, we examine the general equilibrium effects of the introduction of an interest-bearing CBDC on the macroeconomic. In particular, we inspect the effect of transaction costs, required reserves ratio, productivity shock, and monetary policy shock through impulse response functions. An illustrative calibration of the model is performed for Indonesia as a middle-income country. Other conventional parameters values are taken from relevant references.

The intertemporal discount factor is $\beta = 0.985$, and the relative risk aversion coefficient is $\sigma = 0.5$. Both values are in line with estimates for developing countries [44]. According to [8], elasticity coefficients of having CBDC, cash, and deposits are set to $\eta_e = \eta_m = \eta_d = 0.95$. The relative utility weights or preference parameters of CBDCs, cash, and deposits are assigned to $\alpha_e = \alpha_m = \alpha_d = 0.125$, while that of labor time is $\alpha_l = 3.409$. The coefficient relates to Frisch elasticity of labor supply is $\varphi = 0.276$ [43].

In the production sector, as is standard in the literature, the depreciation rate of physical capital is $\delta = 0.034$ and the elasticity of substitution between intermediate goods is $\theta = 10$. The elasticity of output with respect to capital is set to be $\alpha = 0.33$ as in [38]. These values are consistent with estimates for developing countries. The portion of total wages borrowed from bank, i.e., the strength of the cost channel, is taken to be $k_Q = 0.75$ [44]. In price determination mechanism, we assume that there is a $\phi = 0.779$ probability of keeping the price fixed in the next period, and thus a $1 - \phi = 0.221$ probability of optimally setting the price [43].

In banking sector, we assume that the constant interest elasticity of the supply of loan by the wholesale firm is $\phi_L = -0.5$ and that of deposits by the household is $\phi_D = 0.5$. For the parameters related to the central bank, we use the values suggested by Chawwa [50] based on Indonesia aggregate banking data, the steady state value of required reserves ratio is $\psi = 6.5\%$, the government spending share is $k_G = 9\%$, following the average Indonesia government consumption relative to GDP, and the steady state value of the policy interest rate is $\bar{R}^B = 1.8\%$. For Taylor rule parameters, we use the conventional values of $\phi_\pi = 1.5$ for the feedback coefficient on inflation and $\phi_y = 0.5$ for the output gap coefficient, along with a value of $\rho_R = 0.8$ for interest rate smoothing parameter [43]. According to Bank Indonesia, the inflation target is $\pi^T = 3\%$. The spread of bonds interest rate from central bank rate is assumed to be $\Delta^B = 0.01$ and that of CBDC interest rate is $\Delta^E = 0.005$ [8]. Beside a fixed spread, the dynamics of CBDC interest rate depends also on financial stress as expressed in (61). In this strategy, we set $k_N = 0.01$ as the reaction intensity towards financial stress [8]. Based on [51], we specify the measure of nominal rigidity in cash and CBDC supply processes as $\mu_m = \mu_e = 1$. The degree of persistence in the monetary policy shock is set to be $\rho_u = 0.74$ [52] and that of the productivity shock is $\phi_A = 0.97$ [53]. In the case of liquidity shocks, we assume $\rho_M = 0.85$ and $\rho_E = 0.9$.

The steady state value of all variables are simultaneously calculated based on steady state conditions derived from equations of motion in Appendix A. As initial values, we set $\bar{P} = 1$, $\bar{P}^M = 1/3$, $\bar{A} = 1$, and $\bar{I}^{CB} = 0.01$. Description and value of all parameters are summarized in Table 1.

Table 1. The value of parameters.

No.	Parameter	Description	Value
1	β	intertemporal discount factor	0.985
2	σ	relative risk aversion coefficient	0.5
3	η_m	elasticity of having cash	0.95
4	η_e	elasticity of having CBDC	0.95
5	η_d	elasticity of having bank deposits	0.95
6	φ	coefficient relates to Frisch elasticity of labor supply	0.276
7	α_m	relative utility weights or preference parameters of cash	0.1250
8	α_e	relative utility weights or preference parameters of CBDC	0.1250
9	α_d	relative utility weights or preference parameters of bank deposits	0.1250
10	α_l	relative utility weights or preference parameters of labor time	3.409
11	ρ_M	degree of persistence in cash demand shock	0.85
12	ρ_E	degree of persistence in CBDC demand shock	0.9
13	δ	depreciation rate of physical capital	0.034
14	θ	elasticity of substitution between intermediate goods	10
15	α	elasticity of output with respect to capital	0.33
16	ρ_A	degree of persistence in the supply shock	0.97
17	k_Q	the portion of total wages borrowed from bank (strength of the cost channel)	0.75
18	ϕ	probability of keeping the price fixed in the next period	0.779
19	$1-\phi$	probability of optimally determining the price	0.221
20	ψ	share of required reserves	0.065
21	ϕ_L	constant interest elasticity of the supply of loan by the wholesale firm	−0.5
22	ϕ_D	constant interest elasticity of the supply of deposits by the household	0.5
23	Δ^B	fixed spread of bonds interest rate from central bank rate	0.01
24	Δ^E	fixed spread of CBDC interest rate from central bank rate	0.005
25	k_N	reaction intensity towards financial stress	0.01
26	ρ_R	interest rate smoothing parameter	0.81
27	$\bar{R}^B$	steady state value of the policy interest rate	0.018
28	ϕ_π	relative weights on inflation deviation	1.5
29	π^T	inflation target	0.03
30	ϕ_y	relative weights on output gap	0.125
31	ρ_u	degree of persistence in the monetary policy shock	0.74
32	μ_m	measure of nominal rigidity in the cash supply process	1
33	μ_e	measure of nominal rigidity in the CBDC supply process	1

6. Policy Analysis

In this section, we present the simulation result of the model to explore the responses of variables with respect to liquidity demand shock, productivity shock, and monetary policy shock. We use Matlab Dynare to produce the impulse response functions with one period is a quarter.

6.1. Effects of Liquidity Demand Shock

As stated in (9), consumptions by households are constrained by transaction cost. The cost is a function of money velocity with two parameters a and b as given in (13) and (14). Smaller a and b contributes cheaper transaction cost. However, the magnitude of the cost depends also on the types of money, where in our case is either cash or CBDC, whose velocities are determined by the model. To assess the effect of transaction costs, we specify the following cost parameters: $a_M = a_E = 1$ and $b_M = b_E = 1.5$. By this setting, we consider a situation where cash and CBDC have the same parameters values, and thus the same transaction cost provided the velocities of cash and CBDC are identical. In this simulation, we apply a negative shock on the transaction cost using CBDC as given in (14) to indicate that CBDC has a lower transaction cost.

Figure 2 shows the impact of negative shock of CBDC transaction cost on several relevant variables of the model. A negative shock is intended to decrease the transaction cost using CBDC by 1%. When the shock hits, consumption purchases using CBDC increase as the cost becomes cheaper, and consumption purchases using cash slightly decrease, see

Figure 2a. However, in total, consumption purchases decrease. This fact informs us that households spend more CBDC in purchasing consumption goods, confirmed by a rise in CBDC demand as a response of shock in Figure 2f, even though the rate of CBDC is decreased by the shock as indicated by Figure 2d. In contrast to CBDC, the demand of bank deposits is decreasing even though its rate is increasing, see Figure 2e,f. From the perspective of price, a negative shock on CBDC cost is responded by a decrease in price of goods using CBDC p_t^E in Figure 2g, which indicates that transaction using CBDC is cheaper than using cash. However, the general price p_t, which is aggregated from prices of cash and CBDC in (19), does not respond the shock very much as it fluctuates around its steady state value for all time. This small change in price is followed by a little drop in inflation rate, see Figure 2c. From the view point of money velocity, the negative shock of CBDC transaction cost is reacted by a decline in the velocity of CBDC as depicted by Figure 2h.

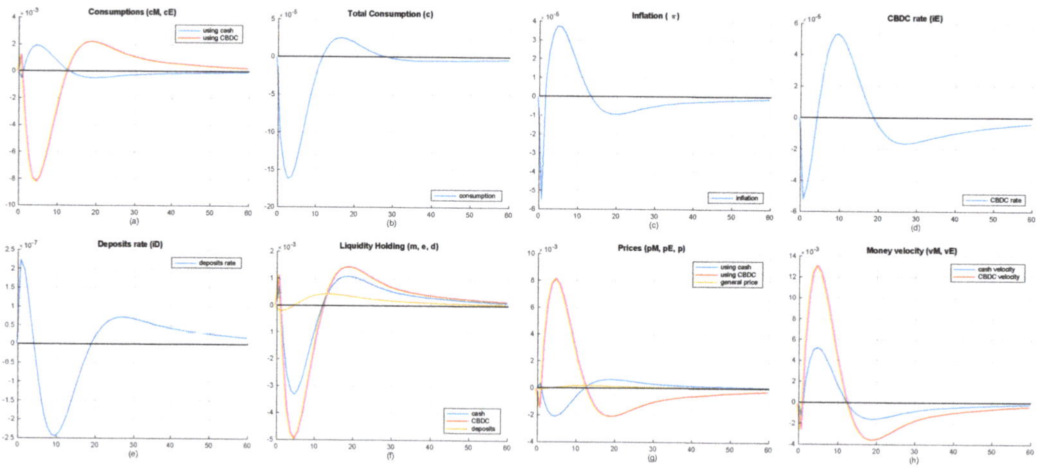

Figure 2. The effect of negative shock of CBDC transaction cost on (**a**) consumption by using cash c_t^M and CBDC c_t^E, (**b**) total consumption c_t, (**c**) inflation π_t, (**d**) CBDC rate i_t^E, (**e**) deposits rate i_t^D, (**f**) liquidity holding m_t, e_t, d_t, (**g**) prices p_t^M, p_t^E, p_t, and (**h**) money velocity $v_t^M = c_t^M - m_t$ and $v_t^E = c_t^E - e_t$.

The simulation results presented in this section, however, indicate that the issuance of an interest-bearing CBDC has the potential to become a profitable means of liquidity storage and to have an impact that does not harm the economy.

6.2. *Effects of Productivity Shock*

The effects of productivity shock on a number of main variables of the model are presented in Figure 3. The productivity shock due to the technological advance causes a rise in the values of the marginal products of labor and capital, and thus firms increase their demand for production inputs, so investment level increased. When one percent shock in productivity hits, the demand for labor increases more than 2% during the first two periods as depicted in Figure 3a. The intensity of labor declines quickly toward steady state. In the same figure, a similar hike in capital demand is shown, but with a more sloping rise and fall. Increasing productivity implies that firms produce more outputs (up to 3% hike), but operate more efficiently so the marginal costs decrease by about 2.5%, see Figure 3e.

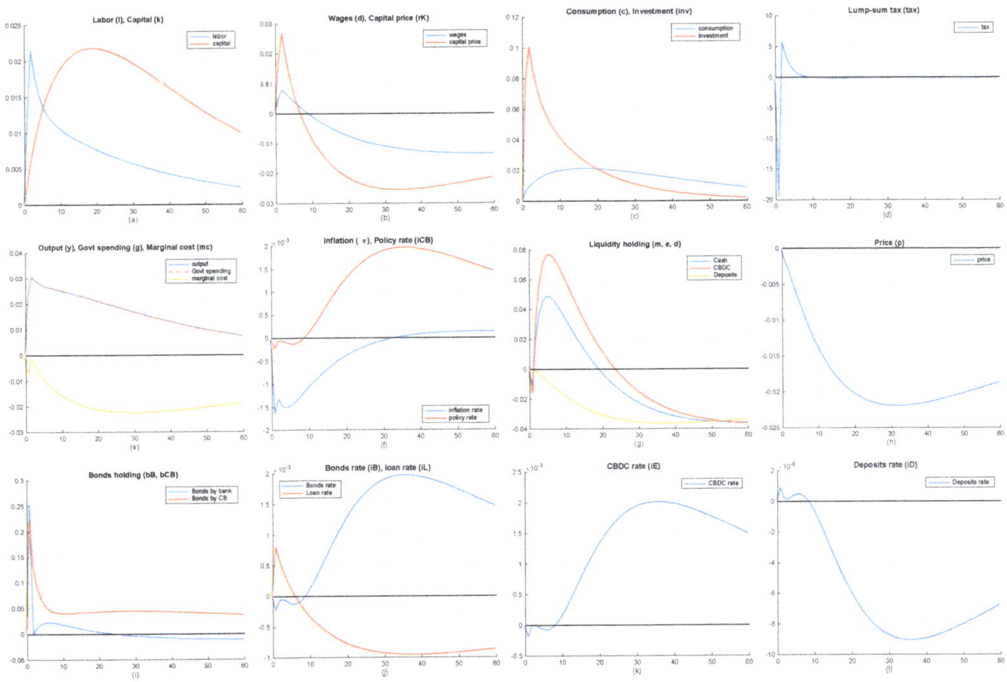

Figure 3. The effect of productivity shock on: (**a**) Labor l_t and capital k_t, (**b**) wages w_t and price of capital r_t^K, (**c**) consumption c_t and investment inv_t, (**d**) lump-sum tax tax_t, (**e**) output y_t, government spending g_t, and marginal cost mc_t, (**f**) inflation π_t and policy rate i_t^{CB}, (**g**) liquidity holding m_t, e_t, d_t, (**h**) price p_t, (**i**) bonds holding b_t^B, b_t^{CB}, (**j**) bond rate i_t^B and loan rate i_t^L, (**k**) CBDC rate i_t^E, and (**l**) deposits rate i_t^D.

Meanwhile, inflations slightly fall in the first ten periods as the production becomes more efficient, see Figure 3f. A small drop in inflation rate causes an increase in the supply of goods, thus leading to easing in monetary policy. A hike in goods production implies a rise in the wage and capital return as indicated by Figure 3b. Thus, households tend to use their time for consumption rather than saving, thus instantaneously decreasing the holding of cash, CBDC, and deposit about 1% as informed in Figure 3g. Due to the decline in inflation, the base policy rate which is governed by the Taylor rule also decreases. The lower base policy rate induces to a direct decrease in the central bank refinance rate, which in turn decreases the deposit and CBDC rates and thus the demand for bank deposits and interest bearing CBDCs.

Due to an increased aggregate supply of output, the price level decreased by more than 2%, see Figure 3h, followed by a small decrease in the inflation rate in the early periods. The central bank responds with a decline of its policy rate followed by CBDC and banks rates to make an economic contraction by reducing purchasing power. As the consequence, bank capital is decreasing due to the decreasing loans and increased liability due to the rising deposit rate. A decline of policy rate also implies the reduction of bond rate, thus central banks and banks buy more bonds, as depicted in Figure 3i. As the result, the rising interest rate makes consumption and investment decline. Both people and firms tend to save their money in CBDC rather than the deposit due to the CBDC attributes of being a risk-free asset. Decreasing consumption implies reduced firm productivity, thus reducing the wage of the labor, moreover, the technology starting to deteriorate as the technology keeps depreciating. As the sources of tax revenue decreased, see Figure 3d, government spending also decreased. In the end, the aggregate demand will be reduced, thus the output will also be declined.

These results aligned with [40,41]. Both of the results imply that CBDC would likely make monetary policy more effective. It can be seen by the response of the central bank towards inflation using CBDC rate is effective. Moreover, households show that remunerated CBDC is more attractive than bonds to fulfill their liquidity, so it enhances the monetary policy effectiveness.

6.3. Effects of Monetary Policy Shock

Figure 4 depicts the effect of one percent increase in policy interest rate on several main variables of the model. A hike in policy rate means an increase of the borrowing cost from central bank, i.e., a decrease in funding provided by central bank. The dynamics of policy rate are mimicked by the bond rate and the CBDC rate as they are determined according to a fixed spread of the policy rate in (60) and (61). For CBDC, it is revealed that the financial stress term expressed in percentage deviation of banks' equity from steady state gives no effect in this situation. A rise in policy rate is responded differently by the loan rate and deposits rate as they have to be determined optimally according to (58) and (59). The loan rate declines in the first period and increases in the half of remaining periods. While, the deposits rate declines during the first four periods, following by rises toward its steady state value.

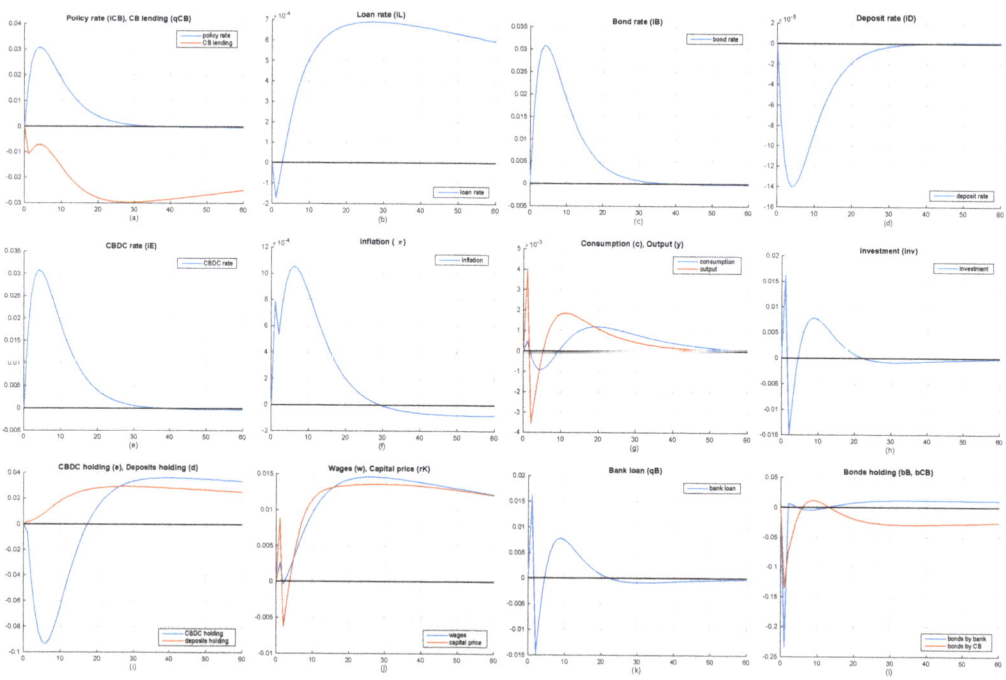

Figure 4. The effect of monetary policy shock on: (**a**) Policy rate i_t^{CB} and central bank lending q_t^{CB}, (**b**) loan rate i_t^L, (**c**) bond rate i_t^B, (**d**) deposit rate i_t^D, (**e**) CBDC rate i_t^E, (**f**) inflation π_t, (**g**) consumption c_t and output y_t, (**h**) investment inv_t, (**i**) CBDC holding e_t and deposits d_t, (**j**) wages w_t and price of capital r_t^K, (**k**) bank's loan q_t^B, and (**l**) bonds holding b_t^B, b_t^{CB}.

The rise of CBDC rate immediately leads to the increase of CBDC demand and the fall of deposits rate directly causes the drop of bank deposits holding. However, the rise of bond rate is not followed by its demand. Bonds holding by bank and central bank drop by 23% and 13%, respectively, in response to monetary policy shock. These occurrences reveal a fact that households already consider CBDC as an alternative instrument of liquidity to bank deposits. Holding CBDC will increase the household's overall liquidity, even though liquidity marginal utility decreased. Therefore, it is more explaining why CBDC is more attractive than the deposit. Since CBDC is remunerated, the households tend to convert more CBDC rather than cash or deposits.

There is lag in monetary policy transmission due to the cost adjustment of investment gradual response. In this lag period, households and firms tend to borrow money from bank to consume and invest before the bank done adjusting the interest rate, respectively. This lag explains why initially there is a short span increment in output when there is increment in the policy rate. After that period, households tend to substitute deposit to cash and CBDC due to the consideration of risk-free assets. CBDC also become an alternative to fulfill liquidity demand. The reduction of the deposit implies that banks have reduced credit supply, thus decreasing their lending power. As a result, there is a decrease in investment, which implies reduced labor as well as wages. Households also tend to save rather than take a loan. Reduced household and firm activity imply a reduction in purchasing power, thus reducing consumption as well as tax revenue. Due to the reduction in tax revenue, the government is also reducing its government spending. Reduced consumption and government spending also imply there is an excess supply of goods, which reduces the price level and inflation rate. Therefore, the reduction of aggregate demand reflects the reduction of output.

6.4. Implementation of the Analytical Model

Given the models in Section 3, it shows that CBDC involves many interactions among agents in the economy. Nonetheless, CBDC implementation itself brings both benefits and consequences [54]. On the high-level, CBDC could increase payment efficiency [55–57], monetary policy effectiveness [19,58,59], higher financial inclusion [60–62], and provide traceability [63–65]. This is also supported by the growing technology [66–68], network effect [17,69], the enthusiasm of CBDC [70–72], and cash inefficiency [73,74].

However, some consequences are the high cost of CBDC infrastructure [56,75], privacy loss potential [76,77], internet coverage limitation [62,78], and electrical outage [79,80]. This could be worsened by cyberattack threats [81,82], bank disintermediation amid crisis times [17], unprepared legal aspects [77,83], and private crypto-asset competitions [84–86].

Following the spirits of both CBDC benefits and consequences, we try to introduce some of the implications. First, CBDC implementation would likely increase budget spending due to its high cost of infrastructure and would disrupt innovation. Therefore, proposing a public–private partnership (PPP) allows us to maintain innovation, and also increase efficiency. The partnership could be with state-owned enterprises or private entities. Second, implementing CBDC implies that people could access their money 24/7, which means CBDC withdrawal could be conducted anytime/anywhere amid crisis times. One idea is to implement the capacity on the CBDC wallet, so there it could limit the withdrawal and will not create bank disintermediation. Third, implementing alternative offline payment (e.g., token-based offline CBDC) implies that people need to be aware of their private keys, otherwise they will lose access to their CBDC. To reduce the risk of losing the whole CBDC, the wallet could be limited so it will reduce the severity of losing CBDC. Fourth, implementing traceable CBDC implies that the central bank needs to govern the legal aspect consisting of the amount of extracted information, CBDC issuance, and eligible authority for CBDC operators. Those efforts are nothing but to maintain public trust. Fifth, central banks need to provide any means of backup plan to prevent a single point of failure risk. Preventing an outage is important because it could disrupt the whole financial system. Sixth, the central banks must use permissioned DLT to gain sufficient accessibility amid a decentralized system. Lastly, even though the central banks need to align their system to achieve interoperability in cross-border transactions, central banks still need to maintain their sovereignty.

7. Conclusions

The development of CBDC has been conducted by central banks across the world with various progress and motivation. From that consideration, implementing CBDC would likely to have macroeconomy consequences and monetary policy implication. However, it needs a comprehensive approach to support monetary policy based on those impacts. We have developed a medium size DSGE model to examine the interaction between CBDC and other variables and to quantify the macroeconomic effects of CBDC issuance. The proposed model consists of seven economic agents, namely households, retail firm, wholesale firms, capital producing firm, commercial bank, the central bank, and the government.

The model consider an economy in which the households may consider CBDC as a liquidity asset in addition to cash and bank deposits. The introduction of CBDC then differentiates the amount of consumption and the price in terms of cash and CBDC. As CBDC is designed to be an interest-bearing, CBDC may compete with cash in consumption process. The attractiveness of CBDC can also be appreciated at the lower transaction cost than cash. Thus, an interest-bearing CBDC can be considered as a profitable transaction instrument.

We have used the model to explain the main macroeconomic variables responses to a negative shock on CBDC transaction cost, as well as a positive supply shock, and a positive shock to the base policy rate. Our findings confirm that CBDC offers a number of macroeconomic benefits. A lower transaction cost offered by CBDC encourages households to consume more using CBDC, and thus reducing the purchase using cash. The price of goods counted in CBDC reduced, while the general price index is about in steady state leading to a small fall in inflation. As responses to an increase of output due to a productivity shock, we have shown that households use cash and CBDC in almost similar manners by reducing the holding for consumption. Responding to a one percent increase in the base policy rate, we have revealed that the dynamics of the policy interest rate is directly followed by that of CBDC. Thus, the accumulation of CBDC can be controlled by the policy rate.

As self-critical and possible limitations and shortcomings, our study considers only the issuance of retail CBDCs. More general situation in which commercial banks are enabled to provide loan to firms and to make settlement reserves in term of wholesale CBDCs will be the future research work. Additionally, the assessment of CBDC issuance in an open economy might be substantial to emerging countries as they have a significant portion of exports.

Author Contributions: Conceptualization, validation, data curation, supervision, F.S.; software, model derivation, writing—original draft preparation, simulation, visualization, T.B.; formal analysis, methodology, writing—review and editing, investigation, F.S. and T.B. All authors have read and agreed to the published version of the manuscript.

Funding: This research received no external funding.

Institutional Review Board Statement: Not applicable.

Informed Consent Statement: Not applicable.

Data Availability Statement: The data used to support the findings of this study are included in this published article.

Conflicts of Interest: The authors declare no conflict of interest.

Appendix A. Log-Linearized Equations

The model consists of 36 variables. Initially, all variables are denoted by capital letters. After log-linearization, they are denoted by small letters. The description of variables are presented in Table A1.

Table A1. The description of variables.

No.	Variable	Description
1	A_t, a_t	Productivity shock
2	B_t, b_t	Government bonds
3	B_t^B, b_t^B	Government bonds held by commercial bank
4	B_t^{CB}, b_t^{CB}	Government bonds held by central bank
5	C_t, c_t	Consumption by households
6	C_t^M, c_t^M	Consumption by households using cash
7	C_t^E, c_t^E	Consumption by households using CBDC
8	D_t, d_t	Bank deposits holding by households
9	E_t, e_t	CBDCs holding by households
10	G_t, g_t	Government spending
11	I_t^B, i_t^B	Nominal interest rate of government bonds
12	I_t^{CB}, i_t^{CB}	Nominal interest rate by central bank (policy rate)
13	I_t^D, i_t^D	Nominal interest rate of bank deposits
14	I_t^E, i_t^E	Nominal interest rate of CBDC
15	I_t^L, i_t^L	Nominal interest rate of loans
16	INV_t, inv_t	Investment level
17	K_t, k_t	Capital stocks
18	L_t, l_t	Labor supply by households
19	M_t, m_t	Cash holding by households
20	MC_t, mc_t	Marginal cost
21	N_t, n_t	Bank's equity
22	P_t, p_t	Price
23	P_t^M, p_t^M	Price in cash
24	P_t^E, p_t^E	Price in CBDC
25	Π_t, π_t	Inflation rate
26	Q_t^{CB}, q_t^{CB}	Loans given to commercial banks by central bank
27	R_t^K, r_t^K	Price of capital
28	S_t^M, s_t^M	Transaction cost for cash
29	S_t^E, s_t^E	Transaction cost for CBDC
30	TAX_t, tax_t	Lump sum tax or transfer
31	TR_t, tr_t	Reserves
32	u_t	Monetary policy shock
33	W_t, w_t	Wages
34	Y_t, y_t	Output
35	Z_t^M, z_t^M	Cash demand shock
36	Z_t^E, z_t^E	CBDC demand shock

The following linear equations, which constitute as the equations of motion of the model, are derived according to log-linearization method in Section 4.

1. Labor supply:

$$\sigma c_t + \varphi l_t = w_t - p_t. \tag{A1}$$

2. CBDC demand:

$$\alpha_e \left(\frac{\bar{E}}{\bar{P}}\right)^{-\eta_e} \eta_e (p_t - e_t) = -\frac{\bar{C}^{-\sigma}}{\bar{P}}(\sigma c_t + p_t) + \beta \frac{\bar{C}^{-\sigma}(1+\bar{I}^E)}{\bar{P}} \mathbb{E}_t \left(\sigma c_{t+1} - \frac{\bar{I}^E}{1+\bar{I}^E} i_t^E + p_{t+1}\right). \tag{A2}$$

3. Cash demand:

$$\alpha_m \left(\frac{\bar{M}}{\bar{P}}\right)^{-\eta_m} \eta_m (p_t - m_t) = -\frac{\bar{C}^{-\sigma}}{\bar{P}}(\sigma c_t + p_t) + \beta \frac{\bar{C}^{-\sigma}}{\bar{P}} \mathbb{E}_t (\sigma c_{t+1} + p_{t+1}). \tag{A3}$$

4. Deposits demand:

$$\alpha_d \left(\frac{\bar{D}}{\bar{P}}\right)^{-\eta_d} \eta_d(p_t - d_t) = -\frac{\bar{C}^{-\sigma}}{\bar{P}}(\sigma c_t + p_t) + \beta\frac{\bar{C}^{-\sigma}(1+\bar{I}^D)}{\bar{P}}\mathbb{E}_t\left(\sigma c_{t+1} - \frac{\bar{I}^D}{1+\bar{I}^D}i_t^D + p_{t+1}\right). \quad \text{(A4)}$$

5. Euler equation:

$$\sigma\bar{P}(\mathbb{E}_t c_{t+1} - c_t) = \beta\bar{R}^K(\mathbb{E}_t r_{t+1}^K - p_{t+1}). \quad \text{(A5)}$$

6. Consumptions using cash and CBDC:

$$c_t^M = -\zeta(p_t^M - p_t) + c_t, \quad \text{(A6)}$$
$$c_t^E = -\zeta(p_t^E - p_t) + c_t. \quad \text{(A7)}$$

7. Total consumption with transaction costs:

$$\bar{C}c_t = \bar{C}^M c_t^M + \bar{C}^M \bar{S}^M(c_t^M + s_t^M) + \bar{C}^E c_t^E + \bar{C}^E \bar{S}^E(c_t^E + s_t^E). \quad \text{(A8)}$$

8. Transaction costs:

$$\bar{S}^M s_t^M = a_M\frac{\bar{C}^M}{\bar{M}}(c_t^M - m_t + z_t^M) + b_M\frac{\bar{M}}{\bar{C}^M}(m_t - c_t^M), \quad \text{(A9)}$$
$$\bar{S}^E s_t^E = a_E\frac{\bar{C}^E}{\bar{E}}(c_t^E - e_t + z_t^E) + b_E\frac{\bar{E}}{\bar{C}^E}(e_t - c_t^E). \quad \text{(A10)}$$

9. General price level:

$$\bar{P}^{1-\theta}p_t = (\bar{P}^M)^{1-\theta}p_t^M + (\bar{P}^E)^{1-\theta}p_t^E. \quad \text{(A11)}$$

10. Capital stocks:

$$k_{t+1} = \delta \cdot inv_t + (1-\delta)k_t. \quad \text{(A12)}$$

11. Cobb–Douglas production function:

$$y_t = a_t + \alpha k_t + (1 \quad \alpha)l_t. \quad \text{(A13)}$$

12. Optimal levels of labor and capital:

$$l_t = mc_t + y_t - \frac{k_Q\bar{I}^{CB}}{1+k_Q\bar{I}^{CB}}i_t^{CB} - w_t, \quad \text{(A14)}$$
$$k_t = mc_t + y_t - r_t^K. \quad \text{(A15)}$$

13. Marginal cost:

$$mc_t = -a_t + (1-\alpha)\left(\frac{k_Q\bar{I}^{CB}}{1+k_Q\bar{I}^{CB}}i_t^{CB} + w_t\right) + \alpha r_t^K. \quad \text{(A16)}$$

14. Phillips curve and inflation rate (complete derivation is given in Appendix D):

$$\pi_t = \frac{(1-\beta\phi)(1-\phi)}{\phi}(mc_t - p_t) + \beta\mathbb{E}_t\pi_{t+1}, \quad \text{(A17)}$$
$$\pi_t = p_t - p_{t-1}. \quad \text{(A18)}$$

15. Capital producing firm:

$$\bar{I}^L i_t^L - (1+\bar{I}^L)(\sigma c_t + p_t) = \beta(1+\bar{R}^K)(1-\delta)(1+\bar{I}^L)\mathbb{E}_t(\sigma c_{t+1} + p_{t+1}) - \beta\mathbb{E}_t(R^K r_{t+1}^K + (1-\delta)\bar{I}^L i_{t+1}^L). \quad \text{(A19)}$$

16. Bank's balance sheet:

$$k_Q \bar{W}\bar{L}(w_t + l_t) + \overline{INV} inv_t + \bar{B}^B b_t^B = \bar{Q}^{CB} q_t^{CB} + (1-\psi)\bar{D} d_t + N n_t. \quad \text{(A20)}$$

17. Bank's equity:

$$\bar{N}(n_{t+1} - n_t) = \bar{I}^L \bar{N}(i_t^L + n_t) + \bar{I}^L \bar{D}(i_t^L + d_t) - \bar{I}^D \bar{D}(i_t^D + d_t) + \bar{I}^L \bar{Q}^{CB}(i_t^L + q_t^{CB}) - \bar{I}^{CB}\bar{Q}^{CB}(i_t^{CB} + q_t^{CB}). \quad \text{(A21)}$$

18. Loan interest rate:

$$\phi_L \overline{INV} inv_t + \phi_L \bar{I}^{CB}\overline{INV}(i_t^{CB} + inv_t) = \bar{N} n_t + (1+\phi_L)\overline{INV} inv_t + \bar{N}\bar{I}^L(n_t + i_t^L) + (1+\phi_L)\overline{INV}\bar{I}^L(inv_t + i_t^L). \quad \text{(A22)}$$

19. Deposits interest rate:

$$\bar{I}^D i_t^D = \frac{\phi_D(1-\psi)\bar{I}^{CB}}{1+\phi_D} i_t^{CB}. \quad \text{(A23)}$$

20. Bonds and CBDC interest rates are already given in linear forms:

$$i_t^B = i_t^{CB} + \Delta^B, \quad \text{(A24)}$$

$$i_t^E = i_t^{CB} - \left(\Delta^E + k_N \frac{\bar{N} - n_t}{\bar{N}}\right). \quad \text{(A25)}$$

21. Taylor rule is also given in linear form:

$$i_t^{CB} = \rho_R i_{t-1}^{CB} + (1-\rho_R)(\bar{R}^B + \pi_t + \phi_\pi(\pi_t - \pi^T) + \phi_y(y_t - \bar{Y}) + u_t. \quad \text{(A26)}$$

22. Central bank's balance sheet:

$$\bar{B}^{CB} b_t^{CB} + \bar{I}^B \bar{B}^{CB}(i_t^B + b_t^{CB}) + \overline{TAX} tax_t + \bar{Q}^{CB} q_t^{CB} + \bar{I}^{CB}\bar{Q}^{CB}(i_t^{CB} + q_t^{CB}) = \psi\bar{D}(d_t - d_{t-1}) + \bar{M}(m_t - \mu_m m_{t-1}) + \bar{E}(e_t - \mu_e e_{t-1}). \quad \text{(A27)}$$

23. Government's budget constraint:

$$\bar{P}\bar{G}(p_t + g_t) + \bar{B}^B b_{t-1}^B + \bar{I}^B \bar{B}^B(i_{t-1}^B + b_{t-1}^B) + \bar{B}^{CB} b_{t-1}^{CB} = \overline{TAX} tax_t + \bar{B}^B b_t^B + \bar{B}^{CB} b_t^{CB} + \bar{I}^B \bar{B}^{CB}(i_t^B + b_t^{CB}) + \bar{I}^{CB}\bar{Q}^{CB}(i_t^{CB} + q_t^{CB}). \quad \text{(A28)}$$

24. Economy-wide budget constraint:

$$\bar{Y} y_t = \bar{C} c_t + \overline{INV} inv_t + \bar{G} g_t. \quad \text{(A29)}$$

25. Government expenditure:

$$\bar{G} g_t = k_G \bar{Y} y_t. \quad \text{(A30)}$$

26. Shock generators:

$$z_t^M = \rho_M z_{t-1}^M + \varepsilon_t^M, \tag{A31}$$
$$z_t^E = \rho_E z_{t-1}^E - \varepsilon_t^E, \tag{A32}$$
$$a_t = \rho_A a_{t-1} + \varepsilon_t^A, \tag{A33}$$
$$u_t = \rho_u u_{t-1} + \varepsilon_t^u, \tag{A34}$$

where ε_t^M, ε_t^E, ε_t^A, and ε_t^u are exogenous shock variables.

Appendix B. Proof of Households Utility Maximization

The Lagrange function $\mathcal{L}^H$ for the problem of maximization (1) subject to budget constraint (2) and capital stock (3) is given by:

$$\mathcal{L}^H = \beta^t(U_t^H + \Lambda_t^H H_t) + \beta^{t+1}\mathbb{E}_t(U_{t+1}^H + \Lambda_{t+1}^H H_{t+1}), \tag{A35}$$

where Λ_t^H is the Lagrange multiplier, while U_t^H and H_t are given as follow after substitution (3) into (2):

$$\begin{aligned} U_t^H = & \frac{C_{h,t}^{1-\sigma}}{1-\sigma} + \frac{\alpha_e}{1-\eta_e}\left(\frac{E_{h,t}}{P_t}\right)^{1-\eta_e} + \frac{\alpha_m}{1-\eta_m}\left(\frac{M_{h,t}}{P_t}\right)^{1-\eta_m} + \frac{\alpha_d}{1-\eta_d}\left(\frac{D_{h,t}}{P_t}\right)^{1-\eta_d} \\ & + \frac{\alpha_l L_{h,t}^{1+\varphi}}{1+\varphi}, \\ H_t = & P_t C_{h,t} + P_t K_{h,t+1} - P_t(1-\delta)K_{h,t} + E_{h,t} + M_{h,t} + D_{h,t} + TAX_{h,t} - W_t L_{h,t} \\ & - R_t^K K_{h,t} - (1+I_{t-1}^E)E_{h,t-1} - M_{h,t-1} - (1+I_{t-1}^D)D_{h,t-1} - \Pi_{h,t}^{FB}. \end{aligned}$$

The Lagrange function (A35) should be maximized with respect to consumption $C_{h,t}$, CBDC holding $E_{h,t}$, cash holding $M_{h,t}$, deposit holding $D_{h,t}$, labor time $L_{h,t}$, and capital stock $K_{h,t+1}$. Respectively, we obtain the following relations:

$$C_{h,t}^{-\sigma} = -\Lambda_t^H P_t, \tag{A36}$$
$$\alpha_e\left(\frac{E_{h,t}}{P_t}\right)^{-\eta_e} = \Lambda_t^H + \beta(1+I_t^E)\mathbb{E}_t\Lambda_(t+1)^H, \tag{A37}$$
$$\alpha_m\left(\frac{M_{h,t}}{P_t}\right)^{-\eta_m} = -\Lambda_t^H + \beta\mathbb{E}_t\Lambda_(t+1)^H, \tag{A38}$$
$$\alpha_d\left(\frac{D_{h,t}}{P_t}\right)^{-\eta_d} = -\Lambda_t^H + \beta(1+I_t^D)\mathbb{E}_t\Lambda_(t+1)^H, \tag{A39}$$
$$\alpha_l L_{h,t}^{\varphi} = -\Lambda_t^H W_t, \tag{A40}$$
$$\Lambda_t^H P_t = \beta\mathbb{E}_t\Lambda_{t+1}^H((1-\delta)P_{t+1} + R_{t+1}^K). \tag{A41}$$

Note that terms in the right-hand side of (A36)–(A41) are independent of index h. It means that expressions in the left-hand side are the same across households. Thus, from now on, we will drop the index h from the expression. From (A36) we have $\Lambda_t^H = -C_t^{-\sigma}/P_t$ and from (A40) we obtain $\Lambda_t^H = -\alpha_l L_t^{\varphi}/W_t$. By equating these two equations we get the following condition:

$$\alpha_l C_t^{\sigma} L_t^{\varphi} = \frac{W_t}{P_t}. \tag{A42}$$

Substitution $\Lambda_t^H = -C_t^{-\sigma}/P_t$ into (A41) provides:

$$\left(\frac{\mathbb{E}_t C_{t+1}}{C_t}\right)^{\sigma} = \beta\left(1 - \delta + \mathbb{E}_t\frac{R_{t+1}^K}{P_{t+1}}\right), \tag{A43}$$

and substitution $\Lambda_t^H = -C_t^{-\sigma}/P_t$ into (A41) gives, respectively, the demand for CBDC, cash, and bank deposits:

$$\alpha_e\left(\frac{E_t}{P_t}\right)^{-\eta_e} = \frac{C_t^{-\sigma}}{P_t} - \beta(1+I_t^E)\mathbb{E}_t\frac{C_{t+1}^{-\sigma}}{P_{t+1}}, \tag{A44}$$

$$\alpha_m\left(\frac{M_t}{P_t}\right)^{-\eta_m} = \frac{C_t^{-\sigma}}{P_t} - \beta\mathbb{E}_t\frac{C_{t+1}^{-\sigma}}{P_{t+1}}, \tag{A45}$$

$$\alpha_d\left(\frac{D_t}{P_t}\right)^{-\eta_d} = \frac{C_t^{-\sigma}}{P_t} - \beta(1+I_t^D)\mathbb{E}_t\frac{C_{t+1}^{-\sigma}}{P_{t+1}}. \tag{A46}$$

Appendix C. Proof of Consumption and Price Indices

The households use either cash M_t or CBDC E_t to purchase consumption goods. In this case, the total consumption C_t can be seen as a composite consumption index using Dixit–Stiglitz aggregator [47]:

$$C_t = \left((C_t^M)^{\frac{\zeta-1}{\zeta}} + (C_t^E)^{\frac{\zeta-1}{\zeta}}\right)^{\frac{\zeta}{\zeta-1}} \tag{A47}$$

Consumption basket (A47) is analogous to the case where there exists non-tradable (domestic) goods and imported goods. The equations defining C_t^M and C_t^E are:

$$C_t^M = \left(\int_0^1 (C_{j,t}^M)^{\frac{a-1}{a}}\, dj\right)^{\frac{a}{a-1}}, \tag{A48}$$

$$C_t^E = \left(\int_0^1 (C_{j,t}^E)^{\frac{b-1}{b}}\, dj\right)^{\frac{b}{b-1}}, \tag{A49}$$

where j is index for goods, a and b are the elasticities of substitution between goods. Their respecting price indices are given as:

$$P_t^M = \left(\int_0^1 (P_{j,t}^M)^{1-a}\, dj\right)^{\frac{1}{1-a}}, \tag{A50}$$

$$P_t^E = \left(\int_0^1 (P_{j,t}^E)^{1-b}\, dj\right)^{\frac{1}{1-b}}. \tag{A51}$$

To derive the cash and CBDC consumer price indices, now we will solve three optimization problems regarding the consumption levels C_t^M, C_t^E and C_t. First we solve households' cost minimization problem of using cash:

$$\min_{C_{j,t}^M} \int_0^1 P_{j,t}^M C_{j,t}^M\, dj,$$

subject to consumption level using cash (A48). The Lagrangian of this problem is given by:

$$\mathcal{L}^M - \int_0^1 P_{j,t}^M C_{j,t}^M\, dj + \Lambda_t^M\left(\left(\int_0^1 (C_{j,t}^M)^{\frac{a-1}{a}}\, dj\right)^{\frac{a}{a-1}} - C_t^M\right),$$

where Λ_t^M is the Lagrange multiplier. The first order conditions with respect to $C_{j,t}^M$ produces:

$$C_{j,t}^M = \left(\frac{-P_{j,t}^M}{\Lambda_t^M}\right)^{-a} C_t^M. \tag{A52}$$

By substituting (A52) into constraint (A48), we may reformulate the Lagrange multiplier as $\Lambda_t^M = -P_t^M$, and hence (A52) becomes:

$$C_{j,t}^{M} = \left(\frac{P_{j,t}^{M}}{P_t^{M}} \right)^{-a} C_t^{M}. \tag{A53}$$

Second we solve households' cost minimization problem of using CBDC:

$$\min_{C_{j,t}^{E}} \int_0^1 P_{j,t}^{E} C_{j,t}^{E}\, dj,$$

subject to consumption level using CBDC (A49). By exploiting the similar way, we obtain the demand of good j purchasing by CBDC:

$$C_{j,t}^{E} = \left(\frac{P_{j,t}^{E}}{P_t^{E}} \right)^{-b} C_t^{E}. \tag{A54}$$

Lastly, we want to minimize the consumption cost of using cash and CBDC:

$$\min_{C_{j,t}^{M}, C_{j,t}^{E}} \int_0^1 \left(P_{j,t}^{M} C_{j,t}^{M} + P_{j,t}^{E} C_{j,t}^{E} \right) dj,$$

subject to total consumption (A47). Using the Lagrange method we obtain the first order conditions with respect to $C_{j,t}^{M}$ and $C_{j,t}^{E}$, respectively, given by:

$$C_t^{M} = \left(\frac{-P_t^{M}}{\Lambda_t^{ME}} \right)^{-\zeta} C_t, \tag{A55}$$

$$C_t^{E} = \left(\frac{-P_t^{E}}{\Lambda_t^{ME}} \right)^{-\zeta} C_t, \tag{A56}$$

where Λ_t^{ME} is the corresponding Lagrange multiplier for this problem. Substitution (A55) and (A56) back into (A47) provides the equivalent form of Lagrange multiplier Λ_t^{ME} as follows:

$$\Lambda_t^{ME} = -((P_t^{M})^{1-\zeta} + (P_t^{E})^{1-\zeta})^{\frac{1}{1-\zeta}}.$$

By denoting:

$$P_t = ((P_t^{M})^{1\ \zeta} + (P_t^{E})^{1\ \zeta})^{\frac{1}{1-\zeta}}, \tag{A57}$$

we can then express (A55) and (A56) as:

$$C_t^{M} = \left(\frac{P_t^{M}}{P_t} \right)^{-\zeta} C_t, \tag{A58}$$

$$C_t^{E} = \left(\frac{P_t^{E}}{P_t} \right)^{-\zeta} C_t. \tag{A59}$$

Appendix D. Derivation of Phillips Curve

Note that all wholesale firms that fix their prices have the same markup on the same marginal cost. Thus, in all periods, the optimal price $P_{j,t}^{*}$ is the same for all the firms that set their prices. Thus, the expression for price:

$$P_t = \left(\int_0^1 P_{j,t}^{1-\theta}\, dj \right)^{\frac{1}{1-\theta}} = \int_0^{\phi} P_{t-1}^{1-\theta}\, dj + \int_{\phi}^1 (P_t^{*})^{1-\theta}\, dj = \phi P_{t-1}^{1-\theta} + (1-\phi)(P_t^{*})^{1-\theta}.$$

By imposing steady state condition $\bar{P} = \bar{P}^{*}$, we obtain the log-linearized form of the price equation:

$$p_t = \phi p_{t-1} + (1-\phi) p_t^{*}. \tag{A60}$$

The first order condition (43) can be written as:
$$\mathbb{E}_t \sum_{s=0}^{\infty} (\beta\phi)^s \left(\frac{P_{j,t}}{P_{t+s}}\right)^{1-\theta} Y_{t+s} = \mathbb{E}_t \sum_{s=0}^{\infty} (\beta\phi)^s \frac{\theta}{1-\theta} \left(\frac{P_{j,t}}{P_{t+s}}\right)^{-\theta} \frac{MC_{t+s}}{P_{t+s}} Y_{t+s}.$$
By denoting $P_{j,t} = P_t^*$, log-linearization procedure yields:

$$\mathbb{E}_t \sum_{s=0}^{\infty} (\beta\phi)^s e^{(1-\theta)(p_t^* - p_{t+s}) + y_{t+s}} = \mathbb{E}_t \sum_{s=0}^{\infty} (\beta\phi)^s e^{-\theta(p_t^* - p_{t+s}) + mc_{t+s} - p_{t+s} + y_{t+s}},$$

where we have applied steady state conditions $\bar{P} = \bar{P}^*$ and $\theta\overline{MC} = (\theta - 1)\bar{P}$ as indicated in (42). Further, by approximation $e^x \approx 1 + x$, we have:

$$\begin{aligned} \mathbb{E}_t \sum_{s=0}^{\infty} (\beta\phi)^s (p_t^* - p_{t+s}) &= \mathbb{E}_t \sum_{s=0}^{\infty} (\beta\phi)^s (mc_{t+s} - p_{t+s}) \\ p_t^* \mathbb{E}_t \sum_{s=0}^{\infty} (\beta\phi)^s &= \mathbb{E}_t \sum_{s=0}^{\infty} (\beta\phi)^s p_{t+s} + \mathbb{E}_t \sum_{s=0}^{\infty} (\beta\phi)^s (mc_{t+s} - p_{t+s}). \end{aligned}$$

By recognizing that the series in the right-hand side is a geometric series with ratio $0 < \beta\phi < 1$ and thus converges, then:

$$\begin{aligned} \frac{p_t^*}{1-\beta\phi} &= \mathbb{E}_t \sum_{s=0}^{\infty} (\beta\phi)^s p_{t+s} + \mathbb{E}_t \sum_{s=0}^{\infty} (\beta\phi)^s (mc_{t+s} - p_{t+s}) \\ p_t^* &= (1-\beta\phi)\mathbb{E}_t \sum_{s=0}^{\infty} (\beta\phi)^s p_{t+s} + (1-\beta\phi)\mathbb{E}_t \sum_{s=0}^{\infty} (\beta\phi)^s (mc_{t+s} - p_{t+s}). \end{aligned} \tag{A61}$$

To avoid terms cancellation, we write the first term in the right-hand side of (A61) as follows:

$$\begin{aligned} (1-\beta\phi)\mathbb{E}_t \sum_{s=0}^{\infty} (\beta\phi)^s p_{t+s} &= \mathbb{E}_t \sum_{s=0}^{\infty} (\beta\phi)^s p_{t+s} - \mathbb{E}_t \sum_{s=0}^{\infty} (\beta\phi)^{s+1} p_{t+s} \\ &= \mathbb{E}_t \sum_{s=0}^{\infty} (\beta\phi)^s p_{t+s} - \mathbb{E}_t \sum_{n=1}^{\infty} (\beta\phi)^n p_{t+n-1} \\ &= p_t + \mathbb{E}_t \sum_{s=1}^{\infty} (\beta\phi)^s p_{t+s} - \mathbb{E}_t \sum_{n=1}^{\infty} (\beta\phi)^n p_{t+n-1} \\ &= p_{t-1} + p_t - p_{t-1} + \mathbb{E}_t \sum_{s=1}^{\infty} (\beta\phi)^s (p_{t+s} - p_{t+s-1}) \\ &= p_{t-1} + \mathbb{E}_t \sum_{s=0}^{\infty} (\beta\phi)^s (p_{t+s} - p_{t+s-1}). \end{aligned}$$

By (A18) we obtain:

$$(1-\beta\phi)\mathbb{E}_t \sum_{s=0}^{\infty} (\beta\phi)^s p_{t+s} = p_{t-1} + \mathbb{E}_t \sum_{s=0}^{\infty} (\beta\phi)^s \pi_{t+s}. \tag{A62}$$

Inserting (A62) back into (A61) gives:

$$\begin{aligned} p_t^* = p_{t-1} + \pi_t + (1-\beta\phi)(mc_t - p_t) + \mathbb{E}_t \sum_{s=1}^{\infty} (\beta\phi)^s \pi_{t+s} \\ + (1-\beta\phi)\mathbb{E}_t \sum_{s=1}^{\infty} (\beta\phi)^s (mc_{t+s} - p_{t+s}). \end{aligned} \tag{A63}$$

Forwarding the time index one step gives:

$$p^*_{t+1} = p_t + \pi_{t+1} + (1-\beta\phi)(mc_{t+1} - p_{t+1}) + \mathbb{E}_{t+1}\sum_{s=1}^{\infty}(\beta\phi)^s\pi_{t+s+1}$$
$$+ (1-\beta\phi)\mathbb{E}_{t+1}\sum_{s=1}^{\infty}(\beta\phi)^s(mc_{t+s+1} - p_{t+s+1}).$$

Taking the expectation at time t and multiplying by $\beta\phi$ provides:

$$\beta\phi\mathbb{E}_t p^*_{t+1} = \beta\phi p_t + \mathbb{E}_t\sum_{s=0}^{\infty}(\beta\phi)^{s+1}\pi_{t+s+1} + (1-\beta\phi)\mathbb{E}_t\sum_{s=0}^{\infty}(\beta\phi)^{s+1}(mc_{t+s+1} - p_{t+s+1})$$

and then:

$$\beta\phi\mathbb{E}_t(p^*_{t+1} - p_t) = \mathbb{E}_t\sum_{\tau=1}^{\infty}(\beta\phi)^{\tau}\pi_{t+\tau} + (1-\beta\phi)\mathbb{E}_t\sum_{\tau=1}^{\infty}(\beta\phi)^{\tau}(mc_{t+\tau} - p_{t+\tau}). \quad \text{(A64)}$$

Replacing the last two terms in the right-hand side of (A63) by the left-hand side of (A64) results:

$$p^*_t = p_{t-1} + \pi_t + (1-\beta\phi)(mc_t - p_t) + \beta\phi\mathbb{E}_t(p^*_{t+1} - p_t). \quad \text{(A65)}$$

Combination of (A18) and (A60) gives:

$$\frac{\pi_t}{1-\phi} = p^*_t - p_{t-1}$$

and substitution into (A65) provides:

$$\frac{\pi_t}{1-\phi} = \pi_t + (1-\beta\phi)(mc_t - p_t) + \beta\phi\mathbb{E}_t(p^*_{t+1} - p_t).$$

Finally we get the Phillips curve:

$$\pi_t = \frac{(1-\beta\phi)(1-\phi)}{\phi}(mc_t - p_t) + \beta\mathbb{E}_t\pi_{t+1}.$$

References

1. Pasuthip, P.; Yang, S. *Central Bank Digital Currency: Promises and Risks*; Academic Press: Cambridge, MA, USA, 2020.
2. Bank for International Settlements (BIS). *COVID-19 Accelerated the Digitalisation of Payments*; Committee on Payments and Market Infrastructures: Basel, Switzerland, 2021.
3. Balz, B. COVID-19 and cashless payments—Has coronavirus changed Europeans' love of cash? In Proceedings of the Small and Medium Entrepreneurs Europe (SME Europe), Virtual Event, 21 October 2020.
4. Kotkowski, R.; Polasik, M. COVID-19 pandemic increases the divide between cash and cashless payment users in Europe. *Econ. Lett.* **2021**, *209*, 110139. [CrossRef] [PubMed]
5. Boar, C.; Holden, H.; Wadsworth, A. *Impending Arrival—A Sequel to the Survey on Central Bank Digital Currency*; BIS: Basel, Switzerland, 2020.
6. Klein, M.; Gross, J.; Sandner, P. *The Digital Euro and the Role of DLT for Central Bank Digital Currencies*; FSBC Working Paper; Frankfurt School Blockchain Center: Frankfurt, Germany, 2020.
7. Alonso, S.L.N.; Jorge-Vazquez, J.; Forradellas, R.F.R. Central banks digital currency: Detection of optimal countries for the implementation of a CBDC and the implication for payment industry open innovation. *J. Open Innov. Technol. Mark. Complex.* **2021**, *7*, 72. [CrossRef]
8. Gross, J.; Schiller, J. A model for central bank digital currencies: Implications for bank funding and monetary policy. *SSRN Pap.* **2021**, *3721965*, 1–46. [CrossRef]
9. Carapella, F.; Flemming, J. *Central Bank Digital Currency: A Literature Review*; FEDS Notes; Board of Governors of the Federal Reserve System: Washington, DC, USA, 2020.
10. Sidrauski, M. Rational choice and patterns of growth in a monetary economy. *Am. Econ. Rev.* **1967**, *57*, 534–544.
11. Blanchard, O.; Fischer, S. *Lectures on Macroeconomics*; MIT Press: Cambridge, MA, USA, 1989.

12. Calvo, G.A. Staggered prices in a utility-maximizing framework. *J. Monet. Econ.* **1983**, *1*, 383–398. [CrossRef]
13. Bindseil, U. *Tiered CBDC and the Financial System*; ECB Working Paper Series No. 2351; European Central Bank: Frankfurt, Germany, 2020.
14. Christiano, L.J.; Eichenbaum, M.; Evans, C.L. Nominal rigidities and the dynamic effects of a shock to monetary policy. *J. Political Econ.* **2005**, *113*, 1–45. [CrossRef]
15. Smets, F.; Wouters, R. Shocks and frictions in US business cycles: A bayesian DSGE approach. *Am. Econ. Rev.* **2007**, *97*, 586–606. [CrossRef]
16. Ferrari, M.M.; Mehl, A.; Stracca, L. *Central Bank Digital Currency in an Open Economy*; Working Paper No. 2488; European Central Bank: Frankfurt, Germany, 2020.
17. Agur, I.; Ari, A.; Dell'Ariccia, G. Designing central bank digital currencies. *J. Monet. Econ.* **2022**, *125*, 62–79. [CrossRef]
18. Andolfatto, D. *Assessing the Impact of Central Bank Digital Currency on Private Banks*; Working Paper 2018-026; Federal Reserve Bank of St. Louis: St. Louis, MO, USA, 2018.
19. Davoodalhosseini, S.M.R. *Central Bank Digital Currency and Monetary Policy*; Staff Working Paper 2018-36; Bank of Canada: Ottawa, ON, Canada, 2018.
20. Williamson, S.D. Central bank digital currency and flight to safety. *J. Econ. Dyn. Control* **2021**, 104146, *in press*. [CrossRef]
21. Chiu, J.; Jiang, J.H.; Davoodalhosseini, S.M.R.; Zhu, Y. Central bank digital currency and banking. In Proceedings of the Society for Economic Dynamics: 2018 Annual Meeting of the Society for Economic Dynamics, Mexico City, Mexico, 28–30 June 2018.
22. Chiu, J.; Jiang, J.H.; Davoodalhosseini, S.M.R.; Zhu, Y. *Bank Market Power and Central Bank Digital Currency: Theory and Quantitative Assessment*; Staff Working Paper No. 2019-20; Bank of Canada: Ottawa, ON, Canada, 2020.
23. Keister, T., Monnet, C. Central bank digital currency: Stability and information. In Proceedings of the 2018 Annual Research Conference of the Swiss National Bank and the Bank of Canada/Riksbank Conference on the Economics of Central Bank Digital Currencies, Ottawa, ON, Canada, 17–18 October 2019.
24. Fernandez-Villaverde, J.; Sanches, D.; Schilling, L.; Uhlig, H. Central bank digital currency: Central banking for all? *Rev. Econ. Dyn.* **2021**, *41*, 225–242. [CrossRef]
25. Kim, Y.S.; Kwon, O. *Central Bank Digital Currency and Financial Stability*; Working Paper; Bank of Korea: Seoul, Korea, 2019.
26. Bitter, L. Banking crises under a central bank digital currency (CBDC). In *Beitrage zur Jahrestagung des Vereins fur Socialpolitik 2020: Gender Economics*; ZBW—Leibniz Information Centre for Economics: Kiel, Germany, 2020.
27. Skeie, D.R. *Digital Currency Runs*; Chief Economists Workshop; Bank of England: London, UK, 2020.
28. Christiano, L.J.; Eichenbaum, M.S.; Trabandt, M. On DSGE models. *J. Econ. Perspect.* **2018**, *32*, 113–140. [CrossRef]
29. Stiglitz, J.E. Where modern macroeconomics went wrong. *Oxf. Rev. Econ. Policy* **2018**, *24*, 70–106. [CrossRef]
30. Vines, D.; Wills, S. The rebuilding macroeconomic theory project: An analytical assessment. *Oxf. Rev. Econ. Policy* **2018**, *34*, 1–42. [CrossRef]
31. Blanchard, O. PB 16-11 Do DSGE Models Have a Future? Peterson Institute for International Economics Policy Brief. August 2016; pp. 1–4. Available online: https://www.piie.com/system/files/documents/pb16-11.pdf (accessed on 28 April 2022).
32. Hurtado, S. DSGE models and the Lucas critique. *Econ. Model.* **2014**, *44*, S12–S19. [CrossRef]
33. Hoffmann, A. An overinvestment cycle in Central and Eastern Europe? *Metroeconomica* **2010**, *61*, 711–734. [CrossRef]
34. Hoffmann, A.; Schnabl, G. A vicious cycle of manias, crises and asymmetric policy responses—An overinvestment view. *World Econ.* **2011**, *34*, 382–403. [CrossRef]
35. Hoffmann, A.; Schnabl, G. *National Monetary Policy, International Economic Instability and Feeback Effects—An Overinvestment View*; Working Papers on Global Financial Markets No. 19; Universität Halle-Wittenberg: Halle, Germany, 2011.
36. Ghironi, F. Macro needs micro. *Oxf. Rev. Econ. Policy* **2018**, *34*, 195–218. [CrossRef]
37. Linde, J. DSGE models: Still useful in policy analysis? *Oxf. Rev. Econ. Policy* **2018**, *34*, 269–286. [CrossRef]
38. Barrdear, J.; Kumhof, M. The macroeconomics of central bank digital currencies. *J. Econ. Dyn. Control* **2021**, 104148, *in press*. [CrossRef]
39. Luo, S.; Zhou, G.; Zhou, J. The impact of electronic money on monetary policy: Based on DSGE model simulations. *Mathematics* **2021**, *9*, 2614. [CrossRef]
40. Lim, K.Y.; Liu, C.; Zhang, S. *Optimal Central Banking Policies: Envisioning the Post-Digital Yuan Economy with Loan Prime Rate-Setting*; Discussion Papers in Economics No. 2021/2; Nottingham Trent University: Nottingham, UK, 2021.
41. George, A.; Xie, T.; Alba, J.D. *Central Bank Digital Currency with Adjustable Interest Rate in Small Open Economies*; Policy Research Paper No. 05-2020; Asia Competitiveness Institute, National University of Singapore: Singapore, 2020.
42. Benigno, P.; Schilling, L.M.; Uhlig, H. *Cryptocurrencies, Currency Competition, and the Impossible Trinity*; NBER Working Papers 26214; National Bureau of Economic Research: Cambridge, MA, USA, 2019. [CrossRef]
43. Gertler, M.; Karadi, P. A model of unconventional monetary policy. *J. Monet. Econ.* **2011**, *58*, 17–34. [CrossRef]
44. Primus, K. Excess reserves, monetary policy and financial volatility. *J. Bank. Financ.* **2017**, *74*, 153–168. [CrossRef]
45. Michaillat, P.; Saez, E. Resolving New Keynesian anomalies with wealth in the utility function. *Rev. Econ. Stat.* **2018**, *103*, 197–215. [CrossRef]
46. Schmitt-Grohe, S.; Uribe, M. Foreign demand for domestic currency and the optimal rate of inflation. *J. Money Credit. Bank.* **2012**, *44*, 1207–1224. [CrossRef]
47. Dixit, A.K.; Stiglitz, J.E. Monopolistic competition and optimum product diversity. *Am. Econ. Rev.* **1977**, *67*, 297–308.

48. Agenor, P.-R.; Alper, K.; da Silva, L.P. Capital regulation, monetary policy, and financial stability. *Int. J. Cent. Bank.* **2013**, *9*, 198–243.
49. Uhlig, H. A toolkit for analysing nonlinear dynamic stochastic models easily. In *Computational Methods for the Study of Dynamic Economies*; Marimon, R., Scott, A., Eds.; Oxford University Press: New York, NY, USA, 1999; pp. 30–61.
50. Chawwa, T. Impact of reserve requirement and liquidity coverage ratio: A DSGE model for Indonesia. *Econ. Anal. Policy* **2021**, *71*, 321–341. [CrossRef]
51. Piazzesi, M.; Rogers, C.; Schneider, M. Money and banking in a New Keynesian model. Bank of Canada Annual Conference—-The Future of Money and Payments: Implications for Central Banking, Canada, ON, USA, 5–7 November 2020.
52. Harmanta; Purwanto, N.M.A.; Rachmanto, A.; Oktiyanto, F. Monetary and macroprudential policy mix under financial frictions mechanism with DSGE model. In Proceedings of the International Economic Modeling Conference 2014 (EcoMod 2014), Bali, Indonesia, 16–18 July 2014; pp. 1–35.
53. Angelini, P.; Neri, S.; Panetta, F. The interaction between capital requirements and monetary policy. *J. Money Credit. Bank.* **2014**, *46*, 1073–1112. [CrossRef]
54. Syarifuddin, F. *Optimal Central Bank Digital Currency (CBDC) Design for Emerging Economies*; Working Paper; Bank Indonesia Institute: Jakarta, Indonesia, 2022.
55. Bordo, M.; Levin, A. *Central Bank Digital Currency and the Future of Monetary Policy*; NBER Working Paper No. 23711; National Bureau of Economic Research: Cambridge, MA, USA, 2017.
56. CPMI. *Central Bank Digital Currencies*; Markets Committee Paper No. 174; BIS: Basel, Switzerland, 2018; pp. 1–34.
57. He, D.; Leckow, R.; Haksar, V.; Griffoli, T.; Jenkinson, N.; Kashima, M.; Khiaonarong, T.; Rochon, C.; Tourpe, H. *Fintech and Financial Services: Initial Considerations*; IMF Staff Discussion Notes No. 17/05; IMF: Washington, DC, USA, 2017.
58. Agur, I.; Bernaga, M.; Bordo, M.; Engert, W.; Lis, S.; Fung, B.; Gnan, E.; Levin, A.; Niepelt, D.; Judson, R.; et al. Do we need central bank digital currency? In Proceedings of the SUERF—The European Money and Finance Forum and BAFFI CAREFIN Centre, Bocconi University, Milan, Italy, 7 June 2018.
59. Nelson, B. *The Benefits and Costs of a Central Bank Digital Currency for Monetary Policy*; BPI Research Paper No. 202.589.2454; BSI: Basel, Switzerland, 2021.
60. Mersch, Y. An ECB digital currency—A flight of fancy? In Proceedings of the Consensus 2020 Virtual Conference, New York, NY, USA, 11–13 May 2020.
61. Wallis, J. Unlocking Financial Inclusion with CBDCs. Ripple Insight. 2021. Available online: https://ripple.com/insights/unlocking-financial-inclusion-with-cbdcs/ (accessed on 28 April 2022).
62. Didenko, A.N.; Buckley, R.P. *Central Bank Digital Currencies: A Potential Response to the Financial Inclusion Challenges of the Pacific*; Issues in Pacific Development No. 3; Asian Development Bank: Mandaluyong, Philippines, 2021; pp. 1–40.
63. Nathan, A.; Galbraith, G.L.; Grimberg, J.; Bhushan, S.; Cahill, M.; Courvalin, D.; Pandl, Z.; Rosenberg, I.; Struyven, D.; Tilton, A.; et al. What's in store for the dollar. *Goldman Sachs*, 10 November 2020; 26p.
64. Adam-Kalfon, P.; Arslanian, H.; Sok, K.; Sureau, B.; Jones, H.; Dou, Y. *PwC CBDC Global Index*, 1st ed.; PwC: London, UK, 2021.
65. Mookerjee, A. What if central banks issued digital currency? *Harvard Business Review*, 15 October 2021, pp. 1–11.
66. Adrian, T. Stablecoins, central bank digital currencies, and cross-border payments: A new look at the international monetary system. *International Monetary Fund*, 14 May 2019, pp. 1–5.
67. An, Y.; Choi, P.; Huang, S. *Blockchain, Cryptocurrency, and Artificial Intelligence in Finance*; Springer: Singapore, 2021. [CrossRef]
68. People's Bank of China (PBoC). *Progress of Research & Development of E-CNY in China. Working Group on E-CNY Research and Development*; People's Bank of China: Hong-Kong, China, 2021.
69. Forner, G. *Network Effects on Central Bank Digital Currencies and Blockchain Protocol Based Ledgers*; Universita Ca' Foscari Venezia: Venezia, Italy, 2020. Available online: http://hdl.handle.net/10579/17133 (accessed on 28 April 2022).
70. Boar, C.; Wehrli, A. *Ready, Steady, Go?—Results of the Third BIS Survey on Central Bank Digital Currency*; BIS Papers No. 114; BIS: Basel, Switzerland, 2021; pp. 77–82.
71. Gross, J.; Sedlmeir, J.; Babel, M.; Bechtel, A. *Designing a Central Bank Digital Currency with Support for Cash-like Privacy*; SSRN Papers No. 3891121; BIS: Basel, Switzerland, 2021.
72. Vives, X. Digital disruption in banking. *Annu. Rev. Financ. Econ.* **2019**, *11*, 243–272. [CrossRef]
73. Brugge, J.; Denecker, O.; Jawaid, H.; Kovacs, A.; Shami, I. *Attacking the Cost of Cash*; McKinsey & Company: Chicago, IL, USA, 2018. Available online: https://www.mckinsey.com/industries/financial-services/our-insights/attacking-the-cost-of-cash (accessed on 28 April 2022).
74. ING Group. Central Bank Digital Currency in a European Context. *ING*, 17 August 2020.
75. Adrian, T.; Mancini-Griffoli, T. Central bank digital currencies: 4 questions and answers. *IMF Blog*, 12 December 2019.
76. Borgonovo, E.; Caselli, S.; Cillo, A.; Masciandaro, D.; Rabitti, G. *Central Bank Digital Currencies, Crypto Currencies, and Anonymity: Economics and Experiments*; SUERF Policy Brief No. 222; SUERF: Wien, Austria, 2021.
77. Jiang, J.; Lucero, K. *Background and Implications of China's Central Bank Digital Currency: E-CNY*; SSRN Papers No. 3774479; Elservier: Amsterdam, The Netherlands, 2021.
78. Shah, D.; Arora, R.; Du, H.; Darbha, S.; Miedema, J.; Minwalla, C. *Technology Approach for a CBDC*; Bank of Canada: Ottawa, ON, Canada, 25 February 2020. [CrossRef]

79. Spivey, J. Technology Downtime: What'S Reasonable? (and What Isn'T?). *WorkWingSwept Blog*, 23 July 2021. Available online: https://www.wingswept.com/technology-downtime-whats-reasonable-and-what-isnt/ (accessed on 28 April 2022).
80. Wadsworth, A. The pros and cons of issuing a central bank digital currency. *Reserv. Bank N. Z. Bull.* **2018**, *8*, 1–21.
81. Auer, R.; Bohme, R. The technology of retail central bank digital currency. *BIS Quarterly Review*, 1 March 2020; pp. 85–100.
82. Minwalla, C. *Security of a CBDC*; Bank of Canada: Ottawa, ON, Canada, 24 June 2020. [CrossRef]
83. Sveriges Riksbank. *E-Krona Pilot Phase 1*; Sveriges Riksbank Report; Sveriges Riksbank: Stockholm, Sweden, 2021; pp. 1–21.
84. Agur, I. Central bank digital currencies: An overview of pros and cons. In Proceedings of the SUERF—The European Money and Finance Forum and BAFFI CAREFIN Centre, Bocconi University, Milan, Italy, 7 June 2018; pp. 121–132.
85. Goodell, G.; Aste, T. Can cryptocurrencies preserve privacy and comply with regulations? *Front. Blockchain* **2019**, *2*, 4. [CrossRef]
86. Morales-Resendiz, R.; Ponce, J.; Picardo, P.; Velasco, A.; Chen, B.; Sanz, L.; Guiborg, G.; Segendorff, B.; Vasquez, J. L.; Arroyo, J.; et al. Implementing a retail CBDC: Lessons learned and key insights. *Lat. Am. J. Cent. Bank.* **2021**, *2*, 100022. [CrossRef]

MDPI
St. Alban-Anlage 66
4052 Basel
Switzerland
Tel. +41 61 683 77 34
Fax +41 61 302 89 18
www.mdpi.com

Mathematics Editorial Office
E-mail: mathematics@mdpi.com
www.mdpi.com/journal/mathematics

www.ingramcontent.com/pod-product-compliance
Lightning Source LLC
Chambersburg PA
CBHW061515210926
51850CB00008B/1927
9783036545714